PERSPECTIVES

INTERMEDIATE

Teacher's Book

Daniel **BARBER**

NATIONAL GEOGRAPHIC
L E A R N I N G

Australia · Brazil · Mexico · Singapore · United Kingdom · United States

Perspectives Intermediate
Teacher's Book

Publisher: Sherrise Roehr

Executive Editor: Sarah Kenney

Publishing Consultant: Karen Spiller

Development Editor: Sue Jones

Director of Global Marketing: Ian Martin

Head of Strategic Marketing: Charlotte Ellis

Product Marketing Manager: Anders Bylund

Director of Content and Media Production:
 Michael Burggren

Production Manager: Daisy Sosa

Manufacturing Manager: Eyvett Davis

Art Director: Brenda Carmichael

Production Management and Composition:
 Lumina Datamatics, Inc.

Cover Image: This image, created by TED
Prize winner JR, was on the cover of
The New York Times Magazine's "Walking New
York" issue. ©JR-art.net/Redux Pictures

For product information and technology assistance, contact us at
Cengage Learning Customer & Sales Support, cengage.com/contact

For permission to use material from this text or product,
submit all requests online at **cengage.com/permissions**
Further permissions questions can be emailed to
permissionrequest@cengage.com

Perspectives Intermediate Teachers Book + Audio CD + DVD

ISBN: 978-1-337-29855-1

National Geographic Learning
Cheriton House, North Way,
Andover, Hampshire, SP10 5BE
United Kingdom

National Geographic Learning, a Cengage Learning Company, has a mission to bring the world to the classroom and the classroom to life. With our English language programs, students learn about their world by experiencing it. Through our partnerships with National Geographic and TED Talks, they develop the language and skills they need to be successful global citizens and leaders.

Locate your local office at **international.cengage.com/region**

Visit National Geographic Learning online at **NGL.Cengage.com/ELT**
Visit our corporate website at **www.cengage.com**

228 (tr) Rvector/Shutterstock.com; **228 (cr)** pnDl/Shutterstock.com; 236 **(tr)** jakkapan/Shutterstock.com; **236 (tl)** Atstock Productions/Shutterstock.com; **236 (cr)** Wiktoria Matynia/Shutterstock.com; **236 (cl)** popular business/Shutterstock.com

Printed in Greece by Bakis SA
Print Number: 02   Print Year: 2018

Contents

Contents

GRAMMAR	TEDTALKS		SPEAKING	WRITING
Talking about the present	**This app knows how you feel – from the look on your face**	**RANA EL KALIOUBY** **Idea worth spreading** By teaching computers how to understand emotions on the faces of users, we can make more personal connections with the devices we use. **Authentic listening skills** Content words	Asking follow-up questions	A review **Writing skill** Emphasis
Narrative forms **Pronunciation** Weak forms: *used to*	**Happy maps**	**DANIELE QUERCIA** **Idea worth spreading** The fastest route may be efficient, but there are times when taking a different route can be more interesting and memorable. **Authentic listening skills** Understanding accents	Asking for and giving directions	A story **Writing skill** *just*
Present perfect simple and continuous **Pronunciation** Weak forms: *for*	**How I swam the North Pole**	**LEWIS PUGH** **Idea worth spreading** Sometimes we have to do extraordinary things to make people pay attention to important issues. **Authentic listening skills** Signposts	Agreeing and disagreeing	An opinion essay **Writing skill** Giving your opinion
Making predictions **Pronunciation** Sentence stress in future continuous and future perfect sentences	**Why I'm a weekday vegetarian**	**GRAHAM HILL** **Idea worth spreading** Cutting meat from our diet – even just part of the time – can have a powerful impact on the planet. **Authentic listening skills** Pausing **Critical thinking** Persuading	Talking about hopes and goals	A social media update **Writing skill** Interesting language
Present and past modal verbs	**Why the best hire might not have the perfect résumé**	**REGINA HARTLEY** **Idea worth spreading** Our résumés tell employers about our experiences, determination and ability to deal with life's challenges. **Authentic listening skills** Understanding contrasts	Job interviews **Pronunciation** *quite*	A formal letter of application **Writing skill** Hedging

Contents

GRAMMAR	TEDTALKS	SPEAKING	WRITING
Second conditional **Pronunciation** *I wish* and *If only*	**SUE AUSTIN** **Idea worth spreading** A wheelchair doesn't have to mean 'disability', it can be an exhilarating new way to see and experience the world. **Authentic listening skills** Following the argument Deep sea diving … in a wheelchair	Describing photos	An informal email describing people **Writing skill** Informal language
have / get something done **Pronunciation** Sentence stress	**SUZANNE LEE** **Idea worth spreading** We can use bacteria to produce materials that we can turn into clothes, as sustainable and biodegradable alternatives to leather, cotton and plastics. **Authentic listening skills** Reformulating Grow your own clothes	Shopping for clothes	An announcement **Writing skill** Relevant information
Reported speech: verb patterns with reporting verbs **Pronunciation** Contrastive stress	**CELESTE HEADLEE** **Idea worth spreading** When we talk and listen with genuine interest in the other person, we will learn amazing things. **Authentic listening skills** Understanding fast speech **Critical thinking** Investigating opinions 10 ways to have a better conversation	Responding sympathetically **Pronunciation** Sympathetic intonation	An email of complaint **Writing skill** Using formal linkers
Defining and non-defining relative clauses **Pronunciation** Relative clauses	**THOMAS HELLUM** **Idea worth spreading** Slow TV provides real-time, surprisingly popular entertainment which viewers can relate to. **Authentic listening skills** Collaborative listening **Critical thinking** Supporting your argument The world's most boring television … and why it's hilariously addictive	Asking for and making recommendations	An email describing a place and its culture **Writing skill** Paragraphing
Modal verbs: past speculation, deduction and regret **Pronunciation** Weak forms: *have*	**TIM URBAN** **Idea worth spreading** Procrastination can keep us from chasing our dreams, and we're all affected by it. **Authentic listening skills** Guessing the meaning of new words Inside the mind of a master procrastinator	Explaining causes and reasons	A for and against essay **Writing skill** Using discourse markers

Introduction

Perspectives encourages students to develop an open mind, a critical eye and a clear voice in English. Here are some teaching tips to help you make this happen in your classroom.

An open mind

As well as developing students' knowledge and use of English, every unit explores one theme from a variety of perspectives and fresh contexts. *Perspectives* encourages students to keep an open mind about the information that they meet throughout the course, and to look at the world in new ways so that they leave every lesson a little smarter.

My perspective activities

In every unit there are several activities called My perspective, which ask students to reflect on the content of the lesson from their personal point of view. Sometimes you'll find a My perspective activity at the beginning of the unit to engage students in the theme and get them thinking about what they already know about it. Here are three ways to use them:

- conduct a class discussion. Let students read the questions, then nominate individuals to share their ideas. Encourage others to respond and welcome contrasting points of view.

- organize students into discussion groups. Group work can get more students talking, even the quieter, less confident class members. Consider giving individuals specific roles like chairperson and spokesperson, the chairperson's job being to make sure everyone stays on task and gets to speak, while the spokesperson summarizes the group's discussion to the whole class.

- let students work on their own to answer the questions in writing or as recorded audio. Not only does this allow students time to prepare, it provides a private space that some students need to be able to express themselves.

Choose activities

Students are motivated by greater control in their learning. In every unit they get the chance to choose a task. There are three options, which include one or more speaking and writing tasks. Which activity is best depends on several things, such as what skills the students need to work on, which is possible with the technology available, and how much time you have. If you expect students to make sensible decisions, they need to be well informed, so make them aware of the issues. Here are three ways to approach Choose activities:

- students choose which task to work on and get into groups with others who have made the same choice. This can create a happy, productive atmosphere, but do bear in mind that some activities take longer to complete than others, and require varying degrees of input from the teacher. Be prepared for these issues by having fast finisher activities ready, for example.

- have a vote on one task the whole class will do. After the vote, if there is a tie, ask one student from each side to explain which is best and take the vote again. If there is still a tie, you can make the decision. Consider holding a secret ballot, since students may be reluctant to choose an activity they like if they feel it may be unpopular with the majority.

- there may be times when it is necessary for you to decide for the class. In cases like these, explain why, e.g. there isn't enough time to do the others, or because one task is better exam preparation than the others.

- let students do more than one task. For example, the writing task may make a suitable preparation step before the speaking task for a class that finds speaking spontaneously challenging.

A critical eye

Students learn the critical thinking skills and strategies they need to evaluate new information and develop their own opinions and ideas to share. Being able to critically evaluate and assess ideas and information is becoming ever-more important as young people have to deal with fake news and one-sided presentations of facts, often distributed online via social media. Being able to think critically involves a range of different skills, including developing the ability to: interpret data, ask critical questions, distinguish between fact and opinion, see other points of view, detect bias, and recognize and assess the merit of supporting arguments.

Critical thinking and Challenge activities

Lesson B of every unit in *Perspectives* is based around a reading text. The texts cover a wide range of genres and students are asked to interact with them in many different ways. Once comprehension of the texts has been fully checked, there is often a Critical thinking focus which encourages students to practise a range of skills in the context of particular texts. The Challenge activities in each Lesson D get students to engage with the big idea of the TED Talk.

Both within the Critical thinking activities and elsewhere, there will be plenty of times where students are asked to work together and discuss their ideas, opinions, thoughts and feelings. Some students may not always be very enthusiastic about taking part in pair or group work, so it is important for them to realize its many benefits. These include:

- giving learners the chance to brainstorm ideas before they have to think about the best language to express those ideas in. To make life easier for lower levels, brainstorming tasks can initially be done in the students' first language.

- giving learners the chance to use language they have only recently studied alongside language they are already able to use well.

- encouraging students to learn from each other. Obviously, this may mean learning new language, but also means being exposed to new ideas and opinions.
- developing the class bond and improving relationships between students. This is especially true if you mix up the pairs and groups and ensure everyone talks to everyone else.
- giving you a chance to see how many ideas students have about any particular topic, the range of language they are using and what content and/or grammar and vocabulary you might want to focus on during feedback.

There are several things you can do to help students get more from pair and group work:

- make sure you always explain the task clearly before splitting students up into pairs/groups.
- give your own models to show students the kind of speaking you want them to do.
- check understanding by asking the class to tell you what they are going to do before they do it.
- set a clear time limit.
- monitor carefully to check everyone is doing what you want them to, and to see how they are handling the task.
- have extra activities ready for any fast finishers. There are ideas on these throughout this book.
- finish with some feedback. This may mean looking at errors, exploring new language and/or asking students to share their ideas. After Critical thinking tasks, you may also want to comment and expand on students' ideas.

A clear voice

Developing a clear voice in English is about learning language and expressing your own views, but it is also about how we can help students with pronunciation, become independent learners and achieve the grades they need in exams.

Help with pronunciation

There are tasks that focus on aspects of pronunciation in every unit of *Perspectives* as well as the Authentic listening skills sections in each Lesson D. These highlight features of connected speech that may cause difficulties. In both these sections, students may attempt to copy different speakers' pronunciation. However, we see these sections more as opportunities for students to experiment with how they sound in English and find their own voice, so:

- don't expect students to be perfectly accurate.
- treat the answer key as a guide.
- judge students' efforts according to their intelligibility.

You can also take the ideas in these sections and apply them to other language sections in the book. So as you go through a vocabulary or grammar task, you might:

- drill individual words, collocations or whole sentences.
- help with individual sounds.
- draw attention to word and sentence stress, elision, linking, etc. by marking these features on examples on the board.
- get students to experiment saying phrases at different speeds or with different intonation or different emotion.

Independent learners

We can't cover all the language students need in class, so it is important that we help them become independent learners. An essential part of that is for students to make good use of dictionaries, both bilingual and monolingual.

A bilingual dictionary is good for when they are looking for a word in English. You could encourage their use, for example, in the brainstorming activities mentioned above. You might give students the topic of the next unit and, for homework, get them to create a phrase book that they think may be useful to talk about the topic.

A monolingual dictionary is better when they have the English word and need to know not just the meaning, but also the grammar, collocations and other aspects of usage connected with it. You can help students become independent by getting them to use a monolingual dictionary when doing vocabulary tasks rather than pre-teaching the key language before they start.

When you go through answers to activities, you can check the meaning and other aspects of the word by asking students questions, such as: *What other things can you X? Why might you Y? Can you give three examples of Z?*

You will see specific examples of such questions in the teaching notes. As well as asking questions like those above, you might also: give extra examples, ask students to find examples in a dictionary and get students to create sentences related to *their* lives.

Exam skills

Throughout the Teacher's Book you will find tips that you might pass on to students to help them achieve good grades in their exams. Some of these tips are about being an independent learner, using a dictionary and knowing what to revise. That's because (as you probably know), fundamentally, students do better when they know more language!

The exam tips also give advice on specific task types commonly found in international and local exams, when these tasks appear in the Student's Book. Some of these tips may be repeated at different levels and you might want to further reinforce the point by checking if students remember them each time that task comes up in class.

Unit walkthrough

Vocabulary

Vocabulary gives students the language they need to respond as they think about the unit theme in new and interesting ways.

High-impact photo engages students' interest in the topic.

Students relate the content to themselves and their own world.

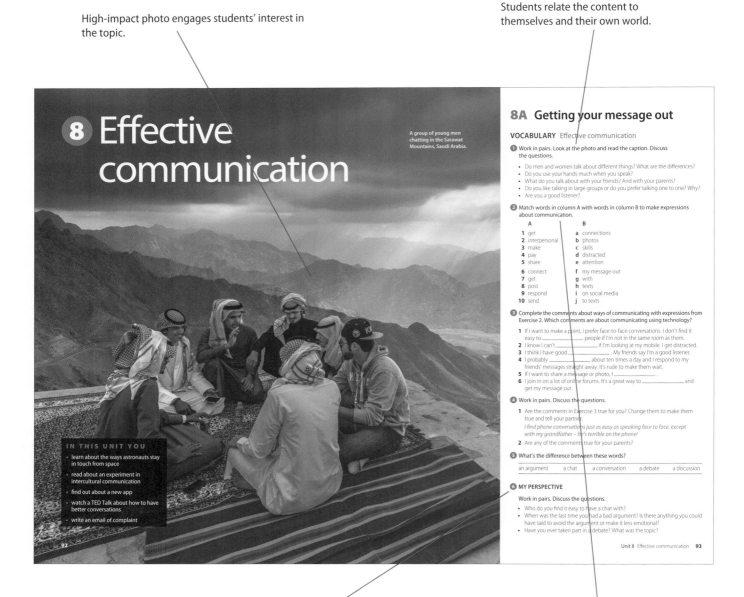

8 Effective communication

A group of young men chatting in the Sarawat Mountains, Saudi Arabia.

IN THIS UNIT YOU
- learn about the ways astronauts stay in touch from space
- read about an experiment in intercultural communication
- find out about a new app
- watch a TED Talk about how to have better conversations
- write an email of complaint

92

8A Getting your message out

VOCABULARY Effective communication

1 Work in pairs. Look at the photo and read the caption. Discuss the questions.
- Do men and women talk about different things? What are the differences?
- Do you use your hands much when you speak?
- What do you talk about with your friends? And with your parents?
- Do you like talking in large groups or do you prefer talking one to one? Why?
- Are you a good listener?

2 Match words in column A with words in column B to make expressions about communication.

	A		B
1	get	a	connections
2	interpersonal	b	photos
3	make	c	skills
4	pay	d	distracted
5	share	e	attention
6	connect	f	my message out
7	get	g	with
8	post	h	texts
9	respond	i	on social media
10	send	j	to texts

3 Complete the comments about ways of communicating with expressions from Exercise 2. Which comments are about communicating using technology?

1 If I want to make a point, I prefer face-to-face conversations. I don't find it easy to _____ people if I'm not in the same room as them.
2 I know I can't _____ if I'm looking at my mobile. I get distracted.
3 I think I have good _____ . My friends say I'm a good listener.
4 I probably _____ about ten times a day and I respond to my friends' messages straight away. It's rude to make them wait.
5 If I want to share a message or photo, I _____ .
6 I join in on a lot of online forums. It's a great way to _____ and get my message out.

4 Work in pairs. Discuss the questions.

1 Are the comments in Exercise 3 true for you? Change them to make them true and tell your partner.
   I find phone conversations just as easy as speaking face to face, except with my grandfather – he's terrible on the phone!
2 Are any of the comments true for your parents?

5 What's the difference between these words?

an argument	a chat	a conversation	a debate	a discussion

6 MY PERSPECTIVE

Work in pairs. Discuss the questions.
- Who do you find it easy to have a chat with?
- When was the last time you had a bad argument? Is there anything you could have said to avoid the argument or make it less emotional?
- Have you ever taken part in a debate? What was the topic?

Unit 8 Effective communication 93

My Perspective activities get students reflecting on their beliefs and behaviours related to the main idea of the unit.

Words are taught with their collocates and practised in context.

Listening and Grammar 1

Listening and grammar exercises continue to develop structures and skills through authentic content. Grammar 1 usually reviews previous knowledge before building on it.

Engaging content teaches students about the world as well as contextualizing the target grammar.

Sustained context provides meaningful and motivating practice.

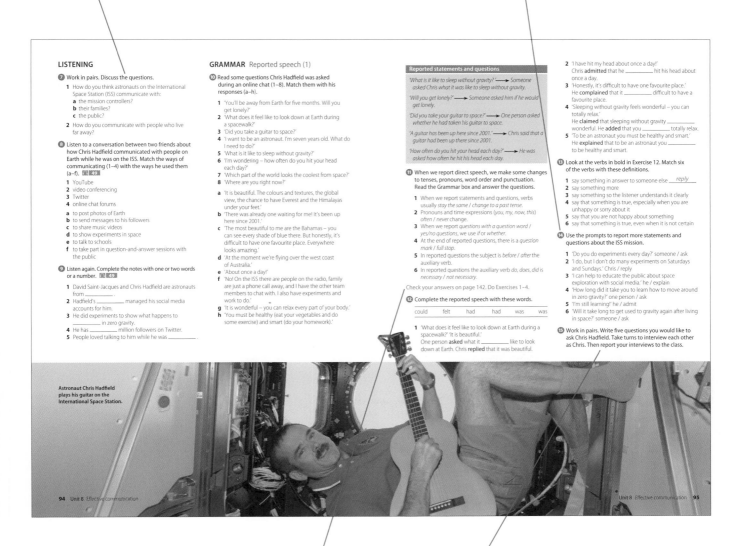

Grammar explanations and further practice at the back of the book provide students with extra support.

A final open-ended activity allows students to personalize the language.

Vocabulary building, Reading and Critical thinking

Reading helps students to become critical consumers of information.

The focus on critical thinking teaches students the skills and strategies they need to evaluate new information.

Reading texts with a global perspective encourage students to think expansively about the world, also recorded for extra listening practice with classes who need it.

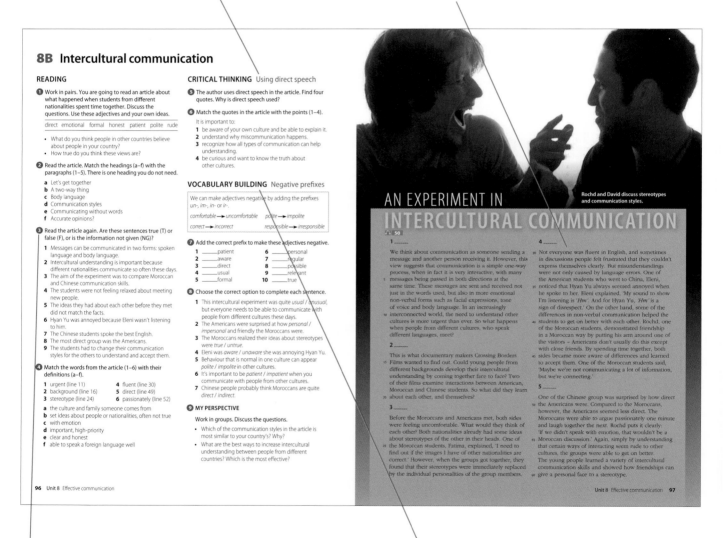

8B Intercultural communication

READING

1 Work in pairs. You are going to read an article about what happened when students from different nationalities spent time together. Discuss the questions. Use these adjectives and your own ideas.

direct emotional formal honest patient polite rude

- What do you think people in other countries believe about people in your country?
- How true do you think these views are?

2 Read the article. Match the headings (a–f) with the paragraphs (1–5). There is one heading you do not need.

- **a** Let's get together
- **b** A two-way thing
- **c** Body language
- **d** Communication styles
- **e** Communicating without words
- **f** Accurate opinions?

3 Read the article again. Are these sentences true (T) or false (F), or is the information not given (NG)?

1 Messages can be communicated in two forms: spoken language and body language.
2 Intercultural understanding is important because different nationalities communicate so often these days.
3 The aim of the experiment was to compare Moroccan and Chinese communication skills.
4 The students were not feeling relaxed about meeting new people.
5 The ideas they had about each other before they met did not match the facts.
6 Hyan Yu was annoyed because Eleni wasn't listening to him.
7 The Chinese students spoke the best English.
8 The most direct group was the Americans.
9 The students had to change their communication styles for the others to understand and accept them.

4 Match the words from the article (1–6) with their definitions (a–f).

1 urgent (line 11)   4 fluent (line 30)
2 background (line 16)   5 direct (line 49)
3 stereotype (line 24)   6 passionately (line 52)

- **a** the culture and family someone comes from
- **b** set ideas about people or nationalities, often not true
- **c** with emotion
- **d** important, high-priority
- **e** clear and honest
- **f** able to speak a foreign language well

CRITICAL THINKING Using direct speech

5 The author uses direct speech in the article. Find four quotes. Why is direct speech used?

6 Match the quotes in the article with the points (1–4).

It is important to:
1 be aware of your own culture and be able to explain it.
2 understand why miscommunication happens.
3 recognize how all types of communication can help understanding.
4 be curious and want to know the truth about other cultures.

VOCABULARY BUILDING Negative prefixes

We can make adjectives negative by adding the prefixes *un-, im-, in-* or *ir-*.

comfortable → uncomfortable   polite → impolite
correct → incorrect   responsible → irresponsible

7 Add the correct prefix to make these adjectives negative.

1 _____patient   6 _____personal
2 _____aware   7 _____regular
3 _____direct   8 _____possible
4 _____usual   9 _____relevant
5 _____formal   10 _____true

8 Choose the correct option to complete each sentence.

1 This intercultural experiment was quite *usual / unusual*, but everyone needs to be able to communicate with people from different cultures these days.
2 The Americans were surprised at how *personal / impersonal* and friendly the Moroccans were.
3 The Moroccans realized their ideas about stereotypes were *true / untrue*.
4 Eleni was *aware / unaware* she was annoying Hyan Yu.
5 Behaviour that is normal in one culture can appear *polite / impolite* in other cultures.
6 It's important to be *patient / impatient* when you communicate with people from other cultures.
7 Chinese people probably think Moroccans are quite *direct / indirect*.

9 MY PERSPECTIVE

Work in groups. Discuss the questions.

- Which of the communication styles in the article is most similar to your country's? Why?
- What are the best ways to increase intercultural understanding between people from different countries? Which is the most effective?

96 Unit 8 Effective communication

AN EXPERIMENT IN INTERCULTURAL COMMUNICATION

🔊 50

1 _____

We think about communication as someone sending a message and another person receiving it. However, this view suggests that communication is a simple one-way process, when in fact it is very interactive, with many
5 messages being passed in both directions at the same time. These messages are sent and received not just in the words used, but also in more emotional non-verbal forms such as facial expressions, tone of voice and body language. In an increasingly
10 interconnected world, the need to understand other cultures is more urgent than ever. So what happens when people from different cultures, who speak different languages, meet?

2 _____

This is what documentary makers Crossing Borders
15 wanted to find out. Could young people from different backgrounds develop their intercultural understanding by coming together face to face? Two of their films examine interactions between American, Moroccan and Chinese students. So what did they learn
20 about each other, and themselves?

3 _____

Before the Moroccans and Americans met, both sides were feeling uncomfortable. What would they think of each other? Both nationalities already had some ideas about stereotypes of the other in their heads. One of
25 the Moroccan students, Fatima, explained, 'I need to find out if the images I have of other nationalities are correct.' However, when the groups got together, they found that their stereotypes were immediately replaced by the individual personalities of the group members.

4 _____

30 Not everyone was fluent in English, and sometimes in discussions people felt frustrated that they couldn't express themselves clearly. But misunderstandings were not only caused by language errors. One of the American students who went to China, Eleni,
35 noticed that Hyan Yu always seemed annoyed when he spoke to her. Eleni explained, 'My sound to show I'm listening is *'Hm'*. And for Hyan Yu, *'Hm'* is a sign of disrespect.' On the other hand, some of the differences in non-verbal communication helped the
40 students to get on better with each other. Rochd, one of the Moroccan students, demonstrated friendship in a Moroccan way by putting his arm around one of the visitors – Americans don't usually do this except with close friends. By spending time together, both
45 sides became more aware of differences and learned to accept them. One of the Moroccan students said, 'Maybe we're not communicating a lot of information, but we're connecting.'

5 _____

One of the Chinese group was surprised by how direct
50 the Americans were. Compared to the Moroccans, however, the Americans seemed less direct. The Moroccans were able to argue passionately one minute and laugh together the next. Rochd puts it clearly: 'If we didn't speak with emotion, that wouldn't be a
55 Moroccan discussion.' Again, simply by understanding that certain ways of interacting seem rude to other cultures, the groups were able to get on better. The young people learned a variety of intercultural communication skills and showed how friendships can
60 give a personal face to a stereotype.

Rochd and David discuss stereotypes and communication styles.

Unit 8 Effective communication 97

Carefully chosen task types provide practice of common task formats found in international exams.

The focus on building vocabulary helps students understand the way words work together.

Grammar 2

Grammar 2 continues to develop students' understanding of grammar.

A Choose task gives students an opportunity for independent learning.

8C Ask me anything

GRAMMAR Reported speech (2)

1 Work in pairs. Discuss the questions.
- What apps do you know that can help people learn languages? What do they do?
- How will computers help us learn languages in the future?
- How could computer technology help if you didn't know how to explain what you wanted in English?

2 Listen to an interview with Nick, who has developed a language learning app. Put the questions the interviewer asks in the order you hear them. 🔊 51
- **a** Did the users know the app's secret?
- **b** How does the app work?
- **c** What do users need to do if they want to use the app?
- **d** Where does the idea come from?
- **e** What does your company do?
- **f** Will the app be available for English learners soon?

3 Work in pairs. Listen again, then discuss the answers to the questions in Exercise 2. 🔊 51

4 Work in pairs. Who says these things? Match the speakers (1–5) with the comments (a–j). Then listen again to check. 🔊 51

1 the interviewer	**3** the app website	**5** Javier
2 Nick	**4** anyone with an iPhone	

- **a** 'Yes, of course I can tell you about it!'
- **b** 'Can you tell me a bit about the app?'
- **c** 'Siri, find a good restaurant near here!'
- **d** 'We should use texting as the way people communicate with the app.'
- **e** 'Text me and I'll help!'
- **f** 'If you want to use the app, add this number to your phone contacts.'
- **g** 'Let's look at an example.'
- **h** 'It isn't actually a chat bot, it's me.'
- **i** 'I really think you should try this app. It's great.'
- **j** 'Remember to come back in five years' time, because computers will keep on learning.'

Verb patterns with reporting verbs
- **a** *The interviewer **asked** Nick to explain where the idea came from.*
- **b** *He **told** Siri to find a good restaurant near there.*
- **c** *Nick **agreed** to talk about his new project.*
- **d** *Nick **suggested** using texting as the way to communicate with the app.*

5 Reporting verbs tell us what the speaker is doing, e.g. suggesting. They are sometimes followed by other verbs, but the structure isn't always the same. Match the verbs in bold in the Grammar box with these structures.
1 Some reporting verbs are followed by *to* + infinitive, e.g. _____ .
2 Some reporting verbs are followed by *someone* + *to* + infinitive, e.g. _____ , _____ .
3 Some reporting verbs are followed by the *-ing* form, e.g. _____ .

Check your answers on page 142. Do Exercises 5 and 6.

6 Match the two parts of the sentences.
1 The app **promises**
2 The website **invited** people
3 Nick **offered**
4 Nick **admitted**
5 The first user **recommended**
6 Nick **reminds** us

- **a** being the app.
- **b** to help.
- **c** to add the app's number to their contacts.
- **d** to show how the app works with an example.
- **e** to come back in five years' time.
- **f** using Nick's app to others on Facebook.

7 Choose the correct options to complete the review of a new app.

A friend (1) *told / suggested* me to download a new app to help me learn vocabulary. He (2) *explained / admitted* not using it himself, but he (3) *offered / suggested* trying it for a few days. It (4) *promises / reminds* to teach you ten new words every day. The premium version is $5, but if you (5) *invite / suggest* a friend to sign up for it, you get $3 off. (You can also (6) *promise / ask* your parents to pay for it – tell them it's for study!) It's quite good fun because it turns learning English into a game. Sometimes I (7) *invite / agree* to let my little sister play it. I (8) *offered / told* to show my English teacher how it works. She thought that some of the vocabulary it teaches isn't very useful. She (9) *reminded / promised* me to do my homework as well, and not to only study with the app. I think she's right – I'd (10) *ask / recommend* spending ten minutes a day on the app, but no more.

8 Work in pairs. Read about the Turing test. Then read items 1–7 and decide which are the best ones to find out if you are speaking to a human or a bot.

The Turing test is a competition for computer 'bots' – programs that try to speak in the way humans do. The person taking the test 'chats' via text message and interacts with either the bot or with a human. The bot wins if the tester believes they are interacting with a human. But what can you do in a Turing test to find out whether you are talking to a human or a computer? Here are some ideas.

1 Could you give me your definition of love, please?
2 Would you like to ask me anything?
3 Why don't we play chess?
4 Are there any problems in your life you would like to talk about? I'd be happy to listen.
5 Do this sum: 34,789 + 74,203.
6 Actually, I'm also a computer. How does that make you feel?
7 I think you should use more emoticons. It will make you seem more human.

9 Choose the correct verb. Report the sentences in Exercise 8.
1 You could ___ask it to give___ you its definition of love. (ask / offer)
2 You could _____ you a question. (invite / promise)
3 You could _____ chess. (admit / suggest)
4 You could _____ to its problems. (offer / tell)
5 You could _____ a sum. (recommend / tell)
6 You could _____ a computer. (admit / ask)
7 You could _____ emoticons. (invite / recommend)

10 **PRONUNCIATION** Contrastive stress

> The same sentence can have different meanings depending on which words are stressed.

a Listen to three sentences. Underline the words that the speaker stresses. 🔊 52
  1 Nick suggested using texting as the way to communicate with the app.
    (He didn't tell people to use texting.)
  2 Nick suggested using texting as the way to communicate with the app.
    (No one else suggested it.)
  3 Nick suggested using texting as the way to communicate with the app.
    (He didn't suggest using voice activation.)

b Listen to the first part of the sentence and choose the correct ending: 1, 2 or 3. 🔊 53
  Ana promised to show me how it worked, …
  1 Felipe didn't promise me anything.
  2 and now she's saying she doesn't have time!
  3 not what it looked like.

c Work in pairs. Practise saying the sentences in a and b in different ways. Can your partner provide the correct ending?

11 Work in pairs. Write questions you would ask to find out if you are chatting to a human or a computer. Work with a different partner. Ask and answer your questions.

12 **CHOOSE**

1 Report the best questions and answers from Exercise 11 to your group.

2 Write a summary of the best questions and answers from Exercise 11. Use reported speech.
  My partner asked me to tell her a joke. I said I didn't know any jokes in English.

3 Search online for a chat bot and have a conversation with it. Tell a partner about your conversation. Decide which chat bot was the best and why.

Students are guided through an analysis of the grammar that gives them a deeper understanding of how it works.

Examples in a grammar box provide clear models for students.

Authentic listening skills and TED Talk

TED Talks help students understand real-world English at their level, building their confidence and allowing them to engage with topics that matter.

The focus on skills needed to deal with authentic pieces of listening prepare students for real-world interactions.

Vocabulary in context activities focus on level-appropriate, high-frequency words and phrases from the TED Talk.

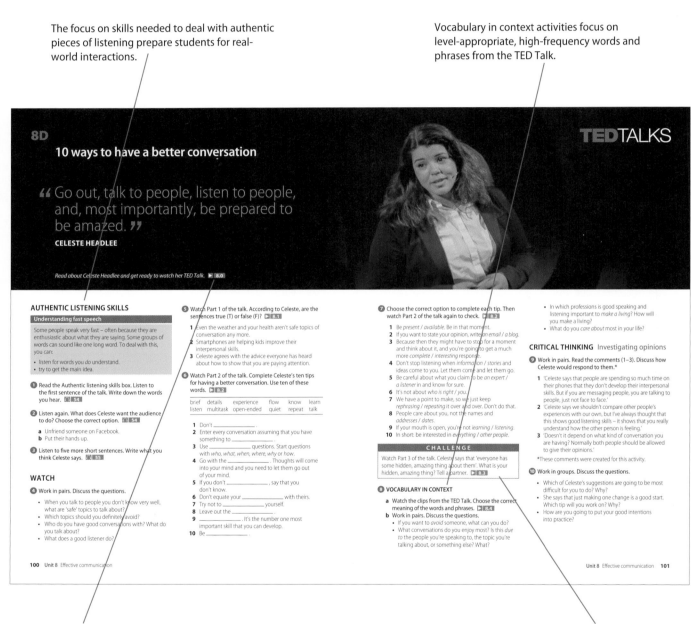

Background information and extra activities on the video help students tune into the themes and language of the TED Talk.

Challenge activities build student confidence through open-ended exercises that go beyond the page.

Speaking and writing

Lesson E allows students to put their own voices to the themes they have been discussing, while developing key strategies for speaking and writing.

Useful language boxes highlight the language students need to communicate in person and in writing.

Each writing section focuses on a common text type and provides training in a useful writing skill.

Writing models at the back of the book provide the text for analysis as well as being a handy reference.

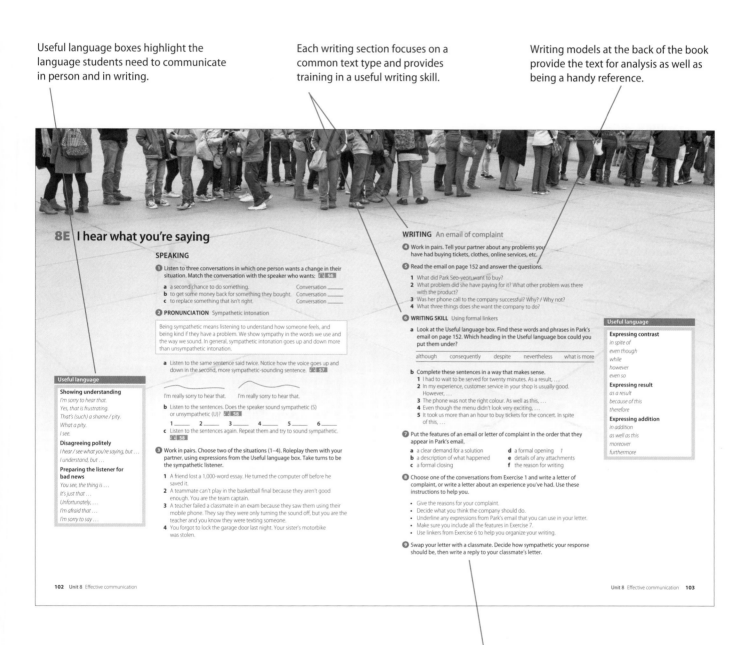

8E | I hear what you're saying

SPEAKING

1 Listen to three conversations in which one person wants a change in their situation. Match the conversation with the speaker who wants: 🔊 56

a a second chance to do something.   Conversation _____
b to get some money back for something they bought.   Conversation _____
c to replace something that isn't right.   Conversation _____

2 **PRONUNCIATION**   Sympathetic intonation

> Being sympathetic means listening to understand how someone feels, and being kind if they have a problem. We show sympathy in the words we use and the way we sound. In general, sympathetic intonation goes up and down more than unsympathetic intonation.

a Listen to the same sentence said twice. Notice how the voice goes up and down in the second, more sympathetic-sounding sentence. 🔊 57

I'm really sorry to hear that.   I'm really sorry to hear that.

b Listen to the sentences. Does the speaker sound sympathetic (S) or unsympathetic (U)? 🔊 58

1 ____   2 ____   3 ____   4 ____   5 ____   6 ____

c Listen to the sentences again. Repeat them and try to sound sympathetic. 🔊 58

3 Work in pairs. Choose two of the situations (1–4). Roleplay them with your partner, using expressions from the Useful language box. Take turns to be the sympathetic listener.

1 A friend lost a 1,000-word essay. He turned the computer off before he saved it.
2 A teammate can't play in the basketball final because they aren't good enough. You are the team captain.
3 A teacher failed a classmate in an exam because they saw them using their mobile phone. They say they were only turning the sound off, but you are the teacher and you know they were texting someone.
4 You forgot to lock the garage door last night. Your sister's motorbike was stolen.

Useful language

Showing understanding
I'm sorry to hear that.
Yes, that is frustrating.
That's (such) a shame / pity.
What a pity.
I see.

Disagreeing politely
I hear / see what you're saying, but …
I understand, but …

Preparing the listener for bad news
You see, the thing is …
It's just that …
Unfortunately, …
I'm afraid that …
I'm sorry to say …

WRITING   An email of complaint

4 Work in pairs. Tell your partner about any problems you have had buying tickets, clothes, online services, etc.

5 Read the email on page 152 and answer the questions.

1 What did Park Seo-yeon want to buy?
2 What problem did she have paying for it? What other problem was there with the product?
3 Was her phone call to the company successful? Why? / Why not?
4 What three things does she want the company to do?

6 **WRITING SKILL**   Using formal linkers

a Look at the Useful language box. Find these words and phrases in Park's email on page 152. Which heading in the Useful language box could you put them under?

although	consequently	despite	nevertheless	what is more

b Complete these sentences in a way that makes sense.

1 I had to wait to be served for twenty minutes. As a result, …
2 In my experience, customer service in your shop is usually good. However, …
3 The phone was not the right colour. As well as this, …
4 Even though the menu didn't look very exciting, …
5 It took us more than an hour to buy tickets for the concert. In spite of this, …

7 Put the features of an email or letter of complaint in the order that they appear in Park's email.

a a clear demand for a solution   **d** a formal opening   *1*
b a description of what happened   **e** details of any attachments
c a formal closing   **f** the reason for writing

8 Choose one of the conversations from Exercise 1 and write a letter of complaint, or write a letter about an experience you've had. Use these instructions to help you.

- Give the reasons for your complaint.
- Decide what you think the company should do.
- Underline any expressions from Park's email that you can use in your letter.
- Make sure you include all the features in Exercise 7.
- Use linkers from Exercise 6 to help you organize your writing.

9 Swap your letter with a classmate. Decide how sympathetic your response should be, then write a reply to your classmate's letter.

Useful language

Expressing contrast
in spite of
even though
while
however
even so

Expressing result
as a result
because of this
therefore

Expressing addition
in addition
as well as this
moreover
furthermore

An open-ended activity allows students to personalize the language.

1 In touch with your feelings

1A Show your emotions
pp8–11

Information about the photo

In March 2014, thousands of faces were collected from the website www.au-pantheon.fr, and at nine national monuments in France through a portable photo booth, to create a monumental installation that surrounded the drum of the Panthéon's dome in Paris, and covered the floor inside the monument. JR's installation *Au Panthéon!* was open to the public from June to October 2014. He wanted to make 'A global art project transforming messages of personal identity into works of art.' JR gave a TED Talk called 'My wish: Use art to turn the world inside out' in March 2011 (from JR's website).

VOCABULARY Describing emotions *p9*

- Focus students' attention on the photo and the caption or project it using the CPT.
- Ask for a show of hands for those who like the photo. Choose one student to explain what they like about it. Choose someone who didn't put their hand up and ask why they *don't* like it.
- Tell students to look at Exercise 1. Put them in pairs to discuss for one or two minutes.
- Nominate students to give their ideas and help them express them in English.

2 MY PERSPECTIVE

- Write up the sentence starter on the board. *Happiness is ....* To model the task, give two examples of your own, ideally showing different patterns. For example,

  Happiness is a strong black coffee first thing in the morning.
  Happiness is lying in bed till 12 on a Saturday morning.
- Tell students to look at Exercise 2 and write at least one idea themselves. Tell them to put up their hand if they need help on how to say something or to use a dictionary.
- When students have completed the sentence, invite them to read out their sentence. Do as many as you like.
- Write errors or new vocabulary on the board as you hear them and ask students about them at the end of the task.

Fast finishers

Students who finish quickly can write one or two more sentences.

- Tell students they are going to learn and practise some vocabulary to describe emotions. Look at the instructions and do the first item with the whole class. Wait for someone to volunteer the answer or nominate someone to answer. If you think students will find the exercise difficult, do the next item as a class before asking them to start. Students can use a dictionary or ask you for help as necessary.

- Tell students to do the rest of the activity on their own. Go round and check students are doing the task correctly and notice words and phrases they look up, ask you about or underline. Focus on these in feedback.
- When most students have finished, get them to compare answers in pairs. Go through the answers by asking different students to read out the full sentence and follow-up comment. Write the number and letter on the board. As you write on the board, ask questions about each item to check the whole class understood the new vocabulary, e.g. *What might someone be scared of? What other things could make someone nervous? What happens to people when they are nervous?*

Answers

1 e   **2** i   **3** b   **4** g   **5** f   **6** h   **7** a   **8** c   **9** d

4

- Look at the instructions and do the first item with the whole class. Wait for someone to volunteer or nominate someone to answer. If you think students will find the exercise difficult, do the next item as a class before asking them to start.
- Tell students to do the rest of the activity on their own. Students can use a dictionary or ask for help as necessary. Go round and check students are doing the task correctly and notice words and phrases they look up, ask you about or underline. Focus on these in feedback.
- Check answers by asking different students to read out the full question. Write the number and missing word on the board. As you write on the board, ask questions about prepositions, e.g. *What's the preposition that comes after 'scared'?*

Answers

1 scared   **2** delighted   **3** embarrassed   **4** lonely
5 nervous / stressed   **6** stressed / nervous
7 confused   **8** angry   **9** relaxed

Exam tip

Dependent prepositions
Tell students that in exams, prepositions and patterns that follow words are often tested, so it is a good idea to notice them and record them as they learn new words. Check that students have recorded in their notebooks not only the adjectives, but also their dependent prepositions, for example, *scared **of**, delighted **with**, confused **about***.

5 **PRONUNCIATION** *-ed* adjectives

- **5a** Tell students they are going to practise the pronunciation of some of the vocabulary. Tell students to look at Exercise 5a and do the first item together. Say *Number one, annoyed – how many syllables a / noyed?* Wait for someone to volunteer the answer or nominate someone to answer.
- Tell students to do the exercise in pairs. Go round and check they are doing the task correctly and notice any errors. You might use this opportunity to show how learners' dictionaries tell them how to pronounce words. Point out that syllables are usually marked with a hyphen, for example *a-nnoyed*.
- **5b** 🔊 **1** Play the audio or if you prefer read the words out yourself for students to listen and check. Give the class one minute to check in pairs. Ask *Do you want to change any of your answers?*
- Check answers by asking different students to read out the full word and say how many syllables there are. Write the number and word on the board with hyphens between the syllables. As you go through, you could ask where the stress is and underline the syllable. You could also ask similar questions to those in Exercises 3 and 4 to further check understanding and teach. You might also get students to repeat the words they are having difficulty with.

Answers

1 a-nnoyed 2   **2** bored 1   **3** con-fused 2
4 de-ligh-ted 3   **5** em-ba-rrassed 3   **6** ex-ci-ted 3
7 in-teres-ted 3 (some may say 4 in-te-res-ted)
8 re-laxed 2   **9** scared 1   **10** stressed 1
11 sur-prised 2   **12** wo-rried 2

- **5c** Read out the instructions and do the first item with the whole class.
- Tell students to do the rest of the activity on their own. Go round and check they are doing the task correctly and notice errors.
- Write two columns on the board as in the book.
- **5d** Elicit the answers from students or play the audio first and then elicit the answers. As you do so, fill in the two columns on the board and get students to repeat as a class and indvidually (if you think it necessary).

Answers

/t/ or /d/ bored, confused, embarrassed, relaxed, scared, stressed, surprised, worried

/ɪd/ delighted, excited, interested

6

- Look at the instructions and ask different students to read out the questions again in Exercise 4. Model the task by giving your own answers. Put students in pairs to ask and answer.
- Go round and check students are doing the task correctly and notice errors, difficulties or where they use L1. Help them by correcting or giving them the English. Write a few interesting things they said on the board or make a note of them for later.
- When the students have finished ask the class to change partners but to start from question 9 this time. Continue listening/noting.
- At the end of the task, give some feedback about new language that came up, errors to correct which you may have written on the board or just interesting things you heard to share with the class.

Fast finishers

Students who finish quickly can find new partners and ask the questions one more time.

LISTENING p10

- Focus students' attention on the photo. Ask for a show of hands of students who have seen a real tiger or other dangerous animal. Choose one student to explain where they saw it and what it was like. Then choose someone who didn't put their hand up and ask what the most unusual wild animal they have seen is or if they know one fact about a tiger.
- Tell students to look at Exercise 7 and read the questions to check they understand them. Give them one or two minutes to discuss in pairs.
- Nominate students to give their ideas.

- Look at the instructions and the vocabulary with the whole class.
- 🎧 **2** Play the audio once straight through. Play it again and tell students to compare their ideas in pairs.
- Check the answers as a whole class and write the number and words on the board. As you get the answers, you might ask students why they think that and for other words they heard which helped them get the answer.

> **Answers**
> 1 nervousness, fear – the speaker is anxious about the possibility of tiger attacks
> 2 anger, worry, unhappiness – the speaker is describing how the boy felt about his sheep being killed because they were his family's livelihood
> 3 excitement – the speaker was thrilled by the speed of the horse

Audioscript 🎧 **2**

1

My name is Matthew Luskin. I'm a conservation biologist and ecologist in Indonesia. There's a chance tigers may become extinct if the forests are cut down or hunters kill them. It would be terrible if they became extinct because so many people love tigers and they help keep the forest ecosystem healthy. To help save tigers, I spent a year in the rainforest looking for them and photographing where they lived. I loved being in the beautiful rainforest but looking for tigers is dangerous because they can attack people. Right before we started our expedition, there were tiger attacks. One man died and three had to hide in a tree for four days. When you know there's a tiger nearby, you're so scared you can't sleep! After I finished the research, I made maps of where tigers live and estimated how many live in each forest. I gave this information to the National Park rangers so they know which forests to protect and where to stop the hunters.

2

I'm William Albert Allard. I've been a National Geographic photographer for more than 50 years. In 1981, I was in Peru, driving along the road, when I saw a boy crying. He looked so unhappy. A driver had come down the road and hit his sheep, killing many of them. Those sheep were all his family had. So, this poor boy, Eduardo, was angry at the driver, and worried what his parents would say.

National Geographic published the photo I took of him, but what I didn't expect was how the readers responded. They collected over $7,000 and bought some new sheep for Eduardo and his family.

3

This is an email from a friend, Chris Bashinelli. He's an explorer and TV host. He's describing an experience he had in Mongolia.

'One of the most important skills for the people who live in Mongolia is horse riding. I had never been on a horse in my life – ever! And my guide warned me not to try. He said I could be seriously injured. But on my last day the men invited me to ride with them. There were no instructions – we just got on our horses and someone shouted "Go!" My horse set off at full speed! I thought I would be scared, but it was so exciting! I'll remember that for the rest of my life.'

- Tell students to look at the instructions and check they understand the questions.
- **2** Tell students to try and complete the task from memory before listening, but don't tell them if they are right or wrong. Play the audio straight through again and then ask students to compare their ideas in pairs.
- Check the answers as a whole class and write the number and name on the board. As you get the answers you might ask students why they think that and for other words or information they heard which helped them get the answer.

> **Answers**
> **1** William (readers raised money to buy sheep for the person in the photo)
> **2** Chris (never been on a horse ever)
> **3** William (talking about the boy in the photo)
> **4** Matthew (trying to stop tiger numbers falling)
> **5** Matthew (can't sleep because you're so nervous)
> **6** Chris (*I thought I would be scared but …*)

Extension

Ask students to discuss in pairs or as a class.

When was the last time you felt any of the emotions the explorers talk about? Why? What happened?

GRAMMAR Subject / object questions *p10–11*

To prepare for teaching the following exercises, see Grammar reference on page 128.

- Look at the instructions and tell students to read the questions. After students have tried to answer the questions in pairs, nominate different students to answer them. Ask another student if they agree and ask them to give an answer if they don't. At this point don't say if they are right or wrong.
- 🎧 **2** Play the second part of the audio once more, unless you think most students are confident of the answers.
- Check the answers by nominating a student to give each answer.

> **Answers**
> **1** He's a photographer.
> **2** a driver
> **3** *National Geographic* readers
> **4** over $7,000

⑪

- To check that students understand subject/object, write *Readers collected money.* on the board. Ask *Which is the subject?* (readers) and *Which is the object?* (money)
- Tell students to look at the Grammar box and do the task in pairs. Alternatively, write the examples on the board and do the task with the whole class. For each sentence, ask for a show of hands for either a or b.
- You can either go through the answers with the whole class, or wait for them to read the Grammar reference on page 128, or nominate individual students to give their answers.

> **Answers**
> **1** a **2** b **3** an object **4** Subject

Grammar reference and practice

Ask students to do Exercises 1 and 2 on page 129 now, or set them for homework.

Answers to Grammar practice exercises

1
1 correct **2** What does Ingrid do? **3** Which bus goes … **4** correct **5** What were you doing … **6** Who did Lina love …

2
2 a Who enjoys their maths classes?
  b Which classes do the children enjoy?
3 a What did Evgeny do yesterday?
  b How many movies did Evgeny watch yesterday?
4 a Who likes the new teacher?
  b Who* do most of the class like?
5 a What has Karina lost?
  b Who has lost her bag?
6 a What did Kei tell Naomi?
  b Who did Kei tell the secret to?

* In object questions, 'who' can be replaced with 'whom'. However, 'whom' is very formal and very few people use it any more, except in a few very formal expressions, such as in a letter addressed to no one specific person: 'To **whom** it may concern …'

 12

- Look at the instructions and do the first item with the whole class. Ask a volunteer the answer or nominate someone to answer. Write the question on the board.
- Tell students to do the exercise on their own. Go round and check students are doing the task correctly and notice errors, help or write the errors on the board as you notice them with an X next to them.
- When most students have finished, get them to check their answers in pairs and to help each other with anything they haven't finished.
- Check the answers as a whole class. When you get the correct answer, say the question out loud and ask everyone to repeat it and maybe one or two individual students to repeat it afterwards. You can correct their pronunciation if necessary.

Answers
1 Whose story happened in Mongolia?
2 What did the men invite Chris to do?
3 What did Chris say about the experience?
4 What was Matthew Luskin studying?
5 How many people did the tigers kill / had the tigers killed before the expedition?
6 How many people hid / were hiding in the tree?

Fast finishers
Students who finish quickly can write two more comprehension questions of their own about the audio.

Extension
Ask students to write the questions they would ask if they were going to interview one of the explorers.

 13

- Tell students to look at the instructions. Put them in pairs and give them a few minutes to do the activity. Students who did the extension could roleplay their interviews.
- Go through the answers by asking different students.

Suggested answers
1 Chris
2 to go horse riding
3 I'll remember that for the rest of my life
4 tigers
5 one
6 three

 14

- Look at the instructions and do the first item with the whole class. You might need to help them by drawing attention to the answer. Ask *Is 'how often' about the subject or object in the answer?* (Strictly speaking, *every time* in sentence 1 is not an object of the verb but an adverbial phrase/complement. However, it can be treated as the object.)
- Go round and check students are doing the task correctly and notice errors, help or write the errors on the board as you notice them with an X next to them.
- As you check the answers, ask *So is it a subject or an object question? So we need/don't need the auxiliary 'do'*, etc.

Answers
1 How often do you laugh?
2 What TV programmes make you angry?
3 Who cries the most in your family?
4 Which horror films you've seen have scared you the most?
5 When you feel confused about homework, what do you do?
6 Who embarrassed you recently?

 15

- Ask different students to read out the questions again in Exercise 14. Model the task by giving your own answers. Put students in pairs to ask and answer.
- Go round and check they are doing the task correctly and notice errors, difficulties or where they use L1. Help them by correcting or giving them the English. Write a few interesting things they said on the board or make a note of them for later.
- When most students have finished ask the class to change partner and start from question 6 this time. Continue listening/noting.
- At the end of the task, give some feedback about new language that came up, errors to correct which you may have written on the board or just interesting things you heard to share with the class.

- Explain the task. Give one or two extra examples yourself, ideally of both kinds of question:

  What do you do when you get stressed?
  Who gets stressed most easily in your family?

- Tell students to write questions on their own. Go round and check they are doing the task correctly.

- If you have time, ask for some ideas from the class and write them on the board. As you do so, make corrections and/or answer them about yourself.

- Explain the task.

- Go round and check they are doing the task correctly. Listen and take notes as students talk.

- At the end of the task, share some interesting things you heard with the class. You can also give some feedback on how well they used the language from the lesson, teach any new language that came up, or focus on errors to correct.

Homework

- Set Workbook Lesson 1A exercises on pages 2–5 for homework.

- Ask students to write part of a quiz for the class. Students each find out some facts about a famous person or place that they are interested in or things which have happened in the news or sport. They should write at least five questions to ask the class to test their knowledge. Remind them they will need to give the answers too. In the next class collect the questions and answers and create a quiz using a variety of the ones students have written (but not necessarily all of them). Then in the following class, put them in teams and ask the different questions as a quiz. See who wins.

1B Fake it until you feel it
pp12–13

LEAD IN

Focus attention on the title of the spread. Ask students if they know what *fake* means. Ask them to give examples of things that can be described as fake and write them on the board, e.g. watches, clothes, sunglasses, credit card number, email address, etc. Ask what the opposite is and teach *genuine*. Ask *What are the good and bad aspects of the fake things on the board?* (Fake things are usually cheaper than genuine things, but may be just as good quality; however, buying fake things means the company that owns the brand is not making any money.) Point out that *fake* can also refer to something intangible, e.g. *a fake smile*, and it can also be used as a verb, e.g. *to fake surprise*, *a headache*, etc.

VOCABULARY BUILDING Suffixes *p12*

- Write the words *embarrassed, depressed* and *friendly* on the board. Alternatively look at the Vocabulary building box. Ask the class if they remember what the words mean or if they can give a translation. Ask if anyone knows what the noun form of these words is and give or write the words up on the board.

- Highlight that *-ed* adjectives are usually based on a verb and we often create a noun from a verb by adding *-ment* or *-ion/-tion*. Ask if students know any other words with these endings and what the verb is and if there is an *-ed* adjective. For other adjectives we often add *-ness* to create the noun. Draw attention to the spelling change of *y* to *i* in *friendliness*. Again, ask if they know any other words ending in *-ness* and what the adjective is.

- Give dictionaries out to students or direct them to a reliable online monolingual dictionary. Look at the instructions in the book and do the first item with the class.

- Students do the rest of the exercise on their own. Go round and check students are doing the task correctly and notice words and phrases they look up, ask you about, or underline. Focus on these in feedback. When most students have finished, get them to compare answers in pairs and to help each other with anything they haven't finished.

- Go through the answers by asking different students to read out the word. Write the answers on the board. As you write, get the class to repeat the word and say where the stress is (see bold in the Answers below).

Answers

1 **ner**vousness 2 **sad**ness 3 ex**cit**ement
4 disa**ppoint**ment 5 **happ**iness
6 ex**haus**tion 7 con**fu**sion 8 **lone**liness

Fast finishers

Students who finish quickly can think of at least three more nouns with each ending.

- Look at the instructions and do the first item together as a class. Encourage students to think about the part of speech first before looking at the actual missing word.

- Tell students to do the rest of the exercise on their own. Go round and check they are doing the task correctly and notice words and phrases they look up, ask you about, or underline. Focus on these in feedback. When most students have finished, get them to compare answers in pairs and to help each other with anything they haven't finished.

- Go through the answers by asking different students to read out each sentence. Write the answers on the board.

> **Answers**
> **1** happiness   **2** lonely   **3** nervous
> **4** disappointment   **5** confusion

Extension

- Write these questions on the board or dictate them to the class.

  If you experience nervousness before an exam, what can you do to help?

  What has created excitement in the world recently? Why?

  Is loneliness something you've experienced? When was that? What helped?

- Get students to discuss the questions as a class or in pairs.

READING *pp12–13*

- Tell students they are going to read a text about smiling and why people smile. Tell them to read the questions and check understanding of *recognize* (see something and know what it is, or know that it is true). NOTE: don't discuss which are the fake smiles at this point.

- Go round and check students are doing the task correctly and notice errors, difficulties or where they use L1. Help them by correcting or giving them the English they need. Write a few interesting things they said on the board or make a note of them for later.

- At the end of the task, share some interesting things you heard with the class. You can also teach any new language that came up, or focus on errors to correct.

- Look at the instructions and ask the class to give another example. Do the task either as a whole class or put students in pairs for a minute or two.

- Elicit ideas and write them on the board correcting their English or providing the English word if they only know how to say it in L1. Don't worry if they don't get many. Tell them they will see some more ideas in the text they will read. (In the text, two reasons for smiling are mentioned: being happy and seeing other people smile.)

- 🎧 **4** Explain the task and set a time limit of three minutes for students to read the text. Stick to the time limit and stop students reading when the time is up.

- At the end of the time limit tell students to check their answer in pairs.

- Check answers, asking students to explain their decision based on the text.

> **Answer**
> Subtitle 2

> **Teaching tip**
>
> **Managing quick reading**
> Students often read at quite different paces, which can cause problems when it comes to managing the class. This can be solved by setting a strict time limit. Alternatively, play the audio or read out the text while students read along. This can also help them connect sound and spelling better. Read at a quick natural pace. However, be aware that school exams tend to demand fast reading for gist and detail and students need to practise different modes of reading for this purpose. Try a variety of reading modes and discuss the advantages and disadvantages with the class.

6

- Explain the task and the difference between false and not given (the answer may be implied, but it is not clearly false or true). Encourage students to find evidence in the text which proves answers to be true or false.

- Do the first item as an example. Students can call out an answer or ask for a show of hands. Don't immediately say if students have given the correct answer but get them to explain their answer. If there's disagreement, let them debate and see if they can persuade each other.

- Give the correct answer. Tell students to complete the exercise on their own. Go round and check they are doing the task correctly. Make sure they make a note of the place in the text where they get the information they need. Get them to compare answers in pairs.

- Check answers, asking students to explain their choices based on the text.

Answers

1 T (the fact people who work on the phone are told to smile when they speak to customers – paragraph 1)

2 T (*you can't stay angry because they're smiling at you* – paragraph 3)

3 NG (the text says that smiling regularly may increase the chances of living longer, but it doesn't say that not smiling will cause illness. This answer is only implied.)

4 T (*And we aren't the only animals that smile to communicate happiness – chimpanzees do it –* paragraph 2)

5 F (*a smile can have the same positive effect on the brain as eating 2,000 bars of chocolate* – paragraph 4 – so neither is more powerful.)

6 F (*why not control your emotions in the same way?* – paragraph 4)

7

- Explain the task. Set a time limit of five minutes.
- Go round and check students are doing the task correctly. Help students by correcting or giving them the English they need, and then write some of these points on the board, or remember them for class feedback.
- If students finish quickly, ask them to see if they can either reduce the summary further or change it to use more words.
- When most students have finished, get them to compare in groups to decide who has the best summary. Give some feedback about new language that came up, and correct any errors that you may have written on the board.
- If you are short of time, you might set this task for homework.

Suggested answer

Smiling is powerful because it makes you happy, has a positive effect on the brain and relationships, and helps you live longer.

8 MY PERSPECTIVE

- Look at the instructions and check students understand the questions. To model the task, give an example answer to one or two questions yourself.
- Put students in groups to discuss the questions. Go round and check students are doing the task correctly and notice errors, difficulties, or where they use L1 and help them by correcting or giving them the English they need.
- Write a few interesting things they said on the board or remember them.
- At the end of the task give some feedback about new language that came up, and look at any errors to correct, which you may have written on the board. You can also tell them interesting things you heard to share with the class.

CRITICAL THINKING Rhetorical questions *p13*

- Write on the board *rhetorical questions*. Give a translation if you know it and ask students if they know what they are and why they are used. Tell students to read the Critical thinking box. You can read it aloud as they do and gloss or translate any words. For example, *emphasize* means to make something very clear, so people notice and remember.
- Explain the task. Set a time limit of ten minutes. Go round and check students are doing the task correctly.
- Check answers by asking different students to give their ideas.

Sugested answers

1 To express enjoyment, affection or friendliness; to connect with other people in social situations; to get out of arguments and embarrassing situations; to increase the chances of living longer; to communicate/ show happiness; to understand others' emotions better; to make ourselves feel happy; to control our emotions

2 (Students' own answers) It encourages people to read and find the answer.

3 *But why should we want people to smile?* (line 9) – tell readers what information they can expect to read
Have you ever been in this situation: you are angry with a friend but you can't stay angry because they're smiling at you? (lines 28–30) – help readers relate text to their own experience
Why not control your emotions the same way? (lines 49–50) – make a suggestion

4 *Can't you hear when the person on the other end of the phone line is smiling?* – to emphasize a point.
Wouldn't it be great if more people smiled? – persuasion

- Either get students to read the text silently, or read it out yourself. Ask questions to check students have understood it.
What was special about the Pan Am smile? (named after Pan Am flight attendants who were famous for always smiling but they weren't genuine)
How did passengers respond to these smiles? (positively)
What's the problem with not smiling in social situations? (you can appear rude)
Which part of the face is important in deciding whether a smile is fake or genuine? (the eyes)
- Tell students to do the exercise on their own. When most students have finished, get them to compare answers in pairs.
- To check answers, take a class vote on each pair. Discuss as a class how easy it is to tell. Ask if the text helped them to decide. It may still not be easy!

- Tell students that another aspect of genuine smiles is that they tend to be less symmetrical, e.g. one eye may be more closed than the other (as in the second c photo). If you have online access, search for the short National Geographic video on the Duchenne smile: 'National Geographic brain games smile .5trial'.

Answers
a first photo is a genuine smile
b first
c second

Homework
Set Workbook Lesson 1B exercises on pages 6–7 for homework.

1C A breath of fresh air
pp14–15

GRAMMAR Talking about the present *pp14–15*

To prepare for teaching the following exercises, see Grammar reference on page 128.

- **Books closed.** Ask students how much they remember about the text on pages 12–13 on why people smile. Put them in pairs or small groups to pool ideas. Then elicit ideas from the whole class, correcting where necessary.

- Tell students they're going to be looking at how to use different present tenses – the present simple, the present continuous and the present perfect simple. Elicit one example of each tense and write it on the board, so weaker students are sure what these structures are.

- Tell students to open their books. Explain the task. Tell them that there may be more than one example in some sentences. Do the first item with the whole class. Ask which tenses students can see (the present perfect simple) and where ('ve known).

- Tell students to do the rest of the activity on their own. Go round and check students are doing the task correctly and notice any problem areas. Focus on these in feedback. When most students have finished, get them to compare answers in pairs and to check they agree on what each tense is.

- Go through the answers by eliciting what they've underlined in each sentence and ask what tense each example is. You may also like to repeat the underlying meaning of each tense as you elicit ideas, so for (a) you might just say: *It's the present perfect simple. From the past to now.* While for (b) you might say: *We're learning more about facial expressions so it's the present continuous. Because it's happening around now*, etc.

Answers
a We've always <u>known</u> that smiling can express enjoyment, affection or friendliness. (present perfect)
b We<u>'re learning</u> more and more about facial expressions. (present continuous)
c We <u>know</u> from studies that smiling may even <u>increase</u> the chances of living longer. (present simple)
d We <u>aren't</u> the only animals that <u>smile</u> to communicate happiness – chimpanzees do it, too. (present simple)
e You <u>are</u> angry with a friend but you <u>can't</u> stay angry because they<u>'re smiling</u> at you. (present simple, present continuous)
f If you <u>know</u> someone who<u>'s always</u> smiling, … (present simple, present continuous)
g If you sometimes <u>feel</u> sad, worried or angry, <u>try</u> smiling. (present simple)

2

- Explain that now students have identified the tenses in the examples, they're going to look at the rules for when to use each tense.
- Look at the instructions and do the first item with the whole class. Give students a minute to read rule 1. Then elicit the tense (the present simple) and ask which sentence in a–g describes 'things that are always or generally true' (d We *aren't the only animals that smile to communicate happiness – chimpanzees do it, too.*).
- You can either go through the answers with the whole class, or wait for them to read the Grammar reference on page 128, or nominate individual students to give their answers. Reject any incorrect answers and get students to explain why they're wrong, if they can.
- Tell students that item 3 is just a brief look at the present perfect – to compare it with the present simple/continuous – and that it will be covered in more detail in Unit 3.

> **Answers**
> **1** present simple
>   - to talk about things that are always or generally true, e.g. scientific facts.
>   (sentence d)
>   - to describe habits and routines (often with words like *sometimes* and *never*).
>   (sentence g – *If you sometimes feel sad …*)
>   - with state verbs, e.g. *enjoy, agree, think*.
>   (sentence c – *We know …*)
> **2** present continuous
>   - to talk about events happening at or around the present time, or at the time of speaking/writing.
>   (sentence e – *… because they're smiling at you.*)
>   - to talk about changing situations.
>   (sentence b – *We're learning more and more …*)
>   - with *always* to describe actions that happen often and might annoy the speaker
>   (sentence f – *… someone who's always smiling*)
> **3** present perfect
>   to describe actions that started in the past and continue to the present.
>   (sentence a – *We've always known that …*)

Grammar reference and practice

Ask students to do Exercises 3–7 on page 129 now, or set them for homework.

> **Answers to Grammar practice exercises**
> **3**
> **1** do you go, is planning
> **2** Are you coming, I need
> **3** normally take, aren't working, I'm cycling, always takes
> **4** have you had, I'm borrowing
> **5** You're always playing, I'm finishing
> **6** I'm looking, haven't seen, I don't know, I'm doing
> **4**
> **1** are getting, are eating / eat
> **2** is going up
> **3** are using / use
> **4** is becoming
> **5**
> **1** How long have you known your best friend?
> **2** How long is your journey to school?
> **3** How long have you been at this school?
> **4** How long does this lesson last?
> **5** How long have you been able to swim?
> **6** How long have you known how to speak English?
> **7** How long have you lived in your house?
> **6**
> **1** b   **2** c   **3** g   **4** a   **5** f   **6** e   **7** d
> **7**
> A: What jobs do your parents do?
> B: Well, my mum is a doctor but my dad isn't working / doesn't work at the moment. He is studying to be a computer programmer.
> A: Oh really? Why's that?
> B: He has been a restaurant manager for most of his life, but he wants to do something different.
> A: And he likes / does he like computers?
> B: Oh, yes, he is always playing / always plays with computers at home. My computer is never working / never works because my dad thinks he can 'improve' it!
> A: Oh no! Well, I hope he learns how to fix your computer on this course!

3

- Explain that students are going to look at a text about getting outside and enjoying the natural world as a way of beating stress. Ask them to discuss these questions in groups.

  Do you ever feel stressed? Why?

  If you do get stressed, how you try to deal with it?

  How much of your time do you think you spend inside? And how much do you spend outside?

  Where's your favourite outdoor place to go to? Why? What do you like most about it?

- Explain the task and do the first item with the whole class and ask how students know this is the answer. (It's at the moment.)

- Tell students to complete the rest of the exercise on their own. When most students seem to have finished, put them in pairs to compare their answers. Tell them to discuss any answers they disagree on.

- Elicit answers from the whole class. In each case, check that students understand why each answer is correct.

Answers

1 Are you feeling   **2** are always sitting
3 usually reads   **4** plays   **5** believe   **6** Do you enjoy
7 need   **8** is becoming   **9** have enjoyed
10 has got

- Explain the task. Point out that again, it's probably best to read the whole text through first to get a feel for it and to understand the time frames better.

- Do the first item with the whole class and ask how they know this is the answer (it's happening now; it's the action within which the other actions in the story happen).

- Tell students to complete the rest of the exercise on their own. When most students seem to have finished, put them in pairs to compare their answers. Tell them to discuss any answers they disagree on.

- Elicit answers from the whole class. In each case, check that students understand why each answer is correct.

Answers

1 are taking   **2** sit   **3** are camping   **4** has spent
5 have known   **6** does   **7** drop   **8** think
9 is destroying   **10** believes

Extension

Ask the whole class what they think of the findings of the research and whether looking at photos from the natural world would help them de-stress. If they say yes, show a few photos you've already found. Students could then discuss where they think each place is, which place they most/least like the look of and why. Finally, ask them whether they feel less stressed after looking at photos of nature.

- Tell students they're going to read about healing forests in South Korea. Ask what they think these might be and then tell them to read through sentences 1–10 quickly to see if they were right. Check they understand what these forests are and ask if there are any places nearby that are similar.

- Explain the task. Do the first item with the whole class.

- Tell students to complete the rest of the activity on their own. When most students seem to have finished, put them in pairs to compare their answers. Tell them to discuss any answers they disagree on. Sometimes more than one correct answer is possible.

- Elicit answers for each item by asking if the sentence is correct. If the sentence is wrong, elicit the correct answer, write it up, and ask why it's correct. For example, item 1 is wrong. It should be *has been* not *is being* because of the time phrase *for hundreds of years*.

Answers

1 wrong, *is being = has been*
2 correct, but could also be *are living*
3 wrong, *become = are becoming*
4 wrong, *go = have gone*
5 wrong, *has believed = believes*
6 correct
7 correct
8 wrong, *have been = are; are becoming* is correct but could also be *have become*
9 correct
10 wrong, *are often going = often go*

- Explain the task and tell students that sometimes more than one tense will be possible and that in these cases, they should choose what they feel is the best – or more natural – option.

- Do the first item with the whole class and ask how they know this is the answer (it's *recently* – from the past to now).

- Tell students to complete the rest of the exercise on their own. When most students seem to have finished, put them in pairs to compare their answers. Tell them to discuss any answers they disagree on.

- Elicit answers from the whole class. In each case, check that students understand the reason for the answers. For example, the question for item (2) is *Where do you usually go...* – because of the prompt *usually*. When you've finished checking the answers, drill the questions as students are going to ask them in Exercise 7.

Answers

1 Have you been to the countryside recently?
2 Where do you usually go to spend time outdoors?
3 What do you like doing in the countryside?
4 Do your parents always make you do activities that you don't enjoy? What? (because it's *always*, so a repeating habit) / Are your parents always making you do activities that you don't enjoy? What? (if you find this an annoying habit)
5 Do you normally feel relaxed when you get home?
6 Are you always checking your mobile phone, or can you leave it at home? (if you think *of* this as an annoying habit) / Do you always check your mobile phone, or can you leave it at home? (because it's *always*, so a repeating habit)
7 If you live in a town or city, are you happy? (if you see the action as permanent) / If you're living in a town or city, are you happy? (if you think of it as temporary and likely to change)
8 Are you planning to go to the countryside any time soon?

Teaching tip

Drilling before freer speaking

If there are sentences in a grammar exercise that students may need to say, it's often fun to quickly drill them. Say each one at normal speed (with weak forms, linking, elision, etc.) in a loud, clear voice. You may sometimes need to remodel particular parts of the sentence, saying them in a slowed-down way, but with the linking still present. After each part, get the whole class to repeat it. Then say the whole sentence again, at normal speed. After each sentence, get the whole class to repeat as one and then point at different students to signal you want them to repeat on their own. Correct or remodel where necessary.

 7

- Read out the instructions. Tell students to give detailed answers and ask any extra questions about things they hear that interest them. To model this, ask a student question 1: *Have you been to the countryside much recently?* and then ask three or four follow-up questions in response to the answers, e.g. *Where have you been? What did you do there? I've never been there. Would you recommend it?* etc. Put students in pairs to ask and answer.
- Set a time limit of five minutes. Go round and check students are doing the task correctly and encourage them to self-correct any errors with the three tenses being practised here if you hear them. Write a few interesting things they said on the board or make a note of them for later.
- At the end of the task, give some feedback about language that came up and errors to correct which you have written on the board. Put students into different pairs and tell them to correct the sentences. Elicit answers, reject any bad corrections, and check why the correct answers are the correct answers. Round up by mentioning a few interesting things that you heard.

 8

- Look at the instructions and ask different students to read out the questions. Put students into groups. Set a time limit of no more than five minutes for students to discuss the questions. For the last three questions, tell them to brainstorm as many ideas as they can, and to use L1 if they're not sure of the English.
- While they work, notice words and phrases they look up, or ask you about, or underline. Focus on these in feedback.
- When most groups have finished, elicit ideas from the whole class. You could maybe list advantages of outdoor activities and popular activities on the board, using their ideas.
- At the end of the task, give some feedback about new language that came up, and focus on errors to correct, which you may have written on the board. You can also share some interesting things you heard with the class. Have a class vote to decide which outdoor activity is most popular.

 9

- Ask students what kind of places / organizations produce leaflets about outdoor activities, where they might find leaflets, and what kind of thing would go into them. For example, a nature park might produce a leaflet that you might find in a tourist information office or hotel, promoting the park, listing the attractions, opening times, prices, etc.
- Read out the instructions. Tell students they are now working together to plan a leaflet. Make one student in each group the 'secretary' and tell them to keep a record of the ideas that come up.
- Set a time limit of five to ten minutes for students to brainstorm their ideas. Allow use of phones / tablets when groups are looking for images for their leaflet.
- Go round and check students are doing the task correctly and notice errors, difficulties or where they use L1. Help them by correcting or giving them the English.
- At the end of the task, give some feedback about new language that came up, errors to correct which you may have written on the board or just interesting things you heard to share with the class. Alternatively move onto Exercise 10.

Teaching tip

Checking if images are cleared for usage

When encouraging students to source images in class, make sure the images they're using are cleared for usage. You may want to demonstrate how this can be done. You could for instance, do a Google search for images of a nearby beauty spot. Look at IMAGES and then click SETTINGS > ADVANCED SEARCH. Then find the USAGE RIGHTS section and choose FREE TO USE OR SHARE, EVEN COMMERCIALLY. See what images are now OK to use. Ask students if they know any other ways of finding images that are OK to use.

⑩ CHOOSE

The idea is for students to make their own choice of activity here. However, you might want to make the decision for the students, in which case explain why. Alternatively, you may decide to let students do more than one task. You could divide the class into groups and have each group do a different task – or you could have a vote on which task the whole class should do. For the vote:

- put students in pairs or groups to decide which they prefer.
- take a vote on each task.
- if the vote is tied, ask one student from each side to explain which is best and take the vote again. You can decide if there is still no change.
- If the class chooses to present their leaflets, they don't need to have written versions; they can simply share ideas and ask/answer questions about other groups' plans.
- If the class chooses to make a video, they can either script and film it in class or else go to a particular location to film for homework. If they decide to do this, they can still script the video in class time.
- If the class chooses to write the leaflet, allow planning time in class so that students can divide the work up, deciding who will work on which part / aspect of the leaflet. They may have time to start writing in class, but will probably need to finish the work at home.

Homework

- Set Workbook Lesson 1C exercises on pages 8–9 for homework.

If students didn't finish the leaflet, set this task for homework.

- Students research one of the following with a view to reporting back in small groups at the start of the next class:
  - healing forests.
  - the most popular outdoor activities for first-time participants.
  - five scientific reasons why being outdoors is good for you.
- You might want to tell students to watch the track called *Unit 1 TED Talk* on the *Perspectives* website before they come to the next class.

1D This app knows how you feel – from the look on your face *pp16–17*

- Tell students they are going to watch a TED Talk about an app that can read facial expressions.
- Put students in small groups and ask them to think of as many different emotions as they can that can be expressed using your face. Elicit ideas from the class and ask for examples of how students would express the feelings on their own faces. Comment by saying things like *Yeah. You do look pretty angry!* Or *You're very good at looking bored! That worries me!*
- Read out the quote and ask students to translate it or say what they think it means in English (or both). Ask the whole class in what ways emotion may have been absent from digital communication, if they can think of any examples of how emotion has always been present in digital communication and how the TED speaker might be trying to bring emotions back. Tell them they'll soon find out the answers.
- ▶ **1.0** Tell them they are going to see a short text on the DVD to introduce the talk and the speaker, and play the *About the speaker* section. Then do the vocabulary exercise.
- After they finish, write the key words from the *About the speaker* section on the board and ask students to retell it aloud, or ask them to write as much of what it said as they can. Correct as necessary.
- Alternatively write the key words from the *About the speaker* section on the board in a random order and read out the *About the speaker* section again, stopping before each key word. Students call out the correct word from the board. Do it again, gradually erasing the words from the board until the students are reciting them from memory.

Answers to About the speaker

1. computer scientist = b (a person who studies how computers work)
2. emotionally intelligent technology = c (computer programs that can understand feelings)
3. connect with = b (have a relationship with, and understand, someone)
4. expressive = a (showing emotions clearly)
5. demonstrates = a (explains how something works)

TED Talk About the speaker ▶ **1.0**

*Rana el Kaliouby is a **computer scientist** who works with **emotionally intelligent technology**.*

*Fifteen years ago, she decided to move from her home in Egypt to study at Cambridge University in England. She communicated with her family by email but she was still lonely, and could not **connect with** them emotionally through her laptop.*

*Rana has helped to develop an app that 'reads' facial muscle movements and recognizes emotions, even on people who are not very **expressive**, and even on small devices such as tablets. She **demonstrates** how it works during her talk.*

Rana's idea worth spreading is that by teaching computers how to understand emotions on the faces of users, we can make more personal connections with the devices we use.

AUTHENTIC LISTENING SKILLS
Content words *p16*

As well as teaching aspects of phonology and listening skills, these tasks also allow:

- you to pre-teach some vocabulary.
- students to read and hear new language before they listen to the whole text.
- students to tune in to the speaker's voice and style.

- Either ask students to read the Authentic listening skills box silently to themselves or read it out yourself as they read along. Ask students what kind of words they find easiest/hardest to hear in normal-speed speech. Explain that this is what they'll now be working on and getting better at.
- Explain the task. Before you play the audio, ask students to work in pairs and practise saying the sentence themselves, stressing the underlined words.
- 🎧 **5** Play the audio and tell students to see how close they were to the recorded version.
- Give them a couple more minutes to practise saying it again – copying what they heard as accurately as possible.

2

- Explain the task. Read out the lists of which words are usually stressed and which words aren't. Check students know what they all mean by asking them for examples.
- Tell students to do the task on their own. When most students have finished, get them to compare answers in pairs.
- 🎧 **6** Play the audio for students to check their ideas.
- Check with the whole class which words were stressed.
- Put students back into pairs. They should take turns to say the sentences as they heard them. Monitor and correct any pronunciation issues that you hear.
- At the end of the task, point out that there are no absolute hard and fast rules – some words that are often stressed won't *always* be stressed. And other stress rules may influence the way a sentence is stressed, such as using stress for emphatic/contrastive reasons.

Answers

Our emotions also influence how we connect with one another. We've evolved to live in a world like this, but instead, we're living more and more of our lives like this … So I'm on a mission to change that. I want to bring emotions back into our digital experiences.

WATCH *p16*

If you are short of time, or want a different approach to the video, you may want to watch the whole talk all the way through with only some brief checking questions. A version of this is on the DVD and is labelled as *TED Talk with activities*. At the end of each section, there is a short gist question. Pause after each question on screen so students can give their answers, then play the answer.

Answers to gist questions on DVD

Part 1

Which question *doesn't* Rana answer?

b How much does it cost?

Part 2

The computer recognizes _____ of Cloe's expressions.

a all

Part 3

Which of these uses of emotionally intelligent software does Rana mention?

a For blind people – to 'see' other people's emotions.

3

- Write *emojis* and *emoticons* on the board and ask if anyone knows what the differences between them are (*emojis* are small digital images or icons used to express an idea or emotion in electronic communication; *emoticons* are representations of facial expressions such as a smile or frown, formed by various combinations of keyboard characters and used in electronic communications to convey the writer's feelings or intended tone, e.g. :) for a smiling face).
- Ask students to read the questions and check they understand them. Then put them in pairs to discuss the questions.
- Go round and check students are doing the task correctly and notice errors, difficulties, or where they use L1. Help them by correcting or giving them the English they need and then write some of these points on the board, or remember them for class feedback.
- At the end of the task, share some interesting things you heard with the class and give some feedback about new language that came up, and correct any errors which you may have written on the board. Ask if there's anyone who never uses emojis and ask why. Find out what their favourite emojis are and why.

Fast finishers

Students who finish quickly can discuss these extra questions. *Which of these 'rules' about emoticons do you agree with?*

- *Emoticons, e.g. :) are old-fashioned. Use emojis, e.g.* *.*
- *You must give your emoticons noses.*
- *Don't invent your own emoticons. People won't understand them.*
- *Don't use any emoticons in emails. Express your emotions in words, e.g. That's fantastic!*

What other 'rules' do you know?

4

- Ask students to read the questions and check they understand them.
- Tell students the sentences on the page are in a different order to how they appear in the DVD. There will be questions about *smirk* here. At 3:02 there is a clear photo showing the difference between a smile and a smirk. You can show the still or look at it before the lesson and just do it to show what it is
- ▶ **1.1** Play Part 1 straight through.
- Ask students to compare their answers in pairs. Ask them to discuss how they made their choice. Go round and notice how well they did in order to decide how quickly to go through answers, and whether you will need to play Part 1 again.
- Elicit answers from the whole class, checking how they decided and repeating the parts of Part 1 that clarified the answers.

Answers

1 T (*as I communicated online with my family back home, I felt that all my emotions disappeared in cyberspace. I was homesick, I was lonely, and on some days I was actually crying, but all I had to communicate these emotions was this*)

2 F (*With the support of my husband, who had to stay in Egypt, I packed my bags and I moved to England*)

3 F (*So we have about 45 of these action units, and they combine to express hundreds of emotions.*)

4 T (*Teaching a computer to read these facial emotions is hard, because these action units, they can be fast, they're subtle, and they combine in many different ways.*)

5 T (*We give our algorithms tens of thousands of examples of people we know to be smiling, from different ethnicities, ages, genders, and we do the same for smirks*)

TED Talk Part 1 script ▶ **1.1**

Our emotions influence every aspect of our lives from our health and how we learn, to how we do business and make decisions, big ones and small. Our emotions also influence how we connect with one another. We've evolved to live in a world like this, but instead, we're living more and more of our lives like this. So, I'm on a mission to change that. I want to bring emotions back into our digital experiences.

I started on this path 15 years ago. I was a computer scientist in Egypt, and I had just gotten accepted to a Ph.D. program at Cambridge University. So, I did something quite unusual for a young newly-wed Muslim Egyptian wife: with the support of my husband, who had to stay in Egypt, I packed my bags and I moved to England. At Cambridge, thousands of miles away from home, I realized I was spending more hours with my laptop than I did with any other human. Yet despite this intimacy, my laptop had absolutely no idea how I was feeling. It had no idea if I was happy, having a bad day, or stressed, confused, and so that got frustrating. Even worse, as

I communicated online with my family back home, I felt that all my emotions disappeared in cyberspace. I was homesick, I was lonely, and on some days, I was actually crying, but all I had to communicate these emotions was this. So, that got me thinking, what if our technology could sense our emotions? What if our devices could sense how we felt and reacted accordingly, just the way an emotionally intelligent friend would?

Our human face happens to be one of the most powerful channels that we all use to communicate social and emotional states, everything from enjoyment, surprise empathy and curiosity. In emotion science, we call each facial muscle movement an action unit. So, for example, action unit 12, it's not a Hollywood blockbuster, it is actually a lip corner pull, which is the main component of a smile. Try it everybody. Let's get some smiles going on. So, we have about 45 of these action units, and they combine to express hundreds of emotions.

Teaching a computer to read these facial emotions is hard, because these action units, they can be fast, they're subtle, and they combine in many different ways. So, take, for example, the smile and the smirk. They look somewhat similar, but they mean very different things. So, the smile is positive, a smirk is often negative. Sometimes a smirk can make you become famous. But seriously, it's important for a computer to be able to tell the difference between the two expressions.

So how do we do that? We give our algorithms tens of thousands of examples of people we know to be smiling, from different ethnicities, ages, genders, and we do the same for smirks. And then, using deep learning, the algorithm looks for all these textures and wrinkles and shape changes on our face, and basically learns that all smiles have common characteristics, all smirks have subtly different characteristics. And the next time it sees a new face, it essentially learns that, you know this face has the same characteristics of a smile, and it says, 'Aha, you know, I recognize this. This is a smile expression.'

5

- Tell students to read through items 1–10 and ask about anything they're unsure of. To show the meaning of 'disgusted', demonstrate by imagining you've just eaten something that tastes horrible. Explain that they won't hear/see all of these emotions mentioned, and they won't be in order, so students should watch and listen and find out which come up.
- ▶ **1.2** Play Part 2 straight through.
- Ask students to compare their answers in pairs. Go round and notice how well they did in order to decide how quickly to go through answers, and whether you will need to play Part 2 again.
- Elicit answers from the whole class.

Answers

6, 10, 1, 9, 3, 4

TED Talk Part 2 script ▶ 1.2

So, the best way to demonstrate how this technology works is to try a live demo, so I need a volunteer, preferably somebody with a face. Cloe's going to be our volunteer today.

So, let's give this a try.

As you can see, the algorithm has essentially found Cloe's face, so it's this white bounding box, and it's tracking the main feature points on her face, so her eyebrows, her eyes, her mouth and her nose. The question is, can it recognize her expression? So, we're going to test the machine. So, first of all, give me your poker face. Yep, awesome. And then as she smiles, this is a genuine smile, it's great. So, you can see the green bar go up as she smiles. Now that was a big smile. Can you try like a subtle smile to see if the computer can recognize? It does recognize subtle smiles as well. We've worked really hard to make that happen. And then eyebrow raised, indicator of surprise. Brow furrow, which is an indicator of confusion. Frown. Yes, perfect. So, on the right side of the demo – look like you're happy. So, that's joy. Joy fires up. And then give me a disgust face. Yeah, wrinkle your nose. Awesome.

So, so far, we have amassed 12 billion of these emotion data points. It's the largest emotion database in the world. We've collected it from 2.9 million face videos, people who have agreed to share their emotions with us, and from 75 countries around the world. It's growing every day. It blows my mind away that we can now quantify something as personal as our emotions, and we can do it at this scale.

6

- Ask students to read the sentences and check they understand them.
- Get students to predict the answers with a show of hands before you watch Part 3, e.g. *Who thinks it's the UK?*
- ▶ 1.3 Play Part 3 straight through. Go round and notice how well they did in order to decide how quickly to go through answers, and whether you will need to play Part 3 again.
- Elicit answers from the whole class.

> **Answers**
> **1** USA   **2** older   **3** wear special glasses   **4** can

TED Talk Part 3 script ▶ 1.3

So, what have we learnt to date? Gender. Our data confirms something that you might suspect. Women are more expressive than men. Let's do culture. So, in the United States, women are 40 percent more expressive than men, but curiously, we don't see any difference in the UK between men and women. Age: people who are 50 years and older are 25 percent more emotive than younger people. Women in their 20s smile a lot more than men the same age, perhaps a necessity for dating.

Where is this data used today? I want to share some examples that are especially close to my heart. Emotion-enabled wearable glasses can help individuals who are visually impaired read the faces of others, and it can help individuals on the autism spectrum interpret emotion, something that they really struggle with. What if your wristwatch tracked your mood, or your car sensed that you're tired, or perhaps your fridge knows that you're stressed, so it auto-locks to prevent you from binge eating. I would like that, yeah.

I think in five years down the line, all our devices are going to have an emotion chip. As more and more of our lives become digital, we are fighting a losing battle trying to curb our usage of devices in order to reclaim our emotions. So, what I'm trying to do instead is to bring emotions into our technology and make our technologies more responsive. So, I want those devices that have separated us to bring us back together. And by humanizing technology, we have this golden opportunity to reimagine how we connect with machines, and therefore, how we, as human beings, connect with one another.

Thank you.

7

- Explain the task.
- ▶ 1.3 Play Part 3 again.
- Elicit from the whole class the different uses that were mentioned:
  - Emotion-enabled wearable glasses can help individuals who are visually impaired read the faces of others.
  - The glasses can also help individuals on the autism spectrum interpret emotion.
  - Your wristwatch could track your mood.
  - Your car could sense that you're tired.
  - Your fridge could sense that you're stressed, so it auto-locks to prevent you from binge eating.
- Put students in pairs to do the activity.
- Elicit answers from the whole class.

8 VOCABULARY IN CONTEXT

- **8a** ▶ 1.4 Tell students that they are going to watch some clips from the talk which contain new or interesting words or phrases. They should choose the correct meaning for each one. Play the Vocabulary in context section. Pause after each question on screen so students can choose the correct definition, then play the answer. If you like, you can ask students to call out the answers.

> **Answers**
> **1** homesick = b (unhappy to be far from home)
> **2** curiosity = b (the feeling of being interested in new things)
> **3** genders = b (sexes (men and women))
> **4** wrinkles = c (lines)
> **5** characteristics = c (qualities)
> **6** joy = a (happiness)

- **8b** Check students understand the words in italics and re-teach if necessary, or ask students if they can recall the example in the talk. Point out that they relate to some of the new words and phrases they have just learnt in Exercise 8a. Tell students to complete the five sentences on their own.

- Put students in pairs to tell each other their ideas. Go round and check they are doing the task correctly and notice errors, difficulties, or where they use L1. Help them by correcting or giving them the English they need. Focus especially on their use of the new words and phrases.

- At the end of the task, give some feedback about new language that came up, and look at any errors which you may have written on the board. You can also retell some stories you heard or nominate one or two students to tell the class the most interesting things they said or heard.

- Explain the task. Check students understand the categories. Elicit from the whole class one idea on how Rana's software could be used in advertising.

- Put students in groups and tell them to brainstorm more ideas. Assign one person in each group to be the group secretary.

- Once the buzz of activity starts to die down a bit, stop the groups and elicit ideas from the whole class.

- Ask extra questions and feed in extra language where necessary to check you understand exactly what students mean.

Suggested answers

advertising – to see how people watching adverts respond to the adverts, and so make them better

entertainment (TV, film, concerts, theatre, etc.) – to give producers information about how funny, sad or exciting different scenes are, so that they can remake them with better emotional impact

health and medicine – to measure patients' pain levels or levels of satisfaction during treatment

people with physical problems and learning difficulties – to help people with autism or visual impairments know what other people are feeling

shopping and fashion – to provide online retailers with information about customers' reactions to items for sale online

social media – to give people who are messaging information about the other person's emotional state

---

- Either do this quickly with the whole class or put students into groups to discuss the questions. Ask the class for ideas about which of the many ideas match each category here and why.

CHALLENGE

- Tell students they're going to have the chance to explore how they feel about the app Rana described. Look at the instructions and the comments and get students to ask about any language they're not sure of.

- Let students do the task on their own. Then put them into pairs to discuss their ideas. Go round and notice errors, difficulties, or where they use L1 and help by correcting or giving students the English they need.

- At the end of the task, ask the whole class which idea they most strongly agree with and see what the popular choice is. Put students back into pairs to discuss how they think Rana would react to each comment. Then elicit ideas from the group as a whole.

Homework

Set Workbook Lesson 1D exercises on page 10 for homework.

1E The feel-good factor *pp18–19*

Information about the photo

The open-air cinema in the castle courtyard, Esslingen am Neckar, Germany is open for about ten days around July and August. It shows a mixture of specially selected films from Hollywood and Europe, blockbusters and art house. You might ask students if they know anywhere similar and whether they would like to go.

SPEAKING *pp18–19*

- Read out this short text as students read and do the first item as a whole class. (A feel-good factor is an aspect of a film that makes people feel happy and positive. We also talk about feel-good movies.)
- Put students in pairs to discuss the other two questions.
- Go round and check students are doing the task correctly and notice errors, difficulties or where they use L1. Help them by correcting or giving them the English they need.
- Write down a few interesting things they said on the board.
- At the end of the task give some feedback about interesting things you heard to share with the class.

- Tell students they are going to learn and practise some vocabulary to talk about films.
- Ask students to look at the sentences and guess the meaning of the words without using a dictionary and write a translation in their language.

Exam tip

Guessing the meaning of unknown words
In an exam or when reading, students might need to guess the meaning of unknown words because they are not allowed to use a dictionary or don't have time. Get them to look at the surrounding words and phrases to help them. For example, linking words like *but* can indicate opposites (if they know one word, they might guess the opposite); or *and* may link to an example of the unknown word or a partial synonym.

- Go round and check students are doing the task correctly.
- In monolingual groups you can check the translation or see if everyone agrees. In multilingual groups the students could try and explain the meaning in English. Explain any the students can't guess.

Answers

special effects – artificial images or sounds in films, often using computer technology

sequel – a film, book, etc. that follows another book and continues the story, e.g. *Cars 2*

soundtrack – all the music that is used in a film

cast – all the actors that appear in the film

plot – the storyline, i.e. what happens

the ending – the conclusion or end of the story, e.g. *a happy ending*

scenes – a part of a book, film, etc. where events happen in the same time and place

Extension

Search online for 'movie soundtrack genre quiz' or similar to find clips of typical music from movies of different genres. Tell students to listen to each clip and write down the genre, or type of film that each makes them think of. They can then compare answers.

- Look at the instructions and do the first item with the whole class. Say *For example 1 I don't think anyone could survive in space for that long …, what kind of movie?* Nominate a student to answer.
- Tell students to do the rest of the activity on their own, using a dictionary if they need to. Go round and check students are doing the task correctly and notice words and phrases they look up, ask you about or underline.
- When most students have finished, go through the answers by reading out the sentence and asking different students to say the kind of film. Write the answers on the board. As you go through the answers, get all the students to say the word and/or ask them what other typical aspects of the movie* genre there are (a sci-fi movie: aliens, astronauts, space ships, alien invasions and battle scenes, etc. a thriller: car chases, bombs, tension, being on the edge of your seat, etc.).

* *movie* and *film* are synonyms. *Movie* is used in America, but it is also very common in British English. *Film* is only commonly used in British English.

Answers
a 6 **b** 4 **c** 2 **d** 3 **e** 1 **f** 5

- Explain the task. Pre-teach any unknown words, e.g. *starring*, *release date*, *set in*, etc.
- 🎧 **7** Play the audio once straight through.
- Ask students to compare their ideas in pairs. Go round and notice how well they did in order to decide how quickly to go through answers, and whether you will need to play the audio again.
- Check answers by pausing the audio after the word or phrase. Ask the class to say the correct option.

> **Answers**
>
> Name of film: *The Way Way Back*
>
> Starring: Steve Carell
>
> Release date: 2013
>
> Type of film: comedy
>
> Set in: a water park
>
> Plot: An unhappy teenager goes on holiday with his family and makes new friends.
>
> Recommended? Yes

Audioscript 🎧 **7**

Male: I watched a great movie last night – The Way Way Back. *Have you seen it?*

Female: Hmm, I don't think so. Who's in it?

Male: It has a great cast. It stars Steve Carell and Toni Collette.

Female: Steve Carell? What else has he been in? I know the name.

Male: You'd recognize him. He was the voice of Gru in Despicable Me, *and many other movies.*

Female: When did it come out?

Male: I think it came out a few years ago – about 2013 or 14. But it's excellent. A real feel-good movie.

Female: Alright. So what's it about? What sort of movie is it?

Male: It tells the story of a teenage boy who has to go on vacation with his mom and her friend. But he doesn't want to go because he hates the friend.

Female: Actually, I think I _have_ seen it. It's a comedy, isn't it?

Male: Yes, I guess so. I mean, it wasn't super funny or anything, but it made me smile.

Female: Where's it set? Isn't there a water park?

Male: A lot of the story is set there, yeah. The family is staying near a water park. Then the boy ends up becoming friends with the manager and getting a job there.

Female: I have seen it. I thought it was funny. I don't usually like comedies, but I enjoyed it.

Male: It _is_ funny, but it's also very emotional at the same time. The boy learns a lot about himself, and there's a happy ending. I'd definitely recommend it.

Female: Me too. The only thing I didn't like was the soundtrack. It made the film feel a little old.

Male: What are you planning to watch this weekend?

- Get students to look at the Useful language box before they listen. Ask questions to check understanding.
- *Which question(s) are about the stars? / the release date? / other films the actor has appeared in? / the place the story takes place? / the genre? / the quality of the actors' work?*
- 🎧 **7** Play the audio again.
- Ask students to compare their ideas in pairs. Go round and notice how well they did in order to decide how quickly to go through answers, and whether you will need to play the audio again.
- Check answers by pausing the audio after the phrase. Ask the class to say the correct option.

> **Answers**
>
> Who's in it?
>
> What else has he been in?
>
> When did it come out?
>
> So what's it about?
>
> What sort of movie is it?
>
> Where is it set?

6

- Look at the instructions and do the first item with the whole class. Say *For example, number 1. It's a sci-fi film. It's the first in a series of four. What's the question?* Nominate someone to answer.
- Tell students to do the rest of the activity on their own, using a dictionary if they need to. Go round and check students are doing the task correctly and notice words and phrases they look up, ask you about or underline.
- When most students have finished, get them to compare answers in pairs and to help each other with anything they haven't finished.
- Check answers around the class. See if anyone guessed the film.

> **Answers**
> 1 What sort of movie is it?
> 2 When did it come out?
> 3 What else has she been in?
> 4 So what's it about?
> 5 Where is it set?
> 6 Who's in it?

The film is *The Hunger Games*. You might show the trailer if you decide that it is suitable and you have time.

- Look at the instructions and choose a student to demonstrate the task with. You start the conversation and encourage the student to ask you follow-up questions. Help them with any new language they try and use. Repeat with one other student. Choose one more student to start a conversation with you (so you ask the questions and the student has to answer). Again help with new language.
- Get students to have similar conversations in pairs. Remind them to use language from the Useful language box. Go round and check they are doing the task correctly and notice errors, difficulties, or where they use L1. Help them by correcting or giving them the English they need, and then write some of these points on the board, or remember them for class feedback.
- When most students have finished, ask the class to change partners and repeat the activity.
- At the end of the task, give some feedback about new language that came up, and focus on errors to correct which you may have written on the board. You can also retell some interesting things you heard to share with the class.

WRITING A review *p19*

- For variety you might do this as a whole class task. Read out each phrase or nominate students to do so. Then ask students to call out *film*, *book* or *both*.
- Correct any errors.
- You could add a competitive element by students starting with two or three lives and they lose one each time they get a wrong answer.

Answers

Film

It stars … It was directed by … It was released in … The soundtrack was amazing. The special effects were a bit disappointing.

Book

It was published in … I couldn't put it down.

Both

It's set in … It tells the story of … / It's about … It came out in … The main character is … The sequel is even better / not as good. It's a moving / inspiring / great / exciting / funny story. I'd definitely recommend it. It made me feel … Unfortunately, I thought it was …

- Tell students they are going to learn to write a review of a book or a film.
- Explain the task.

- Tell students to read the review on page 149. Set a strict time limit or read it out while they read. Ask students to compare the answer in pairs and to give their reasons.
- Check the answer with the whole class.

Suggested answer

4 out of 5 stars (The writer expresses one clear flaw but otherwise strongly recommends it. Students may argue for 3 stars, too.)

- Explain the task. Tell students it's good to give both good and bad points in a review unless it's impossible to think of any!
- Ask students if they can remember any good or bad points from the review *before* they read it again. Tell them to do the activity on their own. Go round and check students are doing the task correctly.
- When most students have finished, get them to compare answers in pairs.
- Go through the answers by asking different students to read out different points.

Answers

Good points

the plot – full of action and mystery

It is an exciting read – I couldn't put it down.

the way the story is told by the three main characters – you get to see the same events in different ways.

All the main characters have qualities that you can understand.

Its vision of the future – it's a reminder to us

Criticisms

sudden change in Alina's personality – didn't understand the change

---

⑪ WRITING SKILL Emphasis

- **11a** Look at the instructions. Elicit the answer. Write *What I really liked was …* on the board.
- **11b** Ask students to find the other ways good and bad points were introduced with a similar emphasis. Give students two minutes to look at the review again. Then ask for the ideas and write them on the board under the previous line.
- **11c** Explain the task. Give some examples yourself as a model. *What I really liked about [name of the film] was …*. You might add a follow-up comment too explaining why.
- Give students a few minutes to complete the three sentences of their own. Set a time limit of about five minutes for this. As students are writing, go round and help them. You might note some common errors for feedback when the time is up.
- Ask if anyone has any sentences they're particularly pleased with, and ask them to read them out.

Fast finishers

Students who finish quickly can write extra sentences.

- Explain the task. Students can use one of the films they have already talked about or a new film or book. Tell them to refer to the model on page 149 for help. Remind them of the structure of the model by reading out the bullet points.

- If you are going to give students a mark, tell them it will be higher if they organize the review in a similar way and use the language they have learnt. Put students in pairs and tell them to talk about or plan their review.

- Set the writing for homework or set a time limit of about twenty minutes to do it in class. As they are writing, go round and help. You might note some common errors for feedback when the time is up.

Fast finishers

Students who finish quickly can check their writing, or a partner's work, for errors, and for new language they used, or they could plan/write a second review.

- Put students in pairs. If there are students who didn't write the review, make sure they are with someone who did.

- Write these questions on the board:
  Did the review follow the pattern in the model and Exercise 12?
  Did it make use of any of the language you learnt?
  Does it sound like a good film or book or not?
  If you have seen it, do you agree with the review?
  Tell students to read their partner's review and answer the questions.

- Tell students to stay in the same pairs but ask them to swap review(s) with another pair. Repeat once or twice more. Go round and monitor. You might note some common errors for feedback. Give some feedback (positive – if they followed the model) and do some error correction on the board.

> **Homework**
> Set Workbook Lesson 1E exercises on pages 11–13 for homework.

2 Enjoy the ride

2A Getting from A to B
pp20–23

Information about the photo

The photo shows the Rio Negro in Colombia, South America, which crosses into Venezuela and eventually becomes a major tributary of the Amazon. The cables cross the canyon of the river in pairs. For some families, these cables are the only way of connecting with the external world.

To find more images or videos of this online, use the search term 'Rio Negro cables'.

LEAD IN

- Focus students' attention on the photo and the caption or project it using the CPT.
- Teach the word *cable* (a strong metal line), *slide* (a children's playground ride) and *cable slide* to describe the thing in the photo. Ask for a show of hands from students who have been on a cable ride such as this. Ask the class:

   Who has been on a cable ride like this? Where did you do it? Did you enjoy it?

   How were the cable rides you have been on different from the one in the photo?

   Where was this photo taken? (the Rio Negro canyon in Colombia)

   Are the children doing it for fun? (No, they are going to school.)

- Ask the class what they think the message of the photo is. Put them in pairs to discuss it for a minute.
- Choose students to give their ideas and help them express them in English.

Suggested answer

The photo shows that the journey to school isn't always easy or safe for children. Children and their families value education so much that they are willing to take great risks to get to school. Alternatively, it could just be that people live very diverse lives and travel in very different ways depending on where they live.

VOCABULARY Travel *p21*

MY PERSPECTIVE

- Tell students to look at Exercise 1 and read the questions to check they understand them.
- Put the class in pairs to discuss the questions for a few minutes. Go round and check students are doing the task correctly and notice errors, difficulties, or where they use L1. Help them by correcting or giving them the English they need, and then write some of these points on the board, or remember them for class feedback.
- Nominate individual students to tell the class some of their answers. You might make a list of the benefits of travel on the board. You might also ask students for reasons it may not always be a good idea to travel, such as for environmental reasons, and to avoid spending money.
- Ask the class: *Who would enjoy going to school in the way the children do? Would you be happy if a younger brother or sister travelled this way?* Ask students to justify their reasons.
- Find out from the class how they get to school. You could ask one person, and then ask *Does anyone else come to school like [name of student]?*
- At the end of the task, give some feedback about new language that came up, and focus on errors to correct (which you may have written on the board). You can also share some interesting things you heard with the class.

Fast finishers

Students can think of other famous sayings and quotations about travel that they may know (e.g. 'Travel broadens the mind' – anonymous; 'The world is a book, and those who do not travel read only one page' – Saint Augustine).

##

- Look at the instructions. Check that students understand that we usually use 'getting around' to describe travelling locally, e.g. 'get around town'. Explain that students are going to compete to see who can think of the most ways of getting around in two minutes. Tell them that after two minutes, they must put their pens down and count how many they have. They will get points for correct answers and extra points for original answers or answers that no one else has written down.
- Point out the expression *go on your skateboard*. Ask how *go somewhere on your skateboard/bike,* etc. is different from *go skateboarding/cycling,* etc. Explain that *go* **on** suggests that you are going on a journey from one place to another, while *go -ing* suggests having fun doing the activity (at a skate park, for example). We *go* **by** *bus/car/taxi/train/plane*.
- Put the class in pairs. Start the clock. Go round and check students are doing the task correctly. Offer help where appropriate. Tell them they can use a dictionary or ask you for help as necessary. Focus on these in feedback.

- After two minutes tell the class to stop. Tell students to swap their papers with a neighbouring pair. Nominate students to provide ways of getting around. Write correct answers on the board, correcting errors where necessary. Ensure correct collocations, e.g. *go ~~by~~ on foot, ~~drive~~ ride a bicycle,* etc. Award students points if they are correct, and ask *Did anyone else have the same one?* If not, award the student extra points. Also award points for interesting, original or fun ones.
- When a winner has been announced and congratulated, ask students in their pairs to answer the questions in question 2.
- Invite suggestions from the class, asking students to justify their answers.

Suggested answers

1 **take the** bus / train / underground (train) (also known as the metro, subway in US cities, the Tube in London) / tram. Also, '**go by** bus / train, etc.'
   go by bike / car
   take a taxi
   go on foot / your bike / roller-skates / rollerblades / your skateboard / your Segway!

2 The cheapest: walking is free.
   The fastest: in cities, motorbikes and bikes are used to get around quickly. Underground trains can be very fast, too.
   The most relaxing: taking a taxi or being driven around means you don't have to worry about anything (except the cost!). Going by train is relaxing outside the city.
   The most stressful: busy public transport, such as buses and underground trains, can be stressful when there are no seats, and everyone pushes to get off.
   Lets you see the most: open-top buses allow you to see the city from high up; bikes mean you can go at your own pace and really experience your surroundings.

---

③

- Tell students they are going to learn some more words and phrases to talk about travel. Look at the instructions and the words in the box. Check which words they already know and which words they aren't sure about. You could read out the words and point out stress and pronunciation. Do the first item with the whole class. Tell students the pairs of words are in the correct order in the box.
- Tell students to do the rest of the activity on their own, using a dictionary if they need to. Go round and check students are doing the task correctly and notice words and phrases they look up, ask you about, or underline. Focus on these in feedback.

- When most students have finished, get them to compare answers in pairs and to help each other with anything they haven't finished.
- Go through the answers by asking for volunteers to read out the full sentence. Quickly check understanding by asking different students: *Which words mean …*

  a long and difficult journey, usually at sea or in space? (voyage)

  a particular way to go from one place to another? (route)

  a short organized trip with school or as part of a holiday? (excursion)

  a trip made for scientific reasons or to discover new places? (expedition)

  a holiday on a ship? (cruise)

  the place where someone is going? (destination)

  travel to and from work and home every day? (commute)

  travelling on foot or using public transport, carrying a bag on your back? (backpacking)

  the journey and everything you did while you were away? (a trip)

  a journey that you take in someone else's car? (a lift)

> **Answers**
>
> **1** commute + lift   **2** flight + destination   **3** cruise + excursion   **4** trip + backpacking   **5** ride + route   **6** expedition + voyage

Extension

Put students in pairs. Tell them to take turns testing each other. One student closes their book while the other reads out the sentences with an 'oral gap fill', e.g. *'My mum and dad BEEEP by car, so they normally give me a BEEEP to school.'* The other student supplies the missing words.

> **Teaching tip**
>
> **Encouraging students to produce new language in feedback**
>
> When asking students for answers, always encourage them to produce the language being studied. Let's say the new vocabulary is *voyage*, and students have to match it with its definition. If you ask: *What's the meaning of 'voyage'?* students will respond with the definition and you won't hear them say the word itself. Ask instead *Which word means a long and difficult journey, usually at sea?* and students get to say *voyage*. There are two reasons for doing it this way:
>
> - it means students get a chance to practise saying the new vocabulary.
> - it allows you to check any pronunciation issues, e.g. /ˈvɔɪɑːʒ/ instead of the correct /ˈvɔɪɪdʒ/ or /kruːɪz/ instead of /kruːz/.

- Look at the instructions and do the first item with the whole class. Point out that you can only *catch* or *miss* vehicles which might leave without you, so *catch/miss my car* is not correct.
- Tell students to do the rest of the activity on their own, using a dictionary if they need to. Go round and check students are doing the task correctly and notice words and phrases they look up, ask you about, or underline. Focus on these in feedback. Check that students understand the answers by asking for alternatives, e.g. *That's right, you can't say 'get school'. Why not? That's right, it's 'get **to** school'.*
- When most students have finished, get them to compare answers in pairs and to help each other with anything they haven't finished.
- Go through the answers. Chorally drill the correct ones, i.e. *Everyone: catch my bus … catch my train … miss my bus … miss my train.* Tell students to record the words and phrases from the lesson in their vocabulary books.

> **Answers**
>
> **1** my car   **2** school (*get **to** school* – see 5)   **3** the car (*get **in / out of** the car*)   **4** a trip   **5** home (*get home*)   **6** a trip (*go **on** a trip* – see 7)   **7** a travel (travel usually a verb; as a noun it is abstract and uncountable)   **8** two kilometres (*The journey is two kilometres long*)

- Look at the instructions. Get students to do the completion first and then check answers. Then finish the first sentence so that it is true for you, as a model for the class.
- Give students two minutes to finish their sentences, then let them compare with a partner.
- Nominate students to share their answers, and elicit a variety of answers for each sentence. Use this opportunity to be interested in students' lives, past travel experiences and future dreams.

> **Suggested answers**
>
> **1** journey / commute (also a noun) / ride (if given a lift) … (students supply time it takes)
> **2** get … (students supply their best way to get to know the city)
> **3** take / go on … (students supply preferred means of public transport and reason)
> **4** went … (students supply last destination of a long journey they went on)
> **5** flight / cruise (*taxi* possible but unlikely … (students supply ideal destination, e.g. *I'd choose Sri Lanka as my destination*)

LISTENING *p22*

6

- Look at the instructions and ask them to look at the table and check they understand what to listen for. Check this by asking *What type of information do you expect in the third column?*
- Do the exercise in the Exam tip, then have the class make similar guesses about the table.

> **Exam tip**
>
> **Listening – Predicting information type**
>
> Many reading and listening tasks ask students to fill in missing information. It is usually possible to guess the kind of information and/or the part of speech that is needed before you listen. Then, while students are listening, they will probably find it easier to hear the actual missing information.
>
> Write the following short text on the board. Elicit possible words, or types of words that are probably missing by asking: *What can you say about the missing information here? The man has lost his _____ with about £_____ in it. He lost it on _____. He thinks he lost it between _____ and _____.*
> (e.g. *wallet / bag*; a number; a form of transport, e.g. *on the bus*; two stations or town names)

- If you think most students will have difficulty listening for all the missing information, you could put students in pairs, A and B, and have the As listen for the information missing from the first two columns, and the Bs from the last two columns.
- Play the audio once straight through. Copy the empty table on the board for feedback afterwards. At the end of the audio, tell students to compare their answers in pairs. Go round and notice how well they did (without saying anything). If you see the majority have not understood, be prepared to play the audio again.
- Encourage students to take turns filling in the missing information on the board. Hand out one or two board pens and tell students to write one piece of missing information each before passing the pen to another student.
- When the table on the board is filled, ask the class whether they agree with all the information, or whether they have different answers. Play the audio again to check.

Audioscript 🎧 8

1

You might think your journey to school takes ages, but Santiago Muñoz has one of the most tiring school commutes in the world. Fourteen-year-old Santiago wants to be a doctor. He lives in New York, down in Queens, but goes to high school all the way up in the Bronx at the Bronx High School of Science because it's a great school for maths and science. It's a journey that takes more than five hours each day. He has to get up at 5:00am. every morning and catch two buses and two subway trains each way. He uses the time to do his homework – if he gets a seat, that is! The good news is that he and his family are moving closer to the school. He's excited about having more time to spend with friends and getting more sleep!

2

Fourteen-year-old Chosing lives in Zanskar, a region in the Himalayan mountains. His school is a hundred kilometres away in a town called Leh, so he stays at school and goes home for the holidays. In winter, after he and his sister have visited their family, the road to Leh is closed because there is too much snow. However, the river is frozen, so their father takes them back to school using the river as an icy road. If they fall in the cold river they could die, so they have to think carefully about where to walk. They don't talk much, but it is never boring. It takes them six days and at the end they are exhausted.

3

For some students living along the Rio Negro river, one of the longest rivers in the country in the rainforest of Colombia, their journey to school is absolutely terrifying. They live on one side of the river, but school is hundreds of metres below them on the other side. The only way down is by riding down an old metal cable slide, which is very fast and dangerous. Injuries happen regularly on the journey. Daisy Mora makes the journey every day. She makes a seat from rope and throws herself out over the river. Then she rides down at about eighty kilometres per hour! It only takes about sixty seconds – if she's frightened, she doesn't show it!

7

- Tell students to look at Exercise 7 and read the questions to check they understand them. Before playing the audio again, let students try to answer from memory. They can write S, C or D.
- 🎧 8 Play the audio. Give students time to compare their answers in pairs.
- Nominate students to answer and write answers on the board.

Answers

	Where they live	How they travel	Time / distance they travel	What they do on the way
1 Santiago Muñoz	New York	bus (x2), subway train (x2)	five hrs / day	does his homework
2 Chosing	the Himalayas	walk along a frozen river	a hundred kilometres, six days	don't speak much, think carefully
3 Daisy Mora	Colombia (near Rio Negro)	on a cable slide	sixty seconds / hundreds of metres below them	

Answers

1 Chosing **2** Daisy **3** Chosing **4** Santiago
5 Santiago **6** Chosing **7** Chosing and Daisy
8 Santiago

GRAMMAR Adjectives ending in -ed and -ing *pp22–23*

To prepare for teaching the following exercises, see Grammar reference on page 130.

8

- Either get students to read the Grammar box silently, or read it out yourself. Tell students to identify all the adjectives in the sentences.
- Write on the board two columns: Describe the journey | Describe how the people feel. Elicit from students the adjectives and write them on the board, each time asking them which column to write them in. Ask them what they notice about the two lists (one group ends in -ed, the other in -ing).

Answers

Adjectives that describe journeys: tiring, boring, terrifying

Adjectives that describe how people feel: excited, exhausted, frightened

9

- Look at the instructions. Tell students to answer the two grammar-checking questions in pairs or ask the questions yourself to the whole class.
- You can either go through the answers with the whole class, or wait for them to read the Grammar reference on page 130 and then ask the class the grammar-checking questions or nominate individual students to give their answers.

Answers

1 -ed **2** -ing

Grammar reference and practice

Ask students to do Exercises 1 and 2 on page 131 now, or set them for homework.

Answers to Grammar practice exercises

1
1 bored **2** surprising **3** worried
4 frightening, relaxed **5** interesting, tired
6 confused **7** terrifying **8** exhausting
2
1 ~~embarrassed~~ embarrassing **2** ~~frightening~~
frightened **3** correct **4** ~~boring~~ bored
5 relaxed ~~relaxing~~ **6** correct **7** ~~depressed~~
depressing **8** correct

10

- Look at the instructions and do the first item with the whole class.
- Tell students to do the rest of the activity on their own, using a dictionary if they need to. Go round and check students are doing the task correctly and notice words and phrases they look up, ask you about, or underline. Focus on these in feedback.
- When you ask for the answers, insist that students provide them in sentence form, e.g. *Terrified means very frightened*. Remind them of the correct pronunciation of -ed words if necessary, which they studied on page 9 of the Student's Book.

Answers

1e, terrifying **2**h, exhausting **3**b, annoying
4c, disappointing **5**f, depressing **6**a, shocking
7d, worrying **8**g, confusing

11

- Explain the task. Tell students to choose the correct option in each item. Quickly go through the answers before putting them in pairs to tell each other one or two experiences based on the prompts. You might tell the class about an experience you have had to illustrate the first prompt.
- Explain that this is a speaking activity so they don't need to write anything. Give them a few minutes to share their experiences. Go round and make a note of any problems students are having with the language, such as pronunciation or meaning.
- When most pairs have finished, stop the activity. Give some feedback about new language that came up, and focus on errors to correct, which you may have written on the board.

Teaching tip

Correcting speaking activities

Students appreciate being corrected during speaking activities; as well as reinforcing learning at the point that they are using language, it helps them to realize the benefits of speaking activities in class. However, it can be demotivating knowing you've made lots of errors. Here are some tips for more friendly feedback!

- Don't interrupt students in the middle of a speaking activity, unless there are serious problems or no one is using the new language correctly. As you listen, quietly take notes of interesting use of English, such as errors or relevant emergent language.

- Make a note of instances where students have used new language well, not just their errors. It is reassuring to know you are on the right track!

- Prioritize errors, those that could cause miscommunication, widespread errors, or errors that are quick to correct because students will be able to immediately self-correct. Most importantly, listen out for students' use of the target language of that lesson, the language they have just learnt.

- Encourage self-correction. Ask questions like: *Is this sentence correct? Why not?* Signpost the error so students have an idea of what's wrong, e.g. *What's the problem with the noun? Was this action before or after that one? How many syllables in this word?*

- Name names! Don't be worried about saying: *Birgit, you said 'x'. What should you have said?* Students know that they all make errors, and they can learn from each other's, but they pay attention more when they know it concerns them. Point out the errors of the stronger students as well as the weaker ones to avoid demotivation.

- Encourage students to record their errors along with the corrected version. You could get them to compile a list in their notebooks called 'My common errors'.

- Explain that students now have a second chance to talk about the experiences in Exercise 11, and that they can try to speak even better this time. Put students in groups of four to six, making sure they are not in groups with their partners in Exercise 11. Point to the questions about the most exciting/boring, etc. experiences.

- After a few minutes, bring the discussion to a close. Nominate students from each group to share their favourite stories with the class.

Homework

- Set Workbook Lesson 2A exercises on pages 14–17 for homework.

- Students write up one or more stories based on experiences they told or heard in Exercises 11 and 12.

- Students find out about other unusual, long or dangerous school journeys. They choose one and present it in the following lesson.

2B Urban explorers pp24–25

VOCABULARY BUILDING Compound nouns p24

LEAD IN

- Point out that the title of the lesson is 'Urban explorers'. Check understanding of *urban*: *Do urban explorers explore the countryside or the city?* (the city) *Do you live in an urban area?* Explain to the class that they're going to learn about things you might see and do when visiting a city.

1

- Look at the instructions. Ask the whole class whether their town or city often gets visitors, or whether there are places in the area that get a lot of tourists. Ask them what they normally see and do there. Start a list of places on the board, e.g. *park, town hall, art gallery*, etc.

2

- Focus students' attention on lists A and B. Point out one or two compound nouns in the list, e.g. *art gallery*. Elicit other compound nouns the students already know, e.g. *alarm clock, classroom, brother-in-law*. Point out that:
  - it is *usually* the second part of the compound that says what something is, e.g. an alarm clock is a type of clock, and a classroom is a type of room.
  - compound nouns can be two separate words, one word, or hyphenated, and that there are no rules about this; they have to learn this as part of the spelling of the compound.
- Tell students to match words in columns A and B to make compound nouns related to places in cities and things to do there. Point out that 1–6 match the words above the line space and 7–12 below the line space. Tell them to use a dictionary if they need to check whether the compound nouns are one word or two (none of these are hyphenated). Alternatively, tell students that four of the compound nouns are one word and challenge them to guess which those are.
- Go round and check that students are doing the task and helping where necessary. Do not give the answers yet.

3

- 🎧 **9** Look at the instructions. First tell students to listen to check their answers. Play the audio.
- Ask for a show of hands. *Who got all twelve correct? Well done! Who got eleven? Ten? Did you know which compound nouns were one word? Good.*
- Tell the students to listen again. This time, they should underline the main stressed part of each compound. Play the first item to check that students are aware of what stress means, and can hear it without difficulty. Play the rest of the audio.
- Invite students to the board to write the compound nouns marking the stress in your preferred way. Ask the class if they are all correct and discuss differences of opinion. Then ask for the general rule.

Teaching tip

Where's the stress?

There are lots of ways of showing where the stress is in a word or phrase, but which is best? Look at the ways of marking stress below and answer the questions.

<u>sight</u>seeing
WALKing tour
skyscraper
rooftop
a-'muse-ment park
building site
● • •
skyscraper
■ ☐☐☐
shopping centre

- Which are quick and easy to mark on the board?
- Which are the clearest to see?
- Which don't distort the normal appearance of the word?
- Which do students need to understand to be able to see word stress in a dictionary?
- Which are often used in teaching materials?
- Which mark all the syllables, not just the stressed ones?

The system you use is up to you, but explain it to students and be consistent. And always ask students: *How many syllables? Where's the stress?*

4

- Look at the instructions for the activity with the class, then give students two minutes to look back at Exercise 2 and decide their answers. Then ask them to compare their ideas in pairs.
- Go through the answers by asking students to read out their lists. Check their pronunciation and stress as they do.

Fast finishers

Students can add more items to each list.

- Decide whether students write or say sentences. Encourage them to make true sentences, even if that means making negative sentences, e.g. *Sightseeing isn't a reason people come to our town.*

- One idea is to do it as a game in pairs. Students close their books and take turns to say sentences, e.g. *There's a bridge over the railway tracks behind the park*, until they cannot think of any more sentences. The last person to say a correct sentence without repeating compound nouns is the winner. They can write their sentences after saying them.

Extension

Get students to explore compound nouns around other topic areas. Put students in pairs and give each pair a different topic around which they should brainstorm compound nouns. Here are some examples:

Sport, e.g. *tennis racket, penalty area*
School and stationery, e.g. *pencil case, blackboard*
Cooking and kitchens, e.g. *tin opener, table lamp*
Computers and technology, e.g. *pen drive, touch pad*
Nature and the environment, e.g. *polar bear, global warming*

READING *pp24–25*

- Focus students' attention on the photo, the title and subtitle. Before they start reading the article, tell them to write three questions that they would like answered in the article. To ensure students aren't reading, you might ask them to close their books, and write the title and subtitle on the board instead.

- Go round the class and check that students are writing questions and not reading. Check that the questions are correctly written. You might prompt a variety of questions by writing on the board *What …? When …? Where …? How …? How many …? Who …? What kind of …? Why …? Is …? Do …? Does …? Has …?* etc.

- When most students have written three questions, ask students to choose their favourite question. Nominate a few students to read theirs out to share with the whole class.

- 🔊 **10** Give students five minutes to read the article to find out whether their questions are answered. Go round and check students' progress. When everyone has finished reading, ask for a show of hands *Hands up if the article answered all three of your questions. Good. Two? Just one? None? OK.*

- Nominate students to read out one of their questions which was answered and to tell the class the answer.

Fast finishers

Students who finish quickly can write another question that is answered in the article.

- Explain the task. Tell students to make a note of the line number in the text where they found the answer. Advise them to read 1–7 carefully first before answering.

> ### Exam tip
> #### Identifying where the answer is in the text
> When answering comprehension questions, students should always make sure they know where in the text the information is that leads them to their answer. It's a good idea to make a note of the line number, or underline the words, phrases or sentences that help them decide. By saying to themselves: *The answer is x and I know this because it says this here*, they can be more confident that they are correct.

- Get whole-class feedback. Ask *For number one, hands up who thinks the answer is a? b? c? Good the correct answer is b.* Then invite volunteers to explain where in the text the information is that led them to that answer.

CRITICAL THINKING Selecting information *p25*

- Ask a student to read the Critical thinking box to the class. Ask the class if they ever have to write articles about a subject which involves choosing what information to include. Ask them what reasons there might be for including information or leaving it out.

- Ask students to decide which of questions 1–9 are answered in the article. After two minutes, get them to compare answers in pairs.

- Go through the answers. When you ask students for the answers, make sure that they tell you where these questions are answered.

Answers

1 is answered in that we hear about stories in London, Paris, Chicago and (probably) China.

4 is answered in the final paragraph. If students wanted to do real urban exploration, the article gives them many ideas about where and how to do it.

6 is answered in that we read about Bradley Garret's adventures in London and Chicago.

7 is answered in the paragraph beginning: *Why do urbexers do it?*

8 is answered in paragraphs 2 and 6

9 is answered in paragraph 2, lines 14–15, and indirectly in paragraph 6

2, 3 and 5 are not answered

- Explain the task and refer students to all the questions they asked in Exercise 6. Put students in groups of four to six to discuss the questions.

- Go round and check that they are doing the task correctly. With the third question, don't accept 'Look online', but make sure they specify, for example what search terms they would use for each question.

- Put students in new groups. Get them to share their ideas.

Teaching tip

Regrouping students for feedback

Normally, students tell the teacher their answers or ideas. After a speaking activity such as a discussion, consider allowing students to give feedback to one another instead. Regrouping students so that they can relay what they have discussed lets them reformulate ideas and say them in a better, more fluent way.

Let's say they discuss in groups of three or four: AAA, BBBB, CCCC, DDD, etc. Assign students in each group a number from 1 to 3 or 4: 1234, 1234, 1234, 123, etc. Then simply tell all the '1's to one corner of the room, all the '2's to another corner, and so on: 1111, 2222, 3333, 444, etc. Now they can share what they have talked about.

- Conclude the lesson by asking students whether the article included mostly relevant, interesting information. Encourage a range of answers if possible, and make sure students justify their answers.

Homework

- Set Workbook Lesson 2B exercises on pages 18–19 for homework.

- Students research the answers to the questions about urbexers they would like answering in Exercise 9.

- Students write an article about a subject of their choice. It should be something they know a lot about, such as a hobby of theirs. they plan it by writing the questions that they imagine a general reader wanting to know.

2C Sydney on $20 *pp26–27*

GRAMMAR Narrative forms *pp26–27*

To prepare for teaching the following exercises, see Grammar reference on page 130.

- **Books closed.** Write the three words in the box in Exercise 1 on the board and ask the class the question. Put students in pairs and get them to tell the story about Bradley and the Chicago skyscraper.

- **Optional step.** If you think that students may already be familiar with narrative tenses, give them a chance to show you how well they have mastered their use. Tell students to write the story from memory. Explain that they need to use the past perfect, past continuous and past simple in the story.

As well as the keywords in Exercise 1, write on the board some more words from the story and tell them to use these, too: *friends, sit, suggest, Legacy Tower, try to get up, walk, get in, residents, open*.

Go round and find out how well students are incorporating the tenses into the story. Gauge their level of understanding of the tenses by how well they use them. This information can help you to focus on the most important aspects of the grammar during the rest of the lesson.

- Tell students to check their ideas with the article on page 25. Invite students to tell you if there were any differences between the original text and their versions.

- Explain the task. Tell students not to refer to the article on page 25 when they're doing the task.

- When most students have finished, get them to compare answers in pairs and to help each other with anything they haven't finished.

- They can then check their answers by looking at the original sentences on page 25.

Answers
a had climbed, had managed, stopped
b was studying, was writing
c were sitting, suggested, walked, got, had opened
d used to work

- Using the sentences in the Grammar box as examples, students complete the rules with the correct narrative tense.

- You can either go through the answers with the whole class, or wait for them to read the Grammar reference on page 130 or nominate individual students to give their answers. When you ask for the answers, check that students can give you an example or examples from the Grammar box.

Grammar reference and practice

Ask students to do Exercises 3–6 on page 131 now, or set them for homework.

- Remind students that urbexers don't do the normal things that tourists and travellers do. Elicit from the class other tourism norms, i.e.
  activities (sightseeing, visiting museums, theme parks, etc.)
  places to stay (hotels, hostels, etc.)
  places to eat (restaurants, cafés, hotels, etc.)
  ways to travel (tourist bus, plane, taxi, hire car, etc.)
- Tell students to read the text about freeganism and ask them how freegans travel differently from normal tourists. (They do it for little or no money, without buying things and travelling for free.)

- Ask students what the advantages of freeganism are as well as to imagine what the disadvantages might be. Make sure they express whether they'd want to live like this and whether they would consider it as a cheap way of travelling.

- **Optional step**. Show the class a video about freeganism. For example, there is a TEDx Talk by Rob Greenfield, 'How To End The Food Waste Fiasco', that explains the reasons people become freegan.

- Look at the instructions. Check that students understand *gap year* (time between leaving school at eighteen and going to university when some people travel). Do the first item with the whole class.
- Tell students to do the rest of the activity on their own. Go round and check how many of the options students are getting correct. Question their ideas by asking them to justify their choices according to the rules in Exercise 4. When most students have finished, get them to compare answers in pairs and to help each other with anything they haven't finished.
- Go through the answers by nominating students to read out each sentence. Check that the rest of the class agrees with each answer before confirming it.

- Explain the task. Tell students that there is sometimes more than one possible choice. Do the first item with the whole class.
- Tell students to do the rest of the activity on their own. Go round and check students' choices. Ask them to justify them according to the rules. Before discussing the answers with the whole class, let students compare with a partner.
- Nominate individual students to give their answers. Write their answers on the board. Ask students what they notice about the possible answers, i.e. that the past simple is very often possible where other narrative tenses might be more accurate.
- At the end of the task, ask the class whether their opinions about freeganism have changed since reading about Becky. Find out what they think now and why.

8 PRONUNCIATION Weak forms: *used to*

- 🔊 **11** Look at the instructions. Play the audio.

- Point out the different pronunciation of *used*. As a main verb it is /ˈjuːz(d)/, but in the *used to* structure to describe past routines it is /ˈjuːs(t)/.

- The preposition *to* is pronounced /tə/ in most sentences. It is not stressed. However, in final position (as in 3), it is in its strong form /tuː/.

- Drill chorally and individually to check everyone can say the different forms of the word. Then let students practise on their own.

Teaching tip

Choral and individual drilling

Students generally appreciate the chance to practise pronunciation in class and to be corrected. Choral drilling is when the teacher makes everyone say the same thing at the same time. Drill chorally first to give students a secure, anonymous space to practise. Individual drilling is when the teacher nominates students to say something on their own. Do individual drilling after choral drilling so that you can check all students are getting it right.

Answers and audioscript 🔊 **11**

1 Our **grand**parents **ne**ver **used** to **throw** their **food** a**way**. /ˈjuːstə/
2 Did **peo**ple **use** to **tra**vel a **lot** when **your pa**rents were **young**? /ˈjuːstə/
3 A: Do you en**joy tra**velling by **plane**?
   B: I **used** to, but **not** any**more**. /ˈjuːstuː/

9

- Look at the instructions and do the first couple of items with the whole class to clarify the instructions and indicate the sort of sentence you expect, e.g. *Before this lesson I didn't know that Karoline and Frieda had been classmates before they came to this school.*

- Show how the different narrative forms may be used for each sentence. You might even ask students what tenses each line suggests, e.g. item 4 may suggest the past simple and the past continuous (*The last time I cried was when I was watching …*, etc.). Go round and offer help to students who need it. Make a note of any difficulties students have with particular tenses, etc.

- When most students have finished, get them to compare answers in pairs and to help each other with anything they haven't finished. Ask them to choose their most interesting sentences and explain to each other why they like them.

Suggested answers

1 … what freeganism is.
2 … play with dolls with my friends. / … believe there were monsters under my bed.
3 … come to school on my own. / think I was any good at maths.
4 … cried … I was watching a film with my family. It was embarrassing!
5 … I went to the shops last week. / … I was saving up for a new bike, so I couldn't do anything with my friends. But it was worth it!
6 … a new T-shirt … looking for a present for my Mum's birthday.

Extension

Play 'Yes, I did/was/had'. This game practises yes/no questions and short answers. The objective of the game is to get three *Yes, I did* answers, two *Yes, I was* answers and one *Yes, I had* answer from your partner before they get them from you. First, ask students to write down as many yes/no questions as they can in the past simple, past continuous and past perfect. Give them an example of each, e.g. *Did you come to school by bus? Were you studying at eight o'clock last night? Had you seen the original Star Wars movies before you watched the latest one?* Then model the game by letting the students ask you questions until they've got the six answers they need from you (you have to be honest!). Students then play the game in pairs. The first student to elicit all six answers wins.

10

- Explain the task. Remind students of the use of narrative tenses to tell stories and anecdotes.

- Point to the questions and tell students that by answering the questions they can prepare what they will say. Also, ask them to identify points in the story when they can use each of the narrative tenses. They can invent a story if they prefer.

11 CHOOSE

The idea is for students to make their own choice of activity here. However, you might want to make the decision for the students, in which case explain why. Alternatively, you may decide to let students do more than one task.

You may be able to divide the class into groups and have each group do a different task – or you could have a vote on which task the whole class should do. For the vote:

- put students in pairs or groups to decide which they prefer.

- take a vote on each task.

- if the vote is tied, ask one student from each side to explain which is best and take the vote again. You can decide if there is still no change.

- Options 1 and 2 are speaking tasks. Encourage students to see this as creating a good text, like a writing activity would be. If you have time, you might suggest they do task 1 before task 2 as preparation.
- Alternatively, ask students to record their story. Let them record it as many times as they like until they are happy with it. They can either keep it for themselves to help them hear their own errors and correct them, or share it with you and/or the rest of the class on a cloud-sharing app like WhatsApp or Padlet.
- Once shared, students can listen to everyone's stories and choose the most exciting, the easiest to understand, the most similar to their own, etc.
- Option 3 is a writing task. Consider displaying the stories on the wall or if students can type their stories and upload them, creating a class webpage for them to read, show their families and so on.

> **Homework**
> - Set Workbook Lesson 2C exercises on pages 20–21 for homework.
> - If students didn't write their stories in Exercise 11, set this task for homework.
> - Students find another freegan experience online and read about it so they can share what they found the following lesson.
> - You might want to tell students to watch the track called *Unit 2 TED Talk* on the *Perspectives* website before they come to the next class.

2D Happy maps *pp28–29*

- Tell students they are going to watch a TED Talk about a new kind of map.
- Read out the quote and ask students to translate it or say what they think it means in English (or both). First of all, ask why adventure is dangerous, and elicit a few ideas. Ask them if that is true, why might someone say its opposite, routine, is not safe. Accept all ideas without imposing any of your own.
- ▶ **2.0** Tell them they are going to see a short text on the DVD to introduce the talk and the speaker, and play the *About the speaker* section. Then do the vocabulary exercise.
- After they finish, you might write the key words from the *About the Speaker* section of the DVD on the board and ask students to retell it aloud, or ask them to write as much of what it said as they can. Correct as necessary.

> **Answers to About the speaker**
> 1 efficiency = a (the ability to use time and energy well to get a job done)
> 2 crowdsource = c (get information from many people, usually using the internet)
> 3 urban = a (connected with cities and towns and not the countryside)
> 4 mapping app = c (software that shows maps)
> 5 path = b (the way from one place to another)

TED Talk About the speaker ▶ 2.0

*Daniele Quercia is a scientist at Yahoo! Labs in Barcelona, where he works on new ways to use online maps to improve our 'offline' lives. His work used to be all about **efficiency**, and getting to where you want to go as quickly as possible. But an experience when he was working in Boston changed all that.*

*Now he is interested in enjoying the journey, not just the quickest route between two places. He and his team **crowdsource** their research. They get members of the public to play an online game. Players have to choose between pairs of photos of **urban** scenes. Daniele has used the information from the game to design a **mapping app** that can show you the happy **path** to your destination.*

Daniele's idea worth spreading is that the fastest route may be efficient, but there are times when taking a different route can be more interesting and memorable.

AUTHENTIC LISTENING SKILLS
Understanding accents *p28*

As well as teaching aspects of phonology and listening skills, these tasks also allow:

- you to pre-teach some vocabulary.
- students to read and hear new language before they listen to the whole text.
- students to tune in to the speaker's voice and style.

- Either ask students to read the Authentic listening skills box silently to themselves or read it out yourself as they read along. Then ask students:

   What accents have you heard spoken in English? (both as a first language, e.g. Irish, Australian, and as a foreign language, e.g. Brazilian English, Japanese English)

   Where do you hear English spoken by a variety of nationalities? (e.g. YouTube videos)

   Which accents are important for you to understand? Why?

   Which accents sound nice to you? Why?

   Which accents are clearest to understand? Why?

- 🎧 **12** Look at the instructions. Focus students' attention on the underlined words in the extract. Play the audio at least twice.
- Invite students who are feeling confident to explain the difference. While you discuss the differences, point out that some native English-speaking accents, such as the traditional London accent, drop the /h/ at the beginning of words, and in normal speech the -ed is sometimes not pronounced by native English speakers.

> **Answers**
>
> The first speaker pronounces *have* /hæv/ while Daniele pronounces it /æv/, dropping the initial /h/.
>
> The first speaker pronounces focused /fəʊkəst/ while Daniele pronounces it /fəʊkəs/, dropping the /t/ sound of -ed.

2

- Tell students to read three more sentences from the TED Talk they are going to hear and to practise saying the sentences as naturally as possible, paying attention to the underlined words. They can listen to each other in pairs if you think this will help them notice differences.
- 🎧 **13** Tell students to listen to the same two voices and notice the pronunciation of the underlined words. Play the audio.
- Play the audio again, but pause to allow students to repeat the sentences. Let them choose whether they want to practise an Italian accent, the native speaker's regional accent, or, perhaps best of all, their own accent! Practising all three allows them to feel as well as hear the differences, of course.

- Check answers as a class. You might ask students what the typical characteristics of English as it is spoken by speakers of their own language are.

> **Answers**
>
> This is how Daniele pronounces these words. Notice that in sentence 1 he pronounces the -ed endings of both verbs (the same as the native speaker), but not in sentence 2. In *smelled* in sentence 3 he drops the -ed but pronounces it clearly in *sounded*. He drops the /h/ in *how* in 3.
>
> **1** I <u>lived</u> in /lɪvdɪn/ Boston and <u>worked</u> in /wɜːktɪn/ Cambridge.
> **2** I <u>teamed</u> up /tiːmʌp/ with Luca and Rossano.
> **3** They also recalled <u>how</u> /aʊ/ some paths <u>smelled</u> /smel/ and <u>sounded</u> /saʊndɪd/.

3 MY PERSPECTIVE

- Ask students to read the statements and decide which of them they agree with, and why. In feedback, encourage students to justify their opinions.
- **Optional step.** Students 'take their stand'. Put up two signs at opposite ends of the classroom, one saying 'AGREE' and the other 'DISAGREE'. Read out each statement in Exercise 3 and ask the students to stand anywhere in the room to reflect their attitude to the statement. They can stand next to either sign or somewhere in the middle. Once everyone has chosen a place to stand, ask them to justify their position.

Extension

Get students to write their 'Pronunciation mission statement' in their notebooks. Tell them that in light of the discussion about accent that they have just participated in, you would like them now to summarize their feelings about pronunciation and accent in their English-learning lives. Dictate the following questions that they should answer in their statement:

Which accents will it be important for you to understand well in your future English-speaking life?

How are you going to improve your pronunciation in English?

What impression do you hope your accent in English gives people in the future?

Whose accent do you hope your accent will be as good as in the future?

Go round and help students write their mission statements. When most of them have finished, invite individual students to read theirs out.

WATCH pp28–29

If you are short of time, or want a different approach to the video, you may want to watch the whole talk all the way through with only some brief checking questions. A version of this is on the DVD and is labelled as *TED Talk with activities*. At the end of each section, there is a short gist question. Pause after each question on screen so students can give their answers, then play the answer.

Answers to gist questions on DVD

Part 1

What did Daniele realize when he took a different route to work one day?

b He had trusted his mobile phone too much.

Part 2

Why did Daniele's team use crowdsourcing to do their research?

a They wanted to understand which parts of the city people find beautiful.

- **Optional first step.** Show the class a still from the talk (at 1:05 in Part 2 or 3:40 in the full talk) that shows two photographs, A and B, of an urban street scene and leafy suburban garden scene respectively. Dictate the following questions for students to write:

  How would you describe the two scenes?

  Is your journey to school more like the first or second photograph? What do you like or dislike about it?

  What do you usually see on your journey to school? What can you hear? What can you smell?

- Alternatively, just ask the class the last question without the image.

- Ask students to read the questions and check they understand them.
- ▶ **2.1** Play Part 1 straight through.
- Ask students to compare their answers in pairs. Go round and notice how well they did in order to decide how quickly to go through answers, and whether you will need to play Part 1 again.
- Check answers by asking the whole class for their ideas.

Answers

1 c **2** b **3** a

TED Talk Part 1 script ▶ 2.1

I have a confession to make. As a scientist and engineer, I've focused on efficiency for many years.

A few years ago, after finishing my Ph.D. in London, I moved to Boston. I lived in Boston and worked in Cambridge. I bought a racing bicycle that summer, and I bicycled every day to work. To find my way, I used my phone. It sent me over Mass Ave, Massachusetts Avenue, the shortest route from Boston to Cambridge. But, after a month, that I was cycling every day on the car-packed Mass Ave, I took a different route one day. I'm not entirely sure why I took a different route that day, a detour. I just remember a feeling of surprise; surprise at finding a street with no cars, as opposed to the nearby Mass Ave full of cars; surprise at finding a street draped by the leaves and surrounded by trees. But after the feeling of surprise, I felt shame. How could I have been so blind? For an entire month, I was so trapped in my mobile app that a journey to work became one thing only: the shortest path. In this single journey, there was no thought of enjoying the road, no pleasure in connecting with nature, no possibility of looking people in the eyes. And why? Because I was saving a minute out of my commute.

Now, let me ask you, am I alone here? How many of you have never used a mapping app for finding directions? Most of you, if not all, have. And don't get me wrong – mapping apps are the greatest game-changer for encouraging people to explore the city. You take your phone out and you know immediately where to go. However, the app also assumes there are only a handful of directions to the destination. It has the power to make those handful of directions the definitive direction to that destination.

- Ask students to read sentences 1–6 and check they understand them.
- ▶ **2.2** Play Part 2 straight through.
- Ask students to compare their answers in pairs. Go round and notice how well they did in order to decide how quickly to go through answers, and whether you will need to play Part 2 again.
- Check answers by asking the whole class for their ideas.

Answers

1 experience **2** most enjoyable **3** play a game
4 London **5** memories **6** many paths

TED Talk Part 2 script ▶ 2.2

After that experience, I changed. I changed my research from traditional data-mining to understanding how people experience the city. The result of that research has been the creation of new maps, maps where you don't only find the shortest path, the blue one, but also the most enjoyable path, the red one. How was that possible?

Einstein once said, 'Logic will get you from A to B. Imagination will take you everywhere.' So, with a bit of imagination, we needed to understand which parts of the city people find beautiful. At the University of Cambridge, with colleagues, we thought about this simple experiment. If I were to show you these two urban scenes, and I were to ask you which one is more beautiful, which one would you say? Don't be shy! Who says A? Who says B? Brilliant! Based on that idea, we built a crowdsourcing platform, a web game. Players are shown pairs of urban scenes, and they're asked to choose which one is more beautiful, quiet and happy. Based on thousands of user votes, then we are able to see where consensus emerges. We are able to see which are the urban scenes that make people happy.

After that work, I joined Yahoo Labs, and I teamed up with Luca and Rossano, and together, we aggregated those winning locations in London to build a new map of the city, a cartography weighted for human emotions. On this cartography, you're not only able to see and connect from point A to point B the shortest segments, but you're also able to see the happy segment, the beautiful path, the quiet path. In tests, participants found the happy, the beautiful, the quiet path far more enjoyable than the shortest one, and that just by adding a few minutes to travel time.

Participants also love to attach memories to places. Shared memories – that's where the old BBC building was; and personal memories – that's where I gave my first kiss. They also recalled how some paths smelled and sounded. So, what if we had a mapping tool that would return the most enjoyable routes based not only on aesthetics but also based on smell, sound and memories? That's where our research is going right now. More generally, my research, what it tries to do is avoid the danger of the single path, to avoid robbing people of fully experiencing the city in which they live. Walk the path through the park, not through the car park, and you have an entirely different path. Walk the path full of people you love and not full of cars, and you have an entirely different path. It's that simple.

If you think that adventure is dangerous, try routine. It's deadly.

Thank you.

7 VOCABULARY IN CONTEXT

- **7a** ▶ **2.3** Tell students that they are going to watch some clips from the talk which contain new or interesting words or phrases. They should choose the correct meaning for each one. Play the *Vocabulary in context* section.

- Pause after each question on the screen so students can choose the correct definition, then play the answer. Give an additional example before moving on to the next question. If you like, you can ask students to call out the answers.

Answers
1 surrounded by trees = c (with trees all around it)
2 shame = b (embarrassment about something bad that you have done)
3 don't get me wrong = b (Please understand me.)
4 a handful of = c (a small number of)
5 shy = b (not confident in public)
6 teamed up = b (started working with)

- **7b** Check students understand the words in italics and re-teach if necessary, or ask students if they can recall the examples in the talk. Tell students to think of examples of the five things. Point out that they relate to some of the new words and phrases they have just learnt in Exercise 7a. Give them two minutes and make sure they note down their ideas.

- Put students in pairs to tell each other their ideas. Go round and check they are doing the task correctly and notice errors, difficulties, or where they use L1. Help them by correcting or giving them the English they need. Focus especially on their use of the new words and phrases.

- At the end of the task, give some feedback about new language that came up, and any errors which you may have written on the board. You can also retell some stories you heard or nominate one or two students to tell the class the most interesting things they said or heard.

CHALLENGE

- Ask students to read the Challenge box and make notes about the three places. Encourage them to think of more than one answer for each category if possible. If you think students may struggle to come up with ideas, you could talk about a place that you know first. Smells might include smells from a factory, the sea, farms, traffic, etc. Sounds could include alarms, planes, music, birds or other animals nearby, etc. Memories could be positive or negative.

- When most students have all their answers, put them in pairs to share their ideas. Go round and notice errors, difficulties, or where they use L1 and help by correcting or giving students the English they need.

- Nominate students to share some of the smells, sounds and memories that they talked about. You could remind students of the structures *It smells/sounds like …* and *It reminds me of …* to help them express their ideas.

8

- Ask students to read the questions and check they understand them. Put them in groups of three to five. Give them five minutes to do discuss them.

- Go around and help groups with their ideas, making suggestions and asking questions.

- After several minutes, regroup students. Tell them to share their groups ideas with the rest of the class.

- Explain the task. To make it more realistic, you might show them photos of two groups of visitors, an older group of tourists with cameras, rucksacks and guide books, and a group of teenagers in a tourist setting.

- If you have physical maps of the local area, you can use them. Otherwise, students may have access to online maps via their mobile devices or class computers.

- It is possible to do this without maps if the students know the town well. In fact, you may decide to get them discussing their routes without a map because that means they have to communicate the routes to one another verbally without resorting to visual support. The next lesson's language focus is on giving directions, so this would be an opportunity to evaluate their competence in this area. Make a note of any errors that they make, e.g. *Turn to left*, *Go through Park Street*, etc. which can then be used for accuracy work in the next lesson.

10

- Explain the task. Join pairs to make groups of four or six students. Give them time to compare their routes and discuss the questions.

- Go round and check they are doing the task correctly and notice errors, difficulties, or where they use L1. Help them by correcting or giving them the English they need.

- Finish with some whole-class discussion about the routes the students have proposed and other issues that came up. Correct any common or interesting errors that you heard.

Homework
- Set Workbook Lesson 2D exercises on page 22 for homework.

- Students explore National Geographic's online map resource and choose their favourite maps from there. They prepare to tell their classmates about it in the next lesson. See http://maps.nationalgeographic.com/maps.

- Students choose and watch another TED Talk about maps from the TED playlist, 'Adventures in mapping'.

2E You can't miss it *pp30–31*

OPTIONAL LEAD IN

- Tell the class that you are going to direct them from the school to somewhere in the town or city. They must listen carefully and decide where the directions lead them. They might prefer to close their eyes so that they can visualize where they are. Choose a place not too far from the school that all the students will know, e.g. a big supermarket, the town hall, the stadium. Give them the directions slowly and clearly, but without repeating them, e.g. *Turn left out of the school entrance. Go along the street for about 100 metres, and take the second turning on the right …*
- Students call out the place as soon as they think they know where you are talking about. The first person to correctly identify the destination is the winner. Congratulate them, then invite them to the front of the class to give directions to the class to another place in town.

SPEAKING *p30*

- Put students in pairs to talk about their experiences and preferences regarding finding their way around unfamiliar places.
- In feedback, if students say they don't ask for directions because they always use their phones these days, ask them what they would do if they had lost or broken their phone, if the signal was weak, or if they were in a foreign country and using the phone was expensive.

- 🎧 **14** Look at the instructions and the table with the whole class. Check they understand the information that they need to listen for. Ask them to give you some possible answers for each question to check that they have understood. Play the audio once straight through.
- When the audio has finished, tell students to compare answers in pairs before nominating students to provide answers.

Audioscript 🎧 14

Conversation 1

Male 1:	Er, excuse me?
Male 2:	Yes?
Male 1:	Can you help me? I'm trying to get to the museum.
Male 2:	The **Science Museum**?
Male 1:	Yes. Do you know where it is?
Male 2:	Yeah. It's quite a long way from here. About **fifteen minutes' walk**.
Male 1:	That's OK.
Male 2:	Right, hmm. The easiest route is to go up Northway Street. Can you see the traffic lights over there, through the park? That's Northway Street. Go up Northway Street for about five minutes until you get to the supermarket on your left. Then take the first … no, second turning on the right.
Male 1:	Right. OK.
Male 2:	As soon as you turn right, you'll see the train station on your left. There's a road just after the station on your left, and you need to go down there.
Male 1:	OK, so it's right, then left after the station?
Male 2:	That's it. It's quite easy after that. The museum is on the other side of the park, and it's really big. You can't miss it.
Male 1:	OK, well, **I can always ask someone else** if I get lost. Thanks very much.
Male 2:	No problem. Bye.

Conversation 2

Melanie:	Hi, Karina!
Karina:	Hi, Melanie.
Melanie:	We were just talking about you.
Karina:	Were you?
Melanie:	Fabien wanted to know if you're still coming tonight.

Answers

	Conversation 1	Conversation 2
1 Do the speakers know each other?	no – they are strangers	yes, they are friends
2 Where do they want to get to?	(science) museum	their friend's house
3 How are they travelling?	on foot / he is walking	by bike / she is cycling
4 How far is it?	15 minutes	1 km from the station
5 What will they do if they get lost?	ask someone	phone their friend

Karina	Yes, that's why I'm calling. **Can you give me directions to your house?**
Melanie	Sure! Are you driving?
Karina	**I'll be on my bike.**
Melanie	OK, well that's easy then. Do you know how to get to the station? **It's probably no more than a kilometre from there.**
Karina	Yes, I know where the station is.
Melanie	Good. So, if the station's behind you, you'll need to turn right …
Karina	OK.
Melanie	At the end of the street you'll see a cinema in front of you.
Karina	Yes, I know where that is.
Melanie	OK. Turn left there.
Karina	Left?
Melanie	Yes!
Karina	That's Northway Street, isn't it?
Melanie	Yeah. OK, so carry on up Northway Street until you get to a supermarket on your right. Just after that, there's a street on the left. That's our street. We're number 15.
Karina	I'll find it. **I'll call you if I have a problem.**

- Focus students' attention on the map on the phone and ask them to look at it carefully. Tell them to listen again in order to work out which of the letters A–E on the map are the four places in Exercise 3. Point out that there are two places for each conversation and that there is one place on the map they don't need.
- 🎧 **14** Play the audio again. Tell students to compare their answers in pairs. Go round and notice how well they did (without saying anything). If you see the majority have not understood, be prepared to play the audio again.
- Check answers by nominating a student to say which letter the Science Museum is. Ask the rest of the class to raise their hands if they disagree.

Answers

1 E **2** A **3** B **4** D

- Explain the task. Tell students to try to remember or guess the missing words from the dialogues. Give them two minutes for this, and let them share ideas before listening.
- 🎧 **14** Play the audio again for students to check.
- When you go through the answers, ask students if they thought of other possibilities for each gap. Accept or reject these ideas according to whether they would be correct or sound natural in these sentences. Possible alternatives are given below.

Answers

1 help, get **2** way (journey), walk **3** until (till), turning (road, street) **4** miss **5** directions
6 behind **7** end **8** Carry (Go), that

- Point out the categories in the Useful language box. Show students how the first sentence in Exercise 4 goes in the first category (A). Ask them to categorize the rest of the sentences.
- Check answers as a class.

Answers

1 A **2** D **3** B / C **4** C **5** A **6** B / C **7** C
8 B / C

6

- Put students in pairs. Tell them to take turns asking for and giving directions between places on the map, e.g. between C and A, between the supermarket and the station.
- Go round and check students are doing the task correctly and listen for good use of the new language of directions as well as any recurring errors.
- Tell the class about any errors that you heard while they were speaking and correct them for the class.

7

- Put students in groups of three to six and explain the game to them. One person should give directions to the group without saying where the directions take them. The first person to correctly identify the destination chooses a new destination and gives new directions to the group.

Extension

- Have students in pairs roleplay encounters in the street with lost tourists. Write on the board the beginning of the dialogue.

Excuse me, do you know the way to `BEEP', please?
Yes, sure, it's not very far from here. You need to go …

- Tell students to take turns being a tourist in their own town. They must first establish in which part of town they are speaking, then ask for directions to another place. Give them a few minutes to perform several conversations like this. Go round and check students are doing the task correctly and notice errors, and make a note of any language points to go over with the class.
- At the end of the task, invite a couple of students from each group to the front of the class to perform a dialogue as if one was a tourist. They should replace the destination with a 'BEEP' so that the rest of the class has to guess the destination.

WRITING A story *p31*

- Tell students they are going to learn how to write stories better. Put them into pairs to describe a time when they got lost. You might prompt ideas by mentioning some likely situations, e.g. on holiday in a new place, in a large city, when you were very young.

- Invite two or three students to tell the class their stories.

- Tell the class to read the story on page 149 and decide at which moments in the story the writer felt uncertain about where he was.

- Nominate students to say the answer for each item. Check that the class agrees.

> **Answers**
>
> He felt uncertain in moments 2, 3, 4 and 5 of the story.

⑩ WRITING SKILL *just*

- Show the class that sentences 1–5 all contain the word *just* but the word means something different in each sentence. Tell them to match the sentences with each meaning. Suggest that they replace *just* with the synonym and read it again, checking it makes sense and has the same meaning.

> **Answers**
>
> **1** b **2** e **3** d **4** a **5** c

- Point out that *just* is a very common word; in one study it is the 57th most common word in the language. One reason is that it has different meanings depending on the context it is found. Ask students to think of other sentences and phrases that they know which contain the word *just*, e.g. The Nike slogan *Just do it*, the song *Just the way you are* by Bruno Mars, etc.

Extension

- Dictate the following sentences, without saying *just*:

  I've (just) seen the local paper.

  They were (just) interested in making money, nothing else.

  Fortunately, I had (just) enough money for the meal.

  I was (just) about to book the holiday when my boss told me she needed me that week.

  He was (just) arriving at the garage when the car finally ran out of petrol.

- Put students in pairs and tell them to decide where to put *just* in each sentence. Ask them to discuss what *just* means in each sentence.

- Explain the task. Make sure they understand that they only need to write one story so must choose an ending from the options. Remind them that the writing advice at the back of the book and the Writing strategies box are there to help them.

- Refer students to the Writing strategies box for useful questions to help them start making notes, and their notes for Exercise 10 on page 27. Remind them of their options for narrative tenses. Go around and make sure that students are making notes. Help them if they can't think of something to write about by making suggestions.

- Explain the task. Tell students to refer to the model text on page 149 for help. Remind them of the structure of the model by reading out the advice at the back of the book and reminding them of the language they have studied.

- If you are going to give students a mark, tell them it will be higher if they organize the description in a similar way and use language they have learnt. Put students in pairs and tell them to talk about or plan their story.

- Set the writing for homework or set a time limit of about twenty minutes to do it in class.

As students are writing, go round and offer help. You might note some common errors for feedback when the time is up.

> **Exam tip**
>
> **Peer review**
>
> It is quite good for students preparing for exams to review each other's material as the exam often tests positive effect on readers. Peer review also provides an opportunity for interaction in the writing lesson.
>
> - Put students in pairs. Write these questions on the board: *Did the story follow the pattern in the model on page 149? Did it make use of any of the language you learnt?* Tell students to read their partner's story and answer the questions.
>
> - Tell students to stay in the same pairs but to swap stories with another pair. Repeat once or twice more. Go round and monitor. You might note some common errors for feedback. Give some feedback (positive – if they followed the model) and do some error correction on the board.
>
> - When they have all read at least two or three stories, ask individual students to talk about the best and worst experiences written about.

Fast finishers

Students who finish quickly can suggest ways that they could make their stories better or better expressed.

> **Homework**
>
> - Set Workbook Lesson 2E exercises on pages 23–25 for homework.
>
> - Students write another travel story beginning with the sentence: *It was a trip I had looked forward to for a long time …*
>
> - Students prepare three questions to test their classmates at the start of the next lesson about the things they have studied in Unit 2.

3 Active lives

3A Pushing the limits
pp32–35

Information about the photo

The photo shows Ian Flanders bike base jumping in Canyon Lands National Park, Utah, in 2014. Base jumping describes parachute jumps from fixed points such as skyscrapers and mountains. A few people – Ian was the first – push the limits of base jumping by riding bikes off mountains.

Ian died in Turkey in August 2015, aged 28, doing a relatively simple base jump.

LEAD IN

- **Books closed.** Activate students' prior knowledge of sports and related vocabulary by playing 'Categories'. Dictate the five categories to the class: *sport*, *person*, *place*, *equipment/clothes* and *action/verb*. Write the letter 'T' on the board and ask for a sport that begins with that letter. Then ask for a person related to sport that begins with 't', a place where sport is played, some equipment or item of clothing used in a sport and an action performed in a sport, e.g. *tennis, triathlete, track, trainers, throw*.

- Put students in teams of two. Tell them that to win they must think of one thing for four of the categories before the other teams. Announce the first letter. Use the letters S, C, P, R

Suggested answers

S: surfing, swimmer, stadium, shirt, score
C: cycling, coach, court, club, catch
P: pole vault, player, pitch, (ice hockey) puck, play
R: rugby, referee, race track, roller skates, run

VOCABULARY Sports *p33*

- Focus students' attention on the photo and caption or project it using the CPT.
- Put students in pairs. Give them two minutes to discuss the questions.
- Start a short class discussion about extreme sports. Ask for a show of hands from students who are adventurous and who might do a sport like this. Choose one person to explain why they like it. Choose someone who didn't put their hand up and ask why they don't like it.

Extension

Show a video of people doing bike base jumping if you have internet access and a projector. Ask them how dangerous it looks, what safety measures they think are there to avoid injury or death, and which of the class would pay to do it, need to be paid to do it (and how much) or would never do it.

> ### Suggested answer
>
> People do it for excitement, because their friends do it, to get outdoors, to have fun, as well as to 'push the limits' (do more and more extreme things to see how far it is possible to go). People who look for exciting things to do like this are called 'thrill seekers'.

- Tell students they are going to learn some words about sport. Explain the task. Tell them to copy the table into their notebooks.
- Tell students to use a dictionary if they need to. Go round and check they are doing the task correctly and notice words and phrases they look up, ask you about, or underline. Focus on these in feedback.
- When most students have finished, get them to compare answers in pairs and to help each other with anything they haven't finished. Check students' understanding with the following instructions and questions to the class:

Show me how you bounce/pass/kick/throw a ball.

What sports do you play on a pitch (e.g. football), *a court* (e.g. tennis, basketball), *a rink* (e.g. ice skating, ice hockey), *a track* (e.g. athletics, the 100-metre sprint)?

Who tries to beat you so that you don't win? (opponent) *Who checks that you are following the rules of the sport?* (referee) *Who watches the sport in the stadium?* (spectators) *Who helps you train?* (coach)

Where does competitive diving take place? (in a pool) *Where does scuba diving take place?* (in the sea)

Which sport is the only contact sport? (karate) *What other martial arts can you think of?* (e.g. judo, tae kwon do)

- Tell students to add more words to each category (with weaker classes, encourage them to add at least one word to each). When they have done that, ask them to call out suggestions for each category. Tell the others to write down words that they haven't yet written. Encourage students to ask each other what the words mean and how you spell them if they don't know.

Answers

Sports	People	Places	Equipment	Actions
climbing	spectator	pitch	net	bounce
gymnastics	coach	court	rope	pass
sailing	referee	rink		kick
karate	opponent	track		throw
the 100-metre sprint				(coach)
diving				(referee)

- Ask students to write the sentences on their own. Go round and check that they are using the words correctly. Help them by correcting or giving them the English they need.
- When most students have finished, invite volunteers to read out their sentences.

Fast finishers

Students who finish quickly can write one or two more sentences.

- Tell students that they are going to learn some verb–noun collocations to do with sports. Explain collocations by writing *play*, *go* and *do* on the board, and eliciting some sports that collocate with these verbs, e.g. *play football*, *go skiing*, *do athletics* – not *play skiing*, *do football*, etc.
- If you think that students will find the exercise difficult, put them in pairs. Go around and check they are doing the task correctly.
- When most have finished, get students to compare in pairs if they worked individually. Otherwise nominate students to share their answers. Teach them the sentence: *You can [verb] [noun]*, e.g. *You can win a prize, win a trophy or win the gold medal.* Make sure they give the answers in this format.

Answers

1 win   **2** go   **3** play   **4** do   **5** encourage
6 train   **7** achieve   **8** represent   **9** score   **10** beat

Fast finishers

Students who finish quickly can add more nouns to each list.

Extension

Tell students to choose five collocations that they would like to learn well. These should be collocations that are less familiar to them and that they think will be useful.

- Read out the task. Do the first item with the whole class as an example. Ask the class for possible sports.
- Tell students to do the rest of the activity in pairs, using a dictionary if they need to. After a few minutes, put pairs together into groups of four to compare ideas.
- Nominate students to share answers with the whole class. Use this opportunity to find out more about individual students and their active lives.

6 MY PERSPECTIVE

- Do this task with the whole class. Show interest in the students' personal answers for the first question by asking follow-up questions and helping them express their ideas in natural English.

Extension

- Ask students to prepare a short statement about their sporting lives or the life of a friend or family member. Present your own example to show students what you mean, e.g. *I go running two or three times a week, and I sometimes play squash. I'm not good enough at running to represent a club or be in a team, but I always want to achieve my personal best. However, I used to play in squash tournaments. I even won a few trophies when I was younger.*
- Help students with their personal statements, making sure that they express themselves naturally using the new language. Tell them to memorize their statements and encourage them to practise saying them off by heart with their classmates.
- When everyone is ready, either hold a presentation at the front of the class, or video them all speaking. Then create a video in which everyone speaks and let them share the video with friends and family, post it on a class blog, or wherever digital content can be shared. (Make sure you have their parents' permission to do this.) Alternatively, students could make their own short videos for homework and share them with you.

LISTENING *p34*

Although in the photo it looks as if Ashima is high up, in fact she is very close to the ground training at Hueco Tanks State Natural Area in west Texas with her coach, who is there just below her to catch her if she falls.

 7

- Focus students' attention on the photo and caption or project it using the CPT. Find out if anyone in the class goes climbing or has heard of Ashima. Invite suggestions as to what the V scale measures.
- Ask if any students have experience of climbing or bouldering and can talk a little about why they like it, how easy or difficult it is, what you need to be a good climber, and so on. Ask who else in the class would like to do it, and why.

Answer

The V scale measures the difficulty of climbs. In bouldering, or climbing low rocks without a rope, V0 is very easy, and V16 is the hardest that has ever been climbed.

 8

- 🔔 **15** Read the instructions. Then play the audio once straight through.
- Give students a minute to compare their answers in pairs. Play the audio again if it's clear that they found it difficult. Nominate students to answer. Ask whether they found the answer to number 1 surprising. Encourage as many answers as possible for question 2.
- Find out what students think is her greatest achievement. You could also ask why climbing for Ashima is similar to other challenges in her life. (She says 'everything in life, even school work, is a problem she can solve.')

Answers

1 Because she likes solving puzzles.
2 She has completed the 'Golden Shadow' problem in South Africa, V 14 climb; she's climbed 'Horizon'; she's the first woman to climb a V15, and the youngest person to do it.

Audioscript 🔔 **15**

Welcome to the podcast that looks at our young sports stars. This week's sporting hero is already pushing the limits of her sport, and she's only a teenager! Her name is Ashima Shiraishi and she's a climber.

Ashima discovered climbing at the age of six and she's loved it ever since. After only a year, she began climbing at a professional level. She enjoys traditional climbing up mountains with ropes to keep her safe, but she has become famous for another type of climbing called 'bouldering'. Bouldering is when you climb just a few metres from the

ground, without ropes. Climbs are measured for difficulty, so a V0 is really easy, while a V16 is almost impossible. Bouldering climbs are called 'problems'. Ashima says that to her, climbing is like a problem or puzzle that she has to find an answer to. And she loves solving puzzles.

Ashima still trains in the gym in New York City, but she has also travelled to many countries in her young life looking for more and more difficult climbs. In 2014, she went to South Africa and completed the 'Golden Shadow' problem. This made her one of only five women to complete a V14 climb. But she's just achieved an even more amazing record – earlier this year Ashima climbed 'Horizon', a V15 climb in Japan. She is not only the first woman to ever climb a V15, she's also the youngest person to do it. Climbing isn't without its dangers, of course. Shortly after she completed Horizon, Ashima fell fourteen metres and injured her back, but she has recovered and is now climbing again.

Ashima is still at school, but sometimes she doesn't start her schoolwork until ten o'clock at night, when she's finished her training. But to her, everything in life, even schoolwork, is a problem she can solve.

 9

- Tell students to read the sentences to check they understand them. Before playing the audio again, let students try to answer from memory or go straight into the task. You could ask what they think the answer to 1 is before they listen, but don't tell them if they are right or wrong.
- 🔔 **15** Play the audio. Go round and notice how well they did in order to decide how quickly to go through answers and whether you will need to play the audio again.
- Check the answers as a class by asking for a show of hands or calling out the answer all together or nominating students. Ask students to justify their answers. Where students agree, write the answer on the board. Where there is a dispute, put a question mark on the board but don't say who is correct. Tell students they will listen again and check. Play the audio again if necessary, telling students to focus on the areas of uncertainty.
- If students are *still* uncertain of the answer, play the audio again and stop at key points. Play these sections two or three times if students are still struggling. Draw attention to the problem sounds or words and explain them when you give the answers.

Answers

1 F (*discovered climbing at the age of six*)
2 F (*After only a year, she began climbing at a professional level*)
3 F (*She enjoys … climbing … with ropes … but … bouldering.*)
4 T (*she has also travelled to many countries …*)
5 F (*This made her one of only five women to complete a V14 climb*)
6 T (*She is not only the first woman to ever climb a V15 …*)
7 T (*Ashima fell fourteen metres and injured her back*)
8 T (*sometimes she doesn't start her school work until ten o'clock*)

Extension

There are many videos of Ashima climbing online. Use the search term 'Ashima Shiraishi'. Show a couple of minutes of one of these. She has also given a TEDx Talk called 'Just climb through it'. You could show a clip from this, or recommend it as something to watch at home.

GRAMMAR Past simple and present perfect *pp34–35*

To prepare for teaching the following exercises, see Grammar reference on page 132.

- Look at the sentences in the Grammar box as a whole class and identify the different tenses.

Answers

Underline *went* and *completed*. Circle *has travelled*.

- Go through the questions with the whole class, nominating different students to answer.

Answers

1 It isn't clear, and it isn't important here; the important information is that Ashima has been to many countries before now.
2 Yes, in 2014.
3 The first timeline illustrates sentence a. Show students that the arrows indicate times she has been abroad in the past and are at any time up to the present. The second timeline illustrates sentence b when we are talking about a specific time in the past.

Exam tip

Learning tenses and time expressions together

A common exam question is to identify the correct tense of a sentence. Often, there are time expressions in the sentences which act as clues to help students decide. Encourage them to learn the typical time expressions that are found with each tense, e.g.
past simple – *yesterday, in 2016*
present perfect – *already, for three years, always*.

- Explain the task. Either get students to read the Grammar box silently, or read it out yourself.
- Go round and help students who are not certain of the answers.
- You can either go through the answers with the whole class, or wait for them to read the Grammar reference on page 132 and then ask the class the grammar-checking questions, or nominate individual students to give their answers.

Answers

1 **d** (The only sentence in the past simple; the time expression is *Earlier this year*)
2 **a** (The action *has loved climbing* never stopped between the age of six and the present)
3 **e** (The action *has recovered* happened in the past but means that now she is better)
4 **b** (This is similar to sentence a in Exercise 9)
5 **c** (Notice the meaning of *just* meaning *it happened very recently*. In US English, it is common to use *just* with the past simple, e.g. *She just achieved a more amazing record*. Both tenses would be correct in US English.)

Grammar reference and practice

Tell students to do Exercises 1 and 2 on page 133. Alternatively, do them after Exercises 13 and 14 if you think students have been having difficulties. You could set them for homework.

Answers to Grammar practice exercises

1

1 have always loved 2 invited 3 have been
4 was 5 turned over 6 didn't give up
7 have spent 8 have just bought 9 haven't taken
10 took 11 haven't seen 12 has gone

2

1 We ~~have~~ played three matches yesterday.
2 She hasn't tried ~~yet rollerblading~~ rollerblading yet, but I'm sure she will.
3 The team ~~competed~~ have / has competed / been competing in the tournament for more than 30 years.
4 Oh no! You ~~hurt~~ have hurt your arm. It looks really sore.
5 A: Where's Tariq?
   B: He's ~~been~~ gone to the changing rooms to get ready.
6 José and I have played together ~~since~~ for three years.
7 They ~~hasn't~~ haven't won many matches so far this year.
8 I've ~~met~~ been meeting him since 2014.

- **Optional step.** Before the students complete the text about speed climbing, show a video of Danyl Boldyrev's world record winning climb in 2014. You could set comprehension questions for the text: *What does the sport consist of?* (climbing a fifteen-metre wall against the clock) *What is the other big news for this sport?* (it's been accepted as an Olympic sport)
- Explain the task, reminding students to apply the rules they have learnt to help them.
- Invite students to read a sentence each out loud and say why each option is correct.

Answers

1 has been 2 became 3 started 4 used
5 have been 6 broke 7 wasn't 8 have just accepted ('just accepted' is correct in US English)

- Look at the instructions and do the first item with the whole class.
- Tell students to do the rest of the activity on their own. Go round and check students are doing the task correctly. Provide help as necessary. When most students have finished, ask them to compare in pairs.
- Check answers by nominating different students to read out their sentences. Say *Put your hands up if you think it is correct. And hands up if you think it's incorrect.* Ask different students to explain their answers.
- Tell them to read out the dialogues, taking turns to play A and B. Go round the room listening to the dialogues. Encourage students to use contractions, and correct pronunciation where necessary.

Answers
1 Have you played, injured, haven't played, saw, were
2 did you play, have always loved, have just started
3 Have you ever won, have played
4 Have you ever done, tried, enjoyed, has ever interested
5 Have you watched, has been*

* See page 132, note about the verb *go*

- Look at the instructions. To model the task, invite a student to interview you. Make sure you extend your answers with extra information. Ask students to imagine being asked each question and to answer it silently in their heads using their inner voice. They should not speak at this stage, just imagine the conversations. Reassure students who are not really interested in sport that they are allowed to be honest and say so. Give them a minute or two for this.
- Put students in pairs to ask and answer. Go round and check students are doing the task correctly and make a note of any problems students are having with the language. Focus on these in feedback.
- When most pairs have finished, stop the activity. Give some feedback on their speaking, including corrections.

Fast finishers
Pairs who finish quickly can continue the dialogues with their own questions.

Teaching tip
Using your inner voice
It isn't true that you need a friend to practise speaking. Or even that you need to speak! Many learners use their 'inner voice' to practise what they are going to say. Ask students what they do when they have to remember a phone number or code, but can't find a pen to write it down for a few seconds. Explain that that voice they hear repeating the number inside their heads is called the 'inner voice'.

Ask if any of them use their inner voice to help them with English. Find out how. Explain that they can use their inner voice to prepare for speaking activities and even to practise pronunciation silently!

Homework
- Set Workbook Lesson 3A exercises on pages 26–29 for homework.
- Students write an imaginary interview with one of their sporting heroes.
- Students find out about another young sporting hero and give a mini presentation about them which includes information about their sport, their experience with the sport and their achievements.

3B Conservation through sport *pp36–37*

VOCABULARY BUILDING Phrasal verbs *p36*

- Tell students that the phrasal verbs they are going to study are all connected to sport in some way.
- First get them to underline the phrasal verbs in sentences 1–8 and check answers. Then tell students to underline the synonyms. Show students that the first has been done as an example.
- When most students have finished, ask them to compare their answers in pairs. Invite individual students to write the answers on the board.

> **Answers**
> 1 taking up (a sport) = start doing it
> 2 join in = participate
> 3 warm up = prepare for sport
> 4 keep up with (someone) = stay with them
> 5 knocked out* (someone) = beat
> 6 take on (someone / something) = challenge them
> 7 gave up (a sport) = stop playing it
> 8 work out = exercise
>
> *****knock out** *to beat someone so that they are no longer in a competition.* In boxing, *knock out* means to make your opponent unconscious.

- Ask students questions to check they understand.

  *What sports have you **taken up** but decided not to continue for some reason? Why?* (e.g. because they didn't enjoy it, or weren't good enough, or because they wanted to do something else)

  *Why might someone not want to **join in** a team sport?* (e.g. they are injured, tired or embarrassed because they don't feel they are good enough)

  *Why is it important to **warm up** before doing sports?* (to avoid getting injured, to perform better)

  *Are you in front of or behind someone if you don't **keep up with** them?* (behind)

  *In the football World Cup, do teams **knock each other out** in the first or second part of the tournament?* (second part)

  *What other synonyms are there for **take on**?* (play, compete against)

  *What phrasal verb is the opposite of **give up**?* (take up)

  *What sort of exercises do people do when they **work out**?* (e.g. running on a machine, lifting weights, using the rowing machine, etc.)

- Look at the instructions. Remind students that they need to write the verbs in the correct form.
- Go round and help any students who are having difficulty before eliciting the answers. Before they give their answers, show how the final consonant sound of the first word in the verb connects with the vowel sound of the second words in the verb in both present tense and with the past form. You could then drill them to ensure natural pronunciation.

  join in sounds like 'joy nin' /dʒɔɪ ˌnɪn/, *joined in* /dʒɔɪ ˌnɪn/
  knock out /nɒ ˌkaʊt/, *knocked out* /nɒk ˌtaʊt/
  take up /teɪ ˌkʌp/, *taken up* /teɪkə ˌnʌp/
  give up /gɪ ˌvʌp/, *given up* /gɪvə ˌnʌp/
  warm up /wɔːˈ ˌmʌp/, *warmed up* /wɔːˈm ˌdʌp/
  work out /wɛːˈ ˌkaʊt/, *worked out* /wɛːˈk ˌtaʊt/

> **Answers**
> 1 join in   2 knocked out / taken on   3 take up
> 4 given up   5 warm up   6 work out

- Put students in pairs and tell them to ask each other the questions. Go round and listen for correct pronunciation, especially of the phrasal verbs.

READING *pp36–37*

- Focus students' attention on the photo and the caption or project it using the CPT.

- Put students in pairs. Tell them to list the similarities and differences between this sports event and the normal high jump event in athletics.

- Get students' answers and write them on the board. Similarities include: the athletes are wearing standard athletics clothes; there looks to be a system whereby the height of the string can be raised. Differences include: the athletes are wearing face paints and unusual footwear; the spectators are close to the event; the athlete is not jumping over the string; he is holding a stick.

- Tell students they are going to read an article about the Maasai Olympics. Tell them to read the article quickly and answer the question. Tell them to ignore the gaps (1–6) at this stage. Do not play the audio now because it would give away the answers to Exercise 5.

- Set a time limit of three minutes for students to read the article.

- When most students have finished reading, ask them to discuss the answer in pairs. Invite a volunteer to explain to the class the reason for the Maasai Olympics. Don't immediately accept or reject their answer, but invite the other students to say whether they agree or not.

Answer

To encourage the Maasai men to use their hunting skills to compete against each other (and each other's villages) rather than to kill the lions.

- Either get students to read about topic sentences silently, or read it out yourself. Explain that sentences a–f are the missing topic sentences from each paragraph and they have been mixed up. Look at the first paragraph with the class. Elicit the main idea (that lion populations have decreased). Ask which sentences in Exercise 5 mention lions (c – famous animals and d – lions). Ask why sentence d is not suitable (because the paragraph mentions 'loss of habitat' as a reason for the decrease, not just trophy hunting; also, it mentions the Maasai, without explaining

who they are). Ask why c makes a good topic sentence (it refers to famous animals which lions are; also, 'needs protection' is a good summary of the information in the paragraph).

- Tell students to do the rest of the activity on their own. While they are reading, go round to gauge how difficult they are finding the task. When most students have finished, get them to compare answers in pairs and to help each other with anything they haven't finished.

- 🎧 **16** Nominate students to share answers and check that the rest of the class agrees. Ask them why these are the correct answers. Then play the audio for them to check the answers.

Answers

1 c **2** d **3** a **4** b **5** f **6** e

Extension

- Tell students to choose the best topic sentence for the paragraph below, which you could copy and give them or project digitally.

  a The athletes are very motivated to win, and not only for the prizes.

  b These prizes are more interesting than the prizes for most sports events.

  c There are similarities between the Maasai Olympics and traditional competitions.

  _____ . Medals are awarded to the top three finishers in each event, but unlike the international Olympic Games, the competitors also win money. As well as this, the winners of the 800m and 5,000m races in the games win the chance to run in the New York Marathon. It isn't just individuals who win; the *manyatta* that has been protecting wildlife best also wins some money, and the manyatta that wins overall is given a valuable bull for their village!

- Discuss the answer, and why sentence b is the best sentence. It summarizes the content of the paragraph (interesting prizes) and compares the prizes with other competitions, which is expanded on in the following paragraph. It isn't a because this suggests the paragraph will be talking about motivating reasons for competing other than prizes. It isn't c because the paragraph talks about differences, not similarities, with other competitions, and because it doesn't point to the specific topic of the paragraph (prizes).

- Ask students to choose the best place to put this paragraph into the article. It fits between paragraphs 4 and 5 of the article. Note '*These* prizes', referring to the prizes just mentioned at the end of paragraph 4.

- Explain the task. Tell students to make a note of the line numbers in the text where they found the answer. To encourage discussion, let students work in pairs.
- Get whole-class feedback by asking for a show of hands for each choice. Nominate a student who got it right to say why. Also encourage students to discuss why the wrong answers are not correct.

Answers

1 b (lines 4–13)   2 c (line 8, topic sentence)
3 b (lines 20–22)   4 c (lines 27–29)   5 c (lines 36–39)
6 a (lines 40–48)

CRITICAL THINKING

Presenting a balanced view *p37*

- Read the Critical thinking box to the class. Ask students whether the writer believes the Maasai Olympics are a good or bad development (he thinks they are a good idea). Ask them whether they think the argument is balanced, and if so, where he presents any negative information regarding the Olympics.
- Tell students to read the article again to find sentences that create that balance. If you think this will be challenging for some students, indicate that they should look towards the end of the article. You could tell them there are two sentences if you think they will find this difficult.

Suggested answers

The following sentences go against the main idea of the article, which is that the Maasai Olympics are a very good idea: *Although nineteen percent of the people asked haven't even heard of the Maasai Olympics …; even though trophy hunting still goes on, they see sports as an effective alternative.*

- Explain the task. Remind students that the point of the exercise is to argue your point, but to do so in a balanced way, so encourage them to think of interesting things to say against their own points of view. To do this, write on the board some introductions to other points of view, e.g. *Even though …, It is true that …, Although …, I would say that …*, etc.
- Do the first statement with the class. Ask for a show of hands who agrees with it. Ask them to say why and elicit two or three ideas (e.g. teamwork is a life skill that sport teaches). Ask if anyone can think of reasons to disagree with the statement (e.g. if teamwork is important for life, you can learn it in other aspects of life, such as at work or school; also, sport promotes competition, and sometimes hatred between people). Be prepared to supply these yourself.
- Tell students to do the rest of the task in pairs. Go round and listen to their discussions. Make a note of good balanced arguments, as well as any useful errors or interesting uses of English.
- When they have finished discussing all five statements, provide any feedback as necessary.

- Put students together in larger groups of four now to practise presenting balanced viewpoints. Again, listen to the conversations, encouraging all students to join in.
- When they have finished, nominate students to summarize what their groups said for the class.

Homework

- Set Workbook Lesson 3B exercises on pages 30–31 for homework.
- Students research where and when the next Maasai Olympics will be held and how to attend as a spectator.
- Students write a balanced viewpoint about one of the statements in Exercise 8, or one of their own.

3C Marathon men and women *pp38–39*

GRAMMAR Present perfect simple and continuous *p38*

To prepare for teaching the following exercises, see Grammar reference on page 132.

- **Books closed.** Before the lesson, write sentences a–e from the Grammar box on the board but with a gap where the verbs should be, e.g. *Maasai tribes ___ lions as trophies for hundreds of years.*
- Remind students of the article in the last lesson about the Maasai and ask them whether they remember the missing verbs. You could make it easier by saying the infinitives in the wrong order and asking them which sentence they go in.
- When they suggest a verb for each gap, ask them how they want you to write it: in the infinitive or in another form. Let them reach a consensus and accept whatever they decide. Write it on the board.
- Let them open their books to check. Ask them to underline and circle the two tenses. Get them to correct and underline or circle the verbs on the board.

> **Answers**
> Present perfect simple: b have decreased, d have (already) chosen, e Have (the Games) been…?
> Present perfect continuous: a have been hunting, c have been heating up.

- Explain the task. Go round and help students who might be finding this hard. You may decide to do this exercise as a whole class if you think it will be difficult for most students.
- You can either go through the answers with the whole class, or wait for them to read the Grammar reference on page 132 and then ask the class the grammar-checking questions, or nominate individual students to give their answers.

> **Answers**
> **1** d (the coaches have finished choosing athletes)
> **2** b (now there are only 20,000 lions left)
> **3** e (*be* is usually used as a state verb)
> **4** c (preparations are still heating up and will continue to heat up)
> **5** a (the important information is how long they've been hunting lions)

Grammar reference and practice

Tell students to do Exercises 3–6 on page 133 now, or set them for homework.

> **Answers to Grammar practice exercises**
> **3**
> **1** taken, been raining
> **2** I've injured, haven't wanted
> **3** has known, started
> **4** swum, I've been swimming
> **5** hasn't chosen, I've been training
> **6** won, been playing
> **7** been reading, finished
> **4**
> **1** A: How long have you been playing hockey?
> B: Six years. In that time, I've played for three different teams.
> A: And have your teams won any tournaments?
> B: We haven't won any big trophies, but we won the local tournament last month.
> A: Congratulations!
> **2** A: Where have you been?
> B: I've been working out at the gym.
> A: You haven't had a shower yet, that's for sure! You smell terrible!
> B: Give me a chance! I've just got home!
> **3** A: Who's that player with the ball? He's been playing well so far.
> B: That's Gareth Bale. You must have heard of him! He's been playing for Madrid all season.
> A: Of course I've heard of him! But I didn't know what he looked like.
> **5**
> **1** How many Grand Slams has she won?
> **2** How much have they spent so far?
> **3** How long has she been a member?
> **4** How long have you known each other?
> **5** How long have you been cycling?
> **6** How much did it cost?
> **6**
> **1** Have you ever run a marathon?
> **2** He's just bought some new trainers.
> **3** They've never won before.
> **4** Has she played for the team yet?
> **5** We've never met a famous person.
> **6** I haven't had time to wash my football boots yet. They're very dirty!
> **7** I've already done some exercise today. / I've done some exercise already today. / I've done some exercise today already.
> **8** Have you just arrived? Get your swimming costume on!

- Focus students' attention on the photo and caption or project it using the CPT.
- Ask students how far a marathon is (42km, or 26.2 miles) and roughly how long it takes the top professionals (men take just over two hours, women just over 2 hours 15 minutes). Tell them that this is Eliud Kipchoge, the Kenyan gold medallist during his winning marathon at the Rio Olympics 2016. At the time of publication, he was the third fastest marathon runner ever.

- Explain the task. Remind students of the rules in Exercise 2.
- Go round and check how many of the options students are getting correct. Question students' ideas by asking them to justify their choices according to the rules in Exercise 2.
- When most students have finished, let them compare their answers in pairs. To check answers, invite students to read the text sentence by sentence. After each answer, nominate students to explain the reason these answers are correct, referring to the rules.

Answers

1 have run **2** given **3** belonged **4** has been sending **5** hasn't been winning **6** been doing
7 have become **8** has created

Extension

Put students in pairs. Ask them to come up with reasons why Kenyans might be better long-distance runners than the rest of the world. As a whole class, discuss possible reasons. Then read the text in the Background information box.

Background information

Kenyan running

Many people have tried to learn the secret to the Kenyan's success at long distance running. The general conclusion is that there is no one secret, but a combination of factors, including the following.

- Running is part of the culture of some people in Kenya. Children start running long distances to school from a very early age. This is because the area is poor, the roads are bad and few people have cars.
- The Kenyans from this mountainous region live high up and their bodies adapt to high altitudes by increasing the oxygen-carrying ability of the blood.
- They eat a high-carbohydrate diet with very little sugar or fat.
- They are highly motivated to work hard to become better runners because it is seen as one of the only ways to make lots of money in their communities. Successful runners become celebrities.

4

- Tell students that they are going to practise making questions with the present perfect simple and continuous now. Ask them to read the interview and complete the questions with the prompts to help. If students find question formation difficult, do the first as an example. Make sure they understand that in the perfect continuous tense, the subject goes after the first auxiliary verb (has/have) but before *been*.
- Check answers around the class. Nominate students to read out each question. Check that the rest of the class agrees with each answer before confirming it. Alternatively ask for a volunteer to 'be' Catherine Ndereba, who will respond to

the questions. Invite other students to interview her with their questions. Remind them to change the questions to the second person, i.e. *you* instead of *she*.

Answers

1 How long has Catherine been running?
2 Has she always loved running?
3 How many marathons has she won?
4 Has she won any Olympic medals?
5 What has she been doing recently? (*What has she done recently?* also possible – the first question suggests that the things she has been doing are not necessarily finished; the second suggests finished actions)
6 How far has she run this week?

5

- Tell students to complete the interview with a runner who is in Kenya to train. Explain that many runners make this journey, and there are training camps for local people and visitors.
- Go round and check that students are comfortable using the time expressions. Refer them to page 132 if they are not sure.
- Choose two students to be José and the interviewer and read their dialogue out. When they have finished, ask the class if they would like to correct anything, but don't confirm the answers yet.
- **17** Play the audio for students to check their answers.

Answers

1 just **2** for **3** ever **4** never **5** since **6** yet
7 already **8** since

6 **PRONUNCIATION** Weak forms: *for*

- **6a** Ask students to read questions a–c out loud and then ask them how they pronounced the word *for*. Focus students' attention on questions 1 and 2. Tell them to think about these questions as they listen to sentences a–c.
- **18** Play the audio twice. Then ask students the questions. You might point out that *for* is sometimes pronounced /fɔː(r)/ like the number, but usually only at the end of a sentence, e.g. *How long have you lived here for?*
- **18** Once you've been through the differences, play the audio again for students to listen for them again.

- **6b** Tell students to practise the sentences. To make them feel less embarrassed about talking to themselves, you could put some background music on or let them mumble the sentences quietly to themselves.

- ⌂ **19** Play the audio so that students can compare their attempts with the model.

- Finally, drill the sentences using the 'back chaining' technique. This may help students to focus on the stressed words and say *for* in its weak form.

Teaching tip

Pronunciation – back chaining

Saying whole sentences with precision and fluency is difficult. To help, divide the sentences into short phrases. Identify the last stressed syllable in the sentence and drill only from that point to the end. Then locate the penultimate stressed syllable and drill from this new point to the end. Continue until students are saying the whole sentence, e.g. **week** ... **here** for a **week** ... **on**ly been **here** for a **week** ... I've **only** been **here** for a **week**.

➐ CHOOSE

The idea is for students to make their own choice of activity here. However, you might want to make the decision for the students, in which case explain why. Alternatively, you may decide to let students do more than one task. You could divide the class into groups and have each group do a different task – or you could have a vote on which task the whole class should do. For the vote:

- put students in pairs or groups to decide which they prefer.

- take a vote on each task.

- If the vote is tied, ask one student from each side to explain which is best and take the vote again. You can decide if there is still no change.

- Option 1 is a speaking task. Encourage students to rehearse first and do it again. The first time they do it they can note down any difficult words, points where the present perfect simple and continuous can be used and common errors in grammar or pronunciation. Be available to help them perfect their interviews.

- Options 2 and 3 are writing tasks. Make sure that students know who they are writing for. It would be a good idea to create a blog in advance of the lesson if they are working digitally, or dedicate a space on the classroom notice board for their work. To ensure use of the present perfect in option 3, tell them to choose a sportsperson who is still active in their field.

Homework

- Set Workbook Lesson 3C exercises on pages 32–33 for homework.

- Students write an imaginary interview with a famous athlete or other celebrity that they admire.

- Students find out some other achievements by Kenyan athletes, or research the history of the marathon.

- You might want to tell students to watch the track called *Unit 3 TED Talk* on the *Perspectives* website before they come to the next class.

3D How I swam the North Pole *pp40–41*

- Tell students to look at the title of the lesson, the quote and the photo of Lewis Pugh. Put them in pairs and tell them to write down three things that they think they will hear or learn today.
- Elicit one or two ideas about the lesson from each pair. Encourage speculation, so don't give away any of the content at this point.
- ▶ **3.0** Tell them they are going to see a short text on the DVD to introduce the talk and the speaker, and play the *About the speaker* section. Then do the vocabulary exercise.
- After they finish, write the key words from the *About the speaker* section on the board and ask students to retell it aloud, or ask them to write as much of what it said as they can. Correct as necessary.

Answers to About the speaker
1 the North Pole = b (the point on Earth that is furthest north)
2 climate change = a (changes in temperature and weather over long periods of time)
3 the Arctic = a (the very cold, most northern part of Earth)
4 melted = a (changed from ice to water)
5 sustainable = c (able to continue)
6 freezing = c (very cold)
7 go numb = b (become impossible to feel)
8 chest monitor = c (a machine that records information from his body)
9 rate = a (speed)

TED Talk About the speaker ▶ **3.0**

Lewis Pugh is probably the greatest cold-water swimmer in history. He is the first person to have swum long-distance in all five oceans of the world; he has swum in a lake 5,300 metres up Mount Everest, and here he talks about swimming across **the North Pole**.

His swims have helped to bring the dangers of **climate change** *to people's attention, and* **the Arctic** *is a place where much of the sea-ice has* **melted**. *Lewis wants us all to think about what we can do to make our world* **sustainable**.

You need years of training and lots of courage to swim in **freezing** *water because it is so dangerous. For example, your fingers can* **go numb** *in just a few seconds. For this swim Lewis wears goggles to protect his eyes, and a* **chest monitor** *so his team can measure his body temperature and heart* **rate**.

Lewis's idea worth spreading is that sometimes we have to do extraordinary things to make people pay attention to important issues.

AUTHENTIC LISTENING SKILLS
Signposts *p40*

As well as teaching aspects of phonology and listening skills, these tasks also allow:

- you to pre-teach some vocabulary.
- students to read and hear new language before they listen to the whole text.
- students to tune in to the speaker's voice and style.

- Tell students what they will be doing during the lesson, using very clear signposts to structure what you tell them, e.g. **Before we begin, I'd like to tell you** *what we are doing today.* **First**, *we're going to practise listening skills.* **After that**… etc.
- Either ask students to read the Authentic listening skills box silently to themselves or read it out yourself as they read along. Then ask the class what signposts they remember you using in the previous step. Say it again to remind them. Invite students to call out common signposting expressions in their own language if your students share the same first language.
- Explain the task. Before you play the audio, ask students to read the extracts.
- 🎧 **20** Play the audio.
- Check answers around the class.

Answers
1 Today I want to talk to you about …
2 And the message was clear …
3 But the most important thing was …

- Read out the instructions. Let students read the sentences before you play the audio.
- 🎧 **21** Play the audio.
- To check answers, have students read out each whole signpost, not just the missing word.

Answers
1 saying 2 things 3 second 4 important

WATCH *p40*

- Put students in pairs to discuss the questions. Go around and listen for any interesting information to share with the whole class, e.g. *Aubert once swam 5 km for charity.*
- Conduct whole class feedback and together decide, for example, who the strongest swimmer is, who enjoys cold water, where are good places to swim, etc.

If you are short of time, or want a different approach to the video, you may want to watch the whole talk all the way through with only some brief checking questions. A version of this is on the DVD and is labelled as *TED Talk with activities*. At the end of each section, there is a short gist question. Pause after each question on screen so students can give their answers, then play the answer.

Answers to gist questions on DVD

Part 1

Why did Lewis swim across the North Pole?

b He wanted people to understand what is happening in the Arctic.

Part 2

How did Lewis's friend David help him?

a He encouraged him when he wasn't feeling confident.

Part 3

Which of these statements is <u>not</u> true, according to Lewis?

b He had to teach children in South Africa about climate change.

- Explain the task. Point out that the numbers are in the order they appear in Part 1. Before you play Part 1, let students try to match the numbers to the reasons. Give them a minute to read and guess. When they have finished, ask if anyone is confident they have one right before they listen. For example, someone may be certain that 0° matches with f.

Exam tip

Predicting before listening

Explain to students that we can use what we already know about a topic to help us listen. In this case, everyone knows that water freezes at 0°, so we can get one question right before we have even listened. Predicting answers does more than this, though; it also forces us to focus on the task, familiarize ourselves with the options, and check our understanding.

- ▶ **3.1** Play Part 1 straight through.
- Ask students to compare their answers in pairs. Go round and notice how well they did in order to decide how quickly to go through answers, and whether you will need to play Part 1 again.
- Check the answers as a class by nominating students to answer.

Answers

1 d **2** e **3** h **4** f **5** g **6** b **7** c **8** a

TED Talk Part 1 script ▶ **3.1**

Today I want to talk to you about swimming across the North Pole, across the most northern place in the whole world. Seven years ago, I went to the Arctic for the first time. And it was so beautiful that I've been back there ever since, for the last seven years. I love the place.

But I have seen that place change beyond all description, just in that short period of time. I have seen polar bears walking across very, very thin ice in search of food. I have swum in front of glaciers which have retreated so much. And I have also, every year, seen less and less sea ice. And I wanted the world to know what was happening up there.

In the two years before my swim, 23 percent of the arctic sea ice cover just melted away. And I wanted to really shake the lapels of world leaders to get them to understand what is happening. So, I decided to do this symbolic swim at the top of the world, in a place which should be frozen over, but which now is rapidly unfreezing. And the message was very clear: climate change is for real, and we need to do something about it. And we need to do something about it right now.

Well, swimming across the North Pole, it's not an ordinary thing to do. I mean, just to put it in perspective, 27 degrees is the temperature of a normal indoor swimming pool. This morning, the temperature of the English Channel was eighteen degrees. The passengers who fell off the Titanic fell into water of just five degrees centigrade. Fresh water freezes at zero. And the water at the North Pole is minus 1.7. It's [bleep] freezing. I'm sorry, but there is no other way to describe it.

But the most important thing was to train my mind to prepare myself for what was going to happen. And I had to visualize the swim. I had to see it from the beginning all the way to the end. I had to taste the salt water in my mouth. I had to see my coach screaming for me, 'Come on Lewis! Come on! Go! Go! Go! Don't slow down!' And so, I literally swam across the North Pole hundreds and hundreds of times in my mind.

And then, after a year of training, I felt ready. I felt confident that I could actually do this swim. So, myself and the five members of the team, we hitched a ride on an icebreaker which was going to the North Pole. And on day four, we decided to just do a quick five-minute test swim. I had never swum in water of minus 1.7 degrees before, because it's just impossible to train in those type of conditions. So, we stopped the ship, as you do. We all got down onto the ice, and I then got into my swimming costume and I dived into the sea.

⑤

- Ask students to read the sentences and check they understand them. Let students predict whether they are true or false before they watch.
- ▶ **3.2** Play Part 2 straight through.
- Ask students to compare in pairs. Go round and notice how well they did in order to decide how quickly to go through answers and whether you will need to play Part 2 again. Check how they did against their predictions.
- Check the answers as a class, making sure you get students to give reasons for their answers. Write up the number and letter on the board.

> **Answers**
> 1 F (*... the paradox is that you're in freezing cold water, but actually you're on fire.*)
> 2 T (*I swam ... for five minutes. I remember just trying to get out of the water.*)
> 3 T (*my fingers had swollen so much that they were like sausages.*)
> 4 F (*There is no possibility that this was going to happen.*)
> 5 T (*... and I know, Lewis, deep down, right deep down here, that you are going to make this swim. And I just, I got so much confidence from him saying that, because he knew me so well.*)

TED Talk Part 2 script ▶ **3.2**

I have never in my life felt anything like that moment. I could barely breathe. I was gasping for air. I was hyperventilating so much, and within seconds my hands were numb. And it was – the paradox is that you're in freezing cold water, but actually you're on fire. I swam as hard as I could for five minutes. I remember just trying to get out of the water. I climbed out of the ice. And I remember taking the goggles off my face and looking down at my hands in sheer shock, because my fingers had swollen so much that they were like sausages.

And I thought, in two days' time, I was going to do this swim across the North Pole. I was going to try and do a 20-minute swim, for one kilometre across the North Pole.

There is no possibility that this was going to happen. And I remember then getting out of the shower and realizing I couldn't even feel my hands. And for a swimmer, you need to feel your hands because you need to be able to grab the water and pull it through with you.

And my close friend David, he saw the way I was thinking, and he came up to me and he said, 'Lewis, I've known you since you were eighteen years old. I've known you, and I know, Lewis, deep down, right deep down here, that you are going to make this swim. I so believe in you Lewis. I've seen the way you've been training. And I realize the reason why you're going to do this. This is such an important swim. We stand at a very, very important moment in this history, and you're going to make a symbolic swim here to try and shake the lapels of world leaders. Lewis, have the courage to go in there, because we are going to look after you every moment of it.'

And I just, I got so much confidence from him saying that, because he knew me so well. So, we carried on sailing and we arrived at the North Pole. And we stopped the ship, and it was just as the scientists had predicted. There were open patches of sea everywhere. And I went down into my cabin and I put on my swimming costume. And then the doctor strapped on a chest monitor, which measures my core body temperature and my heart rate. And then we walked out onto the ice.

⑥

- Let students read the sentences and check they understand them.
- ▶ **3.3** Play Part 3 straight through.
- Ask for a show of hands to see how many students think the first and second options in each sentence. Then give them the answers.

> **Answers**
> 1 break the problem of climate change into smaller parts
> 2 understand climate change.
> 3 tells

TED Talk Part 3 script ▶ **3.3**

We're finally at the North Pole. This is months and months and months of dreaming to get here, years of training and planning and preparation. Ooh. In a couple of hours' time I'm going to get in here and do my swim. It's all a little bit frightening, but err, and emotional.

Amundsen, you ready?

Amundsen: Ready.

Lewis Pugh: Ten seconds to swim. Ten seconds to swim.

Go for it! Go, go, go, go!

Take the goggles off. Take the goggles off!

Man: Take the shoes. Take the shoes. Well done lad! You did it! You did it Lewis! You did it! You did it man!

I'd just like to end by just saying this: it took me four months again to feel my hands. But was it worth it? Yes, absolutely it was. There are very, very few people who don't know now about what is happening in the Arctic. And people ask me, 'Lewis, what can we do about climate change?'

And I say to them, I think we need to do three things. The first thing we need to do is we need to break this problem down into manageable chunks. When it comes to climate change, every single country is going to have to make cuts. Britain, America, Japan, South Africa, the Congo. All of us together, we're all on the same ship together.

The second thing we need to do is we need to just look back at how far we have come in such a short period of time. I've just come back from giving a series of speeches in some of the poorest townships in South Africa to young children as young as ten years old. And even in those poorest conditions, they all have a very, very good grasp of climate change.

We need to believe in ourselves. Now is the time to believe. We've come a long way. We're doing good. But the most important thing we must do is, I think, we must all walk to the end of our lives and turn around and ask ourselves a most fundamental question. And that is, 'What type of world do we want to live in, and what decision are we going to make today to ensure that we all live in a sustainable world?'

7 VOCABULARY IN CONTEXT

- **7a** **3.4** Tell students that they are going to watch some clips from the talk which contain new or interesting words or phrases. They should choose the correct meaning for each one. Play the Vocabulary in context section. Pause after each question on screen so students can choose the correct definition, then play the answer. If you like, you can ask students to call out the answers.

- Where a lot of students have given the wrong answer, explain again and give an additional example before moving on to the next extract.

> **Answers**
> 1 Fresh water = b (water with no salt in it, for example, from a river)
> 2 costume = b (clothes)
> 3 barely = a (with difficulty)
> 4 swollen = b (got bigger than usual)
> 5 I believe in you = a (I know you can do it)
> 6 ensure = b (make certain that something happens)

- **7b** Check students understand the words in italics and re-teach if necessary, or ask students if they can recall the example in the talk. Tell students to think of examples of the five things. Point out that they relate to some of the new words and phrases they have just learnt in Exercise 7a. Give them two minutes and make sure they note down their ideas.

- Put students in pairs to tell each other their ideas. Encourage them to find out as much as they can from their partners, e.g. if they say that they used to swim in the river, find out where, when, who with, etc. Go round and check they are doing the task correctly and notice errors, difficulties, or where they use L1. Help them by correcting or giving them the English they need. Focus especially on their use of the new words and phrases.

- At the end of the task, give some feedback about new language that came up, and errors to correct which you may have written on the board. Nominate one or two students to tell the class the most interesting things they said or heard.

- Look at the instructions and do the first item with the whole class. Tell students to do the rest of the exercise on their own.

- When students have read and categorized the comments, ask the class for their answers. Ask them to justify their answers.

> **Answers**
> Comments 2 and 5 are in favour of the swim. Comments 1, 3 and 4 are against it. Comment 1 criticizes the swim on the basis of personal safety, 3 argues that it didn't achieve anything, and 4 suggests that it was a waste of time, money and resources.

- Put students in pairs. Ask them to discuss which comments they agree with most. When they have been talking for a couple of minutes, stop the class and find out how many students agree most with Comment 1, 2, etc. Ask them why they think that.

10

- With students in the same pairs, tell them to make two lists of ideas: one, a list of ways of stopping climate change and the other, things that they already do about it. This should include things they do to reduce climate change (e.g. turn out lights) and things they do to increase it (e.g. drive to school).

- Create two master lists on the board with students' help, by inviting them to add their ideas to the two columns.

- When each list has lots of ideas, ask the class which ideas are most effective at reducing climate change and of these, which ones are easiest to do. Ask students whether any of the ideas they have identified might be things they could start to put into practice.

> **Suggested answers**
> To reduce climate change we can: cut electricity bills by turning off lights, machines, etc. when we are not using them; take public transport, or walk or cycle, rather than drive to school, the shops etc.; insulate our homes so that they don't lose so much heat energy in cold weather; use fans instead of air conditioning in hot weather; wash clothes in cooler water, and hang clothes to dry; recycle and re-use old things; eat less meat (see the TED Talk in Unit 4); choose green energy sources, e.g. wind and solar power; plant trees; choose not to travel by plane when possible.

- Put students in groups. Explain that each group is going to take another important issue and plan a sporting event to raise awareness of it, like Lewis has done. You may decide the issues for the students or let them decide. Choose topical issues and/or issues that students can relate to in some way. Possible ideas include: education, diseases such as diabetes and cancer, unemployment, racism and sexism.
- Tell them they can use the questions to get them started in planning the event. To make it as realistic as possible, why not suggest that at the end of the lesson the idea is to create a promotional video for the event to post on social media?
- While groups start planning, go round and visit each group, helping with their ideas, making suggestions and asking questions.
- Make time at the end of the lesson for each group to present its event, or if they have created a video, to show it to the class.
- Encourage students to look critically at their own work by asking whether the cause and the event match well, which presentation would be most likely to persuade people, and what potential problems there could be.

Homework

- Set Workbook Lesson 3D exercises on page 34 for homework.
- Students find out more about how the North Pole has been affected by climate change in recent years.
- Students choose and watch another TED Talk about climate change or sport from the TED climate change and sport (extreme sport) playlists.

3E School sports *pp42–43*

WRITING An opinion essay *pp42–43*

- **Books closed.** For variety, and to start the lesson with students active and attentive, dictate the four questions rather than have them read them from the book. Check understanding of *compulsory* (describing something that you have to do, like wear seatbelts in cars).
- Tell students to write one more question of their choice about the topic of school sports so that they have five questions in total. Put students in pairs to discuss the questions. After a couple of minutes, get whole-class feedback and gather students' answers, focusing on the fourth question and their own question.
- Finish by concluding what most of the class feel about school sports.

- Tell the students they are going to learn to write an opinion essay.
- Read out the essay title and explain the task.
- Let students work in pairs before sharing their ideas as a class. Write the number of the questions they think should be answered on the board, but don't confirm the correct answers yet.

Answers

You have to answer questions 2, 5 and 6.

- Tell students to read the essay on page 150 and check their ideas from Exercise 2. Give them three minutes for this.
- Confirm the answers to Exercise 2 once everyone has read the essay. Ask *Does the writer agree or disagree with the statement?* (agree)

- Put students in pairs. Explain the task. You might want to tell one student to have the unit page open and the other student have the Writing bank page open to avoid a lot of flipping backwards and forwards.
- Go round and check that they are doing the task correctly.
- Nominate students to tell you the answer for each question. Check that the class agrees.

Answers

1 … many of us enjoy doing sport …

… Some students do not enjoy academic subjects but they like sport and PE lessons, and this may encourage them to enjoy school more …

… People aren't doing enough exercise in their free time, so schools should help …

… sport is good for the brain as well as the body …

… schools should prepare students for healthy lives as well as future jobs …

2 … if they're spending time at school doing sport, they have to do more work at home …

… there are other important subjects such as Art and Music. Should we give them time, too?

3 Students' own answers

4 (Suggested answers) In support of the writer's opinion: sport teaches life skills like teamwork, dedication and discipline; sport can help classes feel more together and friendly; doing sport at school encourages young people to become professional athletes and potential future champions.

Against the writer's opinion: some children who are not good at sport may feel like failures and should not have to do sport; choice of sports is limited at school, but outside school young people can choose the sport they enjoy most; treating sport as a subject may be the wrong approach and will discourage young people from taking up sports later in life.

5 WRITING SKILL Giving your opinion

• **5a** Ask students to draw on a piece of paper a line like this:

Disagree   Agree

⟷

• Get different students to read out each statement. Tell students to mark on their line how much they agree or disagree with each statement by writing the number of the statement along the line. If they neither agree or disagree, tell them they can write them somewhere in the middle.

• Show students the Useful language for giving your opinion. Give an example of your opinion, e.g. *I disagree with the first statement, so I can say, 'There's no question that many sports are dangerous, but personally, I don't believe the government should try to control whether people do them. Instead …'*

• Tell students to choose two or three statements and write their opinion using the Useful language. Explain that these sentences may be useful later on during the writing stage of the lesson.

5b MY PERSPECTIVE

• Put students in groups of four to six. Tell them to talk about each of the statements in Exercise 5a.

• When they have finished, let them add other arguments they have heard to their notes.

6

• Explain the task. Make sure students understand that they only need to write about one of the statements in Exercise 5a.

• Once they have chosen a statement, remind them that in an opinion essay they must all clearly state whether or not they agree. Ask them to write at least two more questions that they should answer in their essays. For example, for statement 1, good questions to answer include: 'What is a dangerous sport?', and 'Does the government have the power to control whether people do dangerous sports?'

• Show students the paragraphing of the essay on page 150 and compare with the plan in Exercise 6. Tell them to write a topic sentence for each paragraph as part of their plan. (You may need to remind them about topic sentences or do a quick review of them from lesson 3B.)

• Remind them that the advice on page 150 is there to help them. Read out each piece of advice, and point to examples in the text. Tell students to evaluate their own writing by asking whether they have followed the advice.

• If you are going to give the students a mark, tell them it will be higher if they write the essay in a similar way to the model and use language they have learnt.

• Set the writing for homework or set a time limit of twenty minutes to do it in class. As students are writing, go round and offer help. You might note some common errors for feedback when the time is up.

Fast finishers

Students who finish quickly can check their writing for errors, and for new language they used or they could plan/write a second piece of work.

7

• When students have finished writing, tell them to swap with a classmate and read each other's essays. Ask them to evaluate their essays against the guidance in Exercise 6 and on page 150.

SPEAKING *p43*

8

• ⌂ **22** Explain the task. Play the audio.

• Nominate a student to answer and check that the rest of the class agrees.

> **Answer**
>
> They are discussing 3 (which concerns sportspeople's salaries).

Audioscript 🎧 22

Female1: I just think that when you look at all the training that these people do to become the best, it makes sense that they get paid so much.

Male: Yes, but you could say the same for many jobs. Architects spend about seven years of their lives studying, but they don't earn $100,000 every time they go to work.

Female2: That's a good point. It's much more about how much money there is in sports. I mean, TV companies spend millions on football, so the star players are worth a lot of money to the league.

Male: I see what you're saying, but I don't think that's a good enough reason to pay them so much. I mean, there's a ton of money in other industries, like, er …

Female2: Some internet companies are incredibly rich, but software programmers don't make the same amount of money as football players.

Female1: I'm not sure I agree. There are some very rich people at the top of internet companies.

Male: That's true. If we compare star football players with, say, the boss of Amazon or Mark Zuckerberg, then actually the top players don't make that much!

Female1: And there aren't many athletes that make a good salary, are there? It's only the very best in each sport that make millions. They've had to compete against other very talented players to get where they are today.

Female2: And it's only a few sports, like football, golf, and tennis. What about track and field, for example? How much money do long-jumpers make, or even the best marathon runners? It can't be that much.

Female1: You're not wrong there.

❾

- 🎧 22 Look at the instructions. Tell students to read the expressions in the Useful language box. Before playing the audio again, let them try to answer from memory. Then play the audio again.
- Tell students to compare their answers in pairs.
- Elicit answers from the class.

> **Answers**
>
> Agreeing: That's true; That's a good point; You're not wrong there.
>
> Disagreeing: Yes, but …; I'm not sure I agree; I see what you're saying, but …

Exam tip

Interacting with their partner in speaking exams to get higher marks

A lot of speaking exams are done in pairs and part of what is tested is students' ability to listen and respond to their partner when they are speaking. Point out that students will get better marks if they respond with comments like *Really?*, *That's a good idea* or *I'm not sure I agree*, etc. Asking a direct question, e.g. *So what would you do next?* also shows good interaction. To be able to do this naturally in the exam, students need to practise in class, so encourage them to make use of opportunities to speak.

❿

- Ask students to read the task. Give them two minutes. Emphasize the freedom they have to choose any kind of sport here, not just traditional or very active sports.

⓫

- Explain that students are going to practise speaking, but they are also going to practise listening to and responding to each other's opinions.
- Put students in pairs to discuss their choice. Make sure they understand that they must come to an agreement about just three sports between them.
- Go round and check students are doing the task correctly and notice errors, difficulties, or where they use L1. Help them by correcting or giving them the English they need and then write some of these points on the board, or remember them for class feedback.

⓬

- When most pairs have finished, ask students to get into groups of four. Explain that they now need to agree on just three sports between all four of them, so they will need to discuss each sport together.
- At the end of the task, give some feedback about new language that came up, and errors to correct which you may have written on the board. You can also retell some interesting things you heard to share with the class.

> **Homework**
>
> - Set Workbook Lesson 3E exercises on pages 35–37 for homework.
> - Students write another opinion essay in response to a different statement from Exercise 5 or a topical one of your or their choice.

4 Food

4A Learning to cook

pp44–47

Information about the photo

Fridge magnets first appeared in the 1970s. A collector in the United States had a collection of around 45,000 in 2015 and this is thought to be the largest collection of fridge magnets in the world.

VOCABULARY Describing food *p45*

- Focus students' attention on the photo and the caption or project it using the CPT.
- Ask students to say whether the dishes in the photo look delicious in general or not. Ask them why. Ask which country they think the food comes from (these are dishes from Thailand), and where you might see lots of dishes all together like this. Don't explain until they have speculated that these are miniature models of food dishes which contain magnets so that you can decorate the door of a fridge with them. Ask them whether they have fridge magnets at home, and what they are.
- Tell students they are going to learn some words to describe food. Explain the task. They can use a dictionary or ask you for help as necessary. Invite students up to the front of the class to point to the dishes they are thinking of; alternatively, they can try to describe them as best they can. If they can't see one, they should think of one. Write their ideas next to each phrase, e.g. *junk food – hamburgers, hot dogs*.
- Go round the class checking that students are doing the task correctly and arriving at good suggestions for each way of describing food. Ask questions to check that they understand the words in bold, e.g. *Why do you think this dish looks disgusting? Which dish or dishes contain wheat?*
- Write the key words (those in bold) on the board. When students have finished, explain that together, the class will try to decide on one dish, ingredient or type of food, either from the photo or elsewhere, that is the best example for the key words. Invite suggestions for each one in turn, and ensure that the majority of students agree before writing the example.

Suggested answers

1 and **2** Students' own answers

3 There is nothing in the photo that looks like junk food. Typical junk food includes burgers, fried chicken, etc. Junk food is defined as any food that contains lots of fat, salt and sugar and is quick and easy to eat. It is usually quite cheap.

4 Sugary food, e.g. cakes, fizzy drinks; fatty foods, e.g. chips, bacon

5 Many of the dishes in the photo contain lots of vegetables (and therefore contain vitamins). Other foods that contain a lot of vitamins include fruit and vegetables, e.g. oranges, broccoli.

6 The Japanese-style 'California roll' dishes in the centre of the photo, and several other dishes, such as the filled croissant (third row, second from right), could be described as fast food. Other fast foods include pizza, burgers, kebabs, etc.

7 Food which is commonly eaten raw includes: fish, i.e. sushi; meat, e.g. carpaccio, steak tartare, vegetables, e.g. carrot, broccoli, etc. in salads; nuts and grains. Although many ingredients such as fruit is eaten raw, it is not normal to describe it as raw.

8 Food in packets and tins, as well as many baked and frozen food, e.g. breakfast cereals, sweets, biscuits, crisps, soup, burgers, sausages, fish fingers, cheese. Processed food often contains added salt, sugar and fat.

9 Many of the dishes look well-balanced, i.e. containing a good mixture of protein, carbohydrates, fibre and fat, without too much of any one food group.

10 Lots of food in the photo may be steamed, e.g. wrapped vine or banana leaves at the top of the photo. Vegetables are often steamed, and it's considered to be a healthier way of cooking.

11 Anything that doesn't contain meat or fish, e.g. the grey plate with green leaves and a little dish of dark sauce on the right of the photo.

12 The croissant (third row, second from right) contains wheat. Wheat is main ingredient in most bread, pasta, baked cakes and pastries.

Extension

Tell students that there are six words in bold which contain the /st/ sound. Tell them to find them. Point out that as well as the obvious words: ta**st**y, disgu**st**ing, fa**st** and **st**eamed, the sound is also found at the end of proce**ssed** and well-balan**ced**.

- Look at the instructions. Do the first item as a whole class. Tell students to express the answers like this: *'Natural' is the opposite of 'processed'.*
- Tell students to do the rest of the activity on their own When most have finished, get them to compare answers in pairs and to help each other with anything they haven't finished.
- Nominate students to read out their sentences.

Answers

1 *processed* (also *junk food*, which is processed, and seen as of poor quality because it contains added ingredients like sugar, fat and salt)

2 There isn't really an opposite of *fried*, but *steamed* and *raw* are two very different ways of preparing food.

3 *a vegetarian*

4 *disgusting*. (These are both extreme adjectives; *disgusting* is also opposite in meaning to *tasty* but *tasty* isn't an extreme adjective)

5 *raw*

Exam tip

Recording words with related words

If words are learnt and written down with related words, there is a better chance that students will remember them. Relationships between words include synonyms, e.g. *delicious – tasty*, antonyms (opposites), e.g. *natural – processed*, hyponyms (a more specific word than the general category it is in), e.g. *carrot* is a hyponym of *vegetable*, topic, e.g. *to steam* and *saucepan* are both words associated with cooking. Let students explore different ways of recording these words and showing their relationships. For example, teach them to express opposites like this: *natural ≠ processed*.

- Give students two minutes to think of the differences in meaning between these pairs of words. Then put them in pairs to discuss the differences.
- Nominate students to share their ideas with the class.

Answers

1 Fresh vegetables have been picked recently and have not been frozen or canned. They may be cooked. Raw vegetables have not been cooked.

2 Fast food is quick to buy and eat. It may be healthy, unlike junk food, but it often is also unhealthy.

3 Cooked food includes all food that has been heated in preparation for eating, even basic food without added ingredients. Processed food contains many ingredients, often including chemicals to stop it from going off, give it colour or extra flavour.

4 Boiled vegetables are cooked in boiling water. Steamed vegetables are cooked in the steam produced by boiling water, above the water.

5 A strong flavour has lots of flavour and you can notice individual ingredients, e.g. there's a strong meaty flavour in this soup. A spicy flavour is one produced by chilli or pepper that some people find difficult to eat. We often say 'spicy food' is 'hot'.

- Explain the task. Ask students to write the sentences on their own. Tell them to write them in random order without numbering them. Go round and check that they are doing the task correctly, offering help where needed.
- When students have finished, put them in pairs to compare their ideas. Tell them to ask each other questions, e.g. *Why did you write burger and chips?* (It's a type of junk food that I think is tasty.) *Is a doughnut something containing wheat that you'd like right now?* (Yes, that's right!)
- At the end of the task, elicit a few examples of each category from the whole class.

Suggested answers

1, **3**, **5**, **6**, **8** Students' own answers   **2** orange, kiwi, spinach, broccoli, tomato   **4** fish, i.e. sushi; meat, e.g. carpaccio, steak tartare   **7** meat-free pizza (e.g. margarita), falafel, French fries, veggie burger

5 MY PERSPECTIVE

- Look at the instructions and ask students to read the bad habits to check they understand them.
- Ask students to do the exercise on their own. When most students have finished, get them to compare answers in pairs. Write on the board: *I hate it when people … My brother's always …*
- Get feedback from the class. Have a class vote on the worst habit. Find out why these habits annoy them, if they know people who do these things, and if they do them. Encourage them to use the phrases on the board by offering an example, e.g. *My husband's always eating things in the supermarket before we've bought them. It makes me so angry!*
- Have a class discussion on other bad habits to do with food.

LISTENING *p46*

- Tell students that they are going to listen to two people discussing cooking in schools. Ask if they have, or have ever had, cookery lessons at school. Ask how young people normally learn how to cook in their country and whether they enjoy it.
- Read out the questions. Ask students to think about why they agree or disagree.
- 🎧 **23** Play the audio once straight through. Tell students to compare their answers in pairs. Go round and notice how well they did in order to decide how quickly to go through answers and whether you will need to play the audio again.
- Nominate a student to give the answer. Check with other students whether they agree or not, and what the speakers disagree about, before giving the correct answer.

Answer

No, the speakers don't agree – Mali thinks children should learn cooking at school, but Terry thinks it should be done at home.

Audioscript 🎧 **23**

T = Terry, M = Mali

T: Thanks for subscribing to What's news? I'm here with Mali. Hello, Mali.

M: Hi, Terry.

T: Mali is a good friend.

M: You only like me because I cook for you!

T: No! I must say that Mali is a fantastic cook. But that's not the only reason we're friends! You are going to cook for me later, though, aren't you?

M: I thought you were taking me out for lunch! No, I'm going to make a tasty Thai meal for you.

T: OK, I'll do the washing up if you like. How about that?

M: That's a deal!

T: So, what's the secret to being a good cook?

M: I think it helps if you don't wait until you're an adult – my mum taught me when I was growing up.

T: Really? So, what would you say if I told you that food and cooking is going to be compulsory in schools?

M: Oh, that's good. How old will the children be when they start?

T: I expect children will learn some simple dishes at about eight years old.

M: Eight years old is a good time to start.

T: I agree that you should start young. I just don't know that school is the right place to learn.

M: No?

T: To me, home is where you should learn. Schools have enough to do to teach all the other subjects.

M: So why are they introducing this now?

T: The government thinks children should learn about basic food preparation before they leave school.

M: And what about the effect food can have on health? They may be able to teach them about the dangers of a poor diet in those lessons, too.

T: That's true, I suppose.

M: It's about making sure they use fresh ingredients – vegetables, meat and fish.

T: Right.

M: So you never learnt cookery at school or at home, Terry. And you still can't cook?

T: Actually, I've recently decided I'm going to learn one new recipe each week. My brother's showing me how to make vegetable lasagne at his house tomorrow. He's a good cook.

M: That's sounds delicious! Will you make it for me next week?

T: If you do the washing up afterwards.

M: That's a deal!

T: OK, well, thanks for joining us today, Mali. Next week, the podcast goes out at the same time and it's all about eating raw food. Happy eating!

7

- Explain the task. Ask students to read the questions and check they understand them. You could ask what they think the answer to 1 is before they listen, but don't tell them if they are right or wrong.
- 🎧 **23** Play the audio again. Let students compare their ideas in pairs. Go round and notice how well they did in order to decide how quickly to go through answers and whether you will need to play the audio again.
- Check the answers as a class by asking for a show of hands, e.g. *Number 1, who thinks it's Terry? And hands up for Mali.* Alternatively, get students to call out their answers all together or nominate two students to give their answers.
- Where students agree, write the answer on the board. Where there is a difference of opinion, ask students to justify their different answers, but *don't* say who is correct – put a question mark on the board. Tell students they will listen again and check. Go through all the answers like this and then play the audio again if necessary, telling students to focus on the areas of uncertainty.
- If students are *still* uncertain of the answer, play the audio again and stop at key points. Play the section again two or three times if students are still struggling. Draw attention to the problem words and explain them when you give the answers.
- Ask for a show of hands which speaker they agree with more, Terry or Mali.

Answers
1 M (*I'm going to make a tasty Thai meal for you.*)
2 T (*I'll do the washing up if you like*)
3 M (*I think it helps if you don't wait until you're an adult*)
4 T (*… food and cooking is going to be compulsory in schools?*)
5 T (*home is where you should learn. Schools have enough to do …*)
6 M (*They may be able to teach them about the dangers of a poor diet in those lessons, too.*)
7 T (*I've recently decided I'm going to learn one new recipe each week*)
8 T (*My brother's showing me how to make vegetable lasagne … He's a good cook*)

- Put students in pairs to discuss the questions.
- When students have finished, accept answers from the class, and then encourage a whole-class discussion about whether they think schools should teach cooking, and which dishes should be taught if so. Ask students to explain their reasons.

Teaching tip

Playing devil's advocate
Students are usually happy to give their opinion but may do so only briefly, so it is sometimes hard to get them talking extensively. One way to prompt them to say more is to 'play devil's advocate', or pretend to disagree with them to keep an interesting discussion going. For example, if they say that cooking should be taught in schools, you might say: 'But what school subject would you teach less of in order to make time for cookery?' If they say that cooking is not a subject for school, you could challenge them to say where or who should teach them cooking instead.

GRAMMAR Future plans, intentions and arrangements *p46–47*

To prepare for teaching the following exercises, see Grammar reference on page 134.

- 🎧 **23** **Optional step.** If you think that students know future grammar quite well, tell them to close their books. Put the different possible structures on the board, i.e. present simple, *'ll, will, going to, may/might*, present continuous. Dictate the sentences in the Grammar box but replace the verbs in bold with an oral gap fill, e.g. *OK, I BEEP the washing up if you like* and tell them the missing verb, e.g. *'ll do.* Put students in pairs and ask them to complete the sentences. When they have finished, play the audio again for them to check.
- Focus students' attention on the Grammar box and explain the task. Tell them that sentences a–g all come from the audio.

- Go around and check that students understand the concepts, e.g. *arrangements, schedules*.
- Nominate students to share their answers with the class.

Answers

1 a **2** f **3** b **4** e **5** d **6** c **7** g

10

- Look at the instructions and do the first item with the whole class.
- Tell students to do the rest of the activity on their own. Go round and check they are doing the task correctly. When most students have finished, get them to compare answers in pairs and to help each other with anything they haven't finished.
- You can either go through the answers with the whole class, or wait for them to read the Grammar reference on page 134 and then ask the class the grammar-checking questions, or nominate individual students to give their answers.

Answers

1 e **2** c **3** e **4** a **5** b **6** d **7** d

Grammar reference and practice

Tell students to do Exercises 1–4 on page 135 now, or set them for homework.

Answers to Grammar practice exercises

1
1 going to work   **2** does the plane   **3** I'll
4 I'm going to   **5** are you going to   **6** are you
going to   **7** I'm spending, visit   **8** might

2
1 will get, arrives
2 gets, won't be
3 'll / will understand, talk
4 find out, will (you) text
5 'll / will call, give

3
1 'll carry
2 'm helping / going to help
3 won't be
4 'll call
5 'm cooking / going to cook
6 'll make

4
1 What are you doing / going to do this weekend?
2 I'll text you after I speak to her.
3 Are you seeing anyone this evening?
4 I won't make a noise.
5 Do you think you'll go back to that restaurant?
6 I'm not going to see / not seeing her

Teaching tip

When grammar rules have exceptions
Teaching and learning future grammar is difficult because many of the rules we think are true have too many exceptions for us to trust them. You will hear *will* used to talk about plans and intentions, for example, and *going to* to talk about arrangements. Some rules are more reliable: it is very unusual to use anything other than the present simple to talk about the future in clauses introduced by *when, until, as soon as, if* and so on. *Will* or *'ll* are almost always used to talk about decisions made at the moment of speaking.

What should we tell our students if they notice exceptions to rules? It's important to be honest with students and tell them that speakers may choose different structures in a particular situation for different reasons, but that the rules, imperfect as they are, may help them make the right choices most of the time, especially in examinations where these rules are explicitly tested.

A good approach in discussing exercises like Exercise 13 in this lesson, where some of the gaps have more than one possible answer, is to ask why each option is possible. Encourage students to explore the reasons for each possible answer.

11

- Get a student to read out the information about 18- to 25-year olds in Britain. Ask the class whether they think it is similar or different from Britain in their country. Ask for a show of hands to find out who in the class can cook one, two, five or lots of recipes.
- Ask students to read the three comments by Ana, Fumio and Mohammed and to complete them by choosing the correct options. Let them work in pairs if you think that some students need support.
- Go around and check students understand the grammar by asking why they have chosen particular verb forms. Refer them back to the grammar explanations on page 134 if necessary.

Answers

1 I'm going to   **2** start   **3** might teach   **4** I'll
5 going to cook   **6** I'm moving   **7** they'll practise
8 I'm   **9** won't   **10** I need   **11** I might   **12** I'll pick

12 MY PERSPECTIVE

- Put students in pairs to discuss the questions.
- After two minutes, get the students' attention, stop the discussion and find out who is most like each of the characters. Ask students to justify their opinions.

Extension

Have students write their own comments about their attitudes to learning to cook, in the same style as Ana, Fumio and Mohammed's.

- Set the task, making sure students understand not to use the present continuous or *might* in this exercise. Remind them that *might* and *may* are synonyms, so *might* can be used where *may* is a possibility.

Answers

1 'm going to do (intentional plan) / will do (hope)
2 leave
3 will probably be
4 will (belief) / (may (less confident) possibly disappear
5 will cook
6 is going to record / records (to refer to present time, i.e. they have started already)
7 get
8 will go (expectation) / is going to go (intention)
9 will (the makers say this, so a confident expectation) / may (if they are less confident) make
10 'll (after *I think* … – a belief, or perhaps a decision made at the moment of speaking) / may (possibly, not certain) spend

- Tell students to read the questions and then add one more question to ask their classmates about the future of food. Go round the class offering help to any students who can't think of a question. For example, they could ask about specific things we might or might not be eating in the future, or what recipe they would programme their kitchen robot to make for them.

- Put students in pairs or small groups. Remind them that the questions are all about the future, so they can use this as an opportunity to practise the grammar they have studied.

- In feedback, encourage a variety of viewpoints. Make sure students who think robot chefs will happen speak as well as students who don't. Ensure they offer their reasons for their opinions.

Homework

- Set Workbook Lesson 4A exercises on pages 38–41 for homework.

- If they didn't write their own comments about their attitudes to learning to cook in Exercise 12, have them write those for homework.

- Students find out about automated kitchens: how much they will cost, what kinds of recipes they will be able to do, how they work, and so on.

4B Street food *pp48–49*

VOCABULARY BUILDING Compound adjectives *p48*

- **Books closed.** Write on the board:
  It's better to eat oven-baked/oven-baking food that hasn't been fried in oil.
  You'll keep coming back for more great-tasted/great-tasting lemonade.

- Ask students to identify the nouns (food, lemonade). Ask *Where is the food baked?* and elicit the sentence *The food is baked in the oven.* Ask *What tastes great?* (the lemonade) and elicit the sentence *The lemonade tastes great.*

- Ask *Is the food the subject or the object of the sentence?* (the object) Show students that the correct adjective is *oven-baked.* Ask *Is the lemonade the subject or the object of the sentence?* (the subject) Show them that the correct adjective is *great-tasting.*

- Tell students to open their books on page 48, read about compound adjectives and choose the correct options in sentences 1–5. Go round the class and check that students are doing the task correctly. If they are struggling, consider pointing out the rules if you think they might help students understand: if the noun being described (e.g. *food, lemonade*) is the active agent, or subject of the verb (*bake, taste*), we use the present participle, but if the noun is not the agent, we use the past participle.

- To check the answers, read the first sentence in item 1 and nominate a student to read the second sentence. Then tell that student to read the first sentence in item 2 and to nominate the next student, and so on.

Answers

1 deep-fried 2 good-looking 3 sweet-tasting
4 rice-filled 5 undercooked

- Look at the instructions and do the first item with the whole class.

- Tell students to do the rest of the activity on their own and to use a dictionary if they need to. Go round and check students are doing the task correctly and notice words and phrases they look up, ask you about, or underline. Focus on these in feedback. When most students have finished, get them to compare answers in pairs and to help each other with anything they haven't finished.

- Go through the answers by asking different students to read out the full sentences.

Answers

1 home-made 2 well-known 3 old-fashioned
4 modern-looking 5 overcooked

- Look at the instructions and use the model sentence to illustrate the task. Ask students to shout out popular dishes to help all students think of food to describe and write them on the board.
- Set a time limit of two minutes for students to write their three sentences. Go round and check they are doing the task correctly. Provide help if necessary.
- For feedback, you could ask students to read out their descriptions without saying the name of the dish, while the rest of the class try to guess which dish they are talking about.

READING *p49*

- Put students in pairs to discuss the questions. Tell them to try and agree on the three most important characteristics of street food.
- In feedback, after some general discussion about street food where they live (question 1), write the characteristics in question 2 on the board and collect everyone's top three characteristics by tallying their answers, i.e.
  It's tasty |||
  It's convenient |||| ||
  etc.

- Look at the instructions. Set a time limit of three minutes for students to read the article for gist. If they protest that three minutes is not enough time, reassure them that it is enough to answer the question, that they don't need to understand every word, and that they will have a chance to read the article again. Do not play the audio at this point, since this will prevent students from skim reading.

Exam tip

Gist reading tasks

In exams, there are different tasks which test different understanding of the text. Sometimes the tasks test a general understanding of a paragraph, or the 'gist' of the text (as in this task); sometimes they test students' ability to find a particular piece of information in a text (as in Exercise 5); sometimes they test close understanding of particular vocabulary and sentences. Tasks that require general understanding usually come first in the exam, and students should only need to read the text once. They shouldn't spend too much time on this. For later tasks, students may need to read the text quite quickly once and then re-read sections as they answer each question.

Answers

Five characteristics are mentioned: it is varied and multicultural; it has many flavours but is not hot; it uses local ingredients; it is not expensive; and it is unusual food.

- 🎧 **24** Explain the task. Point out that the writer uses typical dishes as examples to illustrate particular ideas about Filipino food. Explain that unlike the last exercise, students here can look for specific words in the text (the names of the dishes) in order to find the information they need quickly. Set a time limit of three minutes to complete the task.
- While students are reading, write some useful sentence stems on the board for giving the answers, *[Champorado with tuyo] is a good example of … / illustrates … / shows …* In feedback, encourage students to use these structures rather than just saying, for example, '*1 is e*'. For example, *Champorado with tuyo illustrates the multicultural past of the country. Lumpia is a good example of a dish which is similar to dishes from other countries.*
- When most students have finished reading, ask them to discuss their answers in pairs.
- Get whole-class feedback by asking for a show of hands for each choice.

Answers

1 e **2** b **3** d **4** a **5** c

- Put students in pairs or small groups. Give them a few minutes to discuss the questions.
- Go round and check students are doing the task correctly and notice errors, difficulties, or where they use L1. Help them by correcting or giving them the English they need and then write some of these points on the board, or remember them for class feedback.
- When most students have finished, stop the activity. Elicit some of the more interesting information from the conversations, such as who in the class is the most adventurous, what strange things students have eaten, and what students would like to try.
- Then give feedback about new language that came up, and errors to correct which you may have written on the board.

Teaching tip

Seeing things from other points of view

In discussions of other countries and people, cultural differences may result in reactions of misunderstanding and even disgust. Make sure you ask students to reflect on how aspects of their own culture may be seen as unattractive to others. Ask questions such as: *What foods do you eat that might seem strange or unattractive to them? What other eating habits that you practise might be difficult for other people to accept?*

- Set up the task as a race. Explain that some of the words used in the article may be new or less familiar to them. Focus attention on definitions 1–6 and tell them to find them as quickly as possible, using the information about which paragraphs to search in. Emphasize the speed aspect of the task by saying *Ready … steady … GO!*

- When the first person claims to have finished, tell them to quickly give all their answers. Invite the rest of the class to agree or disagree and to make any comments they think are relevant.

- Drill the new vocabulary, paying particular attention to the pronunciation of *cuisine* /kwɪˈzɪːn/ and the /ɔː/ sound in *prawn* and *stall*. Elicit other words the students know with an /ɔː/ sound produced by the letter 'a', e.g. *law, call, although, war*. Point out some common spellings that produce the sound ('aw', 'al', 'all', 'ar').

Answers

1 takeout   **2** dishes   **3** seafood, prawns
4 bite   **5** stall   **6** cuisine

Extension

Ask students to think for a minute about their answers to the following questions:

Which words from the text are important, useful or interesting for some reason?
Where will you record these new words?
How will you learn and remember them?

Then get students to record the new vocabulary along with other words they have learnt related to food, e.g. *seafood – prawns, crab, oysters*, etc.

- Ask students where they might read an article such as the one they've been reading and who might have written it. Suggest, if the students don't, that it may be one way to attract tourists to the Philippines and that it could be written by someone for the tourist board.

- Ask students to imagine that the tourist marketing board of their city or region wants local people to comment on their website about local food, and to think about the questions on their own in that role. Write on the board *Come to [region] and try [food]*. Tell students to write a short comment (a paragraph) describing a dish from their region which might attract visitors there. Encourage them to use compound adjectives to make the food sound as delicious or interesting as possible.

- Go round and check students are doing the task correctly and notice errors, difficulties, or where they use L1. Help them by correcting or giving them the English they need, and make a note of any language points to go over with the class.

- When most students have finished, put them in groups to read out and listen to each other's comments. Find out which dishes were the most popular, whether there were any surprise dishes, and which they think will succeed in attracting visitors.

Homework

- Set Workbook Lesson 4B exercises on pages 42–43 for homework.

- Students research the street food of another country or culture and present it at the start of the next lesson.

- Students use a search engine to find out some interesting foods that are described using the compound adjectives they have learnt, and which ones they think are most useful to learn. Show them how the suggestions that search engines offer include common items as well as strange searches people have done. Searching for 'undercooked' may produce a list like this one:

4C Feed the world with ... bugs? *pp50–51*

GRAMMAR Making predictions *pp50–51*

To prepare for teaching the following exercises, see Grammar reference on page 134.

- Write *FOOD GROUPS* on the board. Explain that food groups are the different types of chemicals that we need to eat to survive. Elicit the main food groups by giving well-known example foods in each group, e.g. meat, eggs, beans, etc. for *protein*. Make sure you elicit the following: *protein*, *carbohydrates* (e.g. rice, bread, potato, and including sugar and sugary food like fruit), *fat* (e.g. oil, butter, red meat) *fibre* (in fruit and vegetables), *minerals* (e.g. calcium from milk), *vitamins* (mostly found in dairy products and fruit and vegetables).
- Look at the instructions and do the first item with the whole class.
- Tell students to do the rest of the activity on their own. Go round and check they are doing the task correctly. When most students have finished, get them to compare answers in pairs and to help each other with anything they haven't finished.
- Alternatively, with weaker classes, tell students that you are going to read the paragraph but that they must read out the missing extracts to complete it. Instruct them not to write anything at this stage. Start to read the paragraph, and pause at the first gap. Wait for students to supply the missing extract. If they say the correct extract, continue, but if they suggest the wrong one, start from the beginning. Continue like this until they have got every gap correct in one attempt. Give students two minutes to repeat the exercise on paper, filling in each gap with the correct letter.
- Check answers around the class.

> **Answers**
>
> **1** e **2** a **3** c **4** f **5** b **6** d

- Do this as a whole-class activity. Elicit the problem and the solution from the class.

> **Answers**
>
> The problem is that as the world population rises, there will not be enough protein to feed everyone. The paragraph suggests that eating insects could be a solution to this problem.

Extension

Have a class discussion using these questions as prompts:
How common is eating insects where you live? Do you ever eat insects?
Have you ever accidentally eaten an insect? Where and when was this?

Would you be happy to eat (more) insects as part of your diet? Why? Why not?
Would you rather increase the number of insects in your diet or become a vegetarian? Why?

- Explain the task. Make sure that students are looking at the sentences as a whole to decide the probability. For example, 'we will run out of food' is certain, but 'They think we will run out of food' is probable.
- Let students compare their answers with a classmate before sharing the answers with the class.

> **Answers**
>
> **1** (certain) e, f **2** (probable) a, c **3** (possible) b, d

- Check that students know which structure is which, i.e. future continuous = *will be eating*, future perfect = *will have grown*, etc.
- Tell students to complete the rules with the correct structure and then match an example extract from the Grammar box.
- You can either go through the answers with the whole class, or wait for them to read the Grammar reference on page 134 and then ask the class the grammar-checking questions, or nominate individual students to give their answers.
- Copy the two timelines in the Teaching tip to provide visual support for the two new tenses: the future perfect and future continuous. Use them to show students how the future perfect describes completed future actions before a point in the future, while the continuous describes future actions happening at the same time as a point in the future.

> **Answers**
>
> **1** going to – extract e **2** will – extract c
> **3** will – extract f **4** may / might – extract b **5** future continuous – extract d **6** future perfect – extract a

> **Teaching tip**
>
> **Using timelines**
> Grammar rules about tenses are often difficult to explain and understand. Timelines are a visual way to get these rules across. The conventions for timelines are these:
> - show time as going from left (the past) to right (the future), with the present clearly marked somewhere along the line. An arrow indicates the movement of time.
> - mark actions as either happening in a moment or over a very short period of time as a line or cross on the line; mark longer actions happening over a period of time as a wavy line running parallel with the timeline.
> - label points on the line with the verb in the correct tense, and always accompany a timeline with the sentence it describes.
>
> Here are two examples, for future perfect and future continuous. Do they follow the conventions?

Future perfect

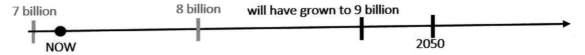

By 2050 the population will have grown to nine billion.

Future continuous

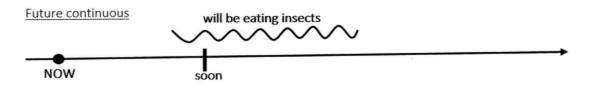

We will soon be eating insects.

Grammar reference and practice

Tell students to do Exercises 5 and 6 on page 135 now, or set them for homework.

Answers to Grammar practice exercises

5

1 'll / will be eating
2 'll / will have passed
3 won't be staying
4 'll / will have gone
5 won't have crossed / won't be crossing*
6 Will you be joining

* The action of crossing the line (or not) can be seen as happening at the same time as it is getting dark (continuous), or before it gets dark (perfect).

6

1 'll / will want
2 'll definitely come
3 Are you / will you be leaving
4 'll / will be
5 won't be
6 'll see
7 'll be wearing

- Look at the instructions. Remind students of the rules in Exercise 4.
- Go round the class and check that students are doing the task correctly and have understood the difference in use between the two tenses. Refer them to timelines if you have them on the board, and ask questions like *Will they be in the middle of the action this weekend, or will it be finished?*
- Ask the whole class or individual students for their answers. Don't say if they are right or wrong, but ask them to support their answer with reasons. Where students agree, write the answer on the board. Where there is a difference of opinion, put a question mark on the board.

6 **PRONUNCIATION** Sentence stress in future continuous and future perfect sentences

- **6 a** 🔊 **25** Explain the task. Play the audio.
- Ask the class if the answers on the board are all correct. Correct any that are not.

Answers

1 will be doing   2 will have tried   3 won't be eating   4 Will you be doing   5 will have finished
6 won't have finished

- **6 b** 🔊 **26** Explain the task. Play the audio.
- Nominate students to share their answers with the class. Point out that in positive sentences 1–2, the auxiliary verbs have contractions or weak forms and that the stress is on the main verb rather than the auxiliary, but in negative sentences 3–4, the emphasis is on the negation.

Answers

1 **what** we'll be **do**ing this week**end**
2 I'll have **tried**   3 I **won't** be **eat**ing any **ants**
4 I **won't** have **fi**nished **mine**

- **6 c** Put students in pairs. Give them two minutes to take turns copying the sentence stress in the audio, while the other listens and pays attention to stress in the future continuous and future perfect forms.

- Tell students that this exercise contains all the verb forms studied in the lesson, not just the future continuous and future perfect forms. If you think that students may still be uncertain of the different uses of the structures, you could let them work in pairs.
- Go round the class and check students are doing the task correctly and check their answers, offering guidance and help as necessary.
- When most students have finished, invite volunteers to read out a sentence at a time with the correct answers.

Extension

Marcel Dicke has given a TED Talk (Why not eat insects?) in which he talks about eating insects. You could show the class the talk now, or sections of it. Alternatively, you could set it as homework.

8 MY PERSPECTIVE

- Put students in pairs to discuss the questions.
- Go round and check students are doing the task correctly and notice errors, difficulties, or where they use L1. Help them by correcting or giving them the English they need and then write some of these points on the board, or remember them for class feedback. When they have been talking for a few minutes, regroup students so that they can tell other classmates what they have been discussing.
- At the end of the task, give some feedback about new language that came up, and errors to correct which you may have written on the board. You can also retell some interesting things you heard to share with the class.

Suggested answers

Advantages of eating insects include:

efficiency – you can get a lot more protein from farming insects than you can from farming cows and other animals.

insects are already a part of our diet, whether we are aware of it or not.

many people enjoy insects as part of their varied diet.

Other advantages include:

insects may be a cheaper source of protein than other kinds of meat.

farming insects will be better for the environment than traditional farming, producing fewer greenhouse gases and using less land and water.

insects are better for your health because they are low in fat.

Extension

Ask students to create promotional videos or radio ads selling the idea of eating insects. They write a script and record themselves.

9

- Explain the task. Tell them that they can invent any kind of dish, either sweet or savoury, for any meal or occasion, and the dish can be as basic or complex as they like.
- Go through the prompts that they can use to describe the dish. Offer to help with new vocabulary, such as the names of insects and other ingredients, and tell students they can use a dictionary as necessary.

- Put students in groups of three to five. As they plan their dishes, go round and visit each group, asking about their recipes and providing help if necessary. Notice any relevant errors and difficulties they are having with English, or where they use L1. Write some of these points on the board, or remember them for class feedback.
- When most groups are ready and have invented their dishes, give some feedback about new language that came up, and errors to correct, which you may have written on the board.

10 CHOOSE

The idea is for students to make their own choice of activity here. However, you might want to make the decision for the students, in which case explain why. Alternatively, you may decide to let students do more than one task. You could divide the class into groups and have each group do a different task – or you could have a vote on which task the whole class should do. For the vote:

- put students in pairs or groups to decide which they prefer.
- take a vote on each task.
- if the vote is tied, ask one student from each side to explain which is best and take the vote again. You can decide if there is still no change.
- Option 1 is a speaking task. You might provide each student with about £20. Dishes cost £10 each, so they are only able to buy two dishes. The group that sells the most dishes wins.
- Option 2 is a writing task. Again, this could be done in class or as homework. You might collect everyone's recipes and create a book of insect recipes.
- Option 3 involves online research. If students have online access in the classroom, this could be done in class, after which they present their findings to the class. If not, this could be set as homework, in which case students present what they found out at the start of the next lesson.

Homework

- Set Workbook Lesson 4C exercises on pages 44–45 for homework.
- See Exercise 10 for research and writing tasks.
- You might want to tell students to watch the track called *Unit 4 TED Talk* on the *Perspectives* website before they come to the next class.

4D Why I'm a weekday vegetarian *pp52–53*

- Tell students they are going to watch a TED Talk about eating meat and being a vegetarian. Ask what *vegetarian* means and find out whether anyone in the class is a vegetarian or knows anyone who is.

- Read out the quote and ask students to translate it or say what they think it means in English (or both).

- ▶ **4.0** Tell them they are going to see a short text on the DVD to introduce the talk and the speaker, and play the *About the speaker* section. Then do the vocabulary exercise.

- After they finish, write the key words from the *About the speaker* section on the board and ask students to retell it aloud, or ask them to write as much of what it said as they can. Correct as necessary.

Answers to About the speaker

1 green = c (good for the planet)
2 log cabin = c (a house made of wood)
3 hippie = a (people who believe in peace and love)
4 commit = a (promise to do something)
5 emissions = c (gas and pollution that we create)
6 footprint = b (the amount of carbon dioxide (CO_2) that we produce)

TED Talk About the speaker ▶ **4.0**

*Graham Hill is a designer who tries to convince people to care about the environment and live **green** lives. His first website, Treehugger.com, was named after a phrase for someone who loves to be out in nature, and he says he grew up in the countryside in a **log cabin** with **hippie** parents.*

*But what does it mean to live a greener life in the city? He looks for ways that we can all care about the environment and **commit** to helping reduce our **emissions** and our **footprint**.*

Graham's idea worth spreading is that cutting meat from our diet – even just part of the time – can have a powerful impact on the planet.

AUTHENTIC LISTENING SKILLS Pausing *p52*

As well as teaching aspects of phonology and listening skills, these tasks also allow:

- you to pre-teach some vocabulary.

- students to read and hear new language before they listen to the whole text.

- students to tune in to the speaker's voice and style.

- **Optional step.** Read the Authentic listening skills box out loud while students follow you by reading from the book. Pause carefully and deliberately at the points indicated by a line | (one line means a short pause, two means a longer pause).

  When people | are speaking to an audience, | | they often pause | to break their sentences up | into short sections, | or chunks. | | This makes it easier| for the listeners to follow. | | Speakers often pause: | at the end of sentences; | | where there is a comma | or other punctuation; | | to separate adverbial phrases, | for example expressions about time or place; | | before an important word or phrase; | | and between the subject of a sentence | and its verb | when the subject is long.

- Ask *What was I doing when I read out that text to make it easier to understand?* Elicit that pausing helps students hear the natural syntax of a sentence or paragraph. Tell them to listen again but to mark the pauses with one line for a short pause or two lines for a long pause. Read the text again in the same careful way.

- If possible, show the text with the pauses marked for them to check their answers.

- If students haven't already read the Authentic listening skills box, have them read it now. Explain the task.

- 🎧 **27** Play the audio.

- Write the sentence on the board and invite students to mark the other pauses they heard.

Answers

About a year ago, | I asked myself a question: |'Knowing what I know, | why am I not a vegetarian?'

- Ask students to do the same for the next two sentences of the TED Talk, and predict where the pauses will be. Refer them to the list of reasons for pausing in the Authentic listening skills box. Give them a minute to do this.

- 🎧 **28** Play the audio for students to check.

- For feedback, invite a volunteer to copy Graham and read out the sentences with the same pausing. Find out whether the rest of the class agrees.

Answers

After all, | I'm one of the green guys: | I grew up with hippie parents | in a log cabin. I started a site called | TreeHugger | – I care about this stuff.

Extension

- If you or your students want to explore the last item on the list of reasons why people pause in the Authentic listening skills box, write the next two sentences from the talk on the board:

  *I knew that **eating a mere hamburger a day** | can increase my risk of dying by a third. Cruelty: I knew that **the 10 billion animals we raise each year for meat** | are raised in factory farm conditions …*

- Point out that the subjects of both sentences are long (*eating a mere hamburger a day*, and *the 10 billion animals we raise each year for meat*).

WATCH *p52*

If you are short of time, or want a different approach to the video, you may want to watch the whole talk all the way through with only some brief checking questions. A version of this is on the DVD and is labelled as *TED Talk with activities*. At the end of each section, there is a short gist question. Pause after each question on screen so students can give their answers, then play the answer.

Answers to gist questions on DVD

Part 1

Which is the best summary of this part of the talk?

b Graham knew why eating meat was bad, but he did nothing to change.

Part 2

Graham knows that he should be a vegetarian but he likes eating meat. What is his solution?

c He has reduced the amount of meat he eats.

- Look at the instructions. Set a time limit of two minutes.
- Go around the class, offering suggestions and questioning the students' ideas, e.g. *Why do you think it's good for your health?*
- Elicit their ideas and write them on the board, correcting their English as you do.

Suggested answers

It's good for your health; it's cheaper than buying meat; it's good for the environment; you may not enjoy the taste of meat; you may disagree with the way animals are treated; it may be against your religion; you may have an allergy to meat.

- Explain the task. Make sure students understand one of the problems is *not* mentioned.
- ▶ **4.1** Play Part 1 straight through.
- Ask students to compare their answers in pairs. Go round and notice how well they did in order to decide how quickly to go through answers, and whether you will need to play Part 1 again.
- Check the answers as a class by nominating students to answer.

Answers

a 3 **b** 2 **c** not mentioned **d** 1 **e** 4

TED Talk Part 1 script ▶ **4.1**

About a year ago, I asked myself a question: 'Knowing what I know, why am I not a vegetarian?' After all, I'm one of the green guys: I grew up with hippie parents in a log cabin. I started a site called TreeHugger – I care about this stuff. I knew that eating a mere hamburger a day can increase my risk of dying by a third. Cruelty: I knew that the 10 billion animals we raise each year for meat are raised in factory farm conditions that we, hypocritically, wouldn't even consider for our own cats, dogs and other pets. Environmentally, meat, amazingly, causes more emissions than all of transportation combined: cars, trains, planes, buses, boats, all of it. And beef production uses 100 times the water that most vegetables do.

I also knew that I'm not alone. We as a society are eating twice as much meat as we did in the 50s. So, what was once the special little side treat now is the main, much more regular. So really, any of these angles should have been enough to convince me to go vegetarian. Yet, there I was – chk, chk, chk – tucking into a big old steak.

- Explain the task. Students should complete the information with between one and three words. Give them a minute to read the sentences and predict possible answers or types of answers.
- ▶ **4.1** Play Part 1 again. Ask students to compare their answers in pairs. Go round and notice how well they did in order to decide how quickly to go through answers, and whether you will need to play Part 1 again.
- Check the answers as a class by nominating students to answer.
- Students may have found item 3 difficult to hear because Graham pronounces the missing word, 'transportation', very quickly, so that the second syllable is almost missing: 'trans…tation' /træns…teɪʃ(ə)n/. If many students got this wrong, play the DVD at this point, and show how the context can help them 'hear' the word; he says … *all of transportation combined – cars, trains, planes, buses, boats…*

- Ask which of the facts they find most surprising.

Answers
1 hamburger   **2** 10 billion   **3** transportation
4 water   **5** twice as much

- Look at the instructions. Give students time to read the options.
- ▶ **4.2** Play Part 2. Ask students to compare their answers in pairs. Go round and notice how well they did in order to decide how quickly to go through answers, and whether you will need to play Part 2 again.
- Check the answers as a class by nominating students to answer. Remember to ask why it isn't the other two options as well.

Answers
1 a (not b or c – his idea is to cut down on meat, not give up entirely, so they don't need to imagine their last burger)
2 c (not a or b – he says *On the weekend, your choice*, i.e. they can eat anything at the weekend)
3 c (he says *Best of all, I'm healthier*)

TED Talk Part 2 script ▶ 4.2

So why was I stalling? I realized that what I was being pitched was a binary solution. It was either you're a meat eater or you're a vegetarian, and I guess I just wasn't quite ready. Imagine your last hamburger. So, my common sense, my good intentions, were in conflict with my taste buds. And I'd commit to doing it later, and not surprisingly, later never came. Sound familiar?

So I wondered, might there be a third solution? And I thought about it, and I came up with one, and I've been doing it for the last year, and it's great. It's called weekday veg. The name says

it all: nothing with a face Monday through Friday. On the weekend, your choice. Simple. If you want to take it to the next level, remember, the major culprits in terms of environmental damage and health are red and processed meats. So, you want to swap those out with some good, sustainably harvested fish. It's structured, so it ends up being simple to remember, and it's okay to break it here and there. After all, cutting five days a week is cutting 70 percent of your meat intake.

The program has been great, Weekday Veg. My footprint's smaller, I'm lessening pollution, I feel better about the animals, I'm even saving money. Best of all, I'm healthier, I know that I'm going to live longer, and I've even lost a little weight.

So, please ask yourselves, for your health, for your pocketbook, for the environment, for the animals: What's stopping you from giving Weekday Veg a shot? After all, if all of us ate half as much meat, it would be like half of us were vegetarians.

Thank you.

- Put students in pairs and ask them to discuss the question. Write the following words and questions on the board to help students think of areas to discuss:

*Where?   Who with?   Who cooks?   What?
   How much?   How often?*

*calories   fast food   food from other countries   fruit
   meat and fish   sugar   variety   vegetables*

- Guide a whole-class discussion by inviting students to contribute with ideas. Find out whether everyone agrees with the ideas, and make sure they justify their answers, e.g. *What makes you say that? Is that true for most people in the country?*

8 VOCABULARY IN CONTEXT

- **8a** ▶ **4.3** Tell students that they are going to watch some clips from the talk which contain new or interesting words or phrases. They should choose the correct meaning for each one. Play the Vocabulary in context section.
- Pause after each question on the screen so students can choose the correct definition, then play the answer. If you like, you can ask students to shout out the answers. If helpful, either you or the students could give an additional example before moving on to the next question.
- Where a lot of students have given the wrong answer, explain again and give an additional example before moving on to the next extract.

Answers
1 risk = c (possibility of something bad happening)
2 raise = b (keep)
3 combined = a (together)
4 in conflict with = a (finding it difficult to exist with)
5 came up with = c (thought of)
6 damage = c (harm or injury)

- **8b** Check students understand the words and phrases in italics and re-teach if necessary, or ask the students if they can recall the example in the talk. Point out that they relate to some of the new words and phrases they have just learnt in Exercise 8a. Give them two minutes and make sure they note down their ideas.
- Put students in pairs to tell their ideas. Go round and check they are doing the task correctly and notice errors, difficulties, or where they use L1. Help them by correcting or giving them the English they need. Focus especially on their use of the new words and phrases.
- At the end of the task, give some feedback about new language that came up, and errors to correct which you may have written on the board. Nominate one or two students to tell the class the most interesting things they said or heard.

Suggested answers

1 Physical sports such as team sports, boxing and climbing; horse riding, cycling, skiing and other fast sports, and adventure activities like scuba diving. Indoor hobbies may carry different kinds of risk: video gaming may be bad for your eyesight; staying indoors suggests a lack of exercise, with all the health risks associated with that.
2 Your age + your father's age + your mother's age + your brothers' and sisters' ages, etc.
3 Distractions, such as talking to friends when you should be studying.
4 Students' own answers
5 This may include breaking things by accident, or getting angry with a family member and breaking their possessions deliberately.

CRITICAL THINKING Persuading *p53*

- Ask students to read the Critical thinking box. Explain the task. Tell them that one extract may illustrate more than one technique. Do the first item with the whole class.
- Tell students to do the rest of the activity on their own. Go around the class checking that students are doing the task correctly. When most students have finished, get them to compare answers in pairs and to help each other with anything they haven't finished.
- Check answers with the class.

Answers

1 e **2** a **3** f **4** a **5** b **6** b, c **7** b, c **8** d

---

10

- Still in their pairs, students discuss the questions about persuading your audience. Go around the class listening for errors as well as well-expressed ideas and good use of English.
- Give feedback on the students' use of English, but do not ask students to share their opinions at this stage. Instead, move straight on to the Challenge task.

CHALLENGE

- Explain that students are going to conduct a survey amongst members of the class. In preparation, tell them to write five questions about the topic which they will put to as many of their classmates as possible in a few minutes.
- To help them think of ideas, suggest that they look back over the lesson. Remind them that good questions are ones that they are interested in finding out about, and should be about people's opinions. For example, asking them to define *weekday vegetarianism* is not a good question (as everyone now knows this) but asking them how likely it is that they will one day become a vegetarian or weekday vegetarian, and why, is. Other possible questions include:

  Meat eaters, if you had to give meat up, how much would you miss it? What would you miss most?
  If you are a vegetarian, do you miss any meats? Which?
  Are there any animals eaten around the world that you wouldn't eat even if you are a meat eater?
  If five days a week is difficult to imagine, would you consider being a vegetarian for 1, 2, 3 or 4 days a week?

- When most students have written five questions, ask the class to stand up. Explain that they should speak to as many classmates as possible in the next five to ten minutes (depending on how much time of the lesson is left). Encourage them to mingle with students they don't often speak to. Participate in the mingle yourself. This is a good way to check that the activity is running smoothly, that students are using English, and to make a note of common or important errors.
- Stop the task. Nominate students to share with the class the most interesting information they have collected as well as to get a general impression of whether weekday vegetarianism is popular.

Homework

- Set Workbook Lesson 4D exercises on page 46 for homework.
- Students research other types of diet, such as weight-loss diets and belief-based diets, and why people follow these diets.
- Students choose and watch another TED Talk about food and diet from the TED playlist, 'What's wrong with what we eat?'

4E Future plans

pp54–55

LEAD IN

- Tell the class about a change that you've been trying to make in your life. This could be any kind of change that you are happy to share with your students, such as: lifestyle changes, e.g. cooking more, getting more sleep; developing skills, e.g. learning a language, car repair; developing professionally, etc. Don't script what you say, but try to use one or two of the Useful language expressions from the box. Talk about your successes as well as any difficulties that you have faced, and mention your future hopes and ambitions, of course.

- Ask students what advice they have for you. Conclude by telling the class that they are going to talk about changes that they would like to make in their lives.

SPEAKING *p54*

- Explain the task. Let students read the question and then ask them to predict five words that they might hear in each one. Elicit one or two examples for each person, then put students in pairs and give them two minutes to think of more. Possible words for each could be: (money) – *save, spend, afford, bank*, etc; (their home life) *brother, sister, space, noise, argument*, etc.; (their diet) *food, weight, fat, healthy*, etc.

> **Exam tip**
>
> **Predicting words they might hear**
> If students try to predict words they might hear before they listen, they start to actively think about the topic, which helps prepare them for listening. However, many comprehension tasks above pre-intermediate level work by using synonyms of words that are in the question. When students hear a word that is in the question, this is usually a way to distract them. It probably won't be the answer and they can ignore it. For example, João mentions *home* even though his home life isn't the thing he is unhappy about.

- 🎧 **29** Play the audio once straight through.
- Tell students to compare their ideas in pairs. Go round and notice how well they did in order to decide how quickly to go through answers and whether you will need to play the audio again.
- Check the answers as a class by asking for a show of hands (e.g. *Number 1 who thinks it's João? And hands up for Emily*, etc.) or nominating students (get two students to give their answer, especially where you noted differences).
- Where students agree, write the answer on the board. Where there is a dispute, ask students to justify their different answers, but don't say who is correct – put a

question mark on the board. Tell students they will listen again and check. Go through all the answers like this and then play the audio again if necessary, telling students to focus on the areas of uncertainty. Tell them to listen for the words they predicted correctly.

- If students are still uncertain of the answer, play the audio again and stop at key points. Play these sections two or three times if students are still struggling. Draw attention to the problem sounds or words and explain them when you give the answers. Ask whether anyone correctly predicted individual words.

Answers

a Emily   **b** Kei   **c** João

Audioscript 🎧 29

1

João: We've always eaten meat at home, and if I'm honest, I quite like it. But I'd really like to become vegetarian. I guess the main reason is because I know how bad eating meat is for the environment – a lot of the rainforests have been cut down to make space for farming animals. But I know it would be healthier for me, too. A meat-free diet would help me lose weight I think. But I don't want to make cooking more difficult for my mother, so I'm hoping to cut down as much as possible without stopping the rest of the family from eating what they want.

2

Emily: I've spent a lot of money recently – friends' and family birthdays, that kind of thing. And with the holidays coming up, I've got to find some money because I expect I'll spend a lot over the summer. So I'm aiming to get a job between now and then. I'm thinking of asking at the local gym. They often need trainers, and I'm quite sporty.

3

Kei: So, I'm finding it quite hard at home at the moment. I love my sisters but it's very hard to concentrate because they're so noisy and we don't have much space. I don't need much to study – just a quiet room, a desk and wi-fi. There isn't a library near here, so I'm stuck with it for now. But I think I might ask one of my friends. If they've got space at their house, maybe I can study there while we're doing exams. In the long term, I'm aiming to have moved out by the beginning of my final year of university.

- Look at the instructions. Tell students to read the expressions in the Useful language box. Before playing the audio again, let them try to answer from memory.
- 🎧 **29** Play the audio again. Tell students to compare their answers in pairs.
- Nominate students to suggest expressions that they heard. Check that the rest of the class agree. You might copy the Useful language box on the board in order to mark the expressions that are heard on the audio.

- Explain the task. Give students a minute to think of their hopes and goals. Put students in pairs to discuss.
- Go round and listen out for some expressions and copy them on the board. Also check that students are using the expressions correctly, such as following *I'm interested in* and *I'm thinking of* with the gerund, and *I'm aiming to have* with the past participle.
- Give the class feedback on some well-expressed hopes and goals you heard as well as any errors. Drill the correct expressions.

- Explain to students that they are going to learn a basic coaching technique for making a change in your life. Ask them to read the four-step process and check understanding of *commit to something* (agree to do something and promise yourself that you will do it). Point out the coach's role in the process involves asking their client questions.
- Tell students to choose one of the goals from Exercise 3 that they would like to work on to achieve. Encourage the class to see this as an opportunity to make real change in their lives, and not just to learn some English.

5

- Put students in different pairs from Exercise 3. Explain that they are going to act as each other's life coach. Ideally, they should work on the goals identified in Exercise 4, but if they prefer to avoid talking about real personal goals, they can roleplay a conversation with a life coach using one of the goals in the bulleted list.
- Remind them of the four-step process in Exercise 4 to follow and the expressions in the Useful language box. Tell them to start. You might play some background music to help students feel less exposed when talking about their goals and hopes.
- Go round and check that students are doing the task correctly but don't intervene in the conversations unless they are off task. Listen for interesting language used by coaches and clients, and make a note of common or important errors.
- After five minutes, tell the class to change roles so that the coaches are now clients and *vice versa*.
- Finish the task. Invite volunteers to tell the class what they have committed to and what time scale they are hoping to achieve their goals within. Make a note of what they say and ask them if you can ask them in a future lesson to tell the class how successful they have been in achieving their goal.

WRITING A social media update *p55*

- Look at the instructions. Make sure students specify the activities they would expect to do on these trips. For example, on a cooking holiday they might go shopping for ingredients and taste each other's meals as well as just cook.
- Stop the task when most pairs have finished. Nominate students to suggest some activities, and to say which trip they would prefer to go on and why.

Suggested answers

A cooking holiday – go shopping for ingredients, learn new cooking techniques, cook interesting food, taste each other's meals, take part in cooking competitions, create your own notebook of recipes.

A cycling holiday – plan routes, repair and maintain their bikes, visit beautiful places, get fit, stay in campsites or hostels.

A photography expedition – learn about photography, take lots of photos, create a portfolio of your best photos, visit interesting and beautiful places to photograph.

A study visit – visit interesting places, listen to a guided tour, attend classes, take photos, keep a learning journal.

A volunteering trip – work hard as part of a team to achieve something, e.g. build a building, write a blog or keep a social media page about the experience.

- Explain that Lali is on a special interest trip such as the ones the students have discussed in Exercise 6 and is recording the experience on her social media page. You might ask students what social media platforms they use and whether they update them regularly.
- Tell students to go to page 150 to quickly read Lali's social media update. Ask them to identify what kind of trip she is on. Set a time limit of two minutes. Nominate a student to identify the type of trip she is on (it's a study trip of some kind that involves learning about the local culture, including its food and cooking, but not only that).
- Ask students to read it again, this time to decide which of the things (1–8) Lali has already done, is hoping to do, and is definitely going to do. Set a time limit of four minutes for this.
- Ask students to shout out their answers.

Answers

She has already done 1, 2, 3 and 4. She's hoping to do 6 and 7. She's going to do 5 and 8.

8 WRITING SKILL Interesting language

- **8a** Explain the task. Do the first item with the whole class to make the task clear. Remind students that they don't have to read the whole text carefully for this, but can scan it to find the words.
- Prepare the board for feedback by copying the words in bold in Exercise 7 and leaving a space for the synonymous words and phrases.
- When students have finished, invite them to come to the board to write what they found. When all the words are on the board, ask why these words are used.

> **Answers**
>
> got to – reached
>
> quickly visited – rushed around
>
> walked around – wandered through
>
> travelled slowly – crawled (along)
>
> nice – tasty
>
> walking – trekking
>
> talk to – interview
>
> seeing – catching

She uses these words because they're more colourful and add interest – words like 'get' and 'nice' are very general and don't say much.

- **8b** Explain the task. You might want to put students in pairs and tell one student to have the unit page open and the other student have the writing bank page open to avoid a lot of flipping backwards and forwards.
- Go round and check that students are doing the task correctly.
- Nominate students to tell you the answer for each question. Check that the class agrees.

> **Answers**
> **1** huge   **2** boiling   **3** fresher   **4** exhausting
> **5** super

 9

- Look at the instructions. Make sure students understand that they can choose to write an account of a real trip that they have been on or one that they would like to go on, but they must imagine that they are in the middle of the trip and writing from that point of view.
- Go round and make sure everyone has chosen a trip to write about.

 10

- Explain the task. Tell students to refer to the model text on page 150 for help. Remind them of the structure of the model by reading out the advice at the back of the book and reminding them of the language they have studied.
- If you are going to give students a mark, tell them it will be higher if they organize the social media update in a similar way and use language they have learnt. Put students in pairs and tell them to talk about or plan their update.
- Set the writing for homework or set a time limit of about fifteen minutes to do it in class. As students are writing, go round and offer help. Make sure that they answer questions 1–3 clearly in their writing. Make suggestions about more interesting words and phrases to avoid general words such as *nice, good* and *go*. You might note some common errors.

Fast finishers

Students who finish quickly can add a comment to their social update, as if it was the next day or a few days later, with some new information about an aspect of their trip. For example, if they said they were looking forward to cooking in a professional restaurant, they could say that they did, and it was a very stressful but rewarding experience.

 11

- When students have finished writing, tell them to read each other's updates. When they have all read at least three or four posts, ask individual students to tell the class whose sounded most interesting, and whose food sounded the tastiest.

> **Homework**
> - Set Workbook Lesson 4E exercises on pages 47–49 for homework.
> - Students write another update of their choice.
> - Students research the food of northern India, Delhi or a region of the world of their choice, and learn about a recipe to share with the class. They could even make it and bring it to class for students to try!
> - Students prepare three questions to test their classmates at the start of the next lesson about the things they have studied in Unit 4.

5 Work

5A New ways of working
pp56–59

Information about the photo

Urban development is the practice of improving the lives of people who live in cities through the design of public living spaces: streets, shopping centres, squares and buildings. Munich is more than 800 years old and is proud of its ancient architecture, but like all cities it is constantly needing to adapt. Colourful and eye-catching design is one of the most immediate ways that town planners can make city living a happier experience.

LEAD IN

- Focus students' attention on the photo or project it using the CPT.
- Ask the class the following questions:
  What's his job? (painter or designer)
  What skills or qualifications does he have? (possibly art or design qualifications, experience doing specialist painting, IT skills using design tools)
  How do you think he got the job? (possibly applied after getting his qualifications, or started without formal qualifications and learnt 'on the job')
  What do you imagine he enjoys about his work? (the creative side of his job is satisfying; he works outside, and in lots of different places)
  Would you enjoy a job like this? Why? Why not? (students' own answers)

VOCABULARY Describing work *p57*

- Explain to the class that there is a lot of discussion these days about '21st Century Skills', and many people talk about the fact that working in the 21st century involves more than just academic qualifications and knowledge of the basic skills needed to do a job. Give an example of 'information literacy' skills, e.g. accessing information efficiently (using search engines for example) as well as communication skills, e.g. the ability to work effectively and respectfully in a team.

- Write on the board other categories of 21st century skills: *financial literacy, global and environmental awareness, communication skills, critical thinking, creativity, information* and *technological literacy.*

- Put students in pairs. Tell them to think of possible 21st century skills under one or more of the categories. After a couple of minutes, nominate students to share their ideas. With each, ask how much they think these are new skills, or have been necessary for a long time.

Extension

Tell students to search online for '21st Century Skills' to investigate further the categories on the board. They could work in teams to find out about each category, then report back to the class.

 2

- Look at the instructions. Do the first item as an example with the whole class. Students can use a dictionary or ask you for help as necessary.
- Go round checking understanding and offering help where needed. Encourage a range of jobs for each description; the more jobs they can compare, the clearer the meanings of the words and phrases in bold will be.
- When most students have finished, nominate students to share their ideas with the class. Check they have understood the meaning of the new vocabulary by asking them to justify their answers, e.g. *Why do you think professional photography is a competitive job market?*

Suggested answers

1 competitive jobs – creative and rewarding jobs, e.g. photographer, designer, engineer, scientist, doctor; well-paid jobs, e.g. accountant, financial trader; high status jobs, e.g. athlete, musician, model.
2 web designer, computer programmer (must keep up with latest skills and technological advances); child minder, nurse (need to be available at all times of day, work extra hours); teacher (need to respond to each student's needs in different ways)
3 accountant, financial trader, footballer, lawyer, doctor (in some countries), dentist
4 builder, architect, safety officer, lorry driver
5 Students' own answers (will depend on the country). In the UK, doctors are well-known for working long hours.
6 Students' own answers. Jobs may be stressful for many reasons.*
7 doctor, lawyer, business manager, software developer, investment banker, soldier or officer in the military
8 military officer, pilot or ship's captain, head teacher, business manager, factory manager
9 soldier, athlete, builder, farmer, physical education teacher, cleaner, nursery teacher, fire fighter
10 jobs in the arts (writer, artist, designer, etc); jobs in science and technology (biologist, engineer, software developer); many jobs require creativity of different types.

* *Stressful* and *demanding* are similar in meaning, but *stressful* has a negative connotation. If a job is *demanding*, it needs a lot of time, ability and energy but this may be what the employee wants.

 3

- Tell students that they are going to read a paragraph about the reasons people leave jobs. Elicit some reasons before they read. Explain the task. Set a limit of three minutes.
- When most students have finished, invite volunteers to read a sentence each.

Answers

1 well-paid 2 work long hours 3 demanding
4 in charge of 5 career prospects 6 industry
7 stressful 8 flexible

 4

- You may need to demonstrate the activity on the board if it is an unfamiliar exercise. Write the first line on the board and elicit the second (h *the sports industry* …). Show how the words in bold help them and show how this is mirrored in Exercise 2, e.g. item 4 – the collocation **in the** construction **industry**.
- When most students have finished, get them to compare answers in pairs and to help each other with anything they haven't finished. Tell them to read the lines through once to check that it sounds right.
- Check answers round the class. As an alternative way of sharing answers as a whole class, have students read a line and pass it on to the student sitting to their right.
- The only new collocation is 'out of work', which means to be not working. Point out the expression and ask students: *Are there many people out of work at the moment? Why? Why not? What reasons might you be out of work? What can you do if you are out of work?*, etc.

Answers

1 a 2 h 3 d 4 b 5 f 6 c 7 g 8 e 9 i

5

- Explain the task. Tell students to think of concrete examples for the terms.
- In feedback, ask follow-up questions to check a good understanding, e.g. *Do you know anyone who works part-time? Do you work in or on an industry? Do you work in or on a project? What would you say are long hours? Do students work long hours?*

Answers

1 If you have a *part-time* job, you might only work a few hours a day or a few days a week. A *temporary* job means you don't keep the job for very long, just a few weeks or months.
2 You work *in* an industry, e.g. *I work in software design. He works in sales.* You work *on* a specific project within your job, e.g. *I'm an engineer. At the moment I'm working on a new bridge for a railway company.*
3 A *full-time job* is normally about eight hours a day, five days a week, so about 40 hours a week. But if you *work long hours*, you do more than this, e.g. ten hours a day.

---

6   **MY PERSPECTIVE**

- Tell students that they are going to write a personal statement about the possible career path they are thinking of taking at the moment. You could model the writing activity by writing one for yourself, either a silly one (*I'd really like to work in the interplanetary space exploration industry, either as a full-time astronaut or something creative like spaceship designer …*) or a realistic one about you when you were their age. Remind them that this is an opportunity to start using the new words and expressions. Give them five minutes to write on their own.

- Put students into pairs to compare their plans and answer the question.

- When most students have finished, use this opportunity to get to know your students better. Spend time listening to as many of the students as you can to get an idea of their plans, their hopes and fears about work, and their attitudes to work. For example, you might want to know to what extent a good salary is a priority, or whether students value other qualities in their careers. You might also ask them how useful a good level of English will be in their chosen field.

LISTENING   *p58*

 7

- Focus students' attention on the photo or project it using the CPT. Ask *What kind of place is this?* (an office) *Is it a traditional office?* (no) *Why not?* (offices don't normally have swings or green spaces, and workers sit at their own desks) *Why do you think this company designed its office in this way?* (perhaps to make the work place an attractive place to be, to encourage workers to relax and collaborate more, to attract a younger workforce, etc.) *What sort of company*

would design an office like this? (tech companies, e.g. online businesses, marketing or advertising companies) *Would you like to work in a place like this? Why? Why not?*

- Explain the task. Check understanding of *productive*, i.e. working hard for the company. Set a time limit of three minutes to discuss the ideas.

- Encourage discussion of why these may be good/bad ideas. Play devil's advocate:
  - if students say idea a is good, ask: *If the employees own part of the company, won't they be angry if they disagree with decisions that the management makes?*
  - if students say idea b is good, ask: *How does the company benefit from this? If they lose five percent (one day in about 20/month) of working time from each employee, won't they lose money?*
  - if students say idea c is good, ask: *What if employees only work from 11 to 4?*
  - if students say idea d is good, ask: *What will that do to the feeling of working in a team if people don't see each other very often?*
  - if students say idea e is good, ask: *What if everyone wants to take holiday at the same time, such as during the school holidays when their families are also on holiday?*

- Aim to conclude with the notion of trust; that the employer–worker relationship can be a healthy one if trust is involved.

- Ask if anyone can think of other interesting ways of motivating workers to be more productive, e.g. giving them bonuses if the company does well; taking turns at management roles; letting them make decisions about the company, such as choosing how the office is organised or what the 'dress code' (what people can wear) is.

 8

- Look at the instructions. Explain that students need to find out which ideas listed in Exercise 7 are used by each employer so tell them to look at a–e as they listen.

- 🎧 **30**   Play the audio once straight through. Give students a minute to compare their answers in pairs. Go around and identify information that students found hard to hear or do not agree on.

- Nominate students to share their answers, and check whether the rest of the class agrees. Don't confirm the correct answers at this point.

- Play the audio again for students to check. You might decide to pause the audio after each answer is given and get students to confirm it.

> **Answers**
>
> Hamdi Ulukaya gave his employees shares in the company (a).
>
> Jenny Biggam lets people decide when to take holidays and where they want to work (e and d).

Extension

Search online for the news story about Ulukaya giving away shares in Chobani Yoghurt in April 2016. Use the search term 'chobani yogurt giving away shares'. Show students a news story video. You might discuss the way that the news story gives Chobani Yoghurt a more positive brand image.

Audioscript 30

(Words in bold refer to Exercise 9)

C = Carlos, S = Shruthi

C: *Welcome back. Today we're looking at what makes a good manager. Shruthi's here with me, and as always, we've got two stories for you. Shruthi?*

S: *Hi, Carlos. OK, so these stories illustrate how two managers remember to show their employees how much they appreciate them.*

C: *So, who have you found?*

S: *This is the story of Hamdi Ulukaya. Ulukaya owns Chobani Yogurt. He started the business a few years ago, and it has **gone on** to become a multi-billion-dollar company. Recently, Ulukaya shared ten percent of the company among all 2,000 workers. Basically that means giving away millions of dollars to the factory workers.*

C: *So, does he just **mean** to be nice, or is this actually good management?*

S: *It's both. Ulukaya came to the United States from Turkey, and he felt very welcomed by people. He **remembers** feeling grateful to his workers for helping him start the business. So, it's a thank-you present. But it's also a way of encouraging them to work harder. If you own part of a company, you'll try to make that company worth even more, won't you?*

C: *True. But it could be a very expensive mistake if it doesn't work. Do you think he might **regret** giving so much of the company away?*

S: *I think he knows what he's doing. It shows he trusts them.*

C: *OK, my story is about everyday working conditions. Jenny Biggam runs a media agency. She decided to **stop** treating her workers like children.*

S: *What do you mean?*

C: *Well, her workers can choose when they go on holiday and for how long, for example, and if they think they'll get more work done at home, they can choose to work there.*

S: *Really? Sounds fantastic! Do they get any work done?*

C: *Ha! Yes, of course! The employees feel appreciated, so they enjoy work and are committed to it.*

S: *I think both of these employers are **trying** to make coming to work a happier experience, because this means creating a more productive company.*

C: *I hope other bosses copy their ideas. What about you? What kind of boss would you like? Don't **forget** to phone in and tell us!*

9

- Tell students to read the sentences to check they understand them. Before playing the audio again, let students try to complete the extracts from memory or go straight into the task.
- 30 Play the audio. Tell students to compare their answers in pairs. Go round and notice how well they did in order to decide how quickly to go through answers and whether you will need to play the audio again. Play the audio again if it's clear that they found it difficult.
- Nominate students to answer and write answers on the board along with the following verbs, e.g. *gone on to become*.

Answers

1 gone on (to become)   **2** mean (to be)
3 remembers (feeling)   **4** regret (giving)   **5** stop (treating)   **6** trying (to make)   **7** forget (to phone in)

GRAMMAR Verb patterns: verb + *-ing* or infinitive with *to* pp58–59

To prepare for teaching the following exercises, see Grammar reference on page 136.

10

- Look at the instructions. Do the activity with the whole class. Use the board to highlight the verbs patterns, e.g. *gone on* <u>to become</u>.

Answers

go on + infinitive
mean + infinitive
remembers + verb *-ing*
regret + verb *-ing*
stop + verb *-ing*
try + infinitive
forget + infinitive

11

- Explain the task. Ask students what they notice and elicit that the same verbs are followed by different patterns, e.g. if *go on* was followed by the infinitive, it is now followed by the *-ing* form of the verb.
- Put students in pairs to discuss the changes in meaning depending on the verb pattern that follows each one. Use the example to help students.
- You can either go through the answers with the whole class, or wait for them to read the Grammar reference on page 136 and then ask the class the grammar-checking questions, or nominate individual students to give their answers.

Notes

- *regret* + infinitive is a very formal construction that is usually only used in formal announcements, such as informing a candidate for a job that they didn't get the job, or letting someone know that someone has died. It is usually followed by verbs like *inform*, *tell* and *say*.
- *forget* + -*ing* is usually used in negative sentences, e.g. *I'll never forget flying for the first time.*
- To make the negative, you can often use *not*: *I regret **not** telling him the truth when I had the chance. Remember **not** to show anyone your cards.*

Grammar reference and practice

Ask students to do Exercise 1 on page 137 now, or set it for homework.

12

- Look at the instructions and do the first item with the whole class.
- Tell students to do the rest of the activity on their own. Go round the class checking the accuracy of their answers and providing help where necessary.
- Let students compare answers in pairs before getting them to call out the answers chorally.

13

- Explain the task. First tell students to complete the topics. Check answers as a class.
- Do the first item as an example and talk about something from your own life.
- As they are making notes on their own, go round and check that students are writing notes. When most students have notes about three or four topics, put them in pairs to tell each other about their chosen topics. As they are discussing, go round and note any common or repeated errors to feedback on afterwards.
- At the end of the task, give some feedback about new language that came up, and errors to correct which you may have written on the board. Nominate one or two students to tell the class the most interesting things they said or heard.

14 MY PERSPECTIVE

- Tell students to stay in their pairs to discuss the questions. Write the following sentence stems on the board to encourage them to talk about the questions in concrete terms:

  I hope that where I work …
  I'd like to be able to … when I'm working, because …
  If I could work for anyone, it would be … because I think …

- Find out about your students' hopes and fears regarding their future work places.

5B An unusual job *pp60–61*

VOCABULARY BUILDING Ways of seeing *p60*

- Explain to students that learners of English at their current level of English have enough vocabulary to express most of what they want to say; there is a lot they can already do in English. However, sometimes it won't be possible to express it in the way they would like to – elegantly and accurately. Offer an example, e.g. *He ran quickly past the teacher's door, hoping not be seen.*
- Ask if anyone can think of a verb that means *ran quickly*. If no one can think of a suitable word, suggest *fly, sped, shot* or *sprinted*.
- Conclude by saying that one way they can express themselves better is to learn words with a related meaning, and that today they are going to study verbs which are related to the meaning of *see*, so that by the end of the lesson they will have seven ways of describing different ways of seeing. Before they start, ask them if they know any different ways of describing seeing.
- Explain the task. Many but not all of the verbs can be replaced by *see* and the sentence will still make sense.
- Go round and check students are doing the task correctly. When most students have finished, get them to compare answers in pairs and to help each other with anything they haven't finished.
- In feedback, ask for the verb and its definition.

> **Answers**
> **1** f – spotted   **2** e – caught   **3** b – glanced
> **4** a – noticed   **5** c – identified   **6** g – observed
> **7** d – recognized

- Look at the instructions and do the first item with the whole class.
- Tell students to do the rest of the exercise on their own.
- In feedback, make sure students read out the whole sentence, not just the verb.

> **Answers**
> **1** recognize   **2** glance   **3** identify   **4** spot
> **5** catch   **6** observing   **7** noticed

Extension
Tell students to write sentences of their own using one of the new verbs. Then have them stand up and mingle around the room saying their sentences but gapping the verb, e.g. *Oh! It's you! I didn't BEEP you. Have you had a haircut?* The other student must supply the missing verb (recognize).

READING *pp60–61*

- **Books closed.** Point out that the title of today's lesson is 'An unusual job'. Ask the class what unusual jobs they have heard of. Elicit as many as they can think of. To get the ideas flowing, you could suggest one or two, e.g. chocolate taster, emoji translator, waterslide tester, crisp inspector, queuer.
- Put students in pairs to discuss the questions. Tell them that the questions are all related to the unusual job they are going to read about.
- Conduct brief whole-class feedback, in which you can determine who in the class are good at recognizing faces, remembering names, and recognizing voices.

- 🎧 **31** Explain the task. Tell students to read the article.
- While they are reading, be available for questions about unfamiliar vocabulary. When most students have finished, remind students to complete the sentences.
- Elicit some possible answers. Accept any that get the main idea right.

> **Suggested answers**
> **1** … recognizing faces
> **2** … in front of CCTV screens / in an office / with CCTV videos

- Explain the task. Tell students you will ask them why they chose true or false for each statement in order to make sure that they record where in the text they found the information. Warn them that not all of the answers come in the order in the article.
- Go round and check students are doing the task correctly and offering help if necessary.
- Check answers as a whole class. Ask for a show of hands for each statement, e.g. *So number one. Who thinks it's true? False?* If there are significant numbers of students who got it wrong, nominate one of them to tell you why they chose that option. Try to clarify any confusion they have with the text. Ask someone who got to right to say why they chose that option.

Answers

1 T (*The police can't identify criminals if they don't have a file on that person; image quality is often too poor for recognition* – lines 9–12)

2 F (*No matter how many cameras, …* – lines 7–9)

3 T (*even if they only see them for a moment* – line 16)

4 T (*At football matches, for example, …* – lines 17–19)

5 F (*the ability to recognize faces is different from other kinds of memory.* – lines 34–35)

6 F (*You might also be in the top one percent and not even know it.* – line 44)

- Put students in pairs and give them three minutes to discuss the questions.
- In feedback, find out who might be interested in doing this job and why.

Extension

If your students have online access in class, you could get them to try one of several tests to find out how good they are at recognizing faces. Before the lesson, search for 'super-recognizer test' and try out one or two in order to choose a suitable one for the lesson. Direct everyone to that website and get them to do the test. Be aware that one or two of the tests available take a long time to complete, but they may still enjoy trying them out. You may also do it as a whole class activity with a projector.

CRITICAL THINKING Exaggerating p60

- Teach the word *exaggerate*. Write on the board *This is the millionth time I've asked you to go to bed!* Find out if anyone's parents ever say things like this. Ask if anyone's parents have asked them to do something one million times! Explain that this is an example of *exaggeration*.
- Ask a student to read the Critical thinking box to the class. Then put students in groups to decide whether extracts 1–6 from the article are exaggerating or not. If they decide that an extract is an exaggeration, they should also discuss why the writer does this.
- Go round and listen to each group's discussion, offering prompts if necessary, e.g. *When it says 'You are being watched', do you think you are always being watched on camera when you are in a big city?*
- Conduct whole class feedback and try to reach consensus about each of the extracts.

Suggested answers

1 You are certainly not being watched all the time, and probably not at this precise moment! This dramatic and exaggerated start is used to get the reader's attention.

2 'Thousands'? This is probably true. In a large city, there will be thousands, or even tens of thousands of cameras (in London there may be as many as 500,000).

3 'Amazing'? Perhaps, but as the article says later on, unless we have prosopagnosia, everyone has this ability to some degree. Most of us do remember thousands (or at least many hundreds) of faces.

4 '190'? Not exaggerated. An article like this is unlikely to use precise numbers like this unless they are factually accurate.

5 Could he remember a very short shopping list? Probably, so it is probably exaggerated.

6 'Allowed to watch TV all day'? First, they're not watching TV if they are actively observing faces on CCTV cameras. Second, they probably do many other things in their day, like have meetings, write reports, attend training, etc.

- Put students in pairs to discuss the questions. You may decide to demonstrate the second question to help the class. For example, you could give an exaggerated description of a job you'd like to do, e.g. *I'd love to be a wildlife photographer. They get to travel to hundreds of different countries! I could get my work published in National Geographic magazine and make thousands of dollars! It's an extremely dangerous job if you're taking photos of large animals like lions and tigers.*
- Once students have had time to talk in pairs, invite a few students to the front of the class to read out their exaggerated job descriptions. Have a class vote on whose job sounds most interesting.

Homework

- Set Workbook Lesson 5B exercises on pages 54–55 for homework.
- Students take one of the online facial recognition tests to find out if they could be super-recognizers (see Exercise 6 **Extension**).
- Students research other unusual jobs (see notes in Exercise 3) or new jobs based on developing technologies, e.g. virtual reality engineer, 3D printing designer, armchair explorer. This provides students with suitable preparation for the next lesson, about 'job evolution'. Alternatively, they find out what most police officers' work involves by searching for 'police job description' or similar.

5C Job evolution *pp62–63*

GRAMMAR Present and past modal verbs *pp62–63*

To prepare for teaching the following exercises, see Grammar reference on page 136.

- **Books closed.** Remind the class of the last lesson's topic: super-recognizers. Explain that this is a job that did not exist a few years ago. Put students in pairs, and ask them to think of other new jobs. Tell them to make a list. Suggestions include: virtual assistant, online teacher, personal coach, web designer. If their homework after the last lesson was to research new jobs, get students to tell their partners about the jobs that they found. Invite students to either share their list with the class or present the jobs that they researched for homework.
- Now ask them to work in their pairs to think of jobs from the past which no longer exist, or which are disappearing because of new technologies. Suggestions include: video rental shop assistant, switchboard operator, lift operator in hotels, driver (may soon be replaced by driverless cars, buses and lorries).
- Nominate students to tell the class some of their best ideas about jobs that no longer exist.
- Write the title of today's lesson on the board: Job evolution. Ask the class what they think job evolution means.

> **Answer**
> Job evolution is the way that jobs appear and disappear as new technologies are developed and the world changes.

- Tell students to open their books on page 62 and explain the task. Tell them the sentences in the Grammar box all come from the article on page 61.
- If your students speak a Romance language such as Spanish, French or Italian, they will have little difficulty understanding the Latinate words *obligation*, *permission*, *deduction*, and so on. However, if these words are not cognates in the students' language, you will need to first of all make sure that they understand the metalanguage – the language to talk about language!
- Check answers as a class.

> **Answers**
> **1** a **2** g **3** c **4** e **5** b **6** f **7** d **8** h

- Look at the instructions. You can do this as a whole class, nominating students to categorize each sentence.

> **Answers**
> present – a, c, d, f, h   past – b, e, g

- Tell students to copy the table but to add an empty third column with the heading 'Past'. Draw a table on the board to guide them. Explain the task.
- Go round and check that students are completing their tables correctly. If they are not, refer them to their answers to Exercises 2 and 3. When most students have finished, get them to compare answers in pairs and to help each other with anything they haven't finished.
- Nominate students for the answers.

Answers

1 must   **2** is / are allowed to   **3** can't   **4** should
5 must

- Tell students to complete the third column labelled 'Past' with the four expressions.
- You can either go through the answers with the whole class, or wait for them to read the Grammar reference on page 136 and then nominate individual students to give their answers.

Answers

didn't have to = no obligation in the past
managed to = ability in the past
needed to = obligation in the past
weren't able to = no ability in the past

Grammar reference and practice

Tell students to do Exercises 2–5 on page 137 now, or set them for homework.

Answers to Grammar practice exercises

2
1 have to (not *must* in questions)
2 are allowed to (permission)
3 managed to (not *could* with specific possibility)
4 couldn't (past lack of ability)
5 should (*ought* followed by *to*)
6 don't often have to (no obligation)
7 didn't need to (not *needn't* in past)
8 aren't allowed (*can't* is not followed by *to*)
3
1 must   **2** can't   **3** must   **4** can't
4
1 had to wear a suit
2 must eat
3 couldn't take breaks
4 Do you have to wear a helmet
5 can't use the printer
6 didn't have to buy a new phone
7 could smoke
8 have to / must arrive
9 mustn't / can't drink coffee or tea

5
1 ~~didn't have~~ wasn't allowed
2 ~~must~~ have to
3 ~~mustn't~~ don't have to / don't need to / needn't
4 needn't ~~to~~ do
5 ~~mustn't~~ can't

- Look at the instructions and do the first item with the whole class. Tell students that these words are used once.
- Tell students to do the rest of the activity on their own. Go round and check that students are completing the text correctly. If you see errors being made, interrupt the student and ask why they have chosen that verb. Help them to understand where they are going wrong.
- When most students have finished, get them to compare answers in pairs and to help each other with anything they haven't finished.
- Go through the answers by asking different students to read out each complete sentence.

Answers

1 can   **2** couldn't   **3** had to   **4** don't have to
5 can't   **6** have to   **7** shouldn't   **8** needed

- Focus students' attention on the photos. Ask them what jobs they think are being done. This is an opportunity to use modals of deduction, and show how they can be used in the continuous form to describe photos; write on the board *He/They must be/may be/can't be …* and encourage students to use these stems to make their guesses, e.g. *He can't be cleaning the window because there isn't any water.*
- Put students in pairs. Listen to their ideas but don't confirm what the real jobs are. Instead, tell them to quickly read the text in Exercise 8.

8

- Once students have checked their guesses about the photos, look at the instructions and do the first item with the whole class.
- Tell students to do the rest of the activity on their own. Go round and check that students are doing the task correctly and notice words and phrases they look up, or ask you about, or underline. Focus on these in feedback.
- When most students have finished, get them to compare answers in pairs and to help each other with anything they haven't finished.
- Check answers round the class.

Answers

1 had to   **2** could   **3** couldn't   **4** had to
5 needed to   **6** could   **7** wasn't allowed to
8 didn't have to

- Explain the task. Make sure they understand that for this exercise, *can't, needn't*, etc. are one word.

- Go round and check students' answers, asking students to justify them.
- Check answers as a class by nominating students to read out a sentence at a time.

Answers

1 couldn't   **2** able   **3** can't   **4** needn't   **5** can / could
6 allowed   **7** should / might / may / could
8 need   **9** managed

Extension

Ask the class what other jobs they think will soon disappear because of technological development. Encourage discussion and debate about their ideas.

🔟 CHOOSE

The idea is for students to make their own choice of activity here. However, you might want to make the decision for the students, in which case explain why. Alternatively, you may decide to let students do more than one task. You could divide the class into groups and have each group do a different task – or you could have a vote on which task the whole class should do. For the vote:

- put students in pairs or groups to decide which they prefer.
- take a vote on each task.
- if the vote is tied, ask one student from each side to explain which is best and take the vote again. You can decide if there is still no change.
- Option 1 is a speaking task. Encourage competition and challenge by thinking of a job that students will probably find hard to guess (not *doctor* or *teacher*, for example, but something like goalkeeper, shopper, customs officer, security guard) and playing with the whole class. Correct any errors in question formation during this demonstration of the game. Then let the students play in groups.
- Options 2 and 3 are writing tasks, although option 2 is a competitive game to be played in pairs or small groups. With option 2, make sure students know they will need to read each other's sentences and can challenge them if they think the sentence is either not true, e.g. *Businessmen have to wear a uniform*, or incorrect grammar or spelling.
- Option 3 requires online access. You could set this for homework. Suggest the search terms *job extinction* and *jobs that have disappeared*.

Homework

- Set Workbook Lesson 5C exercises on pages 56–57 for homework.
- If students didn't write about a job that has disappeared in Exercise 10, set this task for homework.
- Students find out about school rules in the past and write about how the school experience has changed for students in the past hundred years or more.
- You might want to tell students to watch the track called *Unit 5 TED Talk* on the *Perspectives* website before they come to the next class.

5D   Why the best hire might not have the perfect résumé

pp64–65

- Tell students they are going to watch a TED Talk about choosing candidates for a job.
- Ask students for some different ways to choose the best person for a job. Elicit and write on the board: *CV/résumé, interview, qualifications, work experience, references/ recommendations*. Teach the correct pronunciation of *résumé* /ˈrezjuːmeɪ/, the word used in American English for *CV* (stress on second letter), the British English equivalent.
- Ask if they think the university you attend is important, which university in their country is best, and if they know the name of any good universities in the US, e.g. Harvard, Yale. Teach them that a group of some of the best universities in the US is called the 'Ivy League'.
- ▶ **5.0** Tell them they are going to see a short text on the DVD to introduce the talk and the speaker, and play the *About the speaker* section. Then do the vocabulary exercise.
- After they finish, write the key words from the *About the speaker* section on the board and ask students to retell it aloud, or ask them to write as much of what it said as they can. Correct as necessary.
- Alternatively write the key words from the *About the speaker* section on the board and read out the *About the speaker* section again, leaving a blank at each key word. Students call out the correct word from the board. Do it again, gradually erasing the words from the board until the students are reciting them from memory.

Answers to About the speaker

1 human resources = c (the part of a company that is responsible for the people in the company)
2 inconsistency = b (being unable to work in the same way all the time, and be reliable)
3 struggle = c (a great effort to do something or get somewhere)
4 obstacles = b (things which make it difficult to act or move forward)
5 entrepreneurs = a (people who start their own businesses)
6 overcome = a (successfully deal with or defeat)
7 'grit' = a (the ability to continue trying to succeed despite difficulty)

TED Talk About the speaker ▶ **5.0**

*Regina Hartley is a **human resources** director for UPS. In her job she sees people with very different experiences. She knows that a person's résumé tells a story. What story does a series of odd jobs tell?*

*It may indicate **inconsistency** and a lack of focus, or it may signal a committed **struggle** against **obstacles**. Many **entrepreneurs**, for example, have had to **overcome** adversity, and believe that facing these difficulties has helped them develop the necessary '**grit**'. But they don't always have the best qualifications.*

Regina's idea worth spreading is that our résumés tell employers about our experiences, determination, and ability to deal with life's challenges.

AUTHENTIC LISTENING SKILLS
Understanding contrasts *p64*

As well as teaching aspects of phonology and listening skills, these tasks also allow:

- you pre-teach some vocabulary.
- students to read and hear new language before they listen to the whole text.
- students to tune in to the speaker's voice and style.

- Ask students to read the Authentic listening skills box. Explain the task. Tell them to read the extracts. Explain 'odd jobs', perhaps by describing your own or another person's career path, one that has included lots of different, disparate jobs.
- 🎧 **32** Play the audio.
- Let students compare their answers in pairs before eliciting the answers for the whole class to hear.

> **Answers**
> **1** may, may   **2** But

- Ask the class which of the techniques for contrasting ideas mentioned in the Authentic listening skills box is used in each. (In the first extract, Regina repeats the structure with 'may'. In the second, she uses *But*, a contrasting word.)

- Look at the instructions and the sentences. Check understanding of *adversity* (a difficult time in your life when you have many problems to solve). You might write the other less familiar words on the board, i.e. *destined* and *failure*.
- 🎧 **33** Play the audio.
- Play it a second and third time as necessary to give students a chance to write down these longer extracts accurately.
- Let students check their answers in pairs. Then nominate students to share their answers with the class. Point out how Regina emphasizes *success … tough … failure … succeed* in 1, and in *in spite of … know … because …* in 2.
- Encourage the students to practise the contrastive intonation, stressing the key words. You might drill the sentences in manageable chunks, i.e. *They don't think they are who they are in **spite** of adversity … they **know** they are who they are **because** of adversity … etc.*

> **Answers**
> **1** … your whole life is destined for failure and you actually succeed?
> **2** … know they are who they are because of adversity.

WATCH   *p64*

If you are short of time, or want a different approach to the video, you may want to watch the whole talk all the way through with only some brief checking questions. A version of this is on the DVD and is labelled as *TED Talk with activities*. At the end of each section, there is a short gist question(s). Pause after each question on screen so students can give their answers, then play the answer.

> **Answers to gist questions on DVD**
>
> **Part 1**
> **1** The Silver Spoon
> **a** a person with advantages who is likely to find success in life
> **2** The Scrapper
> **b** a person who has had to fight to get where they are
>
> **Part 2**
> Which two statements are true, according to Regina?
> **c** Regina has personal experience of a Scrapper's life.
> **d** Steve Jobs' résumé doesn't look very impressive.
>
> **Part 3**
> Which two personal qualities are *not* mentioned as strengths in the workplace?
> **b** a serious attitude to work
> **c** an ability to work alone

- Explain the task.
- When most students have ranked the reasons, put them in pairs to compare their ideas.
- Check answers as a class. Find out how much students agreed with each other, and why. Then ask the class what they think the most and least important reasons are by a show of hands.

- ▶ **5.1** Play Part 1 straight through.
- Ask students to compare their ideas in pairs. Go round and notice how well they did in order to decide how quickly to go through answers, and whether you will need to play Part 1 again.
- Check answers as a class.

> **Answers**
> **1** A   **2** B   **3** A   **4** B   **5** B   **6** A   **7** both
> **8** B   **9** B   **10** A

TED Talk Part 1 script ▶ 5.1

Your company launches a search for an open position. The applications start rolling in, and the qualified candidates are identified. Now the choosing begins. Person A: Ivy League, 4.0, flawless résumé, great recommendations. All the right stuff. Person B: state school, fair amount of job hopping, and odd jobs like cashier and singing waitress. But remember – both are qualified. So, I ask you: who are you going to pick?

My colleagues and I created very official terms to describe two distinct categories of candidates. We call A 'the Silver Spoon', the one who clearly had advantages and was destined for success. And we call B 'the Scrapper', the one who had to fight against tremendous odds to get to the same point.

- Look at the instructions. Put students in pairs to discuss the question, and say why.
- Invite students to share their opinions. Make sure they justify their opinions. For example, if they prefer the 'Silver Spoon', they may say that employing someone who has had lots of different jobs is risky because they may not stay very long. If they prefer the 'Scrapper', it may be because they bring more varied work experience with them.

- Explain the task. Tell students to read the summary first and predict the correct answers.
- ▶ 5.2 Play Part 2 straight through.
- Ask students to compare their ideas in pairs. Go round and notice how well they did in order to decide how quickly to go through answers, and whether you will need to play Part 2 again.
- Check answers as a class.

> **Answers**
>
> **1** focused   **2** an interview   **3** didn't have   **4** didn't finish   **5** many

TED Talk Part 2 script ▶ 5.2

A résumé tells a story. And over the years, I've learnt something about people whose experiences read like a patchwork quilt, that makes me stop and fully consider them before tossing their résumés away. A series of odd jobs may indicate inconsistency, lack of focus, unpredictability. Or, it may signal a committed struggle against obstacles. At the very least, the Scrapper deserves an interview.

To be clear, I don't hold anything against the Silver Spoon; getting into and graduating from an elite university take a lot of hard work and sacrifice. But if your whole life has been engineered toward success, how will you handle the tough times? One person I hired felt that because he attended an elite university, there were certain assignments that were beneath him, like temporarily doing manual labour to better understand an operation. Eventually, he quit. But, on the flip side, what happens when your whole life is destined for failure and you actually succeed?

I want to urge you to interview the Scrapper. I know a lot about this because I am a Scrapper.

I'm the fourth of five children raised by a single mother in a rough neighbourhood in Brooklyn, New York. We never owned a home, a car, a washing machine, and for most of my childhood, we didn't even have a telephone. So, I was highly motivated to understand the relationship between business success and Scrappers, because my life could easily have turned out very differently. As I met successful business people and read profiles of high-powered leaders, I noticed some commonality.

Many of them had experienced early hardships, anywhere from poverty, abandonment, death of a parent while young, to learning disabilities, alcoholism and violence.

Take this résumé. This guy's parents give him up for adoption. He never finishes college. He job-hops quite a bit, goes on a sojourn to India for a year, and to top it off, he has dyslexia. Would you hire this guy? His name is Steve Jobs.

- Explain that *two* options in the multiple choice questions are *correct*, and that this time they have to choose the one which is *not* correct. Suggest they read the questions first to familiarize themselves with the task.
- ▶ 5.3 Play Part 3 straight through.
- Ask students to compare their ideas in pairs. Go round and notice how well they did in order to decide how quickly to go through answers, and whether you will need to play Part 3 again.
- Nominate students to answer.

> **Answers**
>
> **1 b** (*they now view their learning disability as a desirable difficulty which provided them an advantage*)
> **2 a** (*Scrappers are propelled by the belief that the only person you have full control over is yourself*)
> **3 a** (*I didn't have a car, so I carpooled across two bridges with a woman who was the president's assistant.*)

TED Talk Part 3 script ▶ 5.3

In a study of the world's most highly successful entrepreneurs, it turns out a disproportionate number have dyslexia. In the US, 35 percent of the entrepreneurs studied had dyslexia. What's remarkable – they now view their learning disability as a desirable difficulty which provided them an advantage because they became better listeners and paid greater attention to detail. They don't think they are who they are in spite of adversity, they know they are who they are because of adversity. They embrace their trauma and hardships as key elements of who they've become, and know that without those experiences, they might not have developed the muscle and grit required to become successful.

Scrappers are propelled by the belief that the only person you have full control over is yourself. When things don't turn out well, Scrappers ask, 'What can I do differently to create a better result?' Scrappers have a sense of purpose that prevent them from giving up on themselves, kind of like if you've survived poverty, a crazy father and several muggings, you figure, 'Business challenges? Really? Piece of cake. I got this.'

And that reminds me – humour. Scrappers know that humour gets you through the tough times, and laughter helps you change your perspective.

And finally, there are relationships. People who overcome adversity don't do it alone. Somewhere along the way, they find people who bring out the best in them and who are invested in their success. Having someone you can count on no matter what, is essential to overcoming adversity. I was lucky. In my first job after college, I didn't have a car, so I carpooled across two bridges with a woman who was the president's assistant. She watched me work and encouraged me to focus on my future and not dwell on my past. Along the way, I've met many people who've provided me brutally honest feedback, advice and mentorship. These people don't mind that I once worked as a singing waitress to help pay for college.

So back to my original question. Who are you going to bet on: Silver Spoon or Scrapper? I say choose the underestimated contender, whose secret weapons are passion and purpose.

Hire the Scrapper.

8 VOCABULARY IN CONTEXT

- **8a** ▶ **5.4** Tell students that they are going to watch some clips from the talk which contain new or interesting words or phrases. They should choose the correct meaning for each one. Play the Vocabulary in context section. Pause after each question on screen so students can choose the correct definition, then play the answer. If you like, you can ask students to call out the answers. If helpful, either you or your students could give an additional example before moving on to the next question.

Answers
1 terms = c (names)
2 tough = b (difficult)
3 assignments = b (pieces of work you have to do)
4 turn out = a (have a result)
5 Piece of cake = b (something that is easy to do)
6 count on = a (be confident you can trust them)

- **8b** Check students understand the words in italics and re-teach if necessary, or ask students if they can recall the example in the talk. Tell students to think of examples of the five things. Point out that they relate to some of the new words and phrases they have just learnt in Exercise 8a. Give them two minutes and make sure they note down their ideas.

- Put students in pairs to tell each other their ideas. Go round and check they are doing the task correctly and notice errors, difficulties, or where they use L1. Help them by correcting or giving them the English they need. Focus especially on their use of the new words and phrases.

- At the end of the task, give some feedback about new language that came up, and look at any errors to correct which you may have written on the board. Nominate one or two students to tell the class the most interesting things they said or heard.

CHALLENGE

Teaching tip

Introducing sensitive subjects
This is a potentially very personal and sensitive challenge that could be uncomfortable for students to talk about. Adversity comes in many forms, and could include such issues in the students' lives as academic failure, illness and accident, parents' divorce, death in the family, times of poverty, even the fear of death from war or accidents. You need to decide how far you are prepared to push the discussion.

One way that you can help students understand the kind of experience they can talk about, and at the same time lead by example, is to tell them about a true experience of adversity in your life and how it has helped you become who you are. Think carefully about what information about your life you are prepared to tell your students! But if you show a willingness to open up to them, they may feel freer to open up to each other.

- Ask students to read the Challenge box and answer the questions on their own. You might suggest that they write notes.

- When most students have all their answers, put them in groups to share their ideas. Go round and listen to their stories. Help them with any language difficulties where necessary.

- When most or all of the students have shared their stories in their groups, invite one or two students to share their experiences with the whole class. Respond reassuringly and with praise for volunteering.

Homework
- Set Workbook Lesson 5D exercises on page 58 for homework.
- Students choose and watch another TED Talk about employment from the TED playlist, 'Talks to help you find the right job'.

5E Going for the job *pp66–67*

SPEAKING *p66*

- Focus students' attention on the photo and teach *to pick fruit*. Ask whether the job appeals to anyone, and if so, why. Ask if it is normal in the students' country for young people like them to have part-time or holiday jobs, and whether anyone in the class has had a job like this.
- You might remind them of the phrase *temporary job* to describe work that is not permanent or regular, and *unskilled work* to describe work that doesn't need qualifications or much experience.

- Ask the class to look at the three job adverts. Ask them where they might see adverts like these (on online employment agency websites, in local newspapers, on noticeboards in public places, e.g. supermarkets, job centres). Put students in pairs. Tell them to discuss which they would prefer to do and why.
- Write on the board the heading *Casual employment* and the first item on the list: *fruit picker*, and ask the pairs to think of other jobs that might be suitable for students and young people to make some extra money in their spare time. Some suggestions might include: being a waiter in a café or restaurant, working at busy times in a shop, postal and courier work delivering letters, promotional material, newspapers, etc.
- Ask for a show of hands to find out which of the three jobs is most popular, and why, and invite students to suggest items for the list of casual jobs.

- Tell students that they are going to hear a job interview for one of the three jobs advertised. Tell them that they have two listening tasks: first, to identify the job Roberta is applying for, and second, to decide whether her chances of getting the job are good, and why.
- 🎧 **34** Play the audio.
- Let students compare answers.
- Check answers by nominating students to provide answers.

Answers

Roberta is applying for job 2: Part-time catering staff at AquaParks.

(Suggested answer) Roberta seems like a good candidate, and should get the job. She answers the interviewer's questions well, is polite and well-spoken, her English is good, and she seems interested in the job, and not only for the money.

Audioscript 🎧 **34**

I = interviewer, R = Roberta

I: Thank you very much for coming in, Roberta.

R: You're welcome.

I: Now, as I'm sure you're aware, the job involves people skills.

R: Yes, well, I'm a friendly person, and I'd say I was quite a good listener.

I: That's good. And what other skills do you have that you think would help you in this job?

R: Um, well, I speak English, Spanish and a little bit of German, and I know that you get tourists from many countries coming here.

I: That's true. Your English is quite good.

R: Thank you.

I: Now, although the hours are short, I have to tell you that the work is quite intensive.

R: Yes, I know. I have a friend who works in catering and she says it's physically, er, challenging. But I'm willing to work hard.

I: I'm glad to hear that.

R: And I'm usually quite good at dealing with problems and keeping people calm.

I: And what kind of problems do you expect to deal with?

R: Oh, when customers have to wait a long time to get served, that sort of thing.

I: Would you ever leave your customers waiting long?

R: No, of course not, but restaurants get very busy. I think it's important that we can ask for help. I like to think I'm not afraid to ask for help.

I: And what are your faults?

R: I know I can sometimes talk too much. But I'm working on it!

I: And finally, Roberta, can I ask you why you're interested in this job particularly?

R: Yes, of course. I think this job would give me valuable experience in customer service, and the chance to meet new people.

I: OK. Is there anything you want to ask me?

R: Um, yes, I was just wondering if I would have to buy my own uniform …

4

- Look at the instructions. Tell students to read the expressions in the Useful language box on page 67. Before playing the audio again, let them try to answer from memory.
- 🎧 **34** Play the audio again.
- Tell students to compare their answers in pairs.
- Nominate students to say which expressions they heard.
- Tell them that they are going to hear the interview one more time. This time they should try to write down what

Roberta says after each phrase. You might decide to do the first as an example (*I'd say I was quite a **good listener**.*) Play the audio again.

Answers

I'd say I was quite a good listener
I'm willing to work hard
I'm usually quite good at dealing with problems
I like to think I'm not afraid to ask for help
I know I can sometimes talk too much
I'm working on it
I think this job would give me valuable experience
I was just wondering if I would have to buy my own uniform?

5 PRONUNCIATION *quite*

- **5a** 🎧 **35** Tell students to listen to the same sentence said two ways. Explain that the way the sentence is stressed will change the meaning of the sentence, and they should listen to decide whether *quite* or *good* is stressed.

- Elicit the answers, but to ensure students understand the difference, ask them to repeat after you: '*quite good*' in the two different ways: *quite **good*** (i.e. *very good*) ... **quite** *good* (i.e. *not as good*).

- Drill the whole sentence, back chaining like this: ***good*** ... ***good*** at ***dea**ling* with ***prob**lems* ... *quite **good*** at ***dea**ling* with ***prob**lems* ... *I'm **u**sually quite **good*** at ***dea**ling* with ***prob**lems*. Then drill the other way, starting with *quite*: **quite** *good* ... **quite** *good* at ***dea**ling* with ***prob**lems* ... *I'm **u**sually **quite** good at **dea**ling* with ***prob**lems*.

- Have them listen to you hum the syllables in the two sentences and tell you which one you are saying, i.e. for the sentence where *quite* is stressed:

  *hum **HUM** hum hum **HUM** hum hum **HUM** hum hum **HUM** hum*

  and for the sentence where *good* is stressed:

  *hum **HUM** hum hum hum **HUM** hum **HUM** hum hum **HUM** hum.*

- Play the audio again for students to listen and repeat.

Answers
1 stress on *good* = very
2 stress on *quite* = a little bit

- **5b** Tell students that they can practise saying *quite* in two different ways with sentences 1–5. Encourage them to mumble the words on their own, in a low voice, before saying them louder and clearer the second and third times. Demonstrate this before they begin.

- Once they have had a chance to practise on their own, put them in pairs to test each other, by saying each sentence one of the ways, and letting their partner decide whether *quite* meant *very* or *not very*.

- Invite students to say each sentence in front of the whole class and have the class vote on what *quite* means.

 6

- Explain the task. Tell students to plan what they are going to say in response to the four questions, basing their answers on their own experience and personal skills. Remind them of the Useful language box on page 67, and let them use their inner voice to imagine answering the questions using some of the useful expressions.

- Put students in pairs. Get them to take turns at playing the interviewer and job candidate, asking and answering the questions.

- Go round and check students are doing the task correctly and notice errors, difficulties, or where they use L1. Write some of these points on the board, or remember them for class feedback.

- At the end of the task, ask interviewers whether they would give the job to their candidates, and why. Then give some feedback about new language that came up, and errors to correct which you may have written on the board. You can also retell some interesting things you heard to share with the class.

WRITING A formal letter of application *p67*

 7

- Ask students to explain what they would do if they wanted to do one of the jobs advertised on page 66. Explain the task. Tell them to read the letter of application on page 151.

- Let students compare their answers in pairs before nominating individual students to tell the class.

Answers
She includes 1, 2, 4 and 6

8 WRITING SKILL Hedging

- **8a** Write on the board *I think you should give me the job because I'm a brilliant teacher.* Tell the class that you're applying for a better teaching job and you're wondering whether to include this information. Tell them that although it is, of course, true, you're not sure about it. Ask their opinion.

- Read the Writing skill box. Elicit the meaning of *arrogant* (somebody who is arrogant thinks they are better than others and is therefore over-confident and possibly rude).

- Ask students if sentences 1–5 sound arrogant to them. Ask which sound most arrogant, and which less so. Ask if any of those sentences might be suitable in a letter of application (sentences 2 and 4 may be acceptable).

- Tell students to read Aya's letter again and find sentences in the letter that mean the same as sentences 1–5. As students find the sentences, invite them to write them on the board.

Answers
1 I am perfectly qualified for the job. → **I believe** I am a good candidate for the job.
2 I have a lot of experience. → I have **quite** a lot of experience...
3 I am an awesome cook. → I am **not a bad** cook.
4 I get along with everyone. → **I like to think that** I am a friendly person who gets on well with **most** people.
5 I am really smart, so I'm a fast learner. → **I would say** I am a fast learner.

- **8b** Explain the task.
- When most students have finished writing, let them compare their sentences. Make sure they understand that there will be more than one way to express these ideas.
- Elicit a number of different answers from the class.

Suggested answers
1 I have a good level of Chinese and I would say that my Japanese is also quite good. (More useful would be to state your actual language level, e.g. I am a proficient speaker of Chinese. I have a strong intermediate level of Japanese.)
2 I am not a bad driver. (It is more likely that you would just say: I have a full driving licence.)
3 I did well in my exams. / I did very well in my exams. / I got 'As' and 'Bs' in my exams.
4 I was given a lot of responsibility in my last job, and I feel that I managed my responsibilities well.
5 I like to think that I am a creative thinker. / … I am quite creative.

 9

- Explain the task. Make sure they understand that they can choose a job from the adverts on page 66 or choose their own job. Tell students to refer to the model on page 151 for help. Remind them of the structure of the model by reading out the advice at the back of the book and reminding them of the language they have studied. Remind them too that the Useful language box is there to help them but point out that in formal writing we tend not to use contractions, so if they should use phrases from the Useful language box in uncontracted form, e.g. 'I would say that I was …'.
- If you are going to give students a mark, tell them it will be higher if they organize the letter of application in a similar way and use language they have learnt. Put students in pairs and tell them to talk about or plan their letter.
- Set the writing for homework or set a time limit of about twenty minutes to do it in class. As students are writing, go round and offer help. You might note some common errors for feedback when the time is up. Ask fast finishers to suggest ways that they could improve their letters.

Fast finishers
Students who finish quickly can write another letter to apply for one of the other jobs.

10

- When most students have finished writing, organize them in groups according to which jobs they applied for: *Santa Cruz Fruits, Part-time catering staff, Personal care assistant* or a job of their choice. You can either let them evaluate the letters for their chosen job, i.e. compare their own letters with others' for the same job, or collect the letters together to give to another group to read, i.e. compare letters written for another job written by members of another group.
- Ask them to read all of the letters from the group. Explain that they should each make notes about the letters they have read, making a list of positive and negative points for each. You might decide to model this note taking exercise for the class, by writing on the board something like this:

Positive points	*Negative points*
experience working on a farm	*only seems interested in the money*
well-structured letter, few errors	*hasn't included when he is available to work*

- Give the groups five minutes to discuss and decide which student should get the job.
- When they have reached a decision, invite a spokesperson from each group to offer the job to the best candidate. They should explain why these students got the job and why the others were not as good. Check that the rest of the class agree that their reasons are justified.
- Congratulate the students who got the jobs!

Homework
- Set Workbook Lesson 5E exercises on pages 59–61 for homework.
- Students write a job advert for their ideal summer job and their job application for the job.
- Students prepare three questions to test their classmates at the start of the next lesson about the things they have studied in Unit 5.

6 Superhuman

6A **Amazing bodies** *pp68–71*

Information about the photo

For most of the 20th century, the only way to look inside the body was with X-ray technology (invented in 1895). X-rays are good for looking at the bones, but are not able to give much information about soft tissues. In 1971, the first *Computed Tomography*, or CT scan, of a patient's brain was made using a new technology that creates a three-dimensional image of the internal structure of the body. Since then, this technology has developed enormously, helping us better understand how the body works and treat disease.

This is a coloured 3D computed tomography of a human heart (lower left) with the aorta (red and yellow) and pulmonary blood vessels (blue) – the vessels that carry blood to and from the heart.

VOCABULARY The human body *p69*

- **Books closed**. Ask students to think of one interesting or amazing fact about the human body, and to make a question from it. For example, ask what the combined length of all the nerves that connect the brain to other parts of the body is. Get a few guesses and then tell them the answer (76km).
- Once students have thought of a fact, give them a minute to write their questions, so that you can check that their question formation is accurate. Then tell students to stand up and mingle, asking and answering as many questions as they can in five minutes.
- Stop the activity. Invite students to share the most interesting facts that they heard, any facts that they are not sure are true, etc. If students have online access, you could ask them to investigate whether some of the more controversial facts are true.

- Tell the class that they are going to do a quiz about the human body. Look at the instructions. Remind students they don't need all the numbers in the box. Students do the quiz on their own. Set a time limit of about five minutes.
- Go round checking understanding and offering help where needed.
- When the time is up, let students compare in pairs.
- Tell students that they are going to hear the answers from a longer text. Explain that the information is not necessarily in the order that it is required, or in the same form as the

answers in the book. They will therefore need to listen carefully for the answers.

- Either read out the texts with the answers yourself, or nominate students to take turns and read out each section. The answers to the questions are in bold, and in summary below the texts. You will need to confirm these with the class after they have listened to the explanations.

Answers

1 70ml   **2** 96,000km   **3** 27%   **4** 86,000,000,000 (86 billion) neurons   **5** 100%   **6** 18,000cm^2
7 1   **8** 17mm   **9** 206   **10** 435   **11** 9m
12 300–1000 species

The heart and blood

The blood transports oxygen and essential substances for life to every cell in the body. The lungs are where blood meets the air to transfer gases, but **we only use about a quarter of the oxygen we breathe in***. We also rely on the blood to fight infections, carry chemical messages from one place to another, and take away waste products. Incredibly, most of the blood vessels are so small and so numerous that they would be **almost 100,000 kilometres long**** if you put them in one long line. That's more than twice around the Earth! In each heartbeat, **70 millimetres of blood passes through the heart** on its way around the body. During heavy exercise, more than fourteen litres might be flowing through your heart every minute!

*27%   ** 96,000km

The brain and senses

We need a brain and sense organs such as eyes and ears to help us understand our environment and move around in it. There are approximately **86 billion neurons***, or brain cells, in the human brain. We also have many neurons outside the brain, which send information to and from other parts of the body. The largest sense organ is the skin, where we feel touch over **about 1.8 square metres of skin****.

It is not true that we only use 10% of our brains: **we use our whole brain nearly all of the time**. Another common myth exists about the sense of taste. We now know that the tongue does not have special areas for the different tastes (salty, sweet, etc.) – the whole of the tongue can experience all the different tastes. So really, **there is just one area**.

* Neurons are just one kind of brain cell – there are many more total cells in the brain.
** = 18,000 cm^2

The bones and skeleton

The skeleton and muscles support the body and allow us to move. There are **206 bones** in an adult body, but we have many more when we are babies. Over time, many bones join together. Another interesting fact is that during the day, the weight of your head presses down on the bones in the back and squashes them slightly, making you a little bit shorter. At night, you go back to your morning height, which can be **almost 2cm taller***. Evel Knievel was a famous entertainer who jumped over buses and other objects on his motorbike. He holds the record for the most bones broken by one person – during his long career he broke **435**!

* about 17mm

Food and digestion

We are not very big animals, but food travels **about nine metres** through our body. The nutrients in the food pass into the blood along the way. They get into the blood by passing through the wall of the intestine. The total surface area of the small intestine is 30 square metres! When the food is in our digestive system, **hundreds of species of bacteria** digest it and keep us healthy.

3

- Explain the task. Tell students that the words are in the order that they appear in the sentences.
- Go round checking understanding and offering help where needed.
- Nominate students to read out each sentence during feedback, not just the pairs of words. After each sentence, ask the class to identify and note the useful expressions that the words appear in, i.e. *the human skeleton, a red blood cell, hard to breathe, a lung infection, break a bone, blood vessels, feel your heart beat.*

Answers

1 skeleton + cell   **2** breathe + lung   **3** bone + bacteria   **4** blood + oxygen*   **5** beat + skin
6 muscles + tongue

* Blood is always red. Veins look blue because light penetrates the skin to illuminate them, blue and red light (being of different wavelengths) penetrate with different degrees of success. What gets reflected back to our eyes is the blue light.

---

4 MY PERSPECTIVE

- Put students in groups to discuss the question. Also ask them whether there is any information they would like to know more about because they are not sure if it is true. Ask them how they might find out. Encourage them to do this and tell the class what they discovered in the next lesson.
- Go round and check students are doing the task correctly and notice errors, difficulties, or where they use L1. Write some of these points on the board, or remember them for class feedback.

- At the end of the task, find out which information was most surprising to the class. Give some feedback about new language that came up, and errors to correct. You can also retell some interesting things you heard to share with the class.

LISTENING *p70*

Information about the photo

This is Danuru Sherpa talking to his family on his phone at Camp 1 of the mountain Ama Dablam in Nepal. Ama Dablam is close to Mount Everest and is another popular mountain to climb. The local Sherpas help visiting climbers from all over the world to get to the summit, which is 20,243 feet or 6,170 metres high. At this altitude, there is less than half the oxygen available to you than at sea level. It doesn't seem to be affecting Danuru!

- Tell the class that they are going to listen to a radio programme about how amazing the human body is. Focus students' attention on the photo or project it using the CPT. Ask the class to guess where in the world this is, who the person is, and what amazing fact the photo refers to. Encourage speculation, and accept all ideas as possible without giving the answer at this stage (that some people who live at high altitudes, in the Himalayas and the Andes – this is a Sherpa in the Himalayas – have evolved ways to live at high altitude, where there is less oxygen in the air).
- 🎧 **36** Look at the instructions. Play the audio once straight through. Tell students to compare their answers in pairs. Go round and notice how well they did in order to decide how quickly to go through answers and whether you will need to play the audio again. Play the audio again if it's clear that they found it difficult.

Exam tip

Listening for gist
Usually, the first task in a listening is quite simple. The aim is for students to get the main ideas or to be able to show they have managed to understand something of the text. When you check the answer, stick to this question. If you started asking more detailed questions, students could feel they have failed in their understanding because they didn't know they had to listen for that information.

- Ask the whole class or individual students for their answers. Don't say if they are right or wrong, but ask them why they think what they think and to say other words they heard to support their answer.
- Where everyone agrees on the answer, write the area on the board. If they don't agree or most don't know, you can either give the answer or tell students to listen again and check.

Answers
the bones and skeleton   food and digestion   the heart and blood

Our bodies don't look very impressive if we compare them with other animals. At least, that's what many people think. Most mammals can run faster than us; we can't fly, climb or swim that well. But if you listen to today's show, you'll find out why the human body is extraordinary.

Mammals evolved for walking on four legs, but humans have adapted well to walking on just two. The bones in our back have changed shape so that they can support our heavy brains on top of our bodies, and our feet do a fantastic job taking all our weight! Each foot contains 26 bones and more than 100 muscles. And unless you take the car everywhere, you might walk up to 185,000 kilometres in your lifetime. That's more than four times around the Earth!

Most plant material is very difficult to digest for animals like cows and rabbits, but a number of adaptations to their digestive system help them. Cows, which eat grass, have very long digestive systems. A cow's may be more than 40 metres long, about twenty times longer than the animal itself! It contains bacteria and other organisms which help the animals get nutrients from their food. But you contain bacteria, too. Lots! There are more bacterial cells in your body than human cells! The range of bacteria probably depends on your diet. You may have more types of bacteria in your digestive system if you eat a healthy diet with low levels of protein, fat and sugar.

Most humans live near sea level, but 140 million people live at altitudes of 2,500 metres or more, where there is less oxygen in the air – places such as the Himalayas, the Andes and parts of Africa. Be careful visiting such places – you will probably have difficulty breathing if you go to high altitudes. But local people have adapted to the conditions. In the Himalayas, people who have always lived at high altitude have bigger lungs to take in more air, and people in the Andes can carry more oxygen in their blood than the rest of us. We think these adaptations to the body happened less than 3,000 years ago, so if you think evolution always happens very slowly, think again!

- Tell students to read the multiple choice questions to check they understand them. Before playing the audio again, let students try to do the task from memory or go straight into the task.
- 🎧 **36** Play the audio.
- Tell students to compare their answers in pairs before nominating students to share their answers with the class.
- Play the audio again for students to check. You might decide to pause the audio after each answer is given and get students to confirm them.

7

- Put students in pairs to discuss the questions.

- Go round and check students are doing the task correctly and notice mistakes, difficulties, or where they use L1. Help them by correcting or giving them the English they need, and write some of these points on the board, or remember them for class feedback.

- You may have anticipated some of the language that they need before the lesson. You might remind them of some of the recently learnt phrases in Unit 5E (page 67): *I'd say I was quite a (healthy eater), I wouldn't say that I was (a sporty person), I'm usually quite good at (looking after myself), I know I can sometimes (go to bed too late), I'm working on (doing more exercise)*, etc.

- At the end of the task, elicit different ways that students look after their bodies. Then give some feedback about new language that came up, and focus on errors to correct, which you may have written on the board. You can also share some interesting things you heard with the class.

Teaching tip

Anticipating what students might say

In Exercise 7, students are likely to have plenty to say, but may not express their ideas in a natural way. For example, a student might say *I eat healthy food*, when a more natural sentence might be *I'd say I have a fairly healthy diet*.

It's not easy to think of natural ways to reformulate students' sentences, but you can anticipate the sort of things that students are likely to want to say before the lesson. Having thought about what students might try to say may well make it easier to think of how to improve things that do come up. Here are two ways to do this:
1 Write whole sentences or mini-dialogues that students may try to come up with, and keep these ideas up your sleeve when students are speaking in class.
2 Record yourself doing the speaking activity as if you were a student. Listen to what you say, and importantly, how you say it. Prepare a few sentences to write on the board before, during or after students speak.

Feeling that they're not just speaking for the sake of speaking – or speaking in order for the teacher to pick up on and punish basic grammatical mistakes – can be motivating for students, and can help them see greater value in classroom speaking: they speak so that their teacher can help them to better express what they're trying to say.

GRAMMAR Zero and first conditional *p70*

8

- Decide whether students should do this task on their own or in pairs. Explain the task.

Answers

Sentences b, c and d describe possible future situations. Sentences a and e describe facts that are always true.

9

- Tell them that sentences a and e in the Grammar box are examples of zero conditional, and b, c and d of first conditional sentences. Explain the task.

- Go round and check students' understanding of the grammar. Help any students who are having difficulty.

- You can either go through the answers with the whole class, or wait for them to read the Grammar reference on page 138 and then ask the class the grammar-checking questions or nominate individual students to give their answers.

Answers

1 general facts   **2** possible future situations   **3** two clauses   **4** present   **5** present simple, a, e
6 future, b, d   **7** unless   **8** e, c

Grammar reference and practice

Ask students to do Exercises 1 and 2 on page 139 now, or set them for homework.

Answers to Grammar practice exercises

1

1 wake up   **2** shouldn't drink   **3** continues
4 can / may pass   **5** should cover   **6** may / can pass
7 have   **8** can / may go   **9** gets   **10** don't look after

2

1 ~~he'll feel~~ he feels   **2** ~~if~~ unless / ~~won't~~ will
3 ~~should~~ will / may / can   **4** ~~Unless~~ If / ~~happy~~ not happy / ~~can~~ can't   **5** ~~I phone~~ I'll phone   **6** ~~will rain~~ rains   **7** ~~should~~ will / might / may / can
8 ~~will~~ should / ~~you will~~ see

10

- Tell students to quickly read the text about health advice with the comprehension question: *What is the problem that this writer is expressing?* Give them one minute to skim the text, then elicit the problem (he is confused by all the different health advice these days). Ask them whether they also feel confused, or think that health advice is actually quite clear to them.

- Look at the instructions and do the first item with the whole class.

- Tell students to do the rest of the activity on their own. Go round the class checking the accuracy of their answers and providing help where necessary.

- When most have finished, nominate students to read out a sentence each.

- Tell students to complete the advice.
- Go round and help students to come up with the correct form of the verbs if necessary.
- When most students have finished, elicit the correct sentences. Ask students which advice is the most important in their opinion.

Fast finishers

Students who finish quickly can write one more piece of advice.

Put students in groups of three or four to discuss the questions in order to arrive at some advice that they all agree with.

stages. You or some of the students may have knowledge of primary care in emergency situations, in which case, they could teach the class what they know. Alternatively, you could set this as homework.)

Extension

Get students to find out about primary care in emergency situations. Give each student or group of students a different medical emergency to find out how to treat, or they could choose for themselves, e.g. burns, allergic reactions, broken bones, dangerous substances in the eyes, epileptic seizures, etc. You could review this homework at the beginning of lesson 6C, which is about first aid.

- Pre-teach *first aid kit*. If there is one in the classroom or in the school, you could bring it in to show the students, or you could draw one on the board. Invite students to guess what's in it. Then open the box to find out.
- Keep students in their groups. Explain the task. You could provide extra details about the camping trip, such as where (in the mountains, near a river, in the snow, etc.), who with (children, friends or family, etc.) and what you'll be doing (walking, climbing, swimming, etc.).
- Tell students to plan their first aid kits. You could place a restriction on their list, such as a maximum of ten items (they have to carry everything with them, so can't take too much), in order to encourage prioritization of the most important items.
- When most groups have decided what to take, regroup students so that they can compare their lists with those from other groups.

Teaching tip

Taking the teacher out of the picture in feedback
The norm after any exercise is for students to tell the teacher their answers or ideas. After a free speaking activity such as a discussion, this isn't necessary. Consider allowing students the chance to give feedback to one another rather than telling you their ideas one by one. Regrouping students so that they can relay what they have discussed allows them to reformulate ideas and say them in a better, more fluent way, and gives them greater student talking time.

Let's say they discuss in groups of three or four: AAA, BBBB, CCCC, DDD, etc. Assign students in each group a number from 1 to 4: A1A2A3, B1B2B3B4, C1C2 … Then, simply order all the 1s to one corner of the room, all the 2s to another corner, and so on: → A1B1C1D1, A2B2C2D2, A3B3, etc. Now they can share what they have talked about.

Homework
- Set Workbook Lesson 6A exercises on pages 62–65 for homework.
- Students write an advice pamphlet about first aid when camping.

6B More than human?

pp72–73

READING *p72*

- **Optional step**. Tell students to open their books for a few seconds. Focus students' attention briefly on the lesson title, the title of the article and the photo, or project it using the CPT, then tell them to close their books. Put students in pairs to discuss what the central message of the lesson might be. Get them to write a summarizing sentence.
- Invite students to read out their ideas, e.g. *We think that the lesson might tell us about robots and people with mechanical parts of their bodies.* Praise students for their ideas and don't reject any as wrong or accept any that are correct.

- Read out the definition. Ask students to brainstorm examples of cyborg technologies. They may think of ideas similar to the subject of the photo's cyborg technology, i.e. prosthetic limbs, so encourage them to think about other parts of the body (e.g. the brain), other abilities (e.g. eyesight), and other types of machine.

> **Suggested answers**
> prosthetic arms and legs, hands and feet, robotic hands and arms, mechanical exoskeleton with a brain-computer interface, artificial eye (cosmetic only), cochlear implant
>
> Other technologies which may fit the definition include: glasses for eyesight, hearing aid, a watch, scuba diving gear, a kidney dialysis machine, Captain Hook's hook hand, a notepad and pencil!

- Explain the task. Set a time limit of three or four minutes to encourage students to skim quickly. Tell them not to worry about not understanding everything.
- When most students have finished reading, ask for a show of hands to find out who thinks it is 1, 2 or 3. Ask students to justify their answers.

> **Answer**
> **3** (Although *1* is true (e.g. Michael Chorost is deaf without his implants), it does not explain the message of the whole article. *2* goes against the main message, that cyborg technology is part of most of our lives already.)

- 🎧 **37** Tell students to read the article again and answer the questions. Be available for students to ask you questions about unknown words and to check their answers.
- Nominate students to share their answers with the class. Don't immediately say if students have given the correct answer, but ask others whether they agree, and to explain

their answers. Let students debate and see if they can persuade each other.
- Make sure the final answers are clear to everyone.

Fast finishers
Students who finish quickly can write one more question to ask the class.

> **Answers**
> **1** He thinks that it suggests superhuman abilities, doing things that humans can already do, but doing them better, whereas he thinks we should see cyborg technology as giving people abilities they could not do before.
> **2** He can switch off his hearing completely. He uses this to concentrate when there is unwanted noise around.
> **3** He is able to climb better and change his height.
> **4** The writer mentions glasses, contact lenses, smartphones, calculator, pen and paper.
> **5** It is an extension of our brain that helps us remember things.

  MY PERSPECTIVE

- Put students in pairs to discuss the questions.
- Listen to students' conversations and check that they have understood the main message of the article, which is that there are many aspects of our lives which involve cyborg technology already.
- When most students have finished, invite students to share with the class some of their ideas. Explore any potential negative effects of using technology.

VOCABULARY BUILDING Verbs describing ability *p72*

⑤

- Write the quote on the board *Electronic implants allow Chorost to hear enough to have a phone conversation.* Ask *Could Chorost hear a phone conversation before he had implants?* (no) Get students to identify the verb which means *make something possible* (*allow*). Elicit the structure *allow someone to do something.*
- Look at the instructions and do the first item with the whole class. Point out that the number of spaces indicates the number of letters in the verbs.
- Tell students to do the rest of the activity on their own.
- When most students have finished, invite them to write one verb on the board each. Ask the rest of the class whether they agree.

> **Answers**
> **1** allow (line 2)   **2** lets (line 11)   **3** enable (line 26)
> **4** help (line 29)   **5** prevent (line 30)   **6** stop (line 31)
> **7** saves (line 36)

- Look at the instructions and do the first item with the whole class (3 or 4 – *allow someone to do something*).
- Tell students to do the rest of the activity on their own.
- When you nominate students to tell you the answers, make sure they say the sentence which gave them the information.

Answers

1 let (lets him concentrate better) **2** help (help us extend our brains) **3** allow (allow him to hear) **4** enable (enable us to see better) **5** stop (didn't stop him from climbing) **6** prevent (prevent us from forgetting)
7 save (saves us from having to keep lots of information in our memory)

- Explain the task. Make sure students understand that they may need to add *to* or *from*.
- Go round and check that students are doing the task correctly.
- When most students have finished, get them to compare answers in pairs and to help each other with anything they haven't finished.
- Go through the answers by asking different students to read out each complete sentence.

Answers

1 Glasses enable people with poor eyesight **to** see better.
2 This medicine allows you **to** go to school if you have a cold.
3 The robot suit helps disabled people walk again.
4 Doing exercise prevents you **from** putting on weight.
5 The government hopes the advert will stop young people **from** becoming addicted to cigarettes.
6 Running machines save you **from** having to train in the rain.
7 This machine lets the nurses know if the patient stops breathing.

Exam tip

Avoiding silly mistakes

In exercises like Exercise 7, it's easy for students to miss one of the words in their answers and write it incorrectly. They should use the time they have left in an exam to check that they have done exactly what the question asks them to. Here, for example, they could cross out with a pencil each word as they use it, i.e.

1 ~~enable~~ | ~~glasses~~ | people ~~with~~ poor eyesight | see better

---

- Look at the instructions.
- Set a time limit of three minutes for students to write as many sentences as they can. Go round and offer ideas and language support, paying special attention to their accuracy in using the verbs.
- When most students have finished, get them to compare their ideas in pairs. Remind them to try to think of disadvantages as well as advantages.
- Put students' answers on the board or just let them share their ideas orally. Praise a wide range of different verbs in their ideas.

Suggested answers

They allow you to / let you / enable you to / help you …

communicate with friends and family and let them know where you are; look up information that you want to know straight away; take and store photos and videos, and show them to your friends; check your appearance, like a mirror; send directions to friends; keep notes so you don't forget things; play games; check the weather; time yourself; see in the dark (with a torch); learn English!

They stop you / prevent you from / save you from …

getting lost (using maps); getting bored by playing games and watching movies; having to pay for calls (by using wi-fi).

Possible disadvantages include: they may stop you from learning how to communicate with people face to face; they may be bad for concentration and prevent you from understanding what is going on around you; they may stop you from developing skills such as natural navigation; they may make you so dependent on telecommunication companies that they can force you to spend too much money for their services, etc.

Extension / Fast finishers

Students repeat the exercise but talk about a different topic, e.g. cars, supermarkets, living in cities, the internet.

CRITICAL THINKING Bold claims *p72*

- Ask a student to read the Critical thinking box to the class. Then ask what bold claims they think the writer makes in the article, if any.
- Put students in groups to discuss the questions.
- Go round and visit each group and listen to their ideas and argument. Encourage discussion in quieter groups by asking questions, e.g. *Can you say glasses are really as much a cyborg tool as an eye that can help blind people see? Do Hugh Herr and Michael Chorost think of themselves as cyborgs? Why not?* Also, challenge students to justify their comments.
- With the whole class, invite students to give their answers to the questions and to share their opinions about the issues.

- Explore the issues by describing concrete examples of when differences in how we see cyborgs might matter in real life. For example, should people with prosthetic legs and feet be allowed to run in the Olympics against others if this gives them an advantage? And if you can take a calculator into a maths exam to help you, shouldn't you be allowed to take a smartphone, since our real-life abilities depend on the technology we use?
- Have a class vote on whether they think 'we are all cyborgs'.

Suggested answers

1 *We are all cyborgs* is a bold claim because it is very far from the popular definition of a cyborg, used to mean man-machine creations in sci-fi or cutting edge technology. However, some compelling arguments are given. Firstly, there is very little difference between the technology we use (to make us better at things and able to do things we couldn't do on our own) that we wear or hold temporarily (a pair of glasses, a phone, a pen) and permanent cyborg implants. Secondly, we all use a lot of tools these days to increase our mental abilities. If we use technology as an extension of our bodies or brains, we are acting as cyborgs.

2 You could say that these devices are not implanted and can be easily removed. You could say that people don't have them as a part of themselves all the time. You could say that some of the devices are not very sophisticated, so shouldn't be seen as cyborg technology.

3 Students' own answers (c is the statement most likely to be categorized as a bold claim, because writing is very far from the popular definition of the word *cyborg*.)

Homework

- Set Workbook Lesson 6B exercises on pages 66–67 for homework.
- Students choose a TED Talk to watch about cyborg technology, e.g. Amber Case, 'We are all cyborgs now', Neil Harbisson, 'I listen to color', or Hugh Herr (from the article), 'The new bionics that let us run, climb and dance'.
- Students imagine a cyborg technology for their body or brain and write an application to Hugh Herr to make them one, with reasons why.

6C **First aiders** *pp74–75*

GRAMMAR Second conditional *p74*

- **Optional step.** If you set your students homework to research primary care after Lesson 6A, give them the opportunity today to teach the class what they have learnt. Invite students to present their first aid advice to the class.
- Put students in pairs to look at the photo and discuss the questions.
- Nominate a few students to share what they discussed.

Suggested answers

A runner has probably had an injury – he looks as if he is in pain. He might have broken a leg or other bone, or sprained an ankle. The team are giving him first aid. They are working as a team to move him, and will have made sure that they do not do more harm to the patient.

- 🎧 **38** Tell students that they are going to listen to a report about two first aid stories and need to complete the table. Play the audio once straight through.
- While the audio is playing, copy the table on the board with space to fill in the answers. Let students compare their answers in pairs.
- Invite students to the board to fill in the table.
- Students are unlikely to know the key words *collapse* and *choke*, and will likely ask you about them. Don't teach the words at this stage, but ask *What do you think it means? What did the word sound like? How do you think you spell it?* In both reports, the context provides clues as to the meaning (collapse – *lying on the ground*, choke – *restaurant, couldn't breathe, hit her on the back*, etc.). Then correct their spelling and write the words clearly for students to learn.
- Check that the rest of the class agree with what's written. If there is a dispute, ask students to justify their different answers, but don't say who is correct – put a question mark on the board. Play the audio again (if necessary), telling students to focus on the areas of uncertainty.
- If students are still uncertain of the answer, play the audio again and stop at key points. Play these sections two or three times if students are still struggling. Draw attention to the problem sounds or words and explain them when you give the answers.

The International Red Cross believes educating people in first aid is really important. Here are two true stories that clearly show reasons why.

When 16-year-old Anmol saw a man collapse in a car park, she stopped to help. The teenager calmly observed the situation and called an ambulance. The man was lying on the ground looking very confused, so Anmol stayed with him and kept him calm until the emergency services arrived. She was surprised no one else stopped to help. Anmol knew what to do because they teach first aid at her school. The Red Cross wish more schools taught these essential skills.

Natasha was in a restaurant with her family when another guest started to choke. The woman couldn't breathe and her husband didn't know what to do. Calmly, Natasha went over to their table and stood behind the woman. She hit her on the back five times but there was still a problem. Then she put her arms around the woman and pulled up and in. At last the woman coughed and started to cry – but Natasha knew she could breathe again. The waiters called an ambulance and the driver said Natasha should be proud of her actions. He said: 'If it wasn't for you, she might not be alive.'

Natasha knew what to do thanks to first aid training she does from time to time. A study found that up to 59 percent of deaths from injury could be prevented if first aid was carried out before the emergency services arrive. If only more of us knew what to do in situations like this.

What would you do if you saw someone in trouble? Could you help?

Answers		
	Anmol	**Natasha**
What was the problem?	a man collapsed in a car park, lying on the ground and very confused	a woman started to choke and couldn't breathe
How did they help?	called an ambulance, stayed with the man, kept him calm	stood behind the woman and hit her on the back five times, but this didn't help, so she put her arms around the woman and pulled up and in until the woman could breathe

- Copy the sentence on the board. Ask the whole class the questions, nominating students to answer.

> **Answers**
> 1 No, according to the sentence, not everyone learns first aid at school.
> 2 No, not all the lives are saved that could be.
> 3 past simple (*learned*)
> 4 No, the situation is talking about an imaginary present.

4

- Explain the task.
- Go round and check that students aren't just guessing but can justify their choices based on specific example sentences from the Grammar box.
- You can either go through the answers with the whole class, or wait for them to read the Grammar reference on page 138 and then ask the class the grammar-checking questions, or nominate individual students to give their answers. When you go through the answers in class, check that students can give you an example or examples from the Grammar box.

> **Answers**
> 1 imaginary (all sentences) 2 unlikely (all)
> 3 result clause (a, b) 4 if-clause (a, b, e, f)
> 5 could (e) 6 might (f) 7 past (c, d)

Grammar reference and practice

Ask students to do Exercises 3–5 on page 139 now, or set them for homework.

> **Answers to Grammar practice exercises**
> **3**
> 1 would choose 2 paid 3 was or were (both possible)
> 4 couldn't 5 weren't 6 had 7 didn't 8 might
> **4**
> 1 helped his classmates, wouldn't be angry with him
> 2 could come out / would be able to come out, didn't have
> 3 wouldn't have to look after, their parents didn't both work
> 4 wasn't broken, could print
> 5 wish they could
> 6 wasn't closed, wouldn't have to study at home
> 7 be able to drive to work, a car wasn't parked
> 8 Patricio still lived here / Patricio lived here still
> **5**
> 1 real future possibility – see, I'll
> 2 an unlikely future situation – would, won
> 3 an imagined present situation – had, we'd
> 4 real future possibility – will, pass
> 5 an imagined present situation – wasn't, I'd
> 6 an imagined present situation – would, weren't
> 7 an imagined present situation – would, could
> 8 real future possibility – I'll, is

⑤

- Look at the instructions and do the first item with the whole class.
- Tell students to do the rest of the exercise on their own.
- When most students have finished, get them to compare answers in pairs. Read out the complete text for students to check their answers.
- After you have given the answers, ask for a show of hands: *How many people got all twelve correct? Excellent! What about eleven? Ten? Very good*, etc.

Answers

1 saw   **2** knew   **3** was   **4** wouldn't   **5** found
6 would first   **7** had   **8** would be   **9** Would
10 was   **11** might   **12** If only

---

⑥ PRONUNCIATION *I wish* and *If only*

- **6a** **39** Explain the task. Play the audio.

Answers

(Stressed syllables are in bold)
*1 If **only** I **knew** what to **do**.*
*2 I **wish** I **had** a mobile **phone**.*
*3 I **wish** I **didn't** have a **cold**.*
*4 I **wish** I could **get** to **sleep** at **night**.*

- Have students repeat the sentences dramatically, as if the speakers are desperate and regretting the fact that they don't know what to do, don't have their phone, etc.

Teaching tip

Dramatizing intonation and stress

- Most of the attitude and emotion in the things that we say are communicated not through what we say but through the way that we say it. By dramatizing sentences, or saying them with appropriate feeling, students should arrive at the correct intonation and stress more easily. Here are three ways to dramatize the phonological aspects of language.

1 Ask students to imagine they are the people saying the sentence. Describe the scene, emphasizing how happy, or frustrated, or frightened the person must be. Ask them to adopt the role of the speaker.

2 Physicalize the phonology. For example, if they are angry or determined, have them hit their hand on the table on the stressed syllable of a word or sentence. If a question needs a rising intonation to show uncertainty, have them lift their heads on the tonic syllable. Surprise sounds more surprised if students raise their eyebrows as well as their intonation.

3 Practise saying the sentence with different facial expressions (angry, sad, etc.), with different voice qualities (shouting, whispering, like a robot, etc.) and in different accents (like an American, like a Chinese person, like yourself, etc.). Not only does this help students hear intonation and accent in action, it makes the drilling exercise more entertaining.

- **6b** Explain the task. To model the activity, tell the class one or two of your own.
- Go round and check students are writing correct sentences, paying special attention to the verb forms after *I wish* and *If only*.
- Tell students to identify the stressed syllables in their sentences and practise saying them.

Suggested answers

1 I wish I could play a musical instrument.
2 If only my parents let me stay out late on Saturdays.
3 If only my sister didn't keep borrowing my clothes.
4 I wish society cared more for poor people, the elderly and the disabled.
5 If only I could take some of my father's worry away.

- **6c** Put students in pairs to compare and practise saying the sentences.
- After two minutes, invite students to share some of their wishes with the class.

⑦

- Explain the task.
- Set a time limit of two to three minutes for students to complete the conversations in any way they want.

Fast finishers

Students who finish quickly can add more lines of conversations.

⑧

- Put students in pairs to practise saying their conversations and choose their favourite endings.
- Nominate a few pairs of students to read out their conversations.

Suggested answers

1 … I had my first aid kit with me today. / … Olga was here. She'd know what to do.
2 … can't take me after school, I'll go tomorrow. / … was here, she'd say it was my fault!
3 … I could lie down. / … I hadn't eaten all those oysters! … I had my phone with me. I'd call my sister to pick me up. / … I didn't have such a sensitive stomach.

---

⑨ CHOOSE

The idea is for students to make their own choice of activity here. However, you might want to make the decision for the students, in which case explain why. Alternatively, you may decide to let students do more than one task. You could divide the class into groups and have each group do a different task – or you could have a vote on which task the whole class should do. For the vote:

- put students in pairs or groups to decide which they prefer
- take a vote on each task.

- if the vote is tied, ask one student from each side to explain which is best and take the vote again. You can decide if there is still no change.

- Options 1 and 2 are research tasks. If you have online access, these can be done in class; otherwise, they could be set for home study. Students present their findings to the class. If they want, they could follow up task 1 by actually attending a course!

- Option 2 is a writing task; why not create a first aid information centre in the classroom?

- Option 3 is a speaking task. Students should plan what they are going to say (*Where are they? What is wrong with the victims? Who are the people involved?*, etc.) and try some improvised roleplays before recording, either audio or video, the roleplay. They can show this to the rest of the class or post it on the class social site.

- You may decide to pre-teach some useful language, e.g. *What's the problem? Where does it hurt? Are you on any medication? We need an ambulance, please*, etc.

- As a class project, the students who research one emergency in activity 2 could then create a video based on activity 3 on the same emergency as part of their presentation and poster.

Homework

- Set Workbook Lesson 6C exercises on pages 68–69 for homework.

- Students write an extended essay based on one of their wishes from Exercise 6.

- Students extend one of the conversations in Exercise 7.

- If students didn't do options 1 or 2 in class, they do them for homework.

- You might want to tell students to watch the track called *Unit 6 TED Talk* on the *Perspectives* website before they come to the next class.

6D Deep sea diving … in a wheelchair *pp76–77*

- Tell students they are going to watch a TED Talk called 'Deep sea diving … in a wheelchair'. Ask students how they think diving and wheelchairs are connected. Accept any ideas they may have.

- Read out the quote and ask students to translate it or say what they think it means in English (or both).

- **Optional step**. A great way to introduce the theme of the talk is to show your students a photo of a new style of disability access sign from accessibleicon.org. Ask them to discuss why they think the traditional blue disability access symbol has been changed. After they have given their thoughts, you could read out the following information about Accessibleicon.org:

This organization wants to replace the traditional international disability access sign with their own design because they believe the old symbol portrays wheelchair users as inactive, passive and inhuman. The new one shows a more positive image of disabled people actively moving towards their goals.

- ▶ **6.0** Tell students they are going to see a short text on the DVD to introduce the talk and the speaker, and play the *About the speaker* section. Then do the vocabulary exercise.

- After they finish, you might read the *About the speaker* section out loud, pausing at the key words, and waiting for the class to supply the missing words. Then put students in pairs to discuss the relevance of each word, e.g. *assumptions – people have negative assumptions about disabled people and wheelchairs.*

Answers to About the speaker
1 assumptions = c (beliefs)
2 perspective = b (way of thinking about something)
3 spectacles = b (events or exhibitions)
4 restriction = a (something that stops you doing what you want)
5 associations = c (thoughts or feelings)
6 exhilarating = a (exciting)

TED Talk About the speaker

Sue Austin is an artist who makes videos and other public works of art. Through her work, she challenges people's **assumptions** *about disability and shows them in a new* **perspective**.

She has created **spectacles** *that stop people thinking of the wheelchair as a symbol of* **restriction**, *and begin to make more positive* **associations** *with it.*

Sue's idea worth spreading is that a wheelchair doesn't have to mean 'disability', it can be an **exhilarating** *new way to see and experience the world.*

AUTHENTIC LISTENING SKILLS Following the argument *p76*

As well as teaching aspects of phonology and listening skills, these tasks also allow:

- you to pre-teach some vocabulary.
- students to read and hear new language before they listen to the whole text.
- students to tune in to the speaker's voice and style.

- Ask for a volunteer to read the Authentic listening skills box for the whole class. Point out that *However* helps the listener understand that the next thing they hear will be an opposing idea to the one they have just heard, and *That's why* tells the listener that what they have just heard is the reason for the part they are about to hear.
- 🎧 **40** Explain the task. Let students read the extract first before playing the audio.
- Nominate a student to share their answer with the class.

Answers
But even though   As a result

- 🎧 **41** Explain the task. Make sure students understand that each line indicates a missing word. Play the audio.

Answers
1 So when   So I thought   **2** And the other thing is

Extension

- Here is one way to show students how important words and phrases which help the listener follow the argument are. Write these phrases on the board:

    ... it was closed.
    ... I cooked dinner for six people and I had nothing left.
    ... I wasn't at home when you arrived.
    ... I went to the swimming pool.

- Read the same sentence four times: *I went to the supermarket to buy something for lunch.* Each time, choose a different beginning to the next sentence, either: *However, ..., That's because ..., That's why ...* or *After that, ...* . Ask students to supply the rest of the sentence, from the board. E.g. You say *I went to the supermarket to buy something for lunch. That's why ...* Students decide what the next sentence is based on the linking word you have chosen.

    That's why ... I wasn't at home when you arrived.
    However, ... it was closed.
    After that, ... I went to the swimming pool.
    That's because ... I cooked dinner for six people and I had nothing left to eat.

WATCH *p76*

- Look at the instructions. Do this as a whole-class activity. Try to involve as many students as possible in the discussion. Personalize by asking whether anyone has used a wheelchair or knows people who do, how they feel when they see a wheelchair, and how wheelchair users feel about their wheelchairs.

Suggested answers
The extract suggests that she didn't have a wheelchair once, and so could not move around. The wheelchair allowed her to move in a way that she hadn't been able to do before. Other people may have been happy for her or sad that she needed a wheelchair.

- If you are short of time, or want a different approach to the video, you may want to watch the whole talk all the way through with only some brief checking questions. A version of this is on the DVD and is labelled as *TED Talk with activities*. At the end of each section, there is a short gist question. Pause after each question on screen so students can give their answers, then play the answer.

Answers to gist questions on DVD
Part 1
What was Sue's problem?
b   She was changing in a way she didn't like.
Part 2
For Sue, what was the most interesting aspect of her art?
c   Other people responded to it.
Part 3
What does Sue say about her art's effect on people?
c   It allows them to see the world in a different way.

4

- Explain the task. Give students a minute to read the statements.
- ▶ **6.1** Play Part 1 straight through.
- Ask students to compare their ideas in pairs. Go round and notice how well they did in order to decide how quickly to go through answers, and whether you will need to play Part 1 again.
- Check answers as a class and ask students to justify their answers.

TED Talk Part 1 script ▶ 6.1

It's wonderful to be here to talk about my journey, to talk about the wheelchair and the freedom it has bought me.

I started using a wheelchair sixteen years ago when an extended illness changed the way I could access the world. When I started using the wheelchair, it was a tremendous new freedom. I'd seen my life slip away and become restricted. It was like having an enormous new toy. I could whizz around and feel the wind in my face again. Just being out on the street was exhilarating.

But even though I had this new-found joy and freedom, people's reaction completely changed towards me. It was as if they couldn't see me anymore, as if an invisibility cloak had descended. They seemed to see me in terms of their assumptions of what it must be like to be in a wheelchair. When I asked people their associations with the wheelchair, they used words like 'limitation', 'fear', 'pity' and 'restriction'. I realized I'd internalized these responses and it had changed who I was on a core level.

As a result, I knew I needed to make my own stories about this experience, new narratives to reclaim my identity.

5

- Suggest students read the sentences first to familiarize themselves with the task.
- ▶ 6.2 Play Part 2 straight through.
- Ask students to compare their ideas in pairs. Go round and notice how well they did in order to decide how quickly to go through answers, and whether you will need to play Part 2 again.
- Nominate students to answer.

Answers

1 happiness **2** visual art **3** excited **4** no different
5 excitement and adventure **6** amazing her journey has been

TED Talk Part 2 script ▶ 6.2

I started making work that aimed to communicate something of the joy and freedom I felt when using a wheelchair – a power chair – to negotiate the world. I was working to transform these internalized responses, to transform the

preconceptions that had so shaped my identity when I started using a wheelchair, by creating unexpected images. The wheelchair became an object to paint and play with. When I literally started leaving traces of my joy and freedom, it was exciting to see the interested and surprised responses from people. It seemed to open up new perspectives, and therein lay the paradigm shift. It showed that an arts practice can remake one's identity and transform preconceptions by revisioning the familiar.

So when I began to dive, in 2005, I realized scuba gear extends your range of activity in just the same way as a wheelchair does, but the associations attached to scuba gear are ones of excitement and adventure, completely different to people's responses to the wheelchair.

So, I thought, 'I wonder what'll happen if I put the two together?' And the underwater wheelchair that has resulted has taken me on the most amazing journey over the last seven years.

So, to give you an idea of what that's like, I'd like to share with you one of the outcomes from creating this spectacle, and show you what an amazing journey it's taken me on.

- Explain the task. For struggling students, you might tell them that she mentions three things from the list. Check students' understanding of *inspired*; for example, you could say that watching a friend run a marathon inspired you to do the same.
- ▶ 6.3 Play Part 3 straight through.
- Ask students to compare their ideas in pairs. Go round and notice how well they did in order to decide how quickly to go through answers, and whether you will need to play Part 3 again.
- Nominate students to answer.

Answers
She mentions 1, 4 and 5

TED Talk Part 3 script ▶ 6.3

It is the most amazing experience, beyond most other things I've experienced in life. I literally have the freedom to move in 360 degrees of space and an ecstatic experience of joy and freedom.

And the incredibly unexpected thing is that other people seem to see and feel that too. Their eyes literally light up, and they say things like, 'I want one of those', or, 'If you can do that, I can do anything'.

And I'm thinking, it's because in that moment of them seeing an object they have no frame of reference for, or so transcends the frames of reference they have with the wheelchair, they have to think in a completely new way. And I think that moment of completely new thought perhaps creates a freedom that spreads to the rest of other people's lives. For me, this means that they're seeing the value of difference, the joy it brings when instead of focusing on loss or limitation, we see and discover the power and joy of seeing the world from exciting new perspectives. For me, the wheelchair becomes a vehicle for transformation.

And the other thing is, that because nobody's seen or heard of an underwater wheelchair before, and creating this spectacle is about creating new ways of seeing, being and knowing, now you have this concept in your mind. You're all part of the artwork too.

7 VOCABULARY IN CONTEXT

- **7a** ▶ **6.4** Tell students that they are going to watch some clips from the talk which contain new or interesting words or phrases. They should choose the correct meaning for each one. Play the Vocabulary in context section. Pause after each question on screen so students can choose the correct definition, then play the answer. If you like, you can ask students to call out the answers. If helpful, either you or your students could give an additional example before moving on to the next question.

Answers
1 access = b (get into and move around in)
2 tremendous = a (great)
3 extends = c (makes something bigger or longer)
4 outcomes = b (results)
5 light up = c (look happy and excited)
6 concept = a (idea)

- **7b** Check students understand the words in italics and re-teach if necessary, or ask students if they can recall the example in the talk. Tell students to think of examples of the six things. Point out that they relate to some of the new words and phrases they have just learnt in Exercise 7a. Give them two minutes and make sure they note down their ideas.

Suggested answers
1 We can put in ramps and lifts as well as stairs; make doors and corridors wider.

2–3 Students' own answers

4 Better listening skills including finding it easier to follow a speaker's argument; knowledge of words and phrases that appear in the biographical information about Sue (e.g. *assumptions, exhilarating*) and in the Vocabulary in context section (including *outcomes*!); a new understanding of wheelchair users and disability in general.

5 If you heard some good news, if your friends gave you a present or a surprise party, etc.

6 The concept of sharing your toys; waiting for something good, like chocolate after a meal instead of now.

- **7c** Put students in pairs to tell each other their ideas.
- Go round and check they are doing the task correctly and notice errors, difficulties, or where they use L1. Help them by correcting or giving them the English they need. Focus especially on their use of the new words and phrases.
- At the end of the task, give some feedback about new language that came up, and errors to correct which you may have written on the board. Nominate one or two students to tell the class the most interesting things they said or heard.

8 MY PERSPECTIVE

- Put students in pairs to discuss the questions. Set a time limit of five minutes.
- Go round and help them with their ideas, making suggestions and asking questions.
- Stop the task after five minutes and regroup students. Tell them to share what they have been talking about with the group.
- Invite one or two students to share anything interesting they have heard with the whole class.

CHALLENGE

- Ask students to read the Challenge box and think of their 'anything'. Encourage them to think of goals and ambitions that they have sometimes thought would be good to do, but have never done.
- When most students have all their answers, put them in groups to share their ideas and find out who has similar goals and who has very different goals.
- Invite students to share their ideas with the class. Find out if anyone is close to trying to achieve their goals.

Homework
- Set Workbook Lesson 6D exercises on page 70 for homework.
- Students choose and watch another TED Talk about disability from the TED playlist, 'Designing for disability'.

6E Physical challenges

pp78–79

OPTIONAL LEAD IN

- Do a picture dictation. Choose a photo your students will enjoy. This could be something funny or from your life – a room in your house, for example. It should contain a number of elements, such as people, furniture, a few objects, etc.
- Before the lesson, prepare a description. Include some of the expressions from the Useful language box, e.g. *This photo shows my living room. There's a window and a door in the background, with the door on the left. It's obviously night time, because the light is on. My husband is standing in front of a chair on the right. He's holding our dog and they both look happy. Behind him, you can see …* If possible, choose a photo with a surprise element but don't include this information in the description. For example, it could be the 'living room' of a large tent.
- Tell students you are going to describe a photo which they must draw. Tell them whether the image is portrait (vertical) or landscape (horizontal). Reassure them that this is not an art class, you just want pictures that show they have understood correctly.
- Read the description at a slow, clear pace, but do not pause. Read it again. Then let students compare pictures and discuss the details.
- Invite them to ask any questions. Answer truthfully and give them time to make any changes to their drawings. You might decide to read it one more time.
- Finally, let students show each other their drawings, discuss any differences in the details they've drawn and where the misunderstanding lies, and compliment them on their artistic abilities. Reveal the photo!

SPEAKING Describing photos *p78*

- Put students in pairs to answer the questions. Encourage each pair to think of different dances, perhaps from different regions.
- Invite students to share what they know about the different dances with the class.

2

- 🎧 42 Explain the task. Play the audio once straight through.
- Let students compare answers.
- Check answers by nominating students to provide answers.

> **Answer**
> They are describing the photo on the right. One speaker says: 'it might be a stage show in a theatre'.

Audioscript 🎧 42

A: So, what's the question? 'What feelings are these dancers expressing?'

B: Yes, and 'How do they use their bodies and clothes to show their feelings?'

A: OK, so, this one shows some women dancing. In, um … It's some sort of costume.

B: It's an amazing costume they're wearing. Very colourful and … happy.

A: Right. So it looks as if they're in a show or something, because the clothes look very expensive. It must be during a festival of some kind.

B: Yes, or it might be a stage show in a theatre.

A: So, yes, the feeling is obviously happiness – just look at their faces.

B: Right. They look as if they're really enjoying themselves – all that movement and colour.

A: Yes, it's definitely some sort of celebration.

B: And I'd say they seem proud, with their hands in the air, like they're saying: 'Look at us, we are beautiful!'

A: Ha ha. Yes.

- Tell students that speaking exams in English sometimes involve a task where you need to describe or discuss a photograph or other image. Ask if anyone has done an exam like that and whether they had to describe photos. Elicit other situations where you might describe an image, view or scene, e.g. describing the rooms of a new apartment, during phone conversations, etc.
- Focus students' attention on the Useful language box and ask if anyone remembers any of these expressions when you were describing your photo (if you did the optional lead in). Tell them to complete the sentences with the expressions.
- Go round and check students are doing the task correctly and notice errors, difficulties, or where they use L1. Write some of these points on the board, or remember them for class feedback.
- 🎧 42 Play the audio again for students to check their sentences.
- Let students compare answers in pairs.
- Nominate students to give the answers. Check that everyone agrees with each answer before moving on to the next one.
- In feedback, pay special attention to the structures after the verbs of perception *looks* and *seems*: verb + adjective, verb + *like* + noun, verb + *as if* + phrase. Mention that in everyday speech it is normal to say *looks like* + phrase, though this may be seen as wrong in some exams and in more formal English. Elicit the other verbs of perception, which work with the same patterns: *sounds*, *feels*, *tastes* and *smells*. You might practise them by suggesting some perceived sounds, sights, etc. e.g. *You see a black cloud. Someone is cooking in the kitchen next door.*

- Explain the task.
- Go round and check students are doing the task correctly. Make a note of interesting uses of language, especially errors with expressions from the Useful language box, e.g. ~~They look like happy, In the right, … It can be a festival,~~ etc. Write some of these points on the board, or remember them for class feedback.
- Give the class feedback on their speaking performance, get students to correct their errors and comment on students' level of interaction.

- Look at the instructions. Set a time limit of about two minutes.
- Put students in pairs to describe their photos. They must each find their partner's photo in the book.

Extension

Students dictate a photo which their partner has to draw, like you did at the start of the lesson.

WRITING An informal email describing people *p79*

- Explain the task. Tell them to read the email on page 151.
- Go round and be available for questions about the email. Clarify that the email is a response by Aditi to Mauricio's email, and question 2 asks them to identify what she has done for Mauricio in this email.
- Put students in pairs to compare their answers.
- Nominate students to give answers to the class.

7 WRITING SKILL Informal language

- **7a** Ask if students would expect good friends in English-speaking environments to greet each other with *Hi* or *Hello*. Ask what the effect of using language which is formal with friends might be (it could sound slightly unfriendly). Explain the task. One student should keep page 79 open, the other should have their book open on page 151.
- While students are looking, prepare the board with the words 1–7 so that students can write the informal equivalents next to each one.
- Invite students to write their answers on the board.

- **7b** Explain the task.
- When most students have finished, let them compare their answers.
- Check answers around the class.

- **7c** Look at the instructions. Remind students to look at the expressions in the Useful language box
- Go round and check students are doing the task correctly and notice errors and make suggestions.
- Put students in groups of three or four to compare their versions.
- Give feedback on new language that came up, and errors to correct, which you may have written on the board.

Suggested answers

1 Hi Gurpreet, Thanks for your email. It's been ages since we spoke, so I was thrilled to get your news. How are things with you?

2 BTW, while I'm travelling I'll need somewhere to keep my stuff. I was wondering if I could keep it at your place. I should warn you – there's loads!

3 Anyway, I must go now; I'm in a rush to finish an essay at the mo. I'll write again soon, for sure. Say 'Hi' to Yuki when you see her. Bye for now, Francesca.

- Explain the task. Tell students to think of someone they admire and encourage them to think of people who have overcome challenges. They can be famous people or people the students know. The challenges they have faced could be any kind.
- Tell students to refer to the model on page 151 for help. Remind them that the advice at the back of the book, the informal language and the expressions in the Useful language box are there to help them. Also suggest the questions in Exercise 6 question 3 as prompts for writing.
- Set the writing for homework or set a time limit of about twenty minutes to do it in class. As students are writing, go round and offer help. You might note some common errors

for feedback when the time is up. Visit fast finishers to suggest ways that they could improve their emails.

Fast finishers

Students who finish quickly can write another informal email, this time to a friend about meeting an interesting person.

- When most students have finished, put them in groups to read each other's emails.
- When they have all read at least two or three emails, ask individuals to talk about the most interesting people they have read about.

Homework

- Set Workbook Lesson 6E and Review exercises on pages 71–73 for homework.
- Students write another informal email, this time to a friend about meeting an interesting person if they didn't do it in class.
- Students prepare three questions to test their classmates at the start of the next lesson about the things they have studied in Unit 6.

---

7 Shopping around

7A Money and me
pp80–83

Information about the photo

The Train Night Market, or *Talad Rot Fai* in Thai, is one of many places to shop in Bangkok which open at night to avoid the heat of the day. Night shopping is an important cultural tradition in Thailand, as it is in many hot countries. Shoppers enjoy the great atmosphere while buying clothes, shoes, accessories, smart phone accessories, as well as getting a bite to eat and drink.

OPTIONAL LEAD IN

- Focus students' attention on the photo or project it using the CPT. Elicit the kind of place this is for shopping (a market) and elicit other places people shop (out-of-town retail parks, supermarkets, shopping centres [shopping malls in US English], the high street, online stores, etc.). If possible, show students photos of these places to help comprehension.

- Dictate these instructions: *1 Think of one advantage and one disadvantage for each place. 2 Tick the places that you or your family go shopping. 3 Write something you buy in each place. 4 Choose the place you prefer to go shopping and say why.*

- Put students in pairs to discuss. In whole-class feedback, find out which places are most common and popular, and discuss the advantages and disadvantages of each place.

VOCABULARY Money and shopping *p81*

- Put students in groups to discuss the questions.
- Go round and make a note of difficulties students are experiencing in trying to express their ideas, especially to do with money and shopping.
- Nominate students from each group to share some of their groups' ideas. Encourage students to identify their shopping criteria, e.g. if the company name or brand matters to them, why, and why it might matter where the item was made.
- At the end of the task, give some feedback about new language that came up, and focus on errors to correct, which you may have written on the board.

- Look at the instructions. Students can use a dictionary or ask you for help as necessary.
- When most students have finished, have a competition to check understanding. Tell the class to call out the words and phrases in bold with the following meanings. The quickest

person gets a point. Read the definitions, then wait for a response.

a period when things are cheaper (a sale)
an organization that helps people who need it (a charity)
cheaper than usual because the shop has lowered the price (on special offer)
company symbols (logos)
famous company names, e.g. Adidas (brands)
give money away to someone who needs it (donate)
give someone money with the promise that they will give it back (lend)
look in different companies for the best thing to buy (shop around)
looking in a shop, but not looking for anything specific (browsing)
make money from working (earn)
no longer exists in a shop because they have all been bought (sold out / sell out)
not have enough money (can't afford)
owe money (be in debt)
receive money for something you bought because you give it back (get a refund)
return something to a shop (take it back)
take money from someone with the promise that you will give it back (borrow)
a cheap price for something (a good deal, a bargain)
use money badly (waste)
use money to buy something (spend)
- Congratulate the winner.

- Explain the task. You may decide to get them to give each sentence a score, e.g. *0 = It doesn't describe us at all, 3 = It describes us perfectly.*
- Put students in pairs to discuss the statements.

Fast finishers

Students who finish quickly can rewrite the sentences so that they describe them better. For example, they might rewrite *I'm careful what I spend my money on. I don't waste it on stuff I don't need* as *I'm not very careful what I spend my money on. I waste it on lots of things I don't need.* or *I'm quite careful about what I spend my money on but I sometimes make mistakes.*

4

- Look at the instructions. Let students work in the same pairs. Encourage them to think of example sentences to make the differences clear.
- In whole-class discussion, elicit example sentences as well as explanations.

Answers

1 You might *spend* money on something you really need or want. If you *waste* money, you may buy something you neither need nor want.
2 To *earn* means to make money from working. You only *win* money in a game, competition, lottery, bet, etc.
3 If you *borrow* (receive temporarily) money from me, I *lend* (give temporarily) it to you. They describe the same action but from opposite points of view: *lend ⇄ borrow*
4 In a *sale*, many or all of the items in a shop are cheaper than usual, e.g. after Christmas or in the summer. If an item is a *bargain*, the speaker thinks it is very good value, cheap for what it is worth.
5 If you *shop around*, you look for something specific in different shops to find the cheapest price for that thing; if you *browse*, you look at lots of different items in the same shop.
6 The *brand* is the name of the company and its products, e.g. *Nike*, *Apple*. The *logo* is the little image that shows a brand, e.g. the 'M' symbol for *McDonald's*.

5

- Explain the task. Tell students to try completing the opinions first without looking back at Exercise 2.
- Go round and check students are doing the task correctly and notice errors.
- When most students have finished, let them look at Exercise 2 to check their answers.
- To check answers, have one student read out what Akiko says, and someone else read out what Guillermo says. Ask the rest of the class to tell the speakers to stop if they disagree with a missing word.

Answers

1 deal **2** special offers **3** shopping **4** (special) offer / sale* **5** back **6** refund **7** brands **8** money **9** for **10** debts **11** spending **12** bargains **13** browsing **14** sells **15** pay **16** lending **17** earning / earn **18** donate

* 'on sale' and 'on offer' or 'on special offer' mean the same: the item is sold at a cheaper price than normal.

---

6 **MY PERSPECTIVE**

- Put students in pairs to decide whose attitude to shopping and money is better.
- When most students have finished, hold a whole-class discussion. The class could vote on the best attitude.

Extension / Fast finishers

Tell students to write a statement similar to Akiko and Guillermo's statements summarizing their attitude to money.

LISTENING p82

 7

- Teach the class *alternative*, something you can choose instead of the usual thing. Offer an example that relates to their lives, e.g. *If you don't want to eat lunch from the school cafeteria, an alternative is to bring your own lunch.*
- Look at the instructions. Use the types of shopping you discussed in the optional leadin at the beginning of lesson 7A to exemplify 'normal shopping'. You might ask students to predict what they think those alternatives are. Check students have read the question and that they understand that they may have one, two or three things in common.
- 🔔 **43** Play the audio once straight through.
- Let students compare their answers in pairs. Check answers as a class. Ask students to say why the other options are not possible.

> **Answer**
> a and b
> c isn't mentioned in alternative 3.

Audioscript 🔔 **43**

1

You can get a strange reaction to second-hand clothes around here. People have told me a t-shirt I'm wearing is nice, but when I say I bought it in a second-hand shop, I've been given strange looks! There aren't many second-hand shops around here so shopping around means travelling into the city. You can save a lot of money buying second hand, and good quality, well-made things can be found – a lot of them are better than most new clothes. And I love wearing some of the old fashions! Plus, these clothes weren't thrown away … so less rubbish for the planet to deal with!

2

I heard about these places in Germany where you can borrow things instead of buying them. Like a library, but for things, not just books. Say you need to put up some bookshelves in your bedroom but you need a special piece of equipment that you'll never use again. Instead of buying it, you can borrow it! And that's good for the environment as well as the bank account! The way it works is the things in the shop are donated by the customers. So, they give something they own to the shop, and then they can start borrowing from the shop! I love that idea. I wish one had been set up around here.

3

We live beyond the suburbs, close to farms, so it's ridiculous to waste money on food from the supermarket. We were shown at school how the environment pays a price for our food depending on how far it's been transported to get to us. So, I got my parents to buy our fruit and vegetables locally. And

now some of our neighbours are doing it too. It's delivered right from the farm to our door so it's fresher than the supermarket stuff and it's so much cheaper! There isn't the variety you'd get in the store, but you learn to use what you can get.

 8

- Give students time to read the questions and check any vocabulary.
- 🔔 **43** Play the audio.
- Give students a minute to compare their answers in pairs. Go around and identify information that students found hard to hear or do not agree on.
- Nominate students to share their answers, and check whether the rest of the class agrees.

> **Answers**
> **a** 1 (*less rubbish*), 2 (*good for the environment*)
> **b** 3 (*It's delivered straight from the farm to our door*)
> **c** 1 (*good quality … better than most new clothes*),
>   3 (*it's fresher than the supermarket stuff*)
> **d** 1 (*I've been given strange looks*)
> **e** 2 (*I wish one had been set up around here*)
> **f** 1 (*shopping around means travelling into the city*),
>   3 (*There isn't the variety you'd get in the store*)

9 MY PERSPECTIVE

- Put students in pairs to discuss the questions.
- Go round and check students are doing the task correctly and notice errors, difficulties, or where they use L1. Help them by correcting or giving them the English they need, and make a note of any language points to go over with the class. Encourage further discussion by asking them to consider aspects that may change their attitudes, such as borrowing from friends and family or borrowing from strangers, etc.
- At the end of the task, give some feedback about new language that came up, and focus on errors to correct, which you may have written on the board. You can also share some interesting things you heard with the class.

GRAMMAR The passive p82

 10

- Write the two sentences on the board. Ask the class which sentence they think was used in the audio in Exercise 7 (b - the passive sentence). Ask why they think this.
- Ask questions 1–4 to the class, nominating different students to answer each one.

> **Answers**
> **1** Both are in the present simple.
> **2** A driver is the subject, *the food* is the object.
> **3** *The food* is the subject, there is no object.
> **4** In sentence b *the food* is emphasized.

- Explain the task.
- You can either go through the answers with the whole class, or wait for them to read the Grammar reference on page 140 and then ask the class the grammar-checking questions, or nominate individual students to give their answers.

Answers
a present perfect   b present simple   c past simple
d present simple   e past perfect   f past simple

Grammar reference and practice

Ask students to do Exercises 1–3 on page 141 now, or set them for homework.

Answers to Grammar practice exercises
1
1 a (agent is obvious)   **2** a (agent is people in general)
3 a (agent is repeated)
2
1 is affected   **2** were   **3** are   **4** may have been
5 made   **6** is   **7** has been   **8** isn't
3
1 has been designed   **2** have been put   **3** We were encouraged   **4** are kept   **5** had been encouraged
6 was designed   **7** were also placed   **8** is played

- Explain the task. Tell students that there may be more than one reason.
- Invite volunteers to explain each sentence.

Suggested answers
a Agent unknown / unimportant
b Agent people in general
c Agent people in general / unknown
d Agent is important new information, so included at the end.
e Agent unimportant, unknowable (*someone*)
f Agent obvious (*the teacher*) or unimportant

- Look at the instructions.
- Let students compare with a partner before sharing answers with the whole class.
- Ask the class what other types of shops have been changed by the internet (almost every industry has been affected, and some have almost disappeared, e.g. video shops, bookshops).

Answers
1 Things people don't want any longer have always been bought and sold by second-hand shops.
2 However, in the past, only the most common things were found in these shops.
3 Specialist objects were generally only discovered by experts and collectors.
4 For example, before the internet had been invented, where could you find second-hand camping equipment / where could second-hand camping equipment be found?
5 Now search engines are used to find the right thing at the right price, in the right place.

- Tell students that the next text is about other advantages of online buying and selling. Explain the task.
- Go round and check students are doing the task correctly and notice errors or difficulties. Offer support as necessary.
- Check answers around the class. Get students to take turns reading out completed sentences.

Answers
1 can be made   **2** was invented   **3** had been bought / were bought   **4** were not only sold   **5** could earn
6 have been sent   **7** have been created   **8** was established   **9** is put   **10** offers   **11** are advertised
12 is made

Extension

Write on the board the following prompts: *community, small businesses, tax, exercise, jobs, quality, packaging*. Put students in pairs to discuss any potential disadvantages they can think of regarding online shopping. Explain that the prompts may help them think of ideas, but that they can discuss their own ideas instead.

- Tell the class that they are going to play a game in pairs. Explain the rules, and make sure students understand that they can think of anything, but that you will decide whether their ideas are valid.
- Give one or two examples of things that have been borrowed to help students understand what they can include. For example, you could show them your jacket and explain that it was borrowed by a friend last week.
- Set a time limit of five minutes for students to think of as many things as possible for each category. Go round and check that students are thinking of valid things, not cheating by copying other pairs, etc.
- Stop the activity. Ask for a show of hands for the first category of any pairs who have more than three items on their list. Congratulate them all. Ask for those who have more than five/six/seven, etc. items on their list until there

is only one pair left. Ask them to read out their list. Decide whether all their items are true or interesting, and congratulate them on winning the first point.

- Do the same for the other five categories. Announce the overall winners.

Suggested answers

have been borrowed – items of stationery and clothing, books, bike, personal possessions such as mobile phones, MP3 player, etc.

haven't ever been used – items of stationery, books that have never been read, an item in their bag, etc.

aren't sold any more – old products that have been replaced, e.g. videos, things that have been shown to be bad for the environment, e.g. deodorants containing CFCs, etc.

were made by hand – decorative objects at home, a piece of furniture, e.g. a table, clothing, e.g. a dress or a sweater, etc.

were made in another country – cars, motorbikes, bikes, electronic products, e.g. TVs, computers, phones, clothing (students can look at the labels of items around them), etc.

were designed for a different purpose – a cup or glass that is used to keep pens and pencils, the internet, which was designed to share academic information but has thousands of uses, etc.

- Explain the task. Give them an example of another category, such as 'things bought in the same shop in your town', or 'things that are bought every week by people'.
- Go round and check students are doing the task correctly. Help them come up with ideas if necessary.
- When most students have finished, invite different pairs in turn to come to the front of the class and present their items so that others can guess the category.

Homework

- Set Workbook Lesson 7A exercises on pages 74–77 for homework.
- Students write about a special possession of theirs. They describe what it is, where it was from, what it's made of, what special significance it has for them, and so on.
- Students find out about one industry and how it has been affected by technology. They present it in the following lesson.

7B Waste not, want not
pp84–85

LEAD IN

- Write on the board the title of today's lesson: *Waste not, want not*. Tell the class that this expression is said when you decide not to throw something away but to use it again. For example, you might keep a jar when cooking because it might be useful on another day. *Want* here means 'to need', so the expression means: 'If you don't waste things (throw them away), you'll have everything you need.'
- Ask students what things they tend to keep that other people throw away.

READING p84

- Put students in pairs to discuss the questions.
- Invite students to suggest some ideas for each question.

- Put students in A and B pairs. Explain the task.
- Set a time limit of no more than five minutes. Go round and check students are doing the task correctly and are not reading the other text. Stop the activity after five minutes or when students have finished.
- Check answers around the class.

Answers

A
1 They wanted to make space; save money and change their consumerist lifestyle.
2 No. They bought food.
3 They learned to grow vegetables.
4 It was quite difficult sometimes when they were tired. They had to learn to enjoy cooking every day, for example.

B
1 They wanted to teach the children that shopping and having new things isn't the only way to live.
2 No. They bought food and essential household items, e.g. toothpaste. They also bought things second-hand.
3 They learned how to create a website, make clothes, bags and soap, and to repair clothes.
4 It was easier than they expected.

3

- Tell students to cover up the texts on the right-hand page. Explain the task.
- 🎧 **44** When most students have finished, elicit the answers but don't say if they're correct or not. Tell students to read the whole text to check their answers.
- Check answers as a whole class.

VOCABULARY BUILDING Adverbs *p84*

Look at the instructions. You may decide to do this exercise with the whole class if you think they aren't familiar with adverbs.

Teaching tip

Adverbs

To identify what an adverb is modifying, ask yourself which word or phrase in the sentence the adverb is most closely related to. Adverbs modify:
verbs:
  He **walked slowly** down the road.
other adverbs:
  He walked **extremely slowly** down the road.
adjectives:
  The road was **very quiet**.
and whole sentences:
  Fortunately, a car came along and took him to the next town.
  Normally, just add -*ly* to the adjective. If the adjective ends in -*y*, change the -*y* to -*i* (e.g. *happ**i**ly*). If the adjective ends in -*le*, replace the -*e* with -*y* (e.g. *responsib**ly***). If the adjective ends in -*ic*, add -*ally* (*basic**ally***). There are few exceptions to these rules.
  Some of the most common adverbs are irregular: *wrong, hard, fast, early*. *Well* is the adverb from *good*. Mistakes are often made around this area.

5

- Tell students to make the adverbs. Warn them that there are a couple of irregular adverbs in the list and one or two tricky spellings.
- Let them compare their answers in pairs before inviting confident students to write their answers on the board.

6

- Explain the task.
- Go round and check students are doing the task correctly and offering help if necessary.
- Put students in groups to compare their sentences.

Suggested answers
1 … completely impossible / too hard, actually.
2 … busily, eagerly preparing for my exams / completely busy / lazy, etc.
3 … eat healthily / live independently / go out, realistically.
4 … am often completely exhausted / sleep well / occasionally feel sick of shopping for a long time.
5 … usually do it quite fast / occasionally get my mum to buy things for me.

Fast finishers

Students who finish quickly can take one of the adverbs and make as many sentences as possible which contain it.

7 MY PERSPECTIVE

- Keep students in their groups to discuss the questions.
- In feedback, find out which students are the least consumerist, the most self-sufficient, and so on.

Extension

Get students to roleplay an interview with one of the people involved in the two stories, including one of Jen's kids, perhaps, or between the roommates. Ask them to think of something one of them wants to buy (e.g. pizza, a toy, to rent a movie, a new pair of shoes) and what another member of the house thinks about that. Get students in their groups or pairs to practise the situation and act it out, eventually in front of the class.

CRITICAL THINKING Reading between the lines *p84*

Ask a student to read the Critical thinking box to the class. Then put them in pairs to discuss the questions.

Suggested answers
1 Both groups present it as necessary, but, in fact, the experiment was probably something they really wanted to do because they were interested in becoming less dependent on commercial products and consumerism.
2 They have achieved control over their lives, and can say 'we've done something good'.
3 To show other people that it can be done; to move their careers in new directions; to become famous.
4 For many people, seeing others make big changes in their lifestyle may encourage them to do the same.

9

- Look at the instructions and do the first item with the whole class. Make sure students discuss why they think it was one speaker or the other.
- Tell students to do the rest of the exercise on their own.
- When most students have finished, let them compare in pairs.
- Check answers as a class.

Answers
Geoffrey said 1 (the changes seemed more significant for Geoffrey), 2 (new clothes may be more significant for young single people than parents of children) and 3 (Geoffrey was worried about money).

Jen said 4 (Jen worked on her own more, while Geoffrey and his flatmate worked as a team), 5 (they talked about repairing things), 6 (they have children, more likely to make a Christmas tree) and 7 (£2,000 is not a large saving over a year).

Homework
- Set Workbook Lesson 7B exercises on pages 78–79 for homework.
- Students find out about other experiments in anti-consumerism that people have tried. Suggest search terms they can use: 'make do and mend', 'buy nothing new', 'downshifting', 'use less stuff'.

7C   Services in my town
pp86–87

GRAMMAR *have / get something done* *p86*

Tell students to look at the map of Singapore, where Emma lives, and read the sentences. Ask them to think of as many ways as possible that Emma's life is similar to theirs.

Suggested answers
They both live in a city / near a river / in Asia, etc; they have the same dentist that they always have; they have a bicycle; they can't fix big jobs on their own; they've broken shoes and had them repaired; they like pizza; they sometimes get food delivered, etc.

Ask students to look at the Grammar box and tell you what *it* refers to in each sentence.

Answers
a pizza   b her bicycle

- Explain the task.
- You can either go through the answers with the whole class, or wait for them to read the Grammar reference on page 140 and then ask the class the grammar-checking questions, or nominate individual students to give their answers.

Answers
1 No, it is not important. 'We' (her family) asks them.
2 Again, no, it is unimportant. 'I' (Emma) asked them to do it.
3 c

Grammar reference and practice
Tell students to do Exercises 4 and 5 on page 141 now, or set them for homework.

Answers to Grammar practice exercises
4
1 We had the house cleaned by a cleaning company after the party. / After the party, we had the house cleaned by a cleaning company.
2 Please get the fire alarm fixed before something terrible happens.
3 He received so many unwanted calls from companies that he had his phone number changed.
4 I had / I'm having / I'm going to have my old trainers repaired instead of buying a new pair.

5 Where can I get this suit cleaned?

6 Before they moved in, they had all the walls painted. / They had all the walls painted before they moved in.

7 You should have your car tested every year.

8 Get your university application checked for errors before you send it.

5

1 to get / have the oil changed　**2** to get / have it cleaned

3 got / had some flowers sent　**4** gets / has his hair cut

5 get / have a/my photo taken

6 got / had some (Chinese) food delivered

4

- Explain the task. You could set it as a race to find all three sentences as quickly as possible.
- If done as a race, get the winner to read out the sentences; otherwise, get different students to write them on the board.

Answers

*But instead of occasionally going to a restaurant and **having food prepared** for them, now they always cooked at home.*
(lines 18–20)

*They stopped **getting their hair cut** professionally.*
(lines 20–21)

*They also agreed on a few exceptions to make things easier, like **having the washing machine repaired** if it ever broke down (it didn't). (lines 53–56)*

5

- Tell students to use the prompts to write the three sentences about Emma.
- Let them compare answers in pairs.
- Check answers as a class by nominating students to read out a sentence at a time.

Answers

1 She and her brother have their teeth checked every six months.

2 Last week, she got her eyes tested.

3 She wanted to have her boots repaired.

Extension

- Dictate the following sentences. Explain that there is one mistake in all except one of them.

1 *A stolen car found on our street this morning.*
2 *We had to have cut down the tree in our garden because it was dying.*
3 *How many copies of the song are downloaded since Monday?*
4 *If you manage to talk to the author, you should get your book signed.*
5 *The little girl had already been spotted the present and was trying to open it.*

6 *Are you going to cut your hair in the same style, or will you ask the hairdresser for a new look?*

- Tell students to work on their own and to identify the correct sentence and correct the incorrect ones.
- Now get them to swap their notebooks with a classmate for marking. Tell them to award each other a point for every good correction and five points for identifying the correct one. Elicit the answers and write them clearly on the board.

Answers

1 WRONG: passive – missing auxillary '**was** found'

2 WRONG: causative – word order 'have **the tree cut down**'

3 WRONG: passive – present perfect formation '**have been** downloaded'

4 CORRECT

5 WRONG: passive past perfect structure when active voice needed – 'had already **spotted**'

6 WRONG: causative needed but an active sentence 'to **have your hair cut**'

6

- Explain that students can now use the new structure to talk about their lives. Point to the prompts in the box to help them with ideas, but encourage them to think of other services that they or their families use or have used in the past.
- Go round and help students with vocabulary they need and to check they are doing the task correctly.
- Invite students to share their ideas with the rest of the class.

Suggested answers

We don't get our shoes cleaned. My dad always does everyone's shoes.

My sister had her laptop fixed last year because it had a virus.

I get my hair cut every two or three months.

We usually get the car washed at the garage in one of those machines.

7 PRONUNCIATION Sentence stress

- **7a** Look at the instructions. Students do the exercise on their own. Don't check answers at this stage.
- **7b** 🎧 **45** Play the audio. Tell students to listen and check their answers.
- Tell them to listen again to find out which words are stressed. Play the audio again.
- You may decide to drill the questions chorally and individually to check everyone can say them with natural stress. Then let students practise on their own.

Answers and audioscript 🎧 **45**

1

A: *Have you **ev**er had your **sho**pping de**liv**ered?*

B: *No, I haven't. We live too far from the supermarket. What about you?*

A: *Yes, sometimes we get it delivered.*

2

A: *Have you **ev**er had your **phone** re**paired**?*

B: *Yes, I had to have the screen replaced on my first phone because I dropped it.*

A: *Oh no!*

3

A: *Have you **ev**er had **break**fast brought **up** to your bedroom?*

B: *Only when I was sick.*

A: *Me, too.*

4

A: *Have you **ev**er had a **tooth** taken out?*

B: *Yes, I had to have a tooth removed because it was growing in the wrong direction.*

5

A: *Have you **ev**er had your **pho**to **ta**ken with a **fa**mous **per**son?*

B: *Yes, actually, I met Juan Martin Del Potro once and my friend took our photo.*

A: *Who's he?*

Note: The causative *have* or *get* is not normally stressed.

- **7c** Put students in pairs to ask each other the questions.
- Go round and listen carefully for a natural stress pattern in their questions.
- Invite students to share interesting information they have learnt about their partners.

Fast finishers

Students who finish quickly can ask their own questions with *Have you ever had …?*

 8

- Explain that they are going to complete sentences about 'the one percent', the very richest group of people in society. You may decide to share some facts about social inequality here.

> **Background information**
>
> **Social inequality**
> According to an Oxfam report in January 2016, the gap between rich and poor is widening at a faster rate than was previously thought. 'In 2015, just 62 individuals had the same wealth as 3.6 billion people – the bottom half of humanity. This figure is down from 388 individuals as recently as 2010.'

- If you think students are managing the grammar well, have them do this exercise in pairs orally. Tell them to take turns to say alternate sentences correctly, then to swap over and say them again.
- If you feel that the class still needs time to process the structure slowly, let them write the sentences first.
- Check answers as a class.

> **Answers**
> 1 … <u>have/get</u> your clothes <u>chosen</u> for you every morning.
> 2 … <u>had/got</u> your birthday parties <u>planned</u> professionally when you were a child.
> 3 … <u>have had/got</u> your hair <u>cut</u> by a hair stylist at home since you were little.
> 4 … <u>have/get</u> your shoes <u>cleaned</u> for you every day.
> 5 … <u>have/get</u> your dogs <u>walked</u> when you don't feel like doing it.
> 6 … <u>have/get</u> your social media <u>managed</u> by online experts.
> 7 … <u>have/get</u> your holidays <u>arranged</u> by your personal travel agent.
> 8 … <u>have/get</u> your bag <u>carried</u> to school for you.

 9

- Put students in groups to discuss the questions. Point out the argument in the example showing how living in cities may mean you have more things done for you than if you lived in the countryside. Ask students to think of ways that the other factors might affect your use of services.
- Go round and check students are doing the task correctly and notice errors, difficulties or any interesting language they use.
- At the end of the task, give some feedback about new language that came up, and focus on errors to correct, which you may have written on the board. You can also share some interesting things you heard with the class.

> **Suggested answers**
> People live further from their families. Therefore you are more likely to have jobs done that may have been done within the family before, e.g. washing and ironing clothes. Busy people with long days at work may not have time to do these things themselves.
>
> Some people have more money. If you have money to spend, you are more likely to pay others to do jobs that you might have done, e.g. cook and clean.
>
> Social media means that we are more aware of the services on offer. Also, digital services may be offered that can be done anywhere in the world. For example, you can have your photos edited, printed and framed and sent to your house from anywhere in the world. You can have books delivered, when before you would have bought them from a shop, etc.
>
> If more women, who traditionally did most of the household and 'carer' work, are now following careers and are more aware of the inequalities between men and women, they are less likely to accept their role as service providers and will expect businesses to do some of this work for them.

⑩ CHOOSE

The idea is for students to make their own choice of activity here. However, you might want to make the decision for them, in which case explain why. Alternatively, you may decide to let students do more than one task. You could divide the class into groups and have each group do a different task – or you could have a vote on which task the whole class should do. For the vote:

- put students in pairs or groups to decide which they prefer.

- take a vote on each task.

- if the vote is tied, ask one student from each side to explain which is best and take the vote again. You can decide if there is still no change.

- Option 1 is a speaking task. Students can create physical or digital maps to present their information.

- Option 2 is an online research task. Be aware that some people have services done that may not be appropriate for teenagers. Elicit some ideas of what they can look for to direct their searches towards the more appropriate services. Suggest search terms such as 'home delivery services', 'pet pampering', 'unusual home improvements' or 'strange services companies provide'.

- Option 3 is a writing task. Students practise writing opinion essays, so direct them back to page 42 and the Writing bank on page 150 for guidance.

Homework

- Set Workbook Lesson 7C exercises on pages 80–81 for homework.

- If students didn't write their opinion essays in Exercise 10, set this task for homework.

- You might want to tell students to watch the track called *Unit 7 TED Talk* on the *Perspectives* website before they come to the next class.

7D Grow your own clothes *pp88–89*

- Tell students the title of the TED Talk they are going to watch. Invite guesses as to what it might be about.

- ▶ **7.0** Tell them they are going to see a short text on the DVD to introduce the talk and the speaker, and play the *About the speaker* section. Then do the vocabulary exercise.

- To practise the new words further, write them on the board. Read out the definitions in random order. Students have to call out the correct word for each definition.

moves easily without breaking (flexible)
material used to make clothes (fabric)
not damaging the environment (sustainable)
small living things that can only be seen with a microscope (microbes)
stuff from plants that is used to make paper (cellulose)
thin sheets (layers)
things from nature that people can use (resources)

- Erase a couple of the words from the board and repeat the task with the definitions in a different order. Keep doing this until all of the words have been erased but the students can still call them out when you say the definition.

Answers to About the speaker

1 fabric = c (material used to make clothes)
2 microbes = b (small living things that can only be seen with a microscope)
3 layers = a (thin sheets)
4 cellulose = c (stuff from plants that is used to make paper)
5 flexible = b (moves easily without breaking)
6 sustainable = c (not damaging to the environment)
7 resources = b (things from nature that people can use)

TED Talk About the speaker

*Suzanne Lee is a fashion designer but in her research she works more like a biologist. She is developing a new **fabric** that uses bacteria and other **microbes** to create **layers** of **cellulose**.*

*This material, when dried, is light and **flexible**, and may one day be a **sustainable** addition to the **resources** we already have for making clothes and other objects.*

Suzanne's idea worth spreading is that we can use bacteria to produce materials that we can turn into clothes, as sustainable and biodegradable alternatives to leather, cotton and plastics.

AUTHENTIC LISTENING SKILLS
Reformulating *p88*

As well as teaching aspects of phonology and listening skills, these tasks also allow:

- you to pre-teach some vocabulary.
- students to read and hear new language before they listen to the whole text.
- students to tune in to the speaker's voice and style.

- Write on the board *English is a lingua franca, which means you can use it with other people who speak different languages from you.*
- Ask if students have heard the phrase *lingua franca* before. Ask them what it means and how they know this. Point to the second part of the sentence, which reformulates the complex new term into simpler language. Underline *lingua franca*, and circle the rest of the sentence to show the relationship between the term and the reformulation.
- Ask for a volunteer to read the Authentic listening skills box for the whole class. Then tell students to read and listen to the extract, and identify the word or phrase which is made clearer by the second sentence.
- 🎧 **46** Play the audio.
- Check the answer as a class.

Answers
The word *efficiency* is made clearer by the second sentence. (It is efficient because you don't need to grow lots that will be wasted)

- Explain the task.
- 🎧 **47** When students have finished, play the audio so that they can check their answers.
- To check answers, ask students to explain what is reformulated in each instance, and how the reformulation helps understanding.

Answers
1 b **2** a **3** c

WATCH *p88*

- Put students in pairs to discuss the questions. Check that they understand *labels* and *biodegrade* (you could compare plastic and paper shopping bags for this). Tell them to make notes, especially for the second question.
- Go round the class, checking students' understanding of different materials' names and helping them think of advantages and disadvantages of each one.
- Check answers as a class.

Suggested answers
1, **3** and **5** Students' own answers

2 Cotton is cool and lets your skin breathe, but it can be easy to tear; leather may be seen as cruel to animals, and it's also expensive, but it can be fashionable and feels and looks good; plastic may be cheap but it could be sweaty; wool is warm in winter and very comfortable, but is easily damaged by washing and wearing. Other materials include: silk, denim (tough cotton), hemp, polyester.

4 Natural materials can be biodegraded by bacteria easily, i.e. cotton, wool, leather and silk. Artificial materials made from plastics are mostly very difficult to biodegrade.

If you are short of time, or want a different approach to the video, you may want to watch the whole talk all the way through with only some brief checking questions. A version of this is on the DVD and is labelled as *TED Talk with activities*. At the end of each section, there is a short gist question. Pause after each question on screen so students can give their answers, then play the answer.

Answers to gist questions on DVD
Part 1
What is Suzanne talking about?
c How to make the material.

Part 2
Which three of these topics does Suzanne mention?
a a problem with the material
b her future hopes for the material
c how the material is prepared

Part 3
Which of these is <u>not</u> an advantage of the technology?
c The material can replace traditional fabrics.

- Explain the task. Give students time to read the recipe and predict which words and numbers fit in each space. Make sure they understand that not all the words and numbers are used.
- ▶ **7.1** Play Part 1 straight through.
- Ask students to compare their ideas in pairs. Go round and notice how well they did in order to decide how quickly to go through answers, and whether you will need to play Part 1 again.
- Nominate students to give their answers.

Answers
1 tea **2** sugar **3** bath **4** 30 **5** hot **6** 3
7 sheets **8** 2–3

TED Talk Part 1 script ▶ 7.1

So as a fashion designer, I've always tended to think of materials something like this, or this, or maybe this. But then I met a biologist, and now I think of materials like this – green tea, sugar, a few microbes and a little time.

So we start by brewing the tea. I brew up to about 30 litres of tea at a time, and then while it's still hot, add a couple of kilos of sugar. We stir this in until it's completely dissolved and then pour it into a growth bath. We need to check that the temperature has cooled to below 30 degrees C. And then we're ready to add the living organism. And along with that, some acetic acid. And once you get this process going, you can actually recycle your previous fermented liquid. We need to maintain an optimum temperature for the growth. And I use a heat mat to sit the bath on and a thermostat to regulate it. And actually, in hot weather, I can just grow it outside. So, this is my mini fabric farm.

After about three days, the bubbles will appear on the surface of the liquid. So this is telling us that the fermentation is in full swing. And the bacteria are feeding on the sugar nutrients in the liquid. So they're spinning these tiny nano-fibres of pure cellulose. And they're sticking together, forming layers and giving us a sheet on the surface. After about two to three weeks, we're looking at something which is about an inch in thickness. So, the bath on the left is after five days, and on the right, after ten. And this is a static culture. You don't have to do anything to it; you just literally watch it grow. It doesn't need light.

5

- Explain the task. Tell students to read the summary before watching Part 2.
- ▶ 7.2 Play Part 2 straight through.
- Ask students to compare their ideas in pairs. Go round and notice how well they did in order to decide how quickly to go through answers, and whether you will need to play Part 2 again.
- Nominate students to give their answers.

> **Answers**
> **1** wash **2** water **3** thinner **4** paper **5** leather
> **6** is still wet **7** water **8** weak

TED Talk Part 2 script ▶ 7.2

And when it's ready to harvest, you take it out of the bath and you wash it in cold, soapy water. At this point, it's really heavy. It's over 90 percent water, so we need to let that evaporate. So I spread it out onto a wooden sheet. Again, you can do that outside and just let it dry in the air. And as it's drying, it's compressing, so what you're left with, depending on the recipe, is something that's either like a really lightweight, transparent paper, or something which is much more like a flexible vegetable leather. And then you can either cut that out and sew it conventionally, or you can use the wet material to form it around a three-dimensional shape. And as it evaporates, it will knit itself together, forming seams.

What I can't yet do is make it water-resistant. So, if I was to walk outside in the rain wearing this dress today, I would immediately start to absorb huge amounts of water. The dress would get really heavy, and eventually the seams would probably fall apart – leaving me feeling rather naked. Possibly a good performance piece, but definitely not ideal for everyday wear. What I'm looking for is a way to give the material the qualities that I need. So what I want to do is say to a future bug, 'Spin me a thread. Align it in this direction. Make it hydrophobic. And while you're at it, just form it around this 3D shape.'

6

- Explain the task. Tell students to read questions 1–7 before watching Part 3.
- ▶ 7.3 Play Part 3 straight through.
- Ask students to compare their ideas in pairs. Go round and notice how well they did in order to decide how quickly to go through answers, and whether you will need to play Part 3 again.
- Nominate students to give their answers.

> **Answers**
> **3, 5, 7**
> **3** (*at the end of use, we could biodegrade it naturally …*)
> **5** (*We could … imagine growing a lamp, a chair …*)
> **7** (*this one is actually biodegrading in front of your eyes … Okay, we'll let you go and save it …*)

TED Talk Part 3 script ▶ 7.3

BG = Bruno Giussani, SL = Suzanne Lee

What excites me about using microbes is their efficiency. So, we only grow what we need. There's no waste. And in fact, we could make it from a waste stream – so for example, a waste sugar stream from a food processing plant. Finally, at the end of use, we could biodegrade it naturally along with your vegetable peelings. What I'm not suggesting is that microbial cellulose is going to be a replacement for cotton, leather or other textile materials. But I do think it could be quite a smart and sustainable addition to our increasingly precious natural resources.

Ultimately, maybe it won't even be fashion where we see these microbes have their impact. We could, for example, imagine growing a lamp, a chair, a car or maybe even a house. So I guess what my question to you is: in the future, what would you choose to grow? Thank you very much.

BG: *Suzanne, just a curiosity, what you're wearing is not random.*

SL: *No.*

BG: *This is one of the jackets you grew?*

SL: *Yes, it is. It's probably – part of the project's still in process because this one is actually biodegrading in front of your eyes. It's absorbing my sweat, and it's feeding on it.*

BG: *Okay, so we'll let you go and save it, and rescue it. Suzanne Lee.*

SL: *Thank you.*

- Put students in pairs to do the task.
- After a few minutes, join pairs to make groups of four. Let them combine their lists before asking students to help you compile a master list on the board.

Suggested answers

Advantages – It's a sustainable resource, easy to grow, easy to shape, efficient (no waste), could use materials made in the same way to make other things.

Disadvantages – it's not water-resistant yet, people may not like the idea of wearing bacteria!

8 VOCABULARY IN CONTEXT

- **8a** ▶ **7.4** Tell students that they are going to watch some clips from the talk which contain new or interesting words or phrases. They should choose the correct meaning for each one. Play the Vocabulary in context section. Pause after each question on screen so students can choose the correct definition, then play the answer. If you like, you can ask students to call out the answers. If helpful, either you or your students could give an additional example before moving on to the next question.
- Clarify the pronunciation of the new words. Pay special attention to the /ʃ/ sound in *precious* and *efficiency*; also, the vowel sounds in *spread* (/e/), *pour* (/ɔː/), *naked* (/eɪ/) and *bug* (/ʌ/). Point out that although *parent* is pronounced /peərənt/, like *pair*, *transparent* is /trænspærənt/, like *parrot*. Point out the first-syllable stress in *valuable*, and that it has three syllables. Drill the words chorally and individually.

Answers
1 pour = c (make a liquid come out of a container that is in your hand)
2 spread = b (make it flat)
3 transparent = c (possible to see through)
4 naked = b (not wearing any clothes)
5 bug = b (small creature)
6 precious = a (valuable)
7 efficiency = a (how well they use energy)

- **8b** Check students understand the words in italics and re-teach if necessary, or ask students if they can recall the example in the talk. Tell students to think of examples of the five things. Point out that they relate to some of the new words and phrases they have just learnt in Exercise 8a. Give them two minutes and make sure they note down their ideas.
- Put students in pairs to tell each other their ideas. Go round and check they are doing the task correctly and notice errors, difficulties, or where they use L1. Help them by correcting or giving them the English they need. Focus especially on their use of the new words and phrases.

- At the end of the task, give some feedback about new language that came up, and look at any errors to correct, which you may have written on the board. Nominate one or two students to tell the class the most interesting things they said or heard.

Suggested answers
1 butter, jam, pâté, chocolate spread, etc.   2 glass, Perspex, ice, diamond, etc.   3 spider, scorpion, etc.
4 students' own answers   5 swimming, exam writing, etc.

CHALLENGE

- Ask students to read the Challenge box and make notes for themselves. Be available for questions about vocabulary and the task.
- When most students have all their answers, put them in pairs or small groups to share their ideas. Go round and help them with any language difficulties where necessary.
- When most students have shared their ideas, nominate students to share their thoughts on each of the questions with the class.

Homework
- Set Workbook Lesson 7D exercises on page 82 for homework.
- Students explore the world of biodegradable packaging and find out five ways that they and their families can create less waste as shoppers.
- Students choose and watch another TED Talk about fashion from the TED playlist, 'Walk, walk, fashion baby'.

7E Buying and selling

pp90–91

SPEAKING *p90*

- Put students in pairs to talk about the photo and answer the questions about buying clothes.
- In feedback, ask what students have bought recently, and find out what their attitudes are to buying clothes as presents and to buying shoes and clothes online.

- Explain the task.
- 🎧 **48** Play the audio once straight through.
- Let students compare answers in pairs.
- Nominate students to share their answers with the class.

> **Answers**
> **1** b **2** c **3** a

Audioscript 🎧 48

1

A: Can I help you?

B: No. It's OK, I'm just looking.

A: No problem. Just let me know if you need any help.

B: Thanks … Er, excuse me.

A: Yes?

B: Um, I'm looking for black t-shirts. Where are they?

A: Over there. They're all women's, though.

B: Yes, I know, thanks. It's not for me.

2

C: Do you need any help?

D: Er, yes, please. Have you got these in a 13?

C: I'm not sure we have that size, Sir. These ones only go up to 12, I think.

D: Oh, really? Hmm.

C: These are very popular. I think we have them in larger sizes.

D: No, I'm not looking for boots. I'm looking for something more classy. Don't worry, thanks anyway.

C: You're welcome.

3

E: Here you are. Is this what you're looking for?

F: Yeah, maybe. But I'm a large. That looks a little small. Hold on … Excuse me!

G: Yes?

F: Do you have this in a larger size?

G: I think so, yes … We only have it in red.

F: That's OK.

G: Here.

F: Oh, thanks. Where can I try it on?

G: The changing rooms are over there.

E: So? Does it fit?

F: I think so. It's very comfortable … What do you think?

E: Ooh, that looks nice. It really suits you.

F: You think so? OK. I'll get it.

- Explain the task.
- 🎧 **48** Play the audio.
- Go round and notice how well students did without giving any feedback. Decide whether you need to play the audio again. If you do, you could stop at key points.
- Let students nominate each other to share their answers with the class. Make sure they say the whole expression, not just the missing words. Drill each expression chorally. After each one, check understanding, by asking students to translate it to L1 if you understand it, and ask for the equivalent from the Useful language box.

> **Answers**
> **1** looking **2** 13 **3** looking for **4** large **5** only have **6** can I try it on **7** it fit **8** suits you
> **9** get it
>
> **1** = *It's OK, I'm just browsing.* **2** = *Do you have these in a larger size?* **3** = *I'm after something smarter.*
> **4** = *I need a size 'L'.* **5** = *We've only got red ones.*
> **6** = *Where are the changing rooms?* **7** = *Is it the right size?* **8** = *It looks really good on you.* **9** = *I'll buy it.*

Extension

- Put students in pairs to practise putting these expressions into mini-conversations. Tell them to think of something you might hear either before or after each expression. Offer a couple of examples to get them started, e.g. *Can I help you? – No, it's OK, I'm just looking, thanks. / Have you got these in a large? – I'll go and see.*
- Go round the class listening for correct pronunciation and stress. Invite volunteers to share their conversations.

4

- Explain the task.
- Let students compare their answers in pairs.
- Go through the answers with the class, checking understanding and drilling the expressions. Check understanding of *plain, pockets, sleeves, stripes* and *shade* using the clothes that people are wearing in class.
- Drill each expression chorally.

Teaching tip

Using the audioscript

For dialogues in everyday situations, such as shops, train stations, etc. consider letting students memorize dialogues that they are likely to use in the future. Memorization may help students gain confidence and fluency in these predictable situations. Here's one way to use the audioscript in preparation for the free-speaking roleplay.

Let students see the audioscript, either by photocopying it enough times for each pair or by projecting it. They first read the audioscripts in pairs out loud, accompanying it with gestures to reinforce learning. Before the lesson, prepare the script with words taken away, forcing them to remember parts of the text. You could do this in a number of ways, e.g.

Can I ____ you?
No. It's ____, I'm ____ looking.
No ____. Just let me ____ if you ____ any help

or

C_n _ h_lp y__?
N_. _t's _K, _'m j_st l__k_ng.
N_ pr_bl_m. J_st l_t m_ kn_w _f y__ n__d _ny h_lp.

or

Can I …
No. It's …, I'm …
No … Just let …

Let them practise with these prompts before taking away the script completely. Doing it in this gradual way motivates students to learn their lines and become independent of the script.

- Ask students to write down three specific items of clothing they might shop for, e.g. a black long-sleeved shirt, so they have notes to work from.
- Put students in pairs to do roleplays based on the items of clothes they have written down. Make sure they repeat the roleplay several times with different items of clothing and footwear.
- Go round and check students are doing the task correctly and notice errors, difficulties, or where they use L1. Help them by correcting or giving them the English they need, and make a note of any language points to go over with the class.
- When most students have finished, ask the class to change partners.
- At the end of the task, give some feedback about new language that came up, and focus on errors to correct, which you may have written on the board.

- Explain the task.
- Give the students enough time for both pairs in each group to act out at least two dialogues.

WRITING An announcement *p91*

- Discuss the questions with the whole class. Find out if students buy or sell things online and, if so, what and where. Find out what they have at home that they could sell online. Suggest old toys and games that might be worth something to collectors, for example.
- Ask the class what the steps might be to sell an item online. These might include: taking a photo of the item, writing an announcement, deciding on a price, uploading the announcement and photo to a website, creating an online bank account, packaging and posting the item, etc.

- Tell students they are going to do a very practical writing task, writing a *for sale* announcement. Explain the task.
- Look at the example with the whole class. Students complete the task on their own.
- When most students have finished, get them to compare answers in pairs and to help each other with anything they haven't finished.
- Check answers as a class.

Suggested answers

At the beginning: 1 (could also be in the middle), 4, 5 (could also be at the end), 9

In the middle: 3, 6

At the end: 2, 7, 8

- Tell students to read the two announcements on page 152 and answer the questions.
- Nominate students to share their answers.

Answers

The first announcement includes all the information: the name of the item, a photo, the price, ways you can pay, a description of the item, the age and condition, the reason for selling it, information about the seller, information about postage, where the seller lives.

The second announcement is missing the size.

10 WRITING SKILL Relevant information

- **10a** Tell students to read the first two points in the Writing strategies box. Explain the task.
- If students are not confident about the task, you could elicit one irrelevant sentence to get them started. Alternatively, tell them that there are three sentences (or parts of a sentence) in each that are not relevant.

> **Answers**
>
> **1**
>
> My first guitar … New one is a Squier Classic Vibe 50, a similar model but even better quality … Personally, I think it's worth a lot more than J$13,000.
>
> **2**
>
> My aunt gave it to me … I'm disappointed because I absolutely love the colour … Bidding closes soon because I need the money to buy a new dress.

- **10b** Explain the task. Put students in pairs. One student should keep page 91 open, the other should have their book open on page 152.
- Check answers as a class.

> **Answers**
> **1** – (3) age and condition of item
> **2** – (1) description
> **3** – (2) details about postage / (8) where seller lives
> **4** – (1) description
> **5** – (3) age and condition of item
> **6** – (2) details about postage
> **7** – (6) reason for selling it
> **8** – (5) price

11

- Explain the task. Suggest students write about something they thought of in Exercise 7. Remind them that the language in Exercise 10b, the advice at the back of the book and the Writing strategies box are all there to help them.
- Set the writing for homework or set a time limit of about twenty minutes to do it in class. As students are writing, go round and offer help. Be available for any vocabulary they may need, especially regarding the description of the item. Encourage them to really 'sell' their items by making them sound attractive and avoiding too much negative detail. You might note some common errors for feedback when the time is up.
- Tell students to create a final version on a small piece of paper, e.g. A5 size, which can be pinned to the wall. If they are working on computers, they will be able to post them digitally.

Fast finishers

Students who finish quickly can write a second announcement for something very different. Alternatively, let them monitor other students and make suggestions as appropriate.

12

- Create a noticeboard area where students post their announcements so that everyone can read them. This could be a physical board in class, a poster that can be moved, or a digital space, e.g. *Padlet*, where students can all share to the same space with the link.
- Students choose the item that they would most like to buy and say why. A fun way to do this is to hold an auction, where each student starts with the same amount of money, say £10. Each student stands up and tries to 'sell' their item, starting at a low price and seeing how much money they can get for it.

> **Homework**
> - Set Workbook Lesson 7E and Review exercises on pages 83–85 for homework.
> - Students write a sketch in a clothes shop where there is a problem of some kind. Or they write a dialogue in a different kind of shop, e.g. a stationery shop, a camera shop, a phone shop, a computer game shop.
> - Students prepare three questions to test their classmates at the start of the next lesson about the things they have studied in Unit 7.

UNIT AT A GLANCE

Students will

- learn about the ways astronauts stay in touch from space
- read about an experiment in intercultural communication
- find out about a new app
- watch a TED Talk about how to have better conversations
- write an email of complaint

8A Vocabulary
Effective communication, e.g. *pay attention, post on social media*
Listening
A conversation about how Chris Hadfield communicated with Earth from the International Space Station
Grammar
Reported speech: statements and questions

8B Vocabulary building
Negative prefixes, e.g. **un***comfortable,* **im***polite*
Reading
An experiment in intercultural communication
Critical thinking
Using direct speech

8C Grammar
Reported speech: verb patterns with reporting verbs
Pronunciation
Contrastive stress

8D TED Talk
10 ways to have a better conversation, Celeste Headlee
Authentic listening skills
Understanding fast speech
Critical thinking
Investigating opinions

8E Speaking
Responding sympathetically
Pronunciation
Sympathetic intonation
Writing
An email of complaint
Writing skill
Using formal linkers, e.g. *in spite of, as a result, in addition*

8A Getting your message out *pp 92–95*

Information about the photo

The photo is of a group of young men enjoying the atmosphere in the Sarawat Mountains, near the city of Mecca in Saudi Arabia. Mecca is the most important place for Muslims, and many people visit the city each year. The Sarawat Mountains are the highest mountains in the Arabian Peninsular and stretch along the western coast of Saudi Arabia and Yemen, next to the Red Sea.

LEAD IN

- Focus students' attention on the photo or project it using the CPT. Ask the class the following questions: *What do you think the relationship of these young people is? What are they doing? Why have they come to this place? What are the similarities between this group of friends and your friends? What are the differences?* Emphasize the similarities, by focusing on their friendship, the relaxed situation, the idea of going to the countryside for a day out, etc.
- Discuss any other points students wish to raise, but bear in mind there are more personal questions for students to talk about in Exercise 1.

VOCABULARY Effective communication *p93*

- Explain the task.
- Go round listening to students' ideas, prompting where necessary.
- In whole-class feedback, use the students' knowledge of each other to illustrate the concepts of effective communication. Find out which students are thought to be good listeners by the group, who gets on well on a one-to-one basis, who prefers large groups, and why, and who uses their hands a lot. Talk about the strengths of these characteristics. You might make a list of the things the students say men and women talk about, but question any stereotypes or generalizations that may or may not be true, such as that only men talk about sports, or that women are more interested in feelings.

- Explain that the theme of the unit is communication, especially good communication skills. Tell the class to find the collocations. Make sure they understand that 1–5 match with a–e, and 6–10 with f–j.

- Do the first item (*1d get distracted*) with the whole class to remind them what a collocation is. You might even mention some easy collocations, such as *take a photo* or *ride a horse*. Point out that these are all verb collocations, but that others exist (they learned *on special offer* in the previous unit, for example, which is a prepositional phrase).
- Tell students to do the rest of the activity on their own. Go round and check they are doing the task correctly. When most students have finished, get them to compare answers in pairs and to help each other with anything they haven't finished.
- Check the answers as a class. Write the collocations on the board as you get the answers.

> **Answers**
> **1** d   **2** c   **3** a   **4** e   **5** b   **6** g   **7** f   **8** i
> **9** j   **10** h

- Look at the instructions.
- Once students have completed the task, elicit each comment and ask whether it relates to communicating using technology and, if so, how.
- Point out the other expressions related to communication in the sentences, i.e. *face-to-face conversations, get distracted, a good listener, respond to friends' messages, share a message, join in on a forum, get my message out.*
- Point out that although *connect* is a word closely associated with telecommunication, *connect with* in sentence 1 does not relate to technology but to a person's relationships with others. Explain that to *connect with* someone suggests an emotional connection so that you communicate easily with them and find things in common, while *connect to* someone suggests a physical connection, via the internet, for example.
- Explore the meaning of the other expressions. Ask the following questions, as well as your own:
  Why do people 'get distracted' when they're having a conversation? (e.g. because the TV is on)
  What does the prefix 'inter-' mean in terms of 'interpersonal'? (between)
  What apps can you use to 'send' and 'respond to texts' and other messages? (WhatsApp, email, Instagram, Facebook, Snapchat, etc.)
  Where do people 'post on social media'? (Instagram, Facebook, etc.)

  What examples of 'online forums' can you think of? (Reddit, Google Groups, etc. Specific ones will depend on interests,

e.g. Ultimate Guitar for guitar players, Wattpad for fan fiction, etc.)
- Finally, ask students what the advantages of using technology to communicate are (e.g. you can talk over long distances) as well as the disadvantages (e.g. it is easier to misunderstand each other).

> **Answers**
> **1** connect with – this doesn't mention technology, although if a conversation is not face-to-face, it's most likely taking place on the phone.
> **2** pay attention – the communication is not related to technology, although the presence of technology (the phone) is creating a problem.
> **3** interpersonal skills – not related to technology.
> **4** send texts – this relates directly to technology.
> **5** post on social media – this relates directly to technology.
> **6** make connections – this relates directly to technology.

- Put students in pairs to discuss the questions.
- Go round and check students are doing the task correctly and notice errors and difficulties. They are very likely to be using the new expressions, so make a note of any pronunciation errors (e.g. share /ʃeə/), collocational errors (e.g. *connect to people*) or grammatical errors (e.g. *It's hard to pay him attention*) that you hear them making.
- At the end of the task, give some feedback about new language that came up, and focus on errors to correct, which you may have written on the board. You can also share some interesting things you heard with the class.

Extension

Get students to rewrite the sentences in Exercise 3 so that they are true for them.

With the class, explore the differences in meaning between the words. Ask which verb collocates with all of them (*have*). Ask for volunteers to explain what they understand the differences are. Check with the rest of the class that they agree, and encourage others to add their own opinions.

Extension

Have students write an example sentence to illustrate each word, e.g. *We had an argument and now she isn't speaking to me.*

Answers

an argument is a disagreement, sometimes involving anger or shouting

a chat is an informal conversation between people who know each other. It is usually friendly and relaxed

a conversation is a neutral word meaning talking about a subject or series of subjects between two or more people

a debate is a formal disagreement between two sides. Sometimes it is organized so that there are rules, each side taking turns to present their arguments and listen to one another

a discussion is a formal conversation about a particular subject. It is not necessarily a disagreement

6 MY PERSPECTIVE

- Put students in pairs to discuss the questions, or if you think students would benefit from a change in dynamic, in small groups.
- Go round and notice errors, difficulties or useful language.
- In feedback, go through any language that was used well and any errors, correcting them on the board.

Extension

Tell each pair of students to prepare a five-line sketch to illustrate one of the words in Exercise 5. They act it out while the others decide which word is being illustrated, e.g. for an argument, they could act out an argument between two friends, one of whom is unhappy that the other borrowed their phone without asking.

LISTENING *p94*

7

- Focus students' attention on the photo of Chris Hadfield or project it using the CPT. Find out which students would like to go into space, and why. Ask if any of them know something about the International Space Station. Find out if anyone has seen it passing over them at night.
- Put students in pairs to discuss the questions.
- In feedback, ask students to explain their ideas about how the ISS crew keep in touch. Find out who in the class ever talks to people a long way from them, such as friends or family in other countries. Ask them to say what's good (and bad) about their methods, e.g. Skype is fun and you can show people things, but if the connection is poor, it can be frustrating if communication breaks down.

Extension

Use these facts about the ISS to create questions for a quiz. For example, you could ask: *What is the main function of the ISS?* Tell students to write down their answers. Anyone who is correct or close gains a point after showing you their written answer.

8

- Explain the task and give students time to read the ways of communicating and the ways Chris used them.
- 🎧 **49** Play the audio once straight through.
- Let students compare their ideas in pairs. Go round and notice how well students did without saying anything. Be prepared to play the audio again.
- Ask the whole class or nominate students for the answers. Don't say if they are right or wrong, but ask them what they heard to support their answer.
- Where everyone agrees on the answer, write the number and letters on the board. If they don't agree or most don't know, you can either give the answer or tell students to listen again and check.

Answers

1 c (*He played the guitar – 'This is ground control to Major Tom …' That had millions of hits on YouTube.*),
  d (*he did things like science experiments on YouTube.*)
2 e (*And he did these live sessions with schools so that kids could talk to him face to face and ask him questions. … Like video conferencing from space?*)
3 a (*Twitter was his main way of connecting with the general public. He posted photos of Earth*)
  b (*He posted … messages about life on board the space station*)
4 f (*the best thing he did were some live question and answer sessions on chat forums during the mission*)

Audioscript **49**

A: *Who's that?*

B: *His name's David Saint-Jacques. He's a Canadian astronaut on the International Space Station.*

A: *Oh, I didn't know they'd sent another Canadian into space. Chris Hadfield was the first, wasn't he?*

B: *Yes. He was the one who did lots of really cool social media stuff while he was in space.*

A: *That's him. Did you see his version of the David Bowie song, Space Oddity?*

B: *Oh yeah. He played the guitar – 'This is ground control to Major Tom …' That had millions of hits on YouTube.*

A: *Yeah. Even I've seen it!*

B: *The video was great, and he posted many more updates while he was in space. His son helped him get his message out.*

A: *What do you mean?*

B: *His son managed his social media accounts for him. Chris posted thousands of updates while he was away, but his son then shared them more widely. Then he did things like science experiments on YouTube.*

A: *What sort of experiments?*

B: *Well, for example, he did some experiments with water in zero gravity. They're really interesting. And he did these live sessions with schools so that kids could talk to him face to face and ask him questions.*

A: *What? Like video conferencing from space?*

B: *Yeah.*

A: *You know a lot about him!*

B: *I'm a big fan! I love space exploration, and Chris Hadfield is just such a great guy.*

A: *So what else did he use social media for?*

B: *Well, Twitter was his main way of connecting with the general public. He posted photos of Earth and messages about life on board the space station. I still follow him. Hold on … he has … two million followers! But the best thing he did were some live question and answer sessions on chat forums during the mission. I loved those – they were really interesting. For example, someone asked Chris what it was like to sleep in space. It was a chance to talk directly to an astronaut while he was in space!*

A: *So what did you ask him?*

B: *I didn't join in the conversation, I just followed it! Hold on, I'll find one for you. Here … 'Hello out there! My name is Chris Hadfield. I am an astronaut with the Canadian Space Agency who has been living aboard the International Space Station since December, orbiting the Earth sixteen times a day.'*

9

- Look at the instructions. Let students read the notes (1–5) before they listen again. Encourage them to write in any answers they can remember.
- **49** Play the audio.
- Let students compare their answers in pairs.
- Nominate students to answer. If necessary, play the audio again and stop at key points.

Answers
1 Canada   **2** son   **3** water   **4** 2 / two   **5** in space

GRAMMAR Reported speech (1) *p94*

10

- Remind students that the woman in the audio mentions a question and answer session that Chris did with the public. Look at the instructions and do the first item with the whole class.
- Let students do the rest of the activity on their own.
- Check answers. Nominate two students for each item to play the member of the public and Chris.

Answers
1 f   **2** a   **3** b   **4** h   **5** g   **6** e   **7** c   **8** d

11

- Explain the task.
- You can either go through the answers with the whole class, or wait for them to read the Grammar reference on page 142 and then ask the class the grammar-checking questions, or nominate individual students to give their answers.

Answers
1 change to a past tense   **2** often   **3** yes/no questions   **4** full stop   **5** before   **6** not necessary

Note: there are cases when we don't backshift.

The verb does not always go back to a past tense ('backshift') in reported speech. The verb may stay the same when the time reference is still the same, or when the situation has not changed, e.g.

Jack: *It**'s** going to rain tomorrow.*

[Later that same afternoon] *Jack said it**'s** going to rain tomorrow.* (not … *it **was** going to rain* …)

Kriistina: *I **love** him.*

*She said she **loves** him.* (She still loves him, so not … *she **loved** him.*)

Backshifting is usually correct, and it is what is tested in most formal examinations. At this level it is, therefore, important to learn and practise, so, for the sake of clarity and good exam practice in this lesson, insist on the backshift. However, you may want your students to be aware of this aspect of reported speech.

Grammar reference and practice

Tell students to do Exercises 1–4 on page 143 now, or set them for homework.

> **Answers to Grammar practice exercises**
>
> **1**
> **1** say **2** told **3** said **4** asked **5** ask **6** tell
>
> **2**
> **1** went **2** hadn't enjoyed **3** were starting
> **4** would find out **5** couldn't see **6** had visited, had studied **7** had found **8** were, had to visit
>
> **3**
> **1** She told the reporter that she'd been in Antarctica with her team for six months.
> **2** She explained that she was studying small fish that live(d) there.
> **3** She said she had arrived last November (the previous November), at the beginning of summer.*
> **4** She told him that the temperature was -25° that day.
> **5** She said that she didn't want to leave that magical place.
> **6** But she explained that she couldn't stay. She had to catch the plane to New Zealand the next/following day.*
>
> * To replace *tomorrow*, *next week* and so on when the time referenced is no longer *tomorrow* or *next week*, etc. we can use *the next day/week*, etc. or more formally *the following day/week*, etc. To replace *yesterday*, *last week*, etc. we can use *the day/week before* or *the previous day/week*, etc.
>
> **4**
> **1** He asked her what kind of camera she used for her videos.
> **2** He asked her how many videos she had posted on YouTube.
> **3** He asked her if she was happy with the number of people who watch(ed) her videos.
> **4** He asked her if she posted videos every day.
> **5** He asked her if she had ever made a video that people didn't like/hadn't liked.
> **6** He asked her if she would ever stop posting on YouTube.

 12

- Tell students that they are now going to look at the rest of the questions and answers from Chris Hadfield's online forum session. Explain the task.
- Let students compare their answers in pairs.
- Write the answers on the board for students to check themselves.

> **Answers**
> **1** felt **2** had **3** was **4** was, could **5** had

13

- Explain the task. Look at the example.
- Let students compare their answers in pairs.
- When you elicit each answer, elicit an example sentence at the same time and write it on the board next to the verb, e.g. **add** – *He told me that the best preparation for the race was to get some rest. He **added** that I should also eat a good meal the night before.*
- Do some quick-fire grammar practice.

> **Answers**
> **1** reply **2** add **3** explain **4** admit **5** complain
> **6** claim

> **Exam tip**
>
> **Quick-fire grammar practice**
> For students to start using new language correctly and fluently, they need practice producing it correctly and fluently. Teachers can provide quick-fire practice by converting written exercises into spoken ones. Take an exercise that tests reported speech in this case, and instead of presenting it to students on paper, tell them to listen carefully, formulate the reported speech and wait to be chosen to speak, e.g.
> Teacher: *Ellen says: 'I'm cold.'* (Wait two seconds, then nominate Student 1.)
> Student 1: *She complained that she was cold.*
> Teacher: *Good. Lily says: 'OK, OK, I stole the chocolate.'* (Wait two seconds, then nominate Student 2.)
> Student 2: *She admitted that she had stolen the chocolate.*
>
>   You may need to prepare some items before the lesson, or use one of the exercises from the Grammar reference, the Workbook or another source. Prepare at least one quick-fire question for each student, but don't worry about repeating some in random order if you don't have enough!

14

- Explain the task and show students the prompts for each item. Do the first item with the whole class.
- Let students complete the activity on their own.
- When most students have finished, put them in pairs to compare their answers.
- Check answers around the class.

Answers
1 Someone asked Chris if he did experiments every day.
2 Chris replied that he did, but that he didn't do many experiments on Saturdays and Sundays.
3 He explained that he could help to educate the public about space exploration with social media.
4 One person asked him how long it had taken him to learn how to move around in zero gravity.
5 He admitted that he was still learning.
6 Someone asked if it would take long to get used to gravity again after living in space.

- Put students in pairs to write questions for Chris Hadfield. Encourage them to write questions they would be genuinely interested to ask him. Students who finish quickly can write more. Then ask them to guess what Chris's answer might be for their questions.

- Explain that in a minute they are going to perform an interview in front of another member of the class, so they should practise taking turns at playing Chris Hadfield and the interviewer. Give them a few minutes for this.

- Tell one third of the pairs in the class that they are not going to perform the interview, but will listen to the other pairs doing their interviews as reporters. They must report what was said. For example, in a class with twelve students: AA BB CC DD EE FF, the Es and Fs split up to listen to the other four pairs: AAE BBE CCF DDF. Tell the reporters to note down the questions that the interviewers ask as well as the answers that Chris gives.

- Go round the groups checking that students are doing the task correctly and that the reporters are doing their job.

- When most students have finished, nominate the reporters to tell the class what was said. Make sure they use reported speech, and encourage them to use a range of reporting verbs, not just *tell*, *ask* and *say*.

Extension
If you have internet access, finish the class by watching Chris on the ISS doing experiments with water, showing his sleeping quarters, or coming back to earth, etc. Students can make suggestions about, and vote on, what they want to watch.

Homework
- Set Workbook Lesson 8A exercises on pages 86–89 for homework.
- Students write up their imaginary interviews with Chris Hadfield as if they were reporters for an online magazine.
- Students find out the real answers for the questions they wanted to ask Chris Hadfield about life on the ISS. Search terms might include: *How do astronauts wash their hair? Has anyone on the ISS seen an alien?*, etc.

8B Intercultural communication *pp96–97*

READING *p96*

- **Books closed.** Write on the board the following sentence stems:

  People from other countries tend to think that people from my country are …
  Although it's true that …
  In fact, we are actually …
  I'd like to tell people from abroad that …

- Make sure students understand *abroad* (another country) and *tend to* (usually). Give students three minutes to complete the sentences in their notebooks in any way they like.

- Tell students to get into small groups to share what they have written. Then ask for a few volunteers to read out some or all of their sentences. Find out whether the rest of the class agree. You might explain that the assumptions that others have about the people from a country are called *stereotypes* (although this is a question later in the lesson, in Exercise 4).

- Tell students to get into pairs, open their books and answer the questions. Use whole-class feedback to check understanding of the adjectives.

- **Optional step.** Before students read the article, consider showing them a trailer for one of the documentaries discussed in the article, which can be found either at the Crossing Borders website (http://www.cb-films.org/about) or on the National Geographic website (http://education.nationalgeographic.org/media/crossing-borders/).

- Tell students to read the article quickly to do this exercise. Point out that there are six headings but only five paragraphs. Read out the Exam tip below and encourage them to read quickly by setting a strict time limit of three to four minutes.

- Stop the activity. Nominate students for each heading, making sure you ask them to justify their answers.

Exam tip

Fast reading for gist
Some exams don't give students much time to read because they test them on their ability to read quickly for a general understanding, or the 'gist' of the text. Tasks that require general understanding, like matching headings to paragraphs, are usually the first tasks in the exam.

Students should only need to read the text once to do this. Tell them to try reading the first sentence in each paragraph quite quickly and then skim over the rest to get an idea of what the paragraph is about. They shouldn't spend too much time on this so that they have more time for tasks which require them to read more slowly and carefully, such as a true/false task.

• 🔊 **50** Explain that you will give students longer for this task so that they can identify exactly which words and sentences tell them the answer. Set the task and a time limit of between five and seven minutes.
• As they read, go round the class checking on progress and offering help with specific words and phrases.
• In feedback, make sure that students present the evidence for their answers. At the end, ask the class whether any of the information in the article surprised them.

• Explain the task. If you think that students have a good understanding of the words from the context, you could do this quickly as a whole-class activity on the board.
• Make sure students record the new words in their vocabulary books along with an example sentence, either from the article or one they have invented.

CRITICAL THINKING Using direct speech *p96*

• Ask students to find the instances of direct speech first, then to think about the effect these quotes have in the article.
• Discuss the question as a whole class once they have identified the quotes.

6

• Look at the instructions.
• Let students compare their answers in pairs.
• Check answers around the class.

Answers

1 'If we didn't speak with emotion …' (Rochd)
2 'My sound to show I'm listening …' (Eleni)
3 'Maybe we're not communicating a lot …' (a Moroccan student)
4 'I need to find out …' (Fatima)

VOCABULARY BUILDING Negative prefixes *p96*

- Write the four negative adjectives from the Vocabulary building box on the board and underline the four prefixes: *un-*, *im-*, *in-*, *ir-*. Ensure everyone understands the meaning of these prefixes (they make the words negative, e.g. *uncomfortable* means 'not comfortable').
- Explain the task, and tell students to use a dictionary if they need to check. Point out the patterns: that we often add *im-* to adjectives beginning with *p-* and *ir-* to adjectives beginning with *r-*.
- When most students have finished, nominate students to the board to write an answer. Elicit other words students know with those prefixes, or other prefixes they know of.
- Ask students how knowing about prefixes can help develop their reading skills. Make sure that the generative power of prefixes is clear, that it can be useful to work out meanings of unknown words. It is also possible to make new words.

Fast finishers

Students who finish quickly can choose more words containing the negative prefixes *un-*, *im-*, *in-* and *ir-* to learn. They can find them in a dictionary, but they should justify their choices based on usefulness for them as English speakers.

Answers

1 impatient   **2** unaware   **3** indirect   **4** unusual
5 informal   **6** impersonal   **7** irregular   **8** impossible
9 irrelevant   **10** untrue

- Look at the instructions.
- Let students complete the exercise on their own.
- Check the answers as a class. In item 4, both answers are possible depending on whether you are describing her at the time of speaking to Hyan Yu or afterwards, so get students to clarify what they mean.

Answers

1 unusual   **2** personal   **3** untrue   **4** aware
(afterwards) or unaware (at the time)   **5** impolite
6 patient   **7** direct

---

⑨ MY PERSPECTIVE

- Put students in groups of three to five to discuss the questions. Give the second question a practical outcome by asking them to recommend to their school a programme for increasing intercultural understanding among the students.
- Conclude the lesson with a comparison of the groups' ideas, and discuss the strengths and weaknesses of each idea.

Homework

- Set Workbook Lesson 8B exercises on pages 90–91 for homework.
- Students write an article for a travel magazine about stereotypes of their country and which aspects of these stereotypes are true and untrue.

8C Ask me anything

pp98–99

GRAMMAR Reported speech (2) p98

1

- Before you put students in pairs to discuss the questions, elicit one or two apps from the class and one or two ways that technology can help language learners (e.g. computer dictionaries, the CPT).
- Go round and listen to students, making a note of any interesting ideas that you hear.
- Elicit as many different ideas from the class as you can. Ask the students how important they think technology is in language learning, and, if it is so important, how were people able to learn languages in the past.

> **Suggested answers**
> 1 Language course apps, e.g. Babbel, Busuu, Duolingo; flashcard vocabulary learning apps, e.g. Anki, Memrise.
> 2 Computers *may* help learners by: helping them organize their learning, providing learners with opportunities to learn in their own time, away from their teacher; providing motivating and meaningful activities; interacting with learners so that they can practise writing and speaking with them; correcting their errors.
> 3 You could ask the computer to translate for you.

2

- Explain the task. Tell students to read the questions before they listen.
- 🔊 **51** Play the audio once straight through.
- Let students compare their answers in pairs.
- Check answers around the class.

> **Answers**
> 1 e   2 d   3 c   4 b   5 a   6 f

Audioscript 🔊 51

(Answers to the questions for Exercise 3 are in bold.)

I = Interviewer, N = Nick

I: Hi, Nick. Thanks for speaking to us today. What does your company do?

N: **We're interested in how technology is changing English language teaching and learning, and we make digital learning products.**

I: Now, I know you have a new language learning app. Can you tell me a bit about it?

N: Yes, of course!

I: So where does the idea come from?

N: **OK, so it works as a 'chat bot', which is software that can communicate like a human. The most famous example of this is Siri, which comes with Apple's iPhone. So you can say: 'Siri, find a good restaurant near here', and Siri will help. We wanted to know what a language-learning version of Siri would look like.**

I: So, is it like a digital teacher? You ask a question and it will answer?

N: Exactly. A bot that helps users improve their English. But, unlike Siri, it communicates via text message, not voice.

I: Oh? Why's that?

N: Well, text messaging is really popular, so I thought that we should use texting as the way people communicate with the app.

I: What do users need to do if they want to use the app?

N: **Our website says: 'Got a question about English? Text me and I'll help.' The website tells people who are interested that they can just add the app's contact details to their phone contacts.**

I: And how can learners use it?

N: OK, so let's look at an example. Say you need to communicate in English. You're at the train station, but you don't know how to say what you want. Just text your question to the app and it will respond.

I: That sounds amazing! How does the app work?

N: Well, at the moment **it isn't actually a chat bot, it's me.**

I: Ah!

N: We wanted to know whether this was a product that users would be interested in.

I: And did the users know the app's secret?

N: **I think so. A number of people asked whether a robot was answering the questions.** In fact, the first person who texted, a guy called Javier, was very clever. He sent a photo of a cup and the question: 'What can you see?'. Obviously, he wanted to find out if the app was human or not. A few minutes later, Javier shared the conversation he'd had with the app on Facebook, encouraging others to try it. And that's when more users started texting.

I: So finally, Nick, will the app be available for English learners soon?

N: Well, **at the moment, artificial intelligence apps can't answer the sort of questions I was getting. But I'm optimistic – remember to come back in five years' time because computers will keep on learning.**

3

- 🔊 **51** Tell students to listen again but this time to focus on Nick's answers to the questions. Play the audio again.
- Put students in pairs to discuss what they can remember about the answers to the questions in Exercise 2. Go round

and check carefully that all students understand the main ideas well.

Answers
(See audioscript opposite for Nick's answers to the questions in **bold**.)

- Look at the instructions.
- Set a time limit of two minutes.
- Check the answers as a class. For variety, ask for the answers by saying: *What are all the quotes that the interviewer said?*, etc.

Answers
1 b   2 a, d, g, h, j   3 e, f   4 c   5 i

- Read sentences a–d in the Grammar box to the class. Ask the class how the reported speech in these sentences differs from those in lesson 8A. Elicit that reporting verbs are not always followed by a clause with a subject introduced by *that*, and that *agree* and *suggest* show that there is a greater variety of reporting verbs than simply *tell*, *say* and *ask*. Explain that these verbs tell us about the function of what the speaker is doing.
- Use sentence *a* to illustrate what is meant by 'structures' in the instructions for Exercise 5. Write it on the board and underline *asked Nick to explain*. Ask a student to say which of the structures this uses – 1, 2 or 3 (2).
- Have students do the same for the other three verbs on their own.
- You can either go through the answers with the whole class, or wait for them to read the Grammar reference on page 142 and then ask the class the grammar-checking questions, or nominate individual students to give their answers.

Answers
1 agree   2 ask, tell   3 suggest

Grammar reference and practice

- Tell students to do Exercises 5 and 6 on page 143 now, or set them for homework.
- Before students do the exercises, check that they understand the meaning of the reporting verbs, by letting them look up any that they don't understand in a dictionary, for example.

Answers to Grammar practice exercises
5
1 complained that they had
2 asked Paulo if/whether he
3 replied that it hadn't
4 added that he wasn't
5 explained that he was
6 claimed that he had
7 admitted that he had
8 told him/Paulo to buy

6
1 e   2 d   3 c   4 h   5 g   6 f   7 a   8 b

Extension
- If you think your students would benefit from a more challenging task, dictate the following sentences, and ask them to find the mistake in each one and correct it.

  1 You said you are going to France on holiday.
  2 I promised that I buy some more chocolate.
  3 What can you suggest to do to improve our English?
  4 She asked me to not leave her until her mother came back.
  5 They agreed wearing the new school uniform.
- Invite students to write the correct sentences on the board.

Answers
1 You said you ~~are~~ **were** going to France on holiday.
2 I promised ~~that I~~ to buy some more chocolate.
3 What can you suggest ~~to do~~ **doing** to improve our English?
4 She asked me **not** to ~~not~~ leave her until her mother came back.
5 They agreed ~~wearing~~ **to wear** the new school uniform.

- Tell students to do the task and check that the structures used after each reporting verb are correct according to the information on page 142.
- In feedback, insist on students reading out the whole sentences, not just the number and letter.

Answers
1 b   2 c   3 d   4 a   5 f   6 e

- Look at the instructions and do the first item with the whole class.
- Let students complete the activity on their own. Go round and check students are doing the task correctly and question any incorrect answers that you see by telling students to check on page 142 again.
- Let students check their answers with a partner.
- Nominate students to read sentences out to the whole class.

- Ask if anyone can explain what the Turing test is. If they can, let them explain, after which the class can check their accuracy by reading the text. If not, let everyone find out by reading.
- Put students in pairs to judge the best things to say in a Turing test. This is likely to generate a lot of discussion, so you may need to interrupt the conversation. However, don't get feedback or find out the most popular items until students have done Exercise 9, which will help them talk about the ideas more naturally.

- Explain the task. Show students how item 1 in Exercise 8 is connected to the first sentence in Exercise 9. Show them the choice of verb they must make to complete each sentence.
- Give them a few minutes to complete the other sentences.
- Instead of getting the answers from students in order, ask students to give their ideas about which of the things to say in a Turing test. Nominate students to say which items in Exercise 8 they would say, and encourage them to report these using the structures they have formulated in Exercise 9.

10 **PRONUNCIATION** Contrastive stress

- **10a Optional step.** Read out the Pronunciation box. Write on the board the sentence: *If you **think** you have **problems**, you should see your **teacher**.* Read it out loud, stressing the words *think*, *problems* and *teacher* so that it sounds like advice to speak to the teacher. Elicit from students the words which were stressed. Then ask them to listen again and to think how the meaning changes this time. Say it differently, so that it suggests that their teacher's problems are much bigger than theirs: *If you think **you** have problems, you should see your **teacher**!* Elicit the meaning now.
- **🎧 52** Write the sentence on the board. Explain the task. Play the audio.
- Ask students to underline the words on the board. Encourage them to practise saying it the way they heard it, too.

- **10b** Tell students they are going to listen to the first part of a new sentence said in three different ways (a–c). This time they have to choose the correct ending, depending on how the first part is said.

- **🎧 53** Play the audio. You may decide to do it sentence by sentence, stopping after each one and letting students answer.
- Let students compare their answers in pairs.
- Check answers around the class.

- **10c** Drill the sentences in Exercises 10a and 10b stressed three ways, both chorally and individually to check that students can move the primary stress around.
- Put students in pairs to practise them again. One student says the sentence without saying which way they are trying to say it. The other student has to decide which ending they mean.

11

- Explain that students are now going to try writing some better questions for a Turing test. Put them in pairs and give them a few minutes to think of a minimum of five new questions. They must both write the questions so they both have a copy for the next stage.
- Go round offering help and ideas and correcting their questions where necessary. Fast finishers can write more.
- Ask the class to change partners. Tell students to take turns asking and answering their questions. Each time, the person answering the questions must choose to either answer as a human or as an intelligent robot. At the end, the questioner decides if they were talking to a human or a robot.
- When everyone has had a chance to ask their questions, find out from each pair who made the most convincing robots and who made the most convincing humans!

Teaching tip

Three ways to regroup students
If students have been working in the same pairs during the lesson, you may decide to change the groupings, for a variety of reasons. Here are some simple techniques for doing this:

1 Imagine these are the pairs: AA BB CC DD EE. Move the first student A to join the last student E. Immediately, everyone is working with a different student, with minimal disruption:

2 Assign letters to half the class and repeat the same letters to the other half. Tell them to sit with the person with the same letter as them, i.e. AB CD EF GA BC DE FG → AA BB CC DD EE FF GG.

3 Tell students to stand up and organize themselves in a line. You could ask them to line up from tallest to shortest or in order of where their birthdays are in the year, for example, or according to some topical scale, such as according to how many text messages they write each day, with the person who writes the most at one end and the person who writes the least at the other end. Then divide them into pairs like this: AA BB CC DD EE, etc. or like this ABCDEEDCBA.

⑫ CHOOSE

The idea is for students to make their own choice of activity here. However, you might want to make the decision for students, in which case explain why. Alternatively, you may decide to let students do more than one task. You could divide the class into groups and have each group do a different task – or you could have a vote on which task the whole class should do. For the vote:

- put students in pairs or groups to decide which they prefer.
- take a vote on each task.
- if the vote is tied, ask one student from each side to explain which is best and take the vote again. You can decide if there is still no change.
- Option 1 is a speaking task. Tell students to try to agree on a list of the five best questions to ask in a Turing test, i.e. the five questions that a robot would find hardest to answer.
- Option 2 is a writing task.
- Option 3 requires online access. You should find a Turing chat bot before the lesson to recommend to students. Use the search term 'chat bot'.
- Conclude by asking the class how close computer engineers are to creating a genuinely human-like intelligence.

Homework

- Set Workbook Lesson 8C exercises on pages 92–93 for homework.
- Students hold a short conversation in English with a chat bot. They then write up their conversation using reported speech, e.g. *I asked it to tell me its name, but it said it didn't have one . . . .*
- Students try out a language learning app or website every day for a few minutes and report back to the class the following lesson with a recommendation for their classmates whether to use it or not.
- You might want to tell students to watch the track called *Unit 8 TED Talk* on the *Perspectives* website before they come to the next class.

8D 10 ways to have a better conversation *pp100–101*

- Tell students they are going to watch a TED Talk about conversations. Read out the quote and ask students to translate it.
- ▶ **8.0** Tell them they are going to see a short text on the DVD to introduce the talk and the speaker, and play the *About the speaker* section. Then do the vocabulary exercise.
- After they finish, write the key words from the *About the speaker* section on the board and ask students to retell it aloud, or ask them to write as much of what it said as they can. Correct as necessary.

Answers to About the speaker

1 host = b (a person on radio or TV who introduces people and talks to them)
2 competence = b (skill)
3 a compromise = a (an agreement)
4 brief = b (quick)
5 offensive = c (likely to make people angry or unhappy)

TED Talk About the speaker

*Celeste Headlee is the **host** of a daily talk show, On Second Thought, so her job has taught her a lot about how to have conversations, and also, that many of us aren't very good at it!*

*Celeste says that conversational **competence** is about speaking but it is also about listening and finding a **compromise** when we don't share the same point of view. She knows what makes a great conversation – being honest, **brief**, clear, not being **offensive** and most of all, being a good listener.*

Celeste's idea worth spreading is that when we talk and listen with genuine interest in the other person, we will learn amazing things.

AUTHENTIC LISTENING SKILLS
Understanding fast speech *p100*

As well as teaching aspects of phonology and listening skills, these tasks also allow:

- you to pre-teach some vocabulary.
- students to read and hear new language before they listen to the whole text.
- students to tune in to the speaker's voice and style.

- Ask for a volunteer to read the Authentic listening skills box for the whole class. Then ask students if they have experience of trying to understand people who speak too fast in English. Encourage one or two anecdotes about breakdowns in communication, techniques that help, etc. Ask how they can politely get people they are talking to to slow down (e.g. *Sorry, could you slow down a bit? I'm finding it hard to follow you.*)

- **54** Tell students to write down *any* words that they hear. Play the audio at least twice.
- Give students a minute to compare what they heard with two or three classmates. Then ask them to call out the words that they heard. Encourage volunteers to say what they think Celeste says.

2

- **54** Tell students to listen again and choose what Celeste wants the audience to do. Play the audio again. Then get a show of hands for each option.
- Read out the actual words she says more slowly and clearly, so that students can check.

> **Answer**
> b

Audioscript **54**

> *All right, I want to see a show of hands: how many of you have unfriended someone on Facebook because they said something offensive about politics or religion, childcare, food?*

3

- **55** Explain the task. Play the audio one sentence at a time, repeating each at least twice.
- Let them compare in pairs and reconstruct what they think Celeste says. Invite students to share their sentences with the class.

Audioscript **55**

> *I make my living talking to people. I talk to people that I like. I talk to people that I don't like. I talk to some people that I disagree with deeply on a personal level. But I still have a great conversation with them.*

WATCH *p100*

4

- Put students in pairs to discuss the questions.
- After a few minutes, get students' attention and together brainstorm safe topics of conversation and topics to avoid. Conclude with some characteristics of a good listener.

If you are short of time, or want a different approach to the video, you may want to watch the whole talk all the way through with only some brief checking questions. A version of this is on the DVD and is labelled as *TED Talk with activities*. At the end of each section, there is a short gist question. Pause after each question on screen so students can give their answers, then play the answer.

> **Answers to gist questions on DVD**
>
> **Part 1**
>
> Celeste says communication is poor these days because …
>
> **c** We don't spend enough time communicating face to face.
>
> **Part 2**
>
> How many of Celeste's ten tips can you remember?
>
> Students' own answers. For a full list of her 10 tips, see Exercise 6 below.
>
> **Part 3**
>
> Which of these is NOT a correct answer?
>
> When Celeste was growing up, she met a lot of …
>
> **b** boring people

5

- Explain the task. Give students a minute to read the statements.
- **8.1** Play Part 1 straight through.
- Ask students to compare their ideas in pairs. Go round and notice how well they did in order to decide how quickly to go through answers, and whether you will need to play Part 1 again.
- Check answers as a class.

> **Answers**
> **1** T (*Stick to the weather and your health. But these days, with climate change and anti-vaxing, those subjects … are not safe either.*)
> **2** F (*Kids spend hours each day engaging with ideas and each other through screens, but rarely do they have an opportunity to hone their interpersonal communications skills.*)
> **3** F (*I want you to forget all of that.*)

TED Talk Part 1 script **8.1**

> *All right, I want to see a show of hands: how many of you have unfriended someone on Facebook because they said something offensive about politics or religion, childcare, food?*
>
> *And how many of you know at least one person that you avoid because you just don't want to talk to them?*
>
> *You know, it used to be that in order to have a polite conversation, we just had to follow the advice of Henry Higgins in My Fair Lady: Stick to the weather and your health. But these days, with climate change and anti-vaxing, those subjects are not safe either. So, this world that we live in, this world in which every conversation has the potential to devolve into an argument, where our politicians can't speak to one another and where even the most trivial of issues have someone fighting both passionately for it and against it, it's not normal. Pew Research did a study of 10,000 American adults, and they found that at this moment, we are more*

polarized, we are more divided, than we ever have been in history. We're less likely to compromise, which means we're not listening to each other. And we make decisions about where to live, who to marry and even who our friends are going to be, based on what we already believe. Again, that means we're not listening to each other. A conversation requires a balance between talking and listening, and somewhere along the way, we lost that balance.

Now, part of that is due to technology. The smartphones that you all either have in your hands or close enough that you could grab them really quickly. According to Pew Research, about a third of American teenagers send more than a hundred texts a day. And many of them, almost most of them, are more likely to text their friends than they are to talk to them face to face. There's this great piece in The Atlantic. It was written by a high school teacher named Paul Barnwell. And he gave his kids a communication project. He wanted to teach them how to speak on a specific subject without using notes. And he said this: 'I came to realize ...'

'I came to realize that conversational competence might be the single most overlooked skill we fail to teach. Kids spend hours each day engaging with ideas and each other through screens, but rarely do they have an opportunity to hone their interpersonal communication skills.'

Now, I make my living talking to people. I talk to people that I like. I talk to people that I don't like. I talk to some people that I disagree with deeply on a personal level. But I still have a great conversation with them. So, I'd like to spend the next ten minutes or so teaching you how to talk and how to listen.

Many of you have already heard a lot of advice on this, things like look the person in the eye, think of interesting topics to discuss in advance. Look, nod and smile to show that you're paying attention. Repeat back what you just heard or summarize it. So I want you to forget all of that.

There is no reason to learn how to show you're paying attention if you are in fact paying attention.

Now, I actually use the exact same skills as a professional interviewer that I do in regular life. So, I'm going to teach you how to interview people, and that's actually going to help you learn how to be better conversationalists. Learn to have a conversation without wasting your time, without getting bored, and, please God, without offending anybody.

6

- Explain the task. Tell them they won't use two of the words. Give students a minute to read the sentences and predict the gaps.
- ▶ **8.2** Play Part 2 straight through.
- Ask students to compare their ideas in pairs. Go round and notice how well they did in order to decide how quickly to go through answers, and whether you will need to play Part 2 again.
- Check answers as a class.

Answers

1 multitask	**2** learn	**3** open-ended		**4** flow
5 know	**6** experience	**7** repeat		**8** details
9 listen	**10** brief	(quiet and talk are not used)		

TED Talk Part 2 script ▶ 8.2

So I have ten basic rules. I'm going to walk you through all of them, but honestly, if you just choose one of them and master it, you'll already enjoy better conversations.

Number one. Don't multitask. And I don't mean just set down your cell phone or your tablet or your car keys or whatever is in your hand. I mean, be present. Be in that moment. Don't be thinking about your argument you had with your boss. Don't be thinking about what you're going to have for dinner. If you want to get out of the conversation, get out of the conversation, but don't be half in it and half out of it.

Number two. Don't pontificate. If you wanted to state your opinion without any opportunity for response or argument or pushback or growth, write a blog.

Now, there's a really good reason why I don't allow pundits on my show: Because they're really boring. And you don't want to be like that. You need to enter every conversation assuming that you have something to learn. The famed therapist M. Scott Peck said that true listening requires a setting aside of oneself. And sometimes that means setting aside your personal opinion.

Bill Nye: 'Everyone you will ever meet knows something that you don't.' I put it this way: everybody is an expert in something.

Number three. Use open-ended questions. In this case, take a cue from journalists. Start your questions with who, what, when, where, why or how. If you put in a complicated question, you're going to get a simple answer out. If I ask you, 'Were you terrified?' you're going to respond to the most powerful word in that sentence, which is 'terrified', and the answer is 'Yes, I was' or 'No, I wasn't.' 'Were you angry?' 'Yes, I was very angry.' Let them describe it. They're the ones that know. Try asking them things like, 'What was that like?' 'How did that feel?' Because then they might have to stop for a moment and think about it, and you're going to get a much more interesting response.

Number four. Go with the flow. That means thoughts will come into your mind and you need to let them go out of your mind. We've heard interviews often in which a guest is talking for several minutes and then the host comes back in and asks a question which seems like it comes out of nowhere, or it's already been answered. That means the host probably stopped listening two minutes ago because he thought of this really clever question, and he was just bound and determined to say that. And we do the exact same thing.

And we stop listening. Stories and ideas are going to come to you. You need to let them come and let them go.

Number five. If you don't know, say that you don't know. Now, people on the radio are much more aware that they're going *on the record, and so they're more careful about what they claim to be an expert in and what they claim to know for sure. Do that. Err on the side of caution. Talk should not be cheap.*

Number six. Don't equate your experience with theirs. If they're talking about having lost a family member, don't start talking about the time you lost a family member. If they're talking about the trouble they're having at work, don't tell them about how much you hate your job. It's not the same. It is never the same. All experiences are individual. And, more importantly, it is not about you.

Number seven. Try not to repeat yourself. It's condescending, and it's really boring, and we tend to do it a lot. Especially in work conversations or in conversations with our kids, we have a point to make, so we just keep rephrasing it over and over. Don't do that.

Number eight. Stay out of the weeds. Frankly, people don't care about the years, the names, the dates, all those details that you're struggling to come up with in your mind. They don't care. What they care about is you. They care about what you're like, what you have in common. So, forget the details. Leave them out.

Number nine. This is not the last one, but it is the most important one. Listen. I cannot tell you how many really important people have said that listening is perhaps the most, the number one most important skill that you could develop. Buddha said, and I'm paraphrasing, 'If your mouth is open, you're not learning.'

Why do we not listen to each other? Number one, we'd rather talk. When I'm talking, I'm in control. I don't have to hear anything I'm not interested in. I'm the centre of attention. I can bolster my own identity. But there's another reason – we get distracted. The average person talks at about 225 words per minute, but we can listen at up to 500 words per minute. So our minds are filling in those other 275 words.

One more rule. Number ten, and it's this one. Be brief. Be interested in other people.

7

- Explain the task. Give them a minute to read the sentences and predict possible answers from memory.
- ▶ **8.2** Play Part 2 again.
- Ask students to compare their ideas in pairs. Go round and notice how well they did in order to decide how quickly to go through answers, and whether you will need to play Part 2 again.
- Nominate students to give their answers.

Answers
1 present **2** a blog **3** interesting **4** stories
5 an expert **6** you **7** rephrasing **8** dates
9 learning **10** other people

CHALLENGE

- Ask students to read the Challenge box and think about their 'hidden, amazing thing' while they watch.
- ▶ **8.3** Play Part 3 straight through.
- Put students in pairs to discuss what they think their 'hidden, amazing thing' is. You might share something interesting about yourself to encourage students to believe that they also have something interesting to share.
- Find out from a few volunteers what their 'amazing thing' is.

TED Talk Part 3 script ▶ **8.3**

You know, I grew up with a very famous grandfather, and there was kind of a ritual in my home. People would come over to talk to my grandparents, and after they would leave, my mother would come over to us, and she'd say, 'Do you know who that was? She was the runner-up to Miss America. He was the mayor of Sacramento. She won a Pulitzer Prize. He's a Russian ballet dancer.' And I kind of grew up assuming everyone has some hidden, amazing thing about them.

You do the same thing. Go out, talk to people, listen to people, and, most importantly, be prepared to be amazed.

Thanks.

8 **VOCABULARY IN CONTEXT**

- **8a** ▶ **8.4** Tell students that they are going to watch some clips from the talk which contain new or interesting words or phrases. They should choose the correct meaning for each one. Play the Vocabulary in context section. Pause after each question on screen so students can choose the correct definition, then play the answer. If you like, you can ask students to call out the answers. If helpful, either you or your students could give an additional example before moving on to the next question.

Answers
1 avoid = b (try not to talk to or see)
2 due to = a (because of)
3 make my living = c (earn money)
4 nod = c (move your head up and down)
5 have a point to make = a (have something we want to say)
6 don't care about = b (aren't interested in)

- **8b** Check students understand the words in italics and re-teach if necessary, or ask students if they can recall the example in the talk. Point out that they relate to some of the new words and phrases they have just learnt in Exercise 8a. Give them two minutes and make sure they note down their ideas.
- Put students in pairs to share their ideas. Go round and check they are doing the task correctly and notice errors, difficulties, or where they use L1. Help them by correcting or giving them the English they need. Focus especially on their use of the new words and phrases.
- At the end of the task, give some feedback about new language that came up, and errors to correct, which you may have written on the board. Nominate one or two students to tell the class the most interesting things they said or heard.

CRITICAL THINKING Investigating opinions *p101*

- Explain the task. Tell students that these comments criticize some aspect of Celeste's message.
- Set a time limit of five minutes. Go round and help groups with their ideas, making suggestions and asking questions.
- Stop the activity. Put students in groups of four to share their ideas.
- Nominate students to give their responses. You may want to read out the suggested answers as possible responses by Celeste to compare with students' ideas.

> **Suggested answers**
>
> ***1** Isn't there a difference between the type of communication that happens between two people in the same room, and written communication at a distance? Sending lots of texts doesn't improve your communication skills because it doesn't let you respond to body language and it doesn't let the conversation develop and flow in the same way.
>
> ***2** I see what you mean, and I do it too, but talking about yourself means you are taking control of the conversation. The other person might not have finished.
>
> ***3** My point is that if we have conversations where we focus on listening, not speaking, we are more likely to learn something.
>
> * These comments were created for this activity.

- Put students in groups of four to discuss the questions.
- At the end of the task, give some feedback about new language that came up, and focus on errors to correct, which you may have written on the board. You can also share some interesting things you heard with the class. Find out which tips students are going to work on. Make a note of what students say and remember to remind them in subsequent lessons and find out if they have been working on their listening skills.

> **Homework**
> - Set Workbook Lesson 8D exercises on page 94 for homework.
> - Students reflect at the end of each day on the conversations they have had and ask themselves: *What was my best conversation today? Why was it so good? Did I manage to improve the listening skill I identified at the end of the lesson? How? What am I going to do tomorrow to make my conversations even better?*
> - Students choose and watch another TED Talk about communication from the TED playlist, 'The art of meaningful conversation'.

8E I hear what you're saying *pp102–103*

SPEAKING *p102*

1

- Explain the task. Let students read the three situations.
- 🎧 **56** Play the audio once straight through.
- Tell students to compare their ideas in pairs. Go round and notice how well they did in order to decide how quickly to go through answers and whether you will need to play the audio again.
- Nominate students to give their answers. Each of the options mentions 'something'. Ask students what the 'something' is in each case.

> **Answers**
> **a** 3 (the 'something' is a History exam/paper)
> **b** 2 (the 'something' is a train ticket)
> **c** 1 (the 'something' is a computer game)

Audioscript 🎧 56

1

A: *Hi. How can I help you?*

B: *Oh, hello. I bought this game a couple of weeks ago, but it doesn't work on my PC.*

A: *I'm sorry to hear that. Let's have a look. This is for the PlayStation.*

B: *Yes, I know that now, but your colleague told me it worked on a PC.*

A: *That's strange. It does say clearly on the box it's for PlayStation.*

B: *The thing is, I didn't see the box when I bought it. Your colleague got one from the back of the shop and put it straight in the bag.*

A: *Hmm, I see. Yes, that is frustrating. But you've opened the box, I'm afraid. Unfortunately, we don't normally accept returns if they've been opened.*

B: *Yes, but I didn't notice until I opened it. I was hoping I could return it and get the right game for the PC.*

A: *OK. I don't think I can do anything for you, but I'll check with the manager and see what she thinks.*

B: *That would be great.*

A: *Hold on a minute. I'll be right back …*

2

C: *Welcome to Rail Link Web. To book a train ticket for next-day travel, press '1'. For other enquiries, please hold the line.*

D: *Good morning, Rail Link Web. How can I help you?*

E: Oh, hello. I'm phoning about a journey I made yesterday. I wanted to buy my ticket online last week, but I couldn't use my Young Person's railcard to get a discount. The website told me I had to buy the ticket at the station.

D: That's right. You have to show your card.

E: Right, but there was a really long queue at the ticket office. I couldn't buy a ticket …

D: … so you paid on the train.

E: Yes, and it cost me three times what I would have paid online. So I'd like to get the money back, please.

D: Hmm, I see what you're saying, but there's very little I can do for you. You see, you chose to buy the ticket on the train rather than at the station.

E: That was because there was only one ticket office open and I didn't want to miss the train! If the station …

D: I understand, but the only thing you could do is write an email to customer services.

E: I think I might do that.

3

ML = Mr Lebowski, C = Cristina

C: Mr Lebowski?

ML: Hi, Cristina. You wanted to see me. Take a seat.

C: Yes, I just wanted to ask you about my History exam.

ML: You got a D, didn't you?

C: Exactly. I didn't understand the comment you wrote on my paper.

ML: Right, well, it's very simple really. I'm sorry to say you didn't answer the question.

C: I thought I did.

ML: I did say that you needed to explain why you think the war started.

C: It's just that I put so much work into it.

ML: Hmm, that's a shame. You're normally very good at understanding the task.

C: I was hoping that you could give me until Friday to do it again.

ML: I'm sorry, Cristina, I can't. I would have to do the same for all the other students.

C: OK. I knew you'd say that. Thank you anyway.

ML: I'll tell you what. Let me think about it, and I'll get back to you tomorrow, OK?

C: Great! Thank you.

ML: I'm not promising anything!

C: No, I know. Thank you anyway.

2 **PRONUNCIATION** Sympathetic intonation

- **2a** Ask students to read the Pronunciation box. Then ask them for examples of when it's important to be sympathetic to people (e.g. when they are ill, have been disappointed by something or have just received bad news). Note that *sympathetic* is a false friend in some European languages, where it often just means *nice*, as in 'She's a nice person.'

- **57** Explain the task. Play the audio. You may decide to get students to repeat the voice on the audio so that they hear the difference in their own voice.

- **2b** **58** Explain the task. Play the audio.

- Ask for a show of hands to see what the class thought about each sentence. There is likely to be disagreement about sentences 2 and 4. Use this disagreement to discuss how you might make the utterances more or less sympathetic.

> **Answers**
> **1** S **2** S/U **3** S **4** S/U **5** U **6** U

- **2c** **58** Get students to practise the sentences, but making them all sound sympathetic. Play the audio, stopping after each sentence, and conduct choral and individual drilling.

3

- Look at the instructions and tell students to prepare to roleplay two of the situations by first thinking about how the people involved might feel and what they might say. Refer students to the Useful language box.

- Go round and check that students are doing the task correctly. Listen for interesting language, and make a note of common or important errors. Make sure that all pairs have practised at least two of the situations.

- Invite students to the front of the class to perform their roleplays. Set a listening task for the rest of the class: How sympathetic was the friend / team captain / teacher / the brother or sister?

Fast finishers

Students who finish quickly can do another one, or write up one of the roleplays.

Extension

Get students to write their own situations requiring a sympathetic attitude and employing similar language. Have them perform these for their classmates to guess the situation.

WRITING An email of complaint *p103*

4

- Start by telling the class about a problem you have had with a shop or service online, such as not being able to return a damaged product or receiving the wrong item in the post after shopping online. Then put students in pairs to discuss any problems they have had.

- After a minute or two, elicit some of the different problems they have experienced. Find out what they know about their rights as consumers, and the steps they can take to solve these problems. Ask them how acceptable complaining is in their culture and, if not, why not.

 5

- Explain the task. As they read, be available for questions about the vocabulary in the email, e.g. *voucher, helpline, reputation, policy*. Make dictionaries available if possible.
- When most students have finished, let them compare their answers in pairs.
- Check answers around the class.

> **Answers**
> **1** an album (music)
> **2** She couldn't use the voucher to pay for the album; the album was not the one she wanted.
> **3** No, it wasn't. The man she spoke to was unhelpful and rude.
> **4** She wants them to give her a refund as well as a new coupon code; she also expects an apology.

6 WRITING SKILL Using formal linkers

- **6a** Explain that emails of complaint are a common writing text in many English exams. Ask whether these emails are written in a formal or informal style, and why. (They are formal in order to maintain an impersonal distance, so that the reader takes it seriously and acts on it.)
- Explain the task. You could clarify it further by doing the first word (*although*) as an example. Find it in the first line of the third paragraph, elicit that it expresses contrast (the artist was correct, which is good, *but* it was an old album, which is bad), and demonstrate adding it to the first heading.
- Give students two minutes to find and classify the other words.
- Nominate students to give their answers.

> **Answers**
> Expressing contrast: although, despite, nevertheless
> Expressing result: consequently
> Expressing addition: what is more

- **6b** Look at the instructions and do the first item with the whole class.
- Let students complete the activity on their own.
- Go round and check they understand both the meaning and use of the linkers, so a linker expressing result is followed by a result of the previous action, for example. Correct any that are wrong and clarify the misuse for the student.
- Put students in groups. Let them read out their sentences to one another.

> **Suggested answers**
> **1** … I missed my train home! / … everyone else had finished eating before I started!
> **2** … on this occasion, it was very disappointing. / … I've never had such poor service as I have today.
> **3** … the screen was broken. / … it was the wrong model.
> **4** … all the food we had was delicious. / … the restaurant was beautifully decorated and comfortable.
> **5** … we managed to see the beginning of the show. / … my dad didn't get angry.

 7

- Explain to students that they are going to prepare to write their own email or letter of complaint. First, they will look at the typical structure of these forms of correspondence. Explain the task. You might want to put students in pairs and tell one student to have the unit page open and the other student have the writing bank page open to avoid a lot of flipping backwards and forwards.
- Go round and check that students are doing the task correctly.
- Nominate students to tell you the answer for each question. Check that the class agrees.

> **Answers**
> **1** d **2** f **3** b **4** a **5** e **6** c

Background information
Formal letters
Although it is much more common to use email for complaints these days, there are situations when a letter would be more appropriate, or is demanded by the company. Remember when writing a formal letter to include the sender's address in the top right-hand corner of the page, followed by the date immediately below it on the right, then on the next line, the recipient's name, title and address. All of this precedes the greeting: *Dear Mr/Mrs Smith,/Dear Sir or Madam,* on the left-hand side under the recipient's details.

8

- Explain the task. Tell students to refer to the model text on page 152 for help. Remind them of the structure of the model by reading out the advice at the back of the book and reminding them of the language they have studied. Remind them of the guidance they have to refer to: the formal linkers (Exercise 6 and the Useful language box), the structure (Exercise 7), the writing advice on page 152 and the background information on formal letters.

- If you are going to give students a mark, tell them it will be higher if they organize the email or letter in a similar way and use language they have learnt. Put students in pairs and tell them to talk about or plan their email or letter.
- Set the writing for homework or set a time limit of about fifteen minutes to do it in class. As students are writing, go round and offer help. You might note some common errors.

Fast finishers

Students who finish quickly can check their writing with you. Pay special attention to style, formal linkers and structure.

- When students have finished, tell them to swap emails or letters with a classmate, who should respond with a formal reply from the company. They decide how sympathetically to respond.
- Find out which emails or letters of complaint were successful, i.e. they got a positive response to their demands, and why.

Homework
- Set Workbook Lesson 8E and Review exercises on pages 95–97 for homework.
- Students write another email or letter of complaint based on another of the situations in Exercise 1.
- Students prepare three questions to test their classmates at the start of the next lesson about the things they have studied in Unit 8.

---

9 Unexpected entertainment

UNIT AT A GLANCE

Students will

- talk about forms of entertainment
- read about young artists
- learn about FOMO
- watch a TED Talk about Slow TV
- write an email describing a place and its culture

9A Vocabulary
Creative arts, e.g. *performance, stadium, lyrics*
Listening
Four conversations about different types of entertainment
Grammar
Defining relative clauses

9B Vocabulary building
Expressions with *make*, e.g. *make the most of, make a difference*
Reading
Making a splash

9C Grammar
Defining and non-defining relative clauses
Pronunciation
Relative clauses

9D TED Talk
The world's most boring television … and why it's hilariously addictive, Thomas Hellum
Authentic listening skills
Collaborative listening
Critical thinking
Supporting your argument

9E Speaking
Asking for and making recommendations
Writing
An email describing a place and its culture
Writing skill
Paragraphing

9A Entertain me! *pp104–107*

Information about the photo

The photo is of cast members (actors in a production) from the Chinese WeAct Theatre Group, who performed *Titus Andronicus*, Shakespeare's first and bloodiest tragedy, as part of the 2015 Edinburgh Festival Fringe, which takes place every summer in the Scottish capital. Here they are on Calton Hill, where there is a view of the city.

LEAD IN

- Focus students' attention on the photo and the caption or project it using the CPT.
- Read out the caption and ask the class *What sort of theatre performance do you think they are performing in?* You might point out the bloody eye make-up as a clue that this is a tragedy.
- Read out the information about the photo to check their predictions. Ask *In what ways is this form of entertainment traditional? In what ways is it unexpected?* (It is traditional in that it is theatre, and a Shakespearean play. However, the costumes and the fact that a Chinese production is being held in the UK, possibly in Chinese, is unexpected.) *Have you ever been to the theatre? What did you see?*

VOCABULARY Creative arts *p105*

➊ MY PERSPECTIVE

- Put students in pairs to discuss the remaining questions.
- Go round the class and use this as an opportunity to find out students' communicative competence in this area, and make a note of any vocabulary they struggle with or errors talking about the arts. Fast finishers can answer more of the questions.
- Nominate students to feedback to the class some of what they have said, such as the most popular forms of entertainment, their experience with live entertainment and the advantages and drawbacks of watching it live over watching it at home. Give some feedback about new language that came up, and focus on errors to correct, which you may have written on the board. You can also share some interesting things you heard with the class.

➋

- Look at the instructions and do the first item with the whole class.
- Tell students to do the rest of the activity on their own. When most have finished, get them to compare answers in pairs and to help each other with anything they haven't finished.

- Invite students to explain the odd ones out. Do not reject alternative odd ones out if there is a logical argument for them, e.g. in 1, *produce* is the only word where the stress is on the second syllable.

Answers

1 *TV programme* – The others are all verbs to do with making TV shows. *To produce* is to manage the making of the whole show; *to edit* is to choose the different shots and to put them together; *to broadcast* is to send the programme to the public using radio or internet signals. As a noun, a *programme* is a synonym for *TV show*, but as a verb it concerns computing.

2 *characters* – The others are consumers of media: an *audience* in a theatre or concert hall, for example; *listeners* of a radio show, music album or podcast; *viewers* of TV or other visual media-based entertainment.

3 *a theatre* – The others describe the event. A *musical* is a stage or film event with singing and music (e.g. *Lion King - the musical*); a *performance* is one showing of an event (*last night's performance*); a *play* is a piece of theatre (*Hamlet is Shakespeare's most famous play*); a *production* is one theatrical project, which might include many performances. A *theatre* is the place where events take place.

4 *a sculpture* – The others are drawn or painted on a 2D surface. A *drawing* is with pencil, usually black, grey and white; a *mural* is on a wall or building, often very large; a *portrait* is of a person, such as the Mona Lisa. A *sculpture* is a 3D representation of an object, often a person.

5 *exhibition* – The others describe places. A *stadium* is a large place for sports such as football and athletics, although they are often used for rock concerts, too; a *gallery* is a place to see art; a *studio* is either a place for recording music or a room where an artist paints, etc; a *venue* is a general word for a place where an event takes place (e.g. *The venue for tonight's concert has been changed.*) An *exhibition* is an event that takes place, e.g. in a gallery.

6 *concert* - The others are parts of a song. The *lyrics* are the words of a song; the *tune* is the melody; a *verse* is one section of the lyrics which is not repeated (*the chorus* is the repeated part).

Extension

Put students in pairs, one with their book open, one with it closed. The student with the open book tests their partner, by saying the category, e.g. *verbs to do with making TV shows*, and the other has to remember all the words. They then swap roles. This helps students to memorize the new vocabulary.

- Explain the task. Tell students to copy the headings in their vocabulary books, but with an extra column on the right. A minimum of three extra words per category is realistic. Explain that many words can go in more than one category, e.g. *audience* can go under *Theatre*, *TV/radio* and *Music*. Let them use dictionaries, and be available to help with new words.

- When most students have finished the first four columns, tell students to add a fifth category of their choice in the empty column. Brainstorm suggestions for headings on the board and encourage students to use a broad definition of arts and entertainment. You might do so by writing *online video*, *graffiti*, or *hip-hop* on the board, for example.

Answers
(suggested extra words *in italics*)

Art	Music	Theatre	TV / radio
a drawing	produce	produce	broadcast
a mural	audience	audience	edit
a portrait	(at a live	characters	produce
a sculpture	performance)	a theatre	programme
an exhibition	listeners	a musical	audience
a gallery	a performance	a performance	(in the
a studio	a stadium	a play	studio)
a painter	(large live	a production	characters
look at	performances	a venue	listeners
(a piece of	are often	*a comedy*	viewers
art)	performed	*stage*	a (radio)
a landscape	there)	*a scene*	play
	a studio		a production
	a venue		a studio
	a concert		a concert
	the lyrics		(on the
	a tune		radio or on
	a verse		TV)
	rock/pop/folk/		*chat show*
	classical/jazz,		*soap opera*
	etc.		*adverts*
	instrument		

- Look at the instructions. Tell students to be prepared to say why they made each choice.
- Put students in pairs to compare answers.
- Check answers around the class.

Answers
1 *lyrics* – This is a general word for all the verses and the chorus. It's unlikely that someone would only like the verses but not the chorus.
2 *mural* – It mentions the side of the building, and a mural would more likely decorate a flat surface. A sculpture is three dimensional, so more likely to be in the hospital reception or in the centre of a fountain, for example.
3 *broadcast* – A production makes it sound like a complicated show with actors, lighting, editing, etc. whereas this is likely to be just the president talking to the camera. Also, the president wouldn't get involved in the production itself.
4 *viewers* – Viewers watch, listeners listen!
5 *studio* – A gallery is a place for members of the public to see art, not somewhere private where you make art.

5

- Explain the task. Tell students that the pairs of words are in the order that they appear in the sentences.
- Put students in pairs to compare answers.

- For feedback, you might ask students to close their books; then read out the sentences to them, pausing at the gaps and getting them to call out the missing words from memory.
- Tell students to identify and underline useful collocations they see in the sentences. After a minute, write on the board: *to dance to (a song), a* **catchy** *tune, a portrait* **of** *someone, a play* **on at** *the theatre, our* **local** *theatre,* **small** *venues, to* **put on** *a (classical) concert, a* **popular** *TV show.* Check understanding of these expressions by asking, for example, *What catchy tunes are there at the moment?*

Answers
1 tune, lyrics   **2** mural, portrait   **3** play, theatre
4 venues, audience   **5** stadium, concerts
6 broadcast, viewers

- Explain the task. Show students how flexible the expressions in bold in Exercise 5 are, e.g. 3 could be *There's a film on at our local cinema at the moment* …
- You can decide whether students write their sentences first, memorize them, and then stand up and say them to as many classmates as they can, or write their sentences and then work in pairs to share what they have written.
- Go round and check students are doing the task correctly and notice errors, difficulties, or where they use L1. Help them by correcting or giving them the English they need, and make a note of any language points to go over with the class.
- At the end of the task, give some feedback about new language that came up, and focus on errors to correct, which you may have written on the board. You can also share some interesting things you heard with the class.

LISTENING *p106*

- Focus students' attention on the photo or project it using the CPT. Ask *What is it? Do you like it? How do you think the image is created?* Wait for a student to realize that it is in fact a human body, who can then explain it to the others.
- If you can, do a search online for *Angelfish* by Johannes Stötter and show Stötter's 36-second video of the person coming out of the fish position. Ask students whether they consider this sort of thing a form of art or something else. Encourage different opinions.
- Look at the instructions. Tell students to copy the table in Exercises 7 and 8 (i.e. 7 rows x 5 columns). Make it clear by also copying it on the board.
- Tell students that the first time they listen, they only need to complete the first row, i.e. the form of entertainment. Quickly brainstorm possible answers to check they know what this means.
- 🎧 **59** Play the audio once straight through. Tell students to compare their answers in pairs. Go round and notice how well they did in order to decide how quickly to go through answers and whether you will need to play the audio again.

- Check answers around the class. Make sure everyone agrees with the answers before filling in the table on the board.

> **Answers**
> **1** – a photo exhibit / exhibition (the photos are of body paintings, so art / sculpture is also acceptable)
> **2** – a musical / theatre production
> **3** – a podcast
> **4** – a music group / band / pop concert

Audioscript **59**

1

A: *Did you get my email?*

B: *Yes, but I haven't looked at it yet. Hold on while I find it.*

A: *I sent you a link to something you might like to see this weekend. It's a photo exhibit of work by an Italian artist who paints people to look like animals. His name is Johannes Stötter.*

B: *Like face paintings?*

A: *No, their whole bodies. They're like living sculptures. So, he might get two or three people standing in a certain position to create the shape of the animal, and then they're painted to look exactly like that animal. It's incredible!*

B: *OK, just opening the link now … Wow! Is that a person? Oh yeah! OK, so I can see someone sitting down with their knees up. I see her feet!*

A: *Which one are you looking at?*

B: *The angelfish. That's so cool!*

2

C: *'Come From Away' is the new show which opened last night on Toronto's Broadway. Deborah, you went to see it last night.*

D: *Yes, I did. OK, so it's a moving true story of how a small town opened its doors to strangers when they needed help. The production of this musical is not big or expensive, but this reflects the small-town theme of community spirit. The script explores new relationships well, and there are some well-written songs the audience really enjoyed. As far as the acting went, everyone was good, but I particularly liked Kendra Kassebaum's performance. Tickets are on sale now.*

3

E: *So if you could recommend just one podcast that I should listen to, which would it be?*

F: *That's easy. I absolutely love a show called '99% Invisible'. It's a show that's on every week, but I've downloaded all their old episodes. They're free.*

E: *So what's it about?*

F: *It's really interesting, about all the design around us that we don't notice because it's so good. I learn so much just listening to it – it's really cool. And the editing is creative, so it's really easy to follow and understand.*

4

G: *Who are you listening to?*

H: *The Aces.*

G: *I love them! They were the first band I saw live.*

H: *Oh, did you? I'd love to see them!*

G: *Yeah, I love listening to them, but watching them on stage, the performance, the music and the lyrics – the whole thing comes alive.*

8

- Explain the task. Ask students to read the questions and check they understand them. Tell them they should fill in the rest of the table by ticking (✔) the relevant boxes. Before playing the audio again, let students try to do the task from memory or go straight into the task.
- **59** Play the audio.
- Go round and notice how well they did in order to decide how quickly to go through answers and whether you will need to play the audio again.
- Invite a student or students to the board to fill in the table with their answers.

Answers	1	2	3	4
a are in a venue?		✔		✔
b can be enjoyed at home?	✔		✔	✔
c is recommended by one of the speakers?	✔	✔	✔	
d is known by both speakers already?				✔
e is about things that are true?		✔	✔	

9

- Look at the instructions. Make sure students understand they only have to note two more pieces of information. Let students try to do the task from memory.
- **59** Play the audio.
- Put students in pairs to compare their answers.
- Check answers around the class.

Suggested answers

1 He paints people to look like animals; he paints their whole bodies; often, more than one person is involved.
2 It's showing in Toronto; it's about a small town that opened its doors to strangers; it's a small, inexpensive production; it's a musical; the acting was good, especially Kendra Kassebaum; tickets are on sale.
3 It's called *99% Invisible*; it's on every week; it's free to listen to old episodes; it's about design; the editing is creative so it's easy to follow and understand.
4 They're called *The Aces*; they were the first band the speaker saw live; the speaker thinks it's better to see them perform (not just listen to them).

⑩

Explain the task. Alternatively, for speed you could have a class vote. Find out why they like the sound of these forms of entertainment most.

GRAMMAR Defining relative clauses *p106*

⑪

- Explain the task. Say that the sentences all come from the conversations they have just listened to.
- Invite students to read out each sentence and accept correct answers immediately. Alternatively, you could play the audio again and tell students to shout 'stop' when they hear one of the sentences.

> **Answers**
> **1** d **2** b **3** c **4** e **5** a

⑫

- Copy the two sentences in the Grammar box on the board for reference and clarity. Ask students to answer questions 1–3. Clarify the meaning of *omitted* (left out or cut).
- You can either go through the answers with the whole class, or wait for them to read the Grammar reference on page 144 and then ask the class the grammar-checking questions, or nominate individual students to give their answers.
- Use the sentences on the board to go through the answers. Students may need guidance, especially with question 2, so identify the verbs in the relative clauses with the class (*is* and *can listen* respectively), identify the subjects (*that* in both cases), and use arrows to show what *that* replaces in each sentence:

It's a ⟨show⟩ **that** is on every week. (the **show** is on … , i.e. the subject)

He's a ⟨singer⟩ **that** I can listen to all day long. (listen to the **singer** … , i.e. the object)

Answers

1 In b, *that* could be replaced by *who*, because it replaces a person, the *singer*. In a, *that* could be replaced by *which*, because it replaces a thing, the *show*.
2 In a, *that* is the subject of the clause. In b, *that* is the object.
3 b (*He's a singer I can listen to all day long.*)

Grammar reference and practice

Tell students to do Exercises 1–3 on page 145 now, or set them for homework.

> ### Answers to Grammar practice exercises
> **1**
> **1** who **2** – (no relative pronoun necessary)
> **3** which **4** – **5** – **6** which **7** –
> **2**
> **1** My sister is the one who told me about the exhibition.
> **2** This is the book (which/that) I read when I was on holiday.
> **3** This is the song which/that won the award for best R&B track.
> **4** That's the architect who went on to design the new library.
> **5** She's the dancer (who/that) I spoke to after the performance.
> **3**
> **1** All the galleries that/which are taking part in this year's art festival can be found on the website.
> **2** Every picture is made of old glass (which/that) the artists found in rubbish bins and recycling centres.
> **3** Older programmes which/that were made before 2005 won't be available online until 2019.
> **4** Please show tickets which/that were bought online at the main theatre box office.
> **5** Viewers who/that want to vote for the best singer need to call this number.

⑬

- Use the first pair of sentences in number 1 to illustrate the task. Tell students to be careful not to add pronouns where there shouldn't be any, e.g. *The play I saw **it** last week* …
- Go round and check that students are doing the task correctly, and manipulating the relative clauses correctly.
- Put students in pairs to check their answers.
- Check answers around the class.

> ## Answers
> **1** I saw last week wasn't
> **2** which/that only sold 100 tickets closed
> **3** he needed three months to finish, is the longest
> **4** who/that demanded the same salary as her* male colleagues has been given
> **5** who/that was played by Mara Wilson spoiled …
> **6** that documentary we saw together last night
>
> * It is more common to call both men and women actors (traditionally female actors were *actresses*).

- Explain the task. Remind students that a pronoun is not always necessary (this is shown in the answer key below). Tell students that the sentences are in the correct order and that the numbers in the paragraph correspond with the sentence numbers.
- Go round and check students are doing the task correctly.
- When most students have finished, either read out the completed text slowly or project the answers on the board, so that students can check their answers.

Answers

Johannes Stötter is an Italian artist **who uses human models to make art**. He creates images of animals and plants with people **(who) you cannot see because they are covered in paint**. The images **which have made him famous** are sculptures and can take up to eight hours to complete. He painted a tropical frog **which became popular in 2013**. Then a video **(which) he made to show how the image was created** went viral. We seem to love any art **which cleverly tricks the eye in this way**. Johannes Stötter is one of a number of artists **who use the human body as their canvas**, but he is perhaps the best known. In fact, a few years ago, he won the bodypainting championships **which the best international artists compete in each year**.

- Tell students that they are going to play a game. Prepare 11 pieces of paper approximately 10cm x 2cm beforehand or hand out an A4 sheet of paper to every two students and have them divide it up into 24 pieces (there will be two spare pieces).

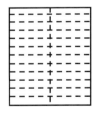

- Each student writes on separate pieces of paper the name of a person that everyone in the class is likely to know. They must not show anyone the names they've chosen. They must think of one for each for the categories, i.e. one actor, one author, etc.
- When they have finished (it's OK if they only have eight or nine names), tell them to fold their pieces of paper in half and half again so that the names are not visible. Now put them in groups of six to eight and divide the groups into two teams of three or four.
- Everyone playing the game puts their names into a hat or box and mixes them up. Students are now ready to play.
- Before they start, ask the class why they are playing the game (other than to have fun, of course) and elicit that it gets them practising relative clauses. Point to the example with Van Gogh to illustrate this. Let them think for a minute about the names they have put in the hat and how they would define them.

- Students take turns to pick out names from the hat and define the famous people to their team mates. They have a minute (the other team can keep time) to elicit as many correct names as possible. At the end of a minute, they count up the number that they got right and add that to their overall score. The other team then takes their turn. Play continues until there are no more names left in the hat. The team with the most names wins.
- Go round and check students are doing the task correctly and notice errors, difficulties, or where they use L1. Help them by correcting or giving them the English they need, and make a note of any language points to go over with the class.
- After congratulating the winners, go through any errors that you heard, by asking *Who's ____?* and eliciting the correct responses.

Homework

- Set Workbook Lesson 9A exercises on pages 98–101 for homework.
- Students write a 'famous things quiz' with ten definitions, e.g. *She's the Mexican artist who painted self-portraits. F____ K____; It's the first book J K Rowling wrote. H____ P____ a____ t____ P____ S____.* They set them for their classmates at the beginning of the next lesson.
- Students find out more about body painting.

9B Fast art, big art *pp108–109*

VOCABULARY BUILDING Expressions with *make* *p108*

- Ask students to read the Vocabulary building box and answer the question. If you know the students' L1, you could get them to translate the phrases in bold. Do they all use the same verb in the L1?
- Ask students to call out other verbs they know in English like *make*, which have different meanings depending on the context. These include *get, have, leave, put, take*, etc.

> **Answers**
> *Make my bed* means to pull the sheets and blankets up and tidy the bed, ready for the next night.
>
> *Make a decision* is another way of saying *decide*, or *arrive at a decision*.
>
> *Makes* in this context means equals or totals (30 x 17 = 510).
>
> *Make friends* means to become, or start being friends.

2

- Explain the task. Suggest that students replace the expressions with their definitions in the sentences to see if the sentences are still understandable.
- Check answers around the class. Write them on the board.

> **Answers**
> **1** f **2** h **3** b **4** e **5** d **6** c **7** g **8** a

3

- Put students in pairs to talk about some of the topics.
- Go round and notice errors, difficulties, or where they use L1.
- Invite volunteers to share what they talked about with the class. At the end of the task, give some feedback about new language that came up, and focus on errors to correct, which you may have written on the board. You can also share some interesting things you heard with the class.

Fast finishers

Students who finish quickly can make up more bullet points using an expression with *make*, e.g. *a song that doesn't make sense* or *a person who has made a big difference in your life*.

READING *p109*

4 MY PERSPECTIVE

- Put students in different pairs from Exercise 3. Explain the task.

- After two minutes, find out what books have made an impression on students. Ask them questions about the books and why they are important to them.

5

- Look at the instructions.
- When most have finished, invite volunteers to share their ideas. When you ask students for the ways that they think are most and least important, make sure they say why they think this.

6

- **60** Explain the task. Tell students to ignore the gaps in the article at the moment. Be available for questions about the article and the language used, and make sure students are doing the task correctly. Make sure dictionaries are available.
- When most have finished, put students in pairs to compare their answers.
- Check answers around the class.

> **Answers**
> **1** Artez started practising graffiti in notebooks at school. He is influenced by other street artists. Sophie-chan moved around a lot when she was a child so she found it hard to make friends. She was influenced by Japanese anime cartoons, and taught herself to draw. She was influenced to go online with her drawing by Marc Crilley.
> **2** Artez makes large murals in public places. He's worked in various countries. Sophie-chan is a manga artist who teaches others to draw manga. She has published a manga book, too.
> **3** Artez uses social media to promote his work, but the local community of artists is also important to him. Sophie-chan makes money from her YouTube channel and has many followers.

7

- Explain the task. Set a time limit of just three minutes for them to put back the missing relative clauses.
- When the time is up, nominate students to tell the class each missing relative clause, but also to identify what the relative pronoun refers to in each case.

> **Answers**
> **1** a (where* refers to Belgrade)
> **2** f (who refers to the Maclaim crew)
> **3** c (which refers to drawing)
> **4** e (who refers to Marc Crilley)
> **5** d (which** refers to her channel being monetized)
> **6** b (which refers to her first book)
> * Students may be interested in this relative pronoun. Tell them that it is used to refer to places in which things happen.
> ** Here, *which* is referring not to a thing but to the idea expressed in the sentence.

Extension

Ask students whether they would like to see some of Sophie-chan's art, or more of Artez's murals. If they would, visit Sophie-chan's channel on YouTube, or go to her website. Artez can be found by searching for 'Artez street art'.

 8

- Explain the task.
- Conduct whole-class discussion by drawing out from each pair the things they discussed. Ask students what Artez and Sophie-chan's main routes to a job in art have been. Make sure you consider each of the bulleted points in Exercise 5.

> **Suggested answers**
>
> Both practised drawing when they were children but they have persevered with their art since then. There is no evidence either of them studied art (in fact, Artez studied Architecture and Sophie-chan's degree is in Engineering) and it's true that in Sophie-chan's case at least, she has that job option if her art doesn't succeed. Both studied other people's work (the Maclaim crew and Marc Crilley are mentioned, and Artez also mentions being part of a community of artists). Both use social media to present and promote their work, with Sophie-chan depending completely on uploading her work to YouTube so that viewers can watch her draw.
>
> It's true that their styles of art are popular because they are attractive and impressive. Would it have been more difficult for them to find success and make a living if they were trying to sell small paintings in art galleries, for example?

 9

- Put students in groups to discuss the questions.
- When most have finished, ask students for some opinions about the nature of art. Invite students to venture a definition of art (or do the extension activity below).

Extension

- Tell the class to write definitions of art. Use the 'Think, pair, share' staging for this.
- Students first write a definition of no more than three sentences on their own; then they get into pairs to compare their definitions and combine them to make a better definition. They then get into groups of four to six to share what they have written. Finally, nominate students to share with the whole class their favourite definitions from each group.
- Your students may enjoy reading other definitions of art online. They could each find one they like and read it out to the class. Use the search terms 'best definitions of art' and 'What is art?'. One interesting collection of definitions is on Maria Popova's *Brain Pickings* blog, for example. Of course, they could also look at the simpler definitions of *art* in dictionaries, in which case, challenge them to think of examples of art that don't fit the descriptions provided.

> **Teaching tip**
>
> **Think, pair, share**
>
> We often ask students to do quite difficult things (such as write a definition of art!). Making them do something challenging and then nominating them to tell the whole class could be intimidating, so one way to facilitate the process is to let them work with their peers first to create a better answer before telling bigger and bigger groups. Here is a basic three-stage process:
>
> **1** Think. Tell students to think about the question and perhaps write an immediate personal reaction to it, or initial notes.
>
> **2** Pair. Put students in pairs to compare their notes, discuss the question further and perhaps bring their ideas together in a new improved answer.
>
> **3** Share. Students then get together in larger groups to share what they have discussed or produced. You may have both members of each pair join the same group or split them up so that their ideas are shared among a larger group, i.e. AA BB CC DD → ABCD ABCD. You may even take it a stage further and combine members of each group into larger groups to share again with more students, or else conclude the activity by getting feedback from the class as a whole.

> **Homework**
>
> - Set Workbook Lesson 9B exercises on pages 102–103 for homework.
> - Students write a biography of an artist or entertainer that they like.

9C A bit of culture

pp110–111

GRAMMAR Defining and non-defining relative clauses *p110*

- Ask students to look at the photos. Ask them what the photos have in common and what the message of the two photos together might be. Elicit their ideas, and make sure you discuss the idea that by spending time on your mobile device or with technology, you might be missing out on important experiences.
- Ask students if it is fair to judge the people with mobile phones in the photos and elicit valid reasons they might be on their phone, e.g. the woman may be finding out information about ancient Egypt, the people may be sharing the experience with friends and family.
- Put students in pairs to roleplay two friends, either at the Pyramid of Giza or at the film premiere, one with their phone and the other without a phone. Suggest that the friend without a phone starts the conversation by saying: *Look at you! You're always on your phone … even here!* Let them improvize for a minute or two before stopping the dialogues and getting whole-class attention.
- Ask the class the question. Invite students to attack and defend the woman's phone use in the photo, and ask students if they ever focus too much on the phone or the screen and so miss out on life. Invite theories as to why the woman without a phone may have a better memory of the event.

- Look at the instructions and do the first item with the whole class.
- Tell students to do the rest of the activity on their own. Go round and check they are making notes and doing the task correctly. When most students have finished, get them to compare answers in pairs and to help each other with anything they haven't finished.
- Find out which class members spend the most time on each of the things. Ask them to comment on whether they think they watch or listen to too much of anything, and what negative and positive effects, if any, these forms of entertainment have on them.

3

- Remind students of the reading they did in lesson 9B. Explain the task. You might read the sentences both ways yourself, or ask students to read them out loud.
- Elicit the answer from the class and discuss why sentence b needs its relative clause to make complete sense.

Answers
Sentence b is missing important information if you leave out the relative clause. The Maclaim crew were **not** some of the first people to create murals; murals were painted by early humans thousands of years ago! So we need to say **which** murals.

4

- Look at the instructions.
- You can either go through the answers with the whole class, or wait for them to read the Grammar reference on page 144 and then ask the class the grammar-checking questions, or nominate individual students to give their answers.

Answers
1 In sentence b, *which* can be replaced by *that*. This is not possible in the other sentences.
2 No, there are no defining relative clauses where the relative pronoun refers to the object of the relative clause. (The pronoun in sentence a refers to the object, but it is a non-defining relative clause.)
3 Non-defining relative clauses are separated from the rest of the sentence by a comma. Sentence b, which has a defining relative clause, does not have a comma.

Grammar reference and practice

Tell students to do Exercises 4–7 on page 145 now, or set them for homework.

Answers to Grammar practice exercises
4
1 I was born in 2001, which was the year the animated movie *Shrek* came out.
2 My favourite author is Marguerite Abouet, who wrote the *AYA* graphic novels.
3 The only musical I've ever seen is *Les Misérables*, which has been playing in the capital for years.
4 *She's Just A Shadow* stars Tao Okamoto, who is one of several new successful Japanese actors.
5 Have a look at his Facebook page, which has a photo of his new baby nephew.

5
1 Commas not necessary – defining relative clause.
2 Commas not necessary – defining relative clause.
3 The music**,** which is played by a DJ**,** is broadcast by radio to the dancers' headphones.
4 Often two or three DJs work at the same time**,** which means that dancers can choose the type of music they want to dance to.
5 Commas not necessary – defining relative clause. (Many nightclub owners are allowed to play loud music late at night, so it is not adding information about *all* nightclub owners.)

6
1 No changes possible (non-defining relative clause).
2 No changes possible (non-defining relative clause).
3 Beyoncé is a singer ~~who~~ I really want to see …
   ('a singer **that** I really want …' also possible)
4 People **that** want to listen …
5 The ballet **that** will be performed next …
6 No changes possible (non-defining relative clause).
7 The member of the band ~~who~~ I thought …
   ('… band **that** I thought …' also possible)
8 This play is set in a city **that** is based on …

7
1 … theatres in the city **which / that** only show …
2 … singer ~~which~~ **who / that** is singing …
3 The woman who ~~she~~ is speaking …
4 The tickets**,** that I bought outside the theatre**,** were twice as expensive as the ones I bought online.
5 The sketch I'm drawing ~~it~~ is part of my art project.
6 … exhibition, which is part of the summer festival**,** goes on …
7 … the *Alien* series, ~~that~~ **which** were some of …
8 Her fourth novel, **which** was published last year, …

 5

- **61** Explain the task. Play the audio.
- Let students discuss their answers in pairs before discussing them with the whole class.
- Elicit a definition of FOMO, but also let its meaning become clear through the examples you and the students provide for it. You might start with an example of FOMO from your life, e.g. checking your emails many times a day; needing to check your phone every time it beeps; receiving notifications from Instagram, etc.
- Invite students to share their FOMO examples. It is important not to judge them at this stage; if they admit to staying up late on their devices, for example, don't tell them how unhealthy this is – they will know that already!

> **Suggested answers**
>
> FOMO, or Fear Of Missing Out, is the fear, or worry, that you are missing something important. It is especially problematic these days because we hear what is going on around us through the media and social networks.
>
> Students' own answers

Audioscript **61**

Do you find yourself checking your phone in the middle of the night? Do you save articles to read later, but never get round to reading them? Perhaps you stay up late just to play the video game that everyone is talking about.

If you're at home one evening after school, what do you do? You check what's on at the cinema on your phone. Oh no! It's the last night they're showing The Last Jedi, *which you've been meaning to see for ages. Too late to go out now, you think. Let's see what's on TV. Aah! It's the final episode of the show that everyone's watching. You know that tomorrow*

you're going to find out what happens from your friends, who'll be watching it right now. Meanwhile, the game of League of Legends you're playing is going on without you.

The problem is, of course, that there is always something going on without you. These days, there's so much good stuff happening out there that it's impossible to catch it all. And the bigger problem is that you know it's going on because you get notifications, reminders, emails and messages telling you. And this creates a worry that won't go away. It's the worry that someone else is having more fun than you. Welcome to the modern disease, Fear Of Missing Out, also known as FOMO.

 6

- Explain the task. You may decide to do a quick-fire review of the rules. Ask *Which ones can you take out of the sentence without changing the central meaning of the sentence? What relative pronouns can defining relative clauses take? What about non-defining relative clauses? Which ones need commas around them?*
- Go round and carefully check students' work to make sure that they understand these complex rules. Let them work in pairs if you think this will help.
- **61** Play the audio again.
- Don't rely on the audio for clarity, though. Also get the answers from students, and make sure the students' answers are completely clear. Get them to say 'comma' when there is one, for example.

> **Answers**
> 1 a Perhaps you stay up late just to play the video game that everyone is talking about.
> 2 e It's the last night they're showing *The Last Jedi***,** which you've been meaning to see for ages.
> 3 b It's the final episode of the show that everyone's watching.
> 4 d You know that tomorrow you're going to find out what happens from your friends**,** who will be watching it right now.
> 5 c And this creates a worry that won't go away.

 7

- Look at the instructions and the example.
- You may get students to write the sentences out in their notebooks. Alternatively, if you think they now understand the grammar well, have them do it orally first in pairs before writing the answers.
- Check answers around the class.

Answers

1 FOMO, which can affect anyone with easy access to the internet, is the secret disease we all suffer from.
2 When people start conversations with *Did you see ...?*, which is a common phrase these days, do you get an uncomfortable feeling in your stomach?
3 The people it affects, who are worried that they might be missing something important, run to their phones when they hear it 'ping'.
4 Most notifications, which might be about music videos, film trailers, funny cat videos or profile photo updates, are really not worth looking at.
5 Some young people, who check Facebook while answering texts and watching TV, spend up to eighteen hours a day* reading or watching things.
6 Studies have shown that we sleep less because of our devices, which include smartphones and tablets.

* This figure totals all the time they spend on different devices even when they are on them at the same time, e.g. watching TV and messaging at the same time. However, it isn't just a problem for young people. According to one website, adults in the UK spend an average of 8 hours 41 minutes a day on screens, while UK children spend only 6 hours 30 minutes.

Teaching tip

Writing to learn, speaking to learn

Students are learning grammar in order to both speak and write English better. Although the priority for most learners is on speaking better, writing gives them more time to get it right and work on accuracy, which is important in lessons when they are meeting new structures for the first time. It's why we do so much writing in class!

But do they sometimes end up doing too much writing, and not enough speaking practice? If your students are finding written exercises very easy, perhaps you should tell them to put their pens down and say the answers instead. That way, they have to think faster. It also speeds up the pace of the lessons and provides variety.

8

- Explain the task. Remind students that non-defining relative clauses provide extra information about nouns, as in the given example (Sophie Kleeman). Suggest that looking for nouns and thinking of the extra information they could add for each may be a good way of doing this.
- Go round and check students are doing the task correctly. Suggest places where relative clauses could go if necessary.
- When most have finished, put pairs of students together to compare their paragraphs. Ask them to choose their three best clauses as a pair. To elicit their ideas, read out the paragraph and ask students to say 'stop' when you reach a place where they have a relative clause.

Suggested answers

(These are possible additions to the text, but it is not a good idea to add all of them!)
There are many ways of fighting FOMO in your life. Sophie Kleeman, **who is a journalist who has written about FOMO / who writes about technology in our lives,** has some advice for us about spending less time on our devices, **which may help you if you are worried / which are beginning to take over our lives**. First of all, phone settings, **which include silent or 'airplane' modes,** can be changed to stop them interrupting you. Phones can be a problem at night, **which is a time you definitely don't want distractions!** Don't keep your phone in your bedroom even if it is on vibrate. Buy an alarm clock instead, **which is how we used to wake up / which wakes you up but nothing else**. Consider your social media, **which can be very distracting,** and decide honestly whether you need 24-hour access to it. Could you just have it on your laptop? Another idea is to play Shame with friends, **who probably have the same problems as you**. The first person to use their phone has to buy the coffees!

9 **PRONUNCIATION** Relative clauses

- **9a** Ask students whether defining or non-defining clauses are separated from the main clause by a comma (non-defining). Ask what the equivalent of a comma is when someone is speaking (a pause). Explain that many relative clauses can be interpreted as either defining or non-defining, depending on the context. Just as commas do in written English, so pausing is used in speech to sound out the difference. Explain the task.
- 🎧 **62** Play the audio.
- Check answers around the class.

Answers

1 She threw away the phone**,** which didn't have a camera. (i.e. non-defining relative clause. There was only one phone**,** and it didn't have a camera.)
2 The men who didn't have tickets were told to leave the theatre. (i.e. defining relative clause. There were many men in the theatre, but only those men without tickets were told to leave.)
3 My sister, who lives in Singapore**,** is studying art. (i.e. non-defining relative clause. I only have one sister, who happens to live in Singapore.)

- **9b** Explain the task.
- 🎧 **63** Play the audio.
- Let students discuss the differences in meaning in pairs before sharing their thoughts with the class.

- **9c** Explain the task. If one student speaks, the other can decide whether they are saying a defining or non-defining relative clause.

⑩ CHOOSE

The idea is for students to make their own choice of activity here. However, you might want to make the decision for the students, in which case explain why. Alternatively, you may decide to let students do more than one task. You could divide the class into groups and have each group do a different task – or you could have a vote on which task the whole class should do. For the vote:

- put students in pairs or groups to decide which they prefer.
- take a vote on each task.
- if the vote is tied, ask one student from each side to explain which is best and take the vote again. You can decide if there is still no change.
- Options 1 and 2 are speaking tasks. However, option 1 is more collaborative. Consider setting them a concrete project goal as a conclusion to the discussion, such as creating a leaflet aimed at students of their school that explains FOMO and offers advice.
- Option 3 follows on from lesson 9B. If they have already done a similar piece of writing for homework, they could work on a second draft of it by incorporating relative clauses were relevant.

Homework

- Set Workbook Lesson 9C exercises on pages 104–105 for homework.
- If they haven't already done so, students do a writing task based on one of the CHOOSE activities.
- Students write about a time when either they were part of an event that they are glad they didn't miss out on, or they talk about a time when they did miss out on something they wanted to go to.
- You might want to tell students to watch the track called *Unit 9 TED Talk* on the *Perspectives* website before they come to the next class.

9D The world's most boring television ... and why it's hilariously addictive *pp112–113*

- Tell students they are going to watch a TED Talk about a TV show. Clarify the meaning of the word *addictive* by asking students what people can be addicted to. Ask them if they know anyone who finds TV addictive. Also check the meaning of *hilarious* (very funny).
- Read out the quote and ask students to translate it or say what they think it means in English (or both).
- ▶ **9.0** Tell them they are going to see a short text on the DVD to introduce the talk and the speaker, and play the *About the speaker* section. Then do the vocabulary exercise.

Answers to About the speaker

1 producer = c (a person who arranges everything needed to make TV and radio programmes)

2 on air … = a (on radio or television)

3 coverage = b (the amount of time that something is on radio or TV)

4 ratings = b (information about how many people watch a TV programme)

5 addictive = b (enjoyable)

6 reality TV = c (a programme which does not use actors or fictional stories)

7 engagement = b (the way people interact with a TV programme)

TED Talk About the speaker

*Thomas Hellum is a **producer** who specializes in documentaries for the Norwegian television channel NRK. He was one of the team that began the 'Slow TV' movement by putting boring events **on air** with full-length **coverage** as they happened.*

*The **ratings** showed that this created exciting, **addictive** television even though this new type of **reality TV** breaks all the rules of TV **engagement**.*

Thomas's idea worth spreading is that Slow TV provides real-time, surprisingly popular entertainment which viewers can relate to.

AUTHENTIC LISTENING
SKILLS Collaborative listening *p112*

As well as teaching aspects of phonology and listening skills, these tasks also allow:

- you to pre-teach some vocabulary.
- students to read and hear new language before they listen to the whole text.
- students to tune in to the speaker's voice and style.

1

- Ask for a volunteer to read the Authentic listening skills box for the whole class. Then ask *Do you ever watch TV or listen to someone and ask the person next to you: 'What did she say?'*?

- Tell the class that they are going to practise collaborative listening. Tell them to write as much as they can of what they hear, like a dictation, but explain that it will be impossible to write everything, and reassure them that if they only write one word the first time they listen, that is OK. You will play the audio at least twice.

- **64** Play the audio twice, and ask students if they would like to hear it a third time. If any students put their pens down in frustration, immediately stop the audio and reassure them again that it's OK if they don't understand very much, because they will get help from each other in a minute.

Audioscript **64**

Norway is a country that gets relatively little media coverage. Even the elections this past week passed without much drama. And that's the Norwegian media in a nutshell: not much drama. A few years back, Norway's public TV channel NRK decided to broadcast live coverage of a seven-hour train ride – seven hours of simple footage, a train rolling down the tracks. Norwegians, more than a million of them according to the ratings, loved it.

 2

- Put students in pairs to compare what they have written and copy from each other's notes.
- **64** Play the audio again, asking students to note down any more words and phrases that they hear.

3

- Back in their pairs, students now rewrite the news report using their notes to help them. Tell them not to worry if it isn't exactly the same as the original. Give them a few minutes to do this, and encourage them to visit other pairs and copy their ideas! Remind them collaboration means helping each other!

- Invite volunteers to read out their news reports, and ask the rest of the class to listen and decide how similar their texts are. Rather than focusing on the exact language, ask if their reports are basically the same from the perspective of the information it provides.

- **64** Play the audio one last time, for students to check their texts.

WATCH *p112*

 4

Put students in pairs to discuss the questions for a minute or two. Then get students' attention and find out about their reality TV viewing habits.

Extension

Brainstorm different kinds of reality TV, such as talent contests and cookery competitions, documentaries, makeover shows, hidden camera shows, shopping (auctions, antiques, etc.). There is even a reality show, called *Gogglebox*, which shows people watching TV!

If you are short of time, or want a different approach to the video, you may want to watch the whole talk all the way through with only some brief checking questions. A version of this is on the DVD and is labelled as *TED Talk with activities*. At the end of each section, there is a short gist question. Pause after each question on screen so students can give their answers, then play the answer.

Answers to gist questions on DVD

Part 1

Choose the best summary for the Al Jazeera news story.

c Norwegian people enjoy television that isn't very exciting.

Part 2

Which two of these topics does Thomas mention?

a where the idea for the programmes came from
c some details about the two journeys

Part 3

Who does Thomas talk about to illustrate the point he is making?

1 Karl, the schoolboy - b	Most of the country watched the show.
2 The people waving - c	People used the show to communicate with their friends and family.
3 The Queen of Norway - a	The show was a success on the internet.

 5

- Explain the task. Give students a minute to read the programmes.
- ▶ **9.1** Play Part 1 straight through.
- Ask students to compare their answers in pairs. Go round and notice how well they did in order to decide how quickly to go through answers, and whether you will need to play Part 1 again.
- Check the answers as a class by nominating students to answer.

Answers
c a b

TED Talk Part 1 script ▶ 9.1

Let's start with a clip from Al Jazeera's Listening Post.

Richard Gizbert: Norway is a country that gets relatively little media coverage. Even the elections this past week passed without much drama. And that's the Norwegian media in a nutshell: not much drama. A few years back, Norway's public TV channel NRK decided to broadcast live coverage of a seven-hour train ride – seven hours of simple footage, a train rolling down the tracks. Norwegians, more than a million of them according to the ratings, loved it. A new kind of reality TV show was born, and it goes against all the rules of TV engagement. There is no storyline, no script, no drama, no climax, and it's called Slow TV. For the past two months, Norwegians have been watching a cruise ship's journey up the coast, and there's a lot of fog on that coast. Executives at Norway's National Broadcasting Service are now considering broadcasting a night of knitting nationwide. On the surface, it sounds boring, because it is, but something about this TV experiment has gripped Norwegians. So, we sent the Listening Post's Marcela Pizarro to Oslo to find out what it is, but first a warning: viewers may find some of the images in the following report disappointing.

- Explain the task. Students should complete the information with one or two words. Give them a minute to read the sentences and predict possible answers.
- ▶ 9.1 Play Part 1 again. Ask students to compare their answers in pairs. Go round and notice how well they did in order to decide how quickly to go through answers, and whether you will need to play Part 1 again.
- Check the answers as a class by nominating students to answer.

> **Answers**
> **1** Slow TV **2** it is **3** disappointing

Put students in pairs to ask each other the questions. Get some whole-class feedback about who would and wouldn't enjoy it, and why.

- Explain the task. Give students a minute to read the sentences. Point out that there are two endings they will not need.
- ▶ 9.2 Play Part 2 straight through.
- Ask students to compare their answers in pairs. Go round and notice how well they did in order to decide how quickly to go through answers, and whether you will need to play Part 2 again.
- Check the answers as a class by nominating students to answer.

> **Answers**
> **1 e** (*except this was just a couple of weeks before the invasion day.*)
> **2 b** (*What other things take a long time? So one of us came up with a train.*)
> **3 c** (*The Bergen Railway had its 100-year anniversary that year.*)
> **4 a** (*1.2 million Norwegians watched part of this programme.*)
> **5 h** (*… it should be live.*)
> **6 f** (*And we asked our viewers out there, what do you want to see? What do you want us to film? How do you want this to look like? Do you want us to make a website? What do you want on it?*)

TED Talk Part 2 script ▶ 9.2

How did we get there? We have to go back to 2009, when one of my colleagues got a great idea. So, he said, why don't we make a radio programme marking the day of the German invasion of Norway in 1940? We tell the story at the exact time during the night. Wow. Brilliant idea, except this was just a couple of weeks before the invasion day. So, we sat in our lunch room and discussed what other stories can you tell as they evolve? What other things take a really long time?

So one of us came up with a train. The Bergen Railway had its 100-year anniversary that year. It goes from western Norway to eastern Norway, and it uses exactly the same time as it did 40 years ago, over seven hours. So we called our commissioning editors in Oslo, and we said, we want to make a documentary about the Bergen Railway, and we want to make it in full-length, and the answer was, 'Yes, but how long will the programme be?' 'Oh,' we said, 'full-length.' 'Yes, but we mean the programme.' And back and forth.

Luckily for us, they met us with laughter, very, very good laughter, so one bright day in September, we started a programme that we thought should be seven hours and four minutes.

Train announcement: We will arrive at Haugastøl Station.

And now we thought, yes, we have a brilliant programme. It will fit for the 2,000 trainspotters in Norway. We brought it on air in November 2009. But no, this was far more attractive. This is the five biggest TV channels in Norway on a normal Friday, and if you look at NRK2 over here, look what happened when they put on the Bergen Railway show: 1.2 million Norwegians watched part of this programme.

So, that's strong and living TV. 436 minute by minute on a Friday night, and during that first night, the first Twitter message came: Why be a chicken? Why stop at 436 when you can expand that to 8,040, minute by minute, and do the iconic journey in Norway, the coastal ship journey Hurtigruten from Bergen to Kirkenes, almost 3,000 kilometres, covering most of our coast. So just a week after the Bergen Railway, we called the Hurtigruten company and we started planning for our next show.

We wanted to do something different. The Bergen Railway was a recorded programme. So, when we sat in our editing room, we watched this picture – it's Ål Station – we saw this journalist. We had called him, we had spoken to him, and when we left the station, he took this picture of us and he waved to the camera, and we thought, what if more people knew that we were on board that train? Would more people show up? What would it look like? So, we decided our next project, it should be live. We wanted this picture of us on the fjord and on the screen at the same time.

But five and a half days in a row, and live, we wanted some help. And we asked our viewers out there, what do you want to see? What do you want us to film? How do you want this to look like? Do you want us to make a website? What do you want on it? And we got some answers from you out there, and it helped us a very lot to build the programme. So, in June 2011, 23 of us went on board the Hurtigruten coastal ship and we put off.

9

- Explain the task. Tell students to read the statements. Emphasize the possibility that some of the information may not be given.
- ▶ **9.3** Play Part 3 straight through.
- Ask students to compare their answers in pairs. Go round and notice how well they did in order to decide how quickly to go through answers, and whether you will need to play Part 3 again.
- Check the answers as a class by nominating students to answer.

Answers

1 F (*he didn't get a note from his teacher, because the teacher had watched the programme.*)

2 T (*… they all had a phone in their hand. And when you take a picture of them, and they get the message, 'Now we are on TV, Dad,' they start waving back.*)

3 NG

4 T (*… we met Her Majesty the Queen of Norway, and Twitter quite couldn't handle it.*)

5 T (*… it's also in the* Guinness Book of Records *as the longest documentary ever.*)

6 F (*… we think that Slow TV is one nice way of telling a TV story …*)

7 T (*… we also think that the good Slow TV idea, that's the idea when people say, 'Oh no, you can't put that on TV.'*)

8 NG

TED Talk Part 3 script ▶ **9.3**

I have some really strong memories from that week, and it's all about people. They made all the stories. This is Karl. He's in the ninth grade. It says, 'I will be a little late for school tomorrow.' He was supposed to be in school at 8am. He came at 9am, and he didn't get a note from his teacher, because the teacher had watched the programme.

We also could take pictures of people waving at us, people along the route, thousands of them, and they all had a phone in their hand. And when you take a picture of them, and they get the message, 'Now we are on TV, Dad,' they start waving back. This was waving TV for five and a half days, and people get so extremely happy when they can send a warm message to their loved ones.

It was also a great success on social media. On the last day, we met Her Majesty the Queen of Norway, and Twitter quite couldn't handle it. And we also, on the web, during this week we streamed more than 100 years of video to 148 nations, and the websites are still there and they will be forever, actually, because Hurtigruten was selected to be part of the Norwegian UNESCO list of documents. And it's also in the Guinness Book of Records as the longest documentary ever. Thank you.

So, we were allowed to be part of people's living room with this strange TV programme, with music, nature, people. And Slow TV was now a buzzword, and we started looking for other things we could make Slow TV about. So, we could either take something long and make it a topic, like with the railway and the Hurtigruten, or we could take a topic and make it long. This is the last project. It's the peep show. It's fourteen hours of birdwatching on a TV screen, actually 87 days on the web.

So, we think that Slow TV is one nice way of telling a TV story, and we think that we can continue doing it, not too often, once or twice a year, so we keep the feeling of an event, and we also think that the good Slow TV idea, that's the idea when people say, 'Oh no, you can't put that on TV.' When people smile, it might be a very good slow idea, so after all, life is best when it's a bit strange.

Thank you.

10 **VOCABULARY IN CONTEXT**

- **10a** ▶ **9.4** Tell students that they are going to watch some clips from the talk which contain new or interesting words or phrases. They should choose the correct meaning for each one. Play the Vocabulary in context section.
- Pause after each question on screen so students can choose the correct definition, then play the answer. If you like, you can ask students to call out the answers. If helpful, either you or your students could give an additional example before moving on to the next question.
- Where a lot of students had given the wrong answer, explain again and give an additional example before moving on to the next extract.

Answers

1 gripped = b (excited)

2 came up with = a (thought of)

3 show up = b (come and watch)

4 in a row = c (without a break)

5 handle = c (deal with)

6 buzzword = a (a fashionable word that is being used a lot in the media)

10b Check students understand the words in italics and re-teach if necessary, or ask the students if they can recall the example in the talk. Point out that they relate to some of the new words and phrases they have just learnt in Exercise 10a. Give them two minutes and make sure they note down their ideas.

- Put students in pairs to share their ideas. Go round and check they are doing the task correctly and notice errors, difficulties, or where they use L1. Help them by correcting or giving them the English they need. Focus especially on their use of the new words and phrases.

- At the end of the task, give some feedback about new language that came up, and errors to correct, which you may have written on the board. Nominate one or two students to tell the class the most interesting things they said or heard.

CRITICAL THINKING Supporting your argument *p113*

- Ask students to read the Critical thinking box. Explain the task.
- Invite volunteers to suggest some of Thomas's techniques. Encourage them to give examples of what he said.

> **Suggested answers**
> **b** He describes events (about the successful production of two shows).
> **d** He lets us experience Slow TV by showing clips.
> **f** He provides statistics (ratings data) and info about the success of the show on social media.

Ask students what other techniques they can remember him using.

> **Suggested answers**
> He introduces his talk with a clip from American TV showing that this is a major phenomenon.
>
> He includes anecdotes that emphasize the popularity, such as the boy who was late for class and the fact that Twitter couldn't handle the number of tweets when the Queen appeared.

CHALLENGE

- Ask students to read the Challenge box and try to think of at least one idea for Slow TV. You might prompt them by asking them to think of things that happen over a long period of time (e.g. long flights, plants growing, the sun and moon rising and setting). From this, students can more easily think of ideas (e.g. a plane journey from the pilot's point of view, a field on a farm where a crop is growing, a TV programme called 'Sun Watch', etc.).

- Put students in groups to discuss the questions and choose and present their best Slow TV idea. Go round and help students with their ideas and the language they need to present it.

- When all of the groups have developed their idea sufficiently, ask them to take turns presenting them. When all ideas have been presented, have a class vote on the ideas according to the criteria in the CHALLENGE box.

> **Homework**
> - Set Workbook Lesson 9D exercises on page 106 for homework.
> - Students write a blog post about a reality TV show that is popular in their country and why it is popular.
> - Students choose and watch another TED Talk about visual media entertainment from the TED playlist, 'Talks for television lovers'.

9E Well worth seeing *pp114–115*

LEAD IN

- Tell the class that they are going to learn about giving recommendations in this lesson. Brainstorm things that people recommend, and write their ideas on the board. Make sure you include the following: *films, books, TV programmes, restaurants, recipes, shops, products, places to go, musicians, songs.*

- Explain that this activity allows them to use the language they already know for recommending things but that they will soon learn more ways to recommend. Elicit one or two ways, e.g. *You should see …, I loved …* and *I think you'll like …*

- Ask students to choose one thing from the list that they want to recommend to everyone in the class. Then tell them to stand up and mingle, giving their recommendations to everyone in the room. Explain that they must try to remember all the recommendations they hear in three minutes.

- Mingle with the students. Call out *Change!* every twenty seconds or so, encouraging students to keep the recommendations as brief as possible.

- When students have spoken to everyone (or most, depending on class size), let them sit down and share some of the recommendations they have been given.

SPEAKING *p114*

1

- Explain the task. Check understanding of *trustworthy* (you can trust them). Explain that different sources may be more trustworthy for some things than others.

- While they work, notice words and phrases they look up, or ask you about, or underline. Focus on these in feedback.

- Conduct a whole-class discussion on the relative trustworthiness of the sources, and where students go for their recommendations. Give some feedback about new language that came up, and focus on errors to correct, which you may have written on the board. You could mention that many online reviews of restaurants, hotels, etc. are probably fake – according to research between six and 30 percent of them!

2

- Tell students to read the questions.
- 🎧 **65** Play the audio.
- Go round and notice how well students did without giving any feedback. Decide whether you need to play the audio again.
- Invite students to give their answers.

> **Answers**
> They agree that the Anthropology Museum is a great place to visit; and that you should not miss the Stone of the Sun.
>
> They disagree about the benefit of paying for a tour guide.

Audioscript 🎧 65

1

*The next place **you might like to go** if the weather isn't great is the Anthropology Museum, which is all about the native people of Mexico and Central America. Now, **I highly recommend this place** because it's such a beautifully designed museum. There is simply so much to see! **You won't want to miss** the 'Stone of the Sun', which is a large stone Aztec calendar and one of the most famous sights in Mexico. There are some amazing examples of Olmec heads, the biggest statues of heads you will probably ever see, and lots of other attractions that are **well worth experiencing**. Make sure to plan your visit, though. You can easily spend all day there, which **will appeal to** the historians among you, but I have to say I got tired after about three hours. One more thing. I **would recommend** hiring a tour guide, who won't charge much but will make the visit much more informative.*

Right, the next rainy day idea is …

2

A: *Guadalupe?*

B: *Hey!*

A: *You've been to the Anthropology Museum, haven't you?*

B: *Yes, I've been a couple of times. Why?*

A: *We have visitors coming next week, and I'd like to take them there. **Is it any good?***

B: *Oh, it's great! You'll love it!*

A: *What is there to do?*

B: *All sorts of things. **I don't normally like** museums and that sort of thing, **but** there's a lot to see there.*

A: *Like what?*

B: *They have the Stone of the Sun there.*

A: *What's that?*

B: *You know, the Aztec calendar, you've probably seen copies around the city.*

A: *Oh yeah, I know what you're talking about. And it's in Chapultepec Park, right?*

B: *Yes, not far from the centre, but **it's worth getting** there when it opens. If you want, **I'll send you a link** with directions.*

A: *I'm sure I'll find it no problem. Did you pay for a tour guide?*

B: *No, **I wouldn't bother if I were you**. That's probably pretty expensive. I'd buy a guide book instead, which you can take home with you.*

A: *Great, well thanks for that. Any other tips?*

B: Take an umbrella if it rains because there are a lot of outdoor spaces with things to see in the gardens.

A: Right. I'll keep my fingers crossed for sun!

- Tell students to think about the style of the expressions in the Useful language box and to categorize them according to the instructions.
- While they are doing the task, set up the board into three columns: *F | TV | B*. When most students have finished, they can write the expressions in the columns they think are correct.
- When all the expressions are on the board, invite students to suggest changes. Explain that different people may have slightly different opinions, and there are no right or wrong answers. If there is any doubt, you can put the expressions in the *both* column.

> **Suggested answers**
> Friends are perhaps more likely to say:
> *Is it any good? / You must go! / I'll send you the link. / It was OK/alright, I suppose. / I wouldn't bother if I were you. / I didn't think it was great.*
>
> TV presenters are perhaps more likely to say:
> *You won't want to miss this. / I highly recommend it. / … is a must-see. / It'll appeal to anyone who enjoys …*
>
> Both friends and TV presenters might say:
> *Is it worth watching/seeing/visiting/reading? / What did you think (about …)? / It's worth watching. / … is well worth seeing. / You might like it if you've got nothing else to do. / If you enjoyed … you'll love … / I don't normally like … but … / I would recommend it to people who …*

- Look at the instructions. Tell students to read the expressions in the Useful language box. Before playing the audio again, let them try to answer from memory.
- **🎧 65** Play the audio again. Tell students to compare their answers in pairs.
- Nominate students to suggest expressions that they heard. Check that the rest of the class agree. You might copy the Useful language box on the board in order to mark the expressions that are heard on the audio.
- Find out whether the National Museum of Anthropology in Mexico is somewhere the students would like to go, and if so, why?

> **Answers**
> See phrases in bold in the audioscript above.

Give students a few minutes to write down examples of each thing. Don't worry too much if some students can't think of an example for each thing; tell them to recommend something else instead. Make sure that they write them clearly on a single piece of paper that their classmate can read.

- Remind them of the lesson aims to practise recommending things using the language given. Put them in pairs to ask questions about what each of them has written.
- Go round making a note of relevant errors from today's lesson and recent lessons (e.g. relative clauses, vocabulary to do with art and entertainment, etc.).
- After a few minutes, stop the conversations and nominate students to share one good recommendation they have been given, as well as one warning that they should remember.
- Point out any common or interesting errors and get students to correct themselves if possible.

WRITING An email describing a place and its culture *p115*

- Put students in pairs to discuss the questions.
- Stop the task when most pairs have finished. Nominate students to suggest some cultural attractions, and to say which they would recommend and why.

- Tell students to go to page 153 and to read the email from Macarena so that they can answer the question.
- Let students compare answers in pairs before they share them with the class.

> **Answers**
> She recommends: the views of the city from the Pablo Neruda museum (but not the museum itself); exploring the city, especially taking the *ascensores* and looking for the street art; the beach at La Caleta Portales.

- Explain the task. Tell them that the relative clauses are not in the same order in the email.
- You might want to put students in pairs and tell one student to have the unit page open and the other student to have the writing bank page open to avoid a lot of flipping backwards and forwards.
- Go round and check that students are doing the task correctly.
- Nominate students to tell you the answer for each relative clause. Check that the class agrees.

Answers

1 There's colour everywhere, which is why I think artists love the place so much. (end of paragraph 3)

2 … a day at the beach, which is where I'm going later with some friends (beginning of paragraph 4)

3 Thanks for your postcard, which I got this morning – what a surprise! (start of paragraph 1)

4 … but unless you're a poetry fan, which I'm not, I wouldn't bother paying … (middle of paragraph 2)

⑩ WRITING SKILL Paragraphing

- **10a** Explain the task. Tell students to write a sentence describing the topic of each paragraph.
- Go round and check that students are doing the task correctly.
- Nominate students to tell you the answer for each paragraph. Check that the class agrees.

Answers

Paragraph 1 talks about the postcard that Aki sent.

Paragraph 2 talks about the museum, Valparaíso's number one tourist attraction.

Paragraph 3 talks about the things you see and do when you explore the city.

Paragraph 4 talks about the beach and fishing port.

Paragraph 5 talks about possibly meeting each other in the future.

- **10b** Explain the task. Tell students that all the different texts in the Writing bank are organized into paragraphs.
- When most have finished, put them in pairs with students who have analyzed a different text. Give them time to explain to each other the organization of their respective texts.

Fast finishers

Students who finish quickly can analyze the paragraphing of another text from the Writing bank.

Suggested answers

(The texts for Units 1, 2, 3 and 10 mention the paragraphing structure in the Writing advice comments in the margins.)

Unit 4 A social media update. Paragraph 1 = A summary of the journey with highlights of their time in Delhi; Paragraph 2 = A summary of the thing that they have already done and are planning to do in Leh.

Unit 5 A formal letter of application. Paragraph 1 = the reason for writing; Paragraph 2 = relevant experience and skills; Paragraph 3 = personal qualities; Paragraph 4 = practical information about availability; Paragraph 5 (one sentence) = request for a reply.

Unit 6 An informal email describing people. Paragraph 1 = acknowledgement of previous email; Paragraph 2 = responding to the receiver's request and introducing the person; Paragraph 3 = details about the person; Paragraph 4 = expression of hope that the information is useful and complete; Paragraph 5 = request for a reply and mention of an attachment.

Unit 7 An announcement. Paragraph 1 = identification of the object (guitar) and who it would benefit; Paragraph 2 = detailed description of the guitar; Paragraph 3 = practical information about price and shipping.

Unit 8 An email of complaint. Paragraph 1 = the reason for writing; Paragraph 2 = description of the situation; Paragraph 3 = account of the complaint procedure so far; Paragraph 4 = clear explanation of what the writer expects the company to do; Paragraph 5 and 6 = mention of an attachment and a request for a reply.

- Explain the task. Make sure they understand that they should spend time planning each paragraph first before they write. Tell students to refer to the Writing advice on page 153, the Useful language on page 114, their ideas from Exercise 7, the grammar of relative clauses to create more interesting sentences, and the model text on page 153, and any useful expressions there.
- If you are going to give students a mark, tell them it will be higher if they organize the email in a similar way and use language they have learnt. Put students in pairs and tell them to talk about or plan their email.
- Go round and check what local attractions students have chosen to write about, the plan they have chosen and why. Tell them they can start writing once they have shown you their plan and they are happy with it.
- Set the writing for homework or set a time limit of about fifteen minutes to do it in class. As students are writing, go round and offer help. Be available for questions about unknown vocabulary, and make dictionaries available. Check for errors and correct as you see them.

Fast finishers

Visit students who finish quickly to suggest ways that they could make their emails better or better expressed. They could also go round and read other people's emails, helping them if they can and asking questions about what they have written. Alternatively, they could write another email about a different place.

- When everyone has finished their emails, get them to swap them with a classmate and answer the questions.
- Round up the lesson by finding out what the most common attractions were that students included in their recommendations.

Homework
- Set Workbook Lesson 9E and Review exercises on pages 107–109 for homework.
- Students write another email describing a different place, somewhere that they know well, such as a holiday destination.
- Students prepare three questions to test their classmates at the start of the next lesson about the things they have studied in Unit 9.

---

10 Time

10A Spend your time wisely *pp116–119*

Information about the photo

The photo is of crowds of travellers at the Churchgate Railway Station in Mumbai. India has one of the largest railway systems in the world. Mumbai is the largest city in India, and the local railway there, the Mumbai Suburban Railway system, carries seven million commuters every day. It has the highest passenger density of any urban railway system in the world. Trains are often very overcrowded.

LEAD IN

- **Books closed.** Write some or all of the following sayings about time, or any others that you know, on the board. Put students in pairs to discuss what they mean and to translate them into their L1. Do they have a similar saying in their language?

  Time flies when you're having fun.
  Time waits for no one.
  Never put off until tomorrow what you can do today.
  Yesterday is history, tomorrow is a mystery, today is a gift – that's why they call it the present.
  Lost time is never found again.

- Invite suggestions from the class as to the meaning of each saying. In a monolingual class, discuss their differing translations, which are best and why. Finally, ask students which of the sayings, if any, they relate to, think are most important in their lives or agree with most.

VOCABULARY Phrasal verbs about time *p117*

1 MY PERSPECTIVE

- Focus students' attention on the photo and the caption or project it using the CPT.
- Put students in different pairs from the previous activity to discuss the questions.
- Elicit a variety of answers from the class. You might draw some conclusions, such as when the busiest times of the day are for the class in general, and what constitutes 'wasted time'.

2

- Explain the task. Tell students to rate the statements on their own first.
- Go round and check students are doing the task correctly and notice errors, difficulties, or where they use L1. Help them by correcting or giving them the English they need.

- When most students have finished, put them in pairs to compare their answers.
- In feedback, ask questions such as *Which of the two of you is more impatient? Why do you say that? Out of the two of you, who is more organized? How do you know?*, etc.
- Do a quick-fire concept-check stage. Ask the class to call out the verb that means:

be excited about something that is going to happen (look forward to)

change the date of an event so that it is sooner (bring forward)

do something after you have been trying to do it for a long time (get round to)

find time for something (fit in)

have no more of something (run out of)

leave a job until later (put off)

spend time with (hang out)

stop working for a few days (take [time] off)

wait for something, often something difficult to wait for (hold on)

work at a quicker pace because you were behind (catch up)

work at a slower pace than other people (fall behind)

waste time doing nothing while other people are doing something (wait around)

- Look at the instructions and do the first item with the whole class making sure students know they may have to change the form of the verb.
- Tell students to do the rest of the activity on their own. Go round and check they are doing the task correctly. When most students have finished, get them to compare answers in pairs and to help each other with anything they haven't finished.
- Nominate students to read out the whole sentence in each item. Check that the rest of the class agree with their answer before accepting it.

> **Answers**
> **1** bring (it) forward **2** get round to **3** ran out of
> **4** hold on **5** waiting around **6** hang out

- Explain the task. Get students to write their answers in their notebooks.
- Go round and check word order, since students may be uncomfortable having the prepositions or particles of the phrasal verbs (the second or third words of the verbs) at the ends of the sentences, as they are in questions 1, 2 and 7.

Fast finishers

Students who finish quickly can make similar jumbled questions which include the phrasal verbs not included in the exercise (*run out of*, *bring forward*, *hold on*). At the end of the exercise, they can write them on the board for the class to do.

- **⌂ 66** When most of the students have finished, play the audio for them to check their answers.
- Check answers by having students repeat the questions slowly and clearly.

> **Answers**
> **1** Who do you like hanging out with?
> **2** What's something you keep meaning to get round to?
> **3** What are you looking forward to doing next holiday?
> **4** What do you always put off for as long as possible?
> **5** What do you try to fit in even when you're busy?
> **6** Do people ever have to wait around for you?
> **7** Which subject would be hardest to catch up with if you fell behind?
> **8** What would you do if you could take a week off right now?

Extension

You might use this opportunity to drill the questions. Point out that the rules for stress in phrasal verbs are complicated but that stress is often on the second word of the verbs: *hang **out** with, get **round** to, put **off***, etc. Also, show how prepositions, which usually have a weak form, e.g. '*to*' in '*I keep meaning to get round to redecorating my room,*' are pronounced with their strong form when in the end position, e.g. '*What's something you keep meaning to get round **to**?*' (strong '*to*')

Answers and audioscript ⌂ 66

1

Who do you like hanging out with?

I love hanging out with my brother when he's home. I don't see him very often.

2

What's something you keep meaning to get round to?

My bedroom has been untidy for weeks, but I haven't got round to cleaning it yet.

3

What are you looking forward to doing next holiday?

Just not getting up early to go to school every day – lying in bed!

4

What do you always put off for as long as possible?

Going to the dentist. I hate that!

5

What do you try to fit in even when you're busy?

I try to do some exercise every day, even if it's just a short jog.

6

Do people ever have to wait around for you?

Yes. I sometimes take a long time to get ready in the morning.

7

Which subject would be hardest to catch up with if you fell behind?

History, I think. There's so much information to learn each week.

8

What would you do if you could take a week off right now?

Ooh, good question. I'd probably read lots of books.

Teaching tip

Drill long sentences in meaningful chunks

Learners need help pronouncing words and saying whole sentences fluently and naturally, but it becomes impossible to get every syllable right in long sentences unless they are broken up into parts. In the first sentence in Exercise 4, consider two meaningful chunks: *Who do you like …* and *… hanging out with?*. Ensure natural connected speech by practising the sentences beforehand: '**Who** *d'you like …*,' '*hanging**out** with?*' Once you've drilled each part separately, drill the whole thing: keeping the natural stress, intonation and connected speech: **Who** *d'you like hanging**out** with?*.

How would you divide questions 2–8 in Exercise 4? What features of connected speech do they contain?

- Put students in pairs to ask and answer the questions.
- Go round and listen to the students, paying special attention to correct use and pronunciation of phrasal verbs. Notice any common or serious errors.
- At the end of the task, give some feedback about new language that came up, and focus on errors to correct, which you may have written on the board. You can also share some interesting things you heard with the class.

LISTENING *p118*

Explain the task. You may decide to stipulate that each group agrees on one piece of advice about each topic and writes it down.

Suggested answers

attitude to life – Life is for living, not planning, so see each new day as an adventure. Live every day as if it was your last.

health – Your body needs to last many years, so don't spoil it.

relationships – Friendships are very important. Look after them.

dreams and ambitions – Don't be afraid to chase your dreams even if they seem impossible.

money and possessions – Money is for spending, not saving. / Save your money for the difficult times.

work and free time – Work to live, don't live to work.

- 🔊 **67** Explain the task. Play the audio once straight through. Encourage students to make a note of which speaker said things that they had predicted.
- Give students a minute to compare their answers in pairs. Go around and identify information that students found hard to hear or do not agree on. Write the numbers 1–8 on the board and invite confident students to write the advice they wrote in Exercise 6 next to the speaker number of the person who gave the same advice. Reassure them that they don't need to use the same words as long as the general message is the same. Check whether the rest of the class agrees.
- Play the audio speaker by speaker, stopping after each one to check whether the class agrees that the advice is roughly the same each time.

Audioscript 🔊 **67**

Speaker 1

Don't take life too seriously. Even if things seem difficult, try to see the lighter side of life. When you really think about it, there's no point worrying about things that haven't happened yet because you only end up worrying about them twice!

Speaker 2

I believe that questioning makes knowledge. If you keep questioning, observing and listening, you will never be lost. So, make good use of your ears and eyes, and your brain, and don't accept anything without first thinking about it and questioning it.

Speaker 3

Trust me, one day you're going to say, 'I wish I had taken better care of myself in my youth.' Look after that beautiful, wonderful body of yours. It deserves it!

Speaker 4

We have one life, so don't wake up and realize you haven't done the things you dreamed of doing. Nothing's impossible, but it will only become more impossible as you get older and are responsible for other people. So, go places. Do things. Even if you haven't got the money. Just pack a bag and go!

Speaker 5

The last time I moved I thought: where has all this stuff come from?! When did I start owning so many possessions? I'm happy, but not because of all my expensive things, and certainly not because of all the money I owe the bank! So, I would say: 'Don't hold on to material objects, hold on to time and experiences instead. And try not to get into debt!'

Speaker 6

Listen, nobody ever dies saying 'If only I hadn't worked so much.' Work hard, sure, but not at the expense of the more important things. If only someone had told me earlier not to prioritize work over family and friends, I wouldn't have wasted so much time at work.

Speaker 7

Maybe this one isn't as special or meaningful as the others, but I think it's important. Brush your teeth regularly – dental problems are awful! And very, very expensive! If someone had told me this years ago, I would have saved a lot of money. And my dentist wouldn't have got so rich!

Speaker 8

I would say: don't accept anyone else's advice as the truth. You can ask for advice from someone you respect, but then you must think about your own situation and come to your own decision. Basically, my advice is: 'Take your own advice.'

- Explain the task. Tell students to use the exact words. Before playing the audio again, let students try to do the task from memory or go straight into the task.
- 🔊 **67** Play the audio again.
- Give students time to compare their answers in pairs.
- Nominate students to share their answers.

> **Answers**
> **1** things that haven't happened   **2** thinking about it and questioning   **3** taken better care of   **4** done the things you dreamed of   **5** objects, time and experiences   **6** work over family and   **7** your teeth regularly   **8** take your own advice

9 MY PERSPECTIVE

- Put students in pairs to decide on the best piece of advice. Insist they justify their choice from the point of view of the best advice for them.
- Ask for a show of hands to find out the most popular advice and get students to share their reasons.

GRAMMAR Third conditional *p118*

- Focus students' attention on the Grammar box and explain the task. Tell them that sentences a–d all come from the audio.
- Go round and check their ideas and question any that are incorrect.
- You can either go through the answers with the whole class, or wait for them to read the Grammar reference on page 146 and then ask the class the grammar-checking questions, or nominate individual students to give their answers.

> **Answers**
> **1** No, she didn't look after them. She didn't save a lot of money.
> **2** No, they cannot (because they are in the past).
> **3** past perfect (*had* + past participle), *would(n't)* + *have* + past participle
> **4** On page 74 they are expressing the present; here they are expressing the past. The emotion being expressed is one of regret (if possible, find the translation in the students' L1 for this concept).
> **5** past perfect (*had* + past participle)
> **6** They are describing imaginary pasts, e.g. in sentence a, she didn't look after her teeth, so looking after them is imaginary.

Grammar reference and practice

Tell students to do Exercises 1–4 on page 147 now, or set them for homework.

> **Answers to Grammar practice exercises**
> **1**
> **1** I'd gone   **2** have learnt   **3** had taken   **4** If only
> **5** wouldn't, hadn't worked   **6** had eaten   **7** I'd spent
> **8** I'd, wouldn't
> **2**
> Sentences 3, 4, 7 and 8 express regret.
> **3**
> **1** had been able, would have kept   **2** would have been, had travelled   **3** had been, wouldn't have got
> **4** would have solved, had followed   **5** had been
> **6** hadn't passed, would have continued
> **4**
> **1** you ever wish you had gone
> **2** only I hadn't eaten that burger
> **3** I hadn't bought an expensive jacket, I would have had enough money
> **4** wouldn't have needed to go back to the shop if he had remembered
> **5** would have been (much) quicker if I had taken

> **Exam tip**
>
> **Sentence transformation tasks**
> Exercise 4 of the Grammar practice is a challenging sentence transformation task, which is used in examinations such as the Cambridge First Certificate. To get maximum points it is important to make sure all the information in the first sentence is also present in the second sentence. It's a good idea for students to check that every word in the first sentence is represented in some way in the second.

- Read out the introduction to the text: *Most hundred-year-olds …*, and explain the task.
- Go round and notice how well students are doing. If they are still having difficulty with the sentence structure, put the basic structure on the board:

  If + *had*(*n't*) + past participle …, … *would*(*n't*) *have* + past participle.

- Put students in pairs to compare answers.
- Check answers around the class. Ask students what they think the secret to a long life is. You might ask them whether they think it is more to do with genetics or lifestyle.

> **Answers**
> **1** wouldn't have lived, had eaten   **2** had worried, would have died   **3** wouldn't have surfed, hadn't eaten
> **4** hadn't lived, would have been   **5** had spent
> **6** had saved

- Look at the instructions and do the first item with the whole class.
- Tell students to do the rest of the activity on their own. Go round and check they are doing the task correctly and notice errors, difficulties, or where they use L1. Help them by correcting or giving them the English they need, and make a note of any language points to go over with the class.
- Nominate students to read out the whole sentence in each item. Check that the rest of the class agree with their answer before accepting it.
- At the end of the task, give some feedback about new language that came up, and focus on errors to correct, which you may have written on the board.

> **Suggested answers**
> If sad things hadn't happened to Frida, it's possible she wouldn't have had such a rewarding life.
> If she hadn't had polio, her father wouldn't have paid her lots of attention. / wouldn't have taught her about art.
>
> (Maybe) she would have become a doctor if she hadn't had the accident.
>
> It's possible she wouldn't have become famous if she hadn't had the accident.
>
> She probably wouldn't have painted self-portraits if she hadn't spent months in bed painting.
>
> If her family hadn't placed a mirror above her bed, it's possible she wouldn't have become famous.
>
> If she had fully recovered, she wouldn't have become as famous as she did.

- Ask the class to imagine they wake up tomorrow morning and find a letter in their letter box. Tell them that the letter is in their own handwriting, but that they don't remember ever writing a letter to themselves. When they open the letter, they see the date written at the top: *10ᵗʰ March 2090*. They look to the bottom of the letter and there is their signature, a little shaky and unsteady, as if an old person has written it. They realize that somehow their 90-year-old selves have managed to travel back in time to the present in order to give them a letter.
- Explain that they are now going to write the letter imagining it is now the year 2090 and they have lived long lives. Ask *What do you want to say to the younger you?* Point to the suggested beginning but allow them to start differently if they prefer.
- Give them plenty of time to write their letters. Be available to check their English, correct any errors and provide any unknown vocabulary. Remember that although one of the aims of the activity is to practise the third conditional, students are free to write anything they like here, and may choose not to regret their actions or talk about what might have been different.
- When students have finished their letters, ask for volunteers to share with the class:

  any advice they gave themselves

  any regrets they expressed

  any good or bad news they received.

Fast finishers

Students who finish quickly can choose to either: draw a timeline of their lives between now and 2090, predicting important dates and events or explain why people in 2090 have started handwriting letters again!

> **Homework**
> - Set Workbook Lesson 10A exercises on pages 110–113 for homework.
> - Students write letters to their younger selves, e.g. at 10 or 12 years old.

10B The man who mastered time *pp120–121*

VOCABULARY BUILDING Expressions with *time* *p120*

LEAD IN

- **Books closed.** Search online using the search term 'Most frequent [or common] words in English'. Have a list of the top 100 available to see. Put students in teams of two or three and tell them to write down what they think are the ten most common words in English. They must not check online, of course. Explain that some words have many forms (e.g. *run*, *runs*, *ran*, *running*) but in this list they are all counted as one word (i.e. *run*). Give them three minutes to discuss and to make their list.

- After three minutes, tell them to swap lists with another team for marking. Read out the top ten, inviting guesses as to what the words are each time. Tell the markers to award ten points for each word that they guessed which appears in the top ten. Then, find out what other words they guessed, and award one point if the word appears in the top 100.

- Congratulate the team with the most points, and then write on the board the following fact: *The 100 most common words make up 50 percent of all the English that you hear and read.* Ask students to think about what that might mean for learners of English. Invite them to suggest conclusions but don't say whether these are right or wrong, just accept them. Possible conclusions include: you don't have to learn many words to understand a lot; and, getting better at English is not about learning lots of complicated new words, it's about learning how to use the common words well.

- Tell students to read the Vocabulary building box to check their conclusions from the lead-in activity. Ask which of the expressions with *time* they use when speaking English. Tell them that even though the word *time* is only the 55th most common word, it is in fact the most common noun in English (all the words in positions 1–54 are verbs, prepositions, articles, etc.).

- Tell students to start a new section in their notebooks or vocabulary books called 'Expressions with *time*'. Have them copy the expressions and write a translation into their L1 and an example sentence next to each one, e.g.
  a long time – mucho tiempo / una larga duración, e.g. 'He looked at her for a long time.'

- Explain the task.
- Go round and check students are doing the task correctly and notice words and phrases they look up. Focus on these in feedback.

- Nominate students to give their answers. Check that the class agrees.

Fast finishers

Students who finish quickly can write an expression on the board for each one. Elicit the meaning in feedback.

> **Answers**
> **1** ahead of their time – very advanced for the time
> **2** from time to time – sometimes, occasionally
> **3** on time – punctual, happening at the time it is supposed to
> **4** in time – before something starts
> **5** at one time – in the past
> **6** pass the time – spend time doing something while you are waiting for something to happen
> **7** in two days' time – two days into the future*
> **8** It's time – The moment has arrived for something (notice the infinitive with *to*: *It's time to* + verb. Also *It's time **for*** + noun.
>
> * Apostrophes are used in time expressions such as *two days' time* and *one years' work*, where the time (*two days*) describes a noun (*time*). You don't need an apostrophe when the time modifies an adjective, e.g. *two days old*.

3

- Pair students up with different classmates. Ask students how well they think they know their partners. Explain that they need to write true sentences about their partners, not about themselves. They cannot ask them any questions until they have finished. To clarify instructions, and if you're feeling brave, invite students to call out sentences about you with *time* expressions that they think are true.

- Go round and check students are using the expressions correctly.

- When most students have five sentences, let them read them out to their partners. Give them time to respond to what has been written about them.

- In feedback, ask whether anyone heard things that were: true and nice to hear, true and not nice to hear, untrue but nice to hear, untrue and not nice to hear.

READING *p120*

4

- Tell students that they are going to read about a man who solved a problem to do with time. Look at the instructions. Set a time limit of three minutes for students to read the article for gist.

- Let students discuss the answers in pairs.

- Invite volunteers to give their answers.

Fast finishers

Students who finish quickly can write a one-sentence summary of the problem, and another one-sentence summary of the way that Harrison solved it.

5

- 🎧 **68** Explain the task. Remind students to keep a record of where they found the evidence in the text for a true or false statement; statements where the information is not given will obviously not be possible to find!
- When most students have finished, ask them to compare their answers in pairs.
- Check answers around the class. Make sure students back up their answers with extracts from the text. Don't go into any detail about whether the 'NG' statements might be true or not at this stage, since this is discussed in much more detail in Exercise 7.

6

- Tell students that there are more time expressions to add to their notebooks. They are either in the article (and the synonyms in Exercise 6 will help them) or they are the synonyms for other words in the article.
- When most have finished, ask students to call out the answers.

CRITICAL THINKING Drawing conclusions *p120*

7

- Ask students to read the Critical thinking box. Ask them which statements in Exercise 5 they were unable to find evidence for. Write the number of these statements on the board: 3, 4, 6, 8.
- Put students in pairs to discuss whether these statements are likely to be true or false, and why.
- After a few minutes, encourage lively class discussion about the answers. Ask for a show of hands for who thinks the statements are true and false, and ask why. Accept any arguments that are well made, even if they do not agree with the Suggested answers below.

8

- Put students in pairs or small groups to discuss the questions. Go round and visit each group, asking them to tell you some of their ideas and checking they are drawing conclusions.
- After a few minutes, reorganize the groups so that students can share their ideas with other classmates.

- Put students in groups to make their lists. Make sure they understand that they must agree on only three inventors, and that they will need to prepare a presentation to persuade the rest of the class that they are right. Weaker classes could come up with fewer inventors, while fast finishers could be given another inventor by the teacher to present.

- Go round and offer help and ideas. Some suggestions include: Tim Berners Lee (inventor of the internet), the Wright brothers (powered flight), Stephanie Kwolek (Kevlar), Josephine Cochran (the dishwasher), Johannes Gutenberg (the printing press), Thomas Edison (electric lighting).

- Remind students of the verbs used to describe ability that they studied on page 72 that might help them explain the importance of their inventions.

- When most groups have finished, let them take turns to present their inventors to the class. As they do, ask them to write the names of their inventors on the board as a record.

- When all the groups have presented their ideas, tell students to vote for the greatest inventor. Congratulate the group who suggested the winner.

Homework

- Set Workbook Lesson 10B exercises on pages 114–115 for homework.

- Students create a page in their vocabulary books, like they did for the word *time*, for one of the nine next most common nouns in English, which are: 2 *person*, 3 *year*, 4 *way*, 5 *day*, 6 *thing*, 7 *man*, 8 *world*, 9 *life*, 10 *hand*.

- Students write a magazine article for a competition in answer to the question: *What invention has had the biggest impact on your life? Why?* Their articles can be serious or light-hearted.

10C Plenty of time! *pp 122–123*

Books closed. Before students open their books, warn them that there is a photograph that might upset them, and to be ready for it. When they open their books, tell them to share their feelings about the photo on page 122 with a partner. Elicit some responses, and ask whether students think they cope with exams well or not. Suggest that today's lesson may help them if they easily get stressed by exams.

GRAMMAR Modal verbs: past speculation, deduction and regret *p122*

- Explain the task. Put students in pairs to discuss the questions.

- After a few minutes, nominate students to share their answers and discuss what they have been talking about with the whole class.

Answers

1 In South Korea, they stop aeroplanes from taking off during the country's main language listening test; in Brazil, huge numbers of people take the college entrance exams; in China, they discuss exam questions on the radio.

2 and 3 (suggested answers) Students might do some of the following: plan a revision schedule; start studying weeks (or months) before the exams; go to a library or somewhere quiet to study; wear earphones to block out sound when studying; copy their notes as a way of studying; try to memorize large amounts of information; take stimulants such as caffeine in coffee in order to study for longer.

- 🎧 **69** Explain the task. Play the audio.

- Tell students to compare their ideas in pairs. Go round and notice how well the students did without saying anything. If you see the majority have not understood, be prepared to play the audio again.

- Ask the whole class or nominate students for their answers. Don't say if they are right or wrong, but ask them why they think what they think and elicit words they heard to support their answer.

- Where everyone agrees on the answer, write the number and words on the board. If students are still uncertain of the answer, play the audio again and stop at key points. Play these sections two or three times if students are still struggling. Draw attention to the problem sounds or words and explain them when you give the answers.

Answers
a 1, 3, 5, 8 **b** 2, 7 **c** 4, 6

1

Start revising early. Giving yourself plenty of time will build your confidence because you know you've prepared as well as you could. I should have given myself more time to revise. In the end, I did a lot of last-minute studying and had too many late nights, and this affected my results.

2

A friend of mine can't have prioritized the questions correctly because she didn't have time for all the questions and failed the exam. I spend five minutes reading through the questions, identifying the ones I can answer easily, then I answer them first.

3

I designed my own revision schedule to help me plan and check my progress. I couldn't have done it without being organized. Most of my friends didn't do anything like that. I don't know how they survived. They must have been very stressed.

4

I didn't get the results I wanted. I was so disappointed at first but then I spoke to the university and now I'm doing an English degree, which I'm really happy about. If I had passed, who knows? I may not have chosen this path. So, it's not the end of the world if you don't get what you want, as long as you know you did your best.

5

I was so worried about the exam that I couldn't sleep well. Around that time, my hair started to fall out, too, which might have been the stress! So please, make sure you allow time for some relaxation. You really don't want to risk your health like I did!

6

I was feeling OK about the exam but I made the mistake of staying to talk about it with my friends. I ended up worrying I'd failed. I shouldn't have listened to them. I felt terrible. And then it turned out I passed! So, I think you need to congratulate yourself for getting through it and then just forget about it and plan to do something nice and relaxing.

7

Stress isn't all bad. I got stuck on the train before a three-hour exam and arrived 45 minutes late. I was so stressed, I wrote really quickly ... and passed the exam! Now, I might have done even better with the full three hours of course, but that's not the point. What I'm saying is that it's natural to feel some stress – and stress gives you energy. So, make it your friend. Just don't panic.

8

Think about where you're going to study. I need to take regular, short breaks – otherwise I lose concentration – so I worked at home, where I could go into the garden or watch TV for a few minutes. Unfortunately, most of the time I just ate snacks from the kitchen and put on lots of weight! If I'd studied at the library, I could have avoided that!

3

 69 Tell students to make a note of the best pieces of advice for them. Play the audio again.

4 **MY PERSPECTIVE**

- Put students in pairs to tell each other the best advice for them and to think of other good advice.
- After a couple of minutes, invite pairs to share their advice with the class.

5

- Direct students' attention to the sentences in the Grammar box and explain the task.
- You can either go through the answers with the whole class, or wait for them to read the Grammar reference on page 146 and then ask the class the grammar-checking questions, or nominate individual students to give their answers.
- You may also decide to clarify further with the whole class (see explanation in the Answers).

> **Answers**
> **a** Group 2, e.g. you could replace sentence e with *My friends were probably very stressed.*
> **b** Group 1, e.g. you would have to replace sentence a with *I chose this path, but if I imagine another life where I did pass the exam, I can see myself choosing a different path.*

Grammar reference and practice

Tell students to do Exercises 5 and 6 on page 147 now, or set them for homework.

> **Answers to Grammar practice exercises**
> **5**
> **1** might   **2** might   **3** must   **4** can't
> **5** should   **6** might / should   **7** can't   **8** shouldn't
>
> **6**
> **1** No, that ~~mustn't~~ **can't** be him.
> **2** I could ~~had~~ **have** done ...
> **3** I ~~must~~ **should/could** have gone yesterday ...
> **4** You ~~can~~ **could** have told me ...
> **5** you ~~might~~ **must** have done something ...

6

- Explain the task. Decide whether to let students work in pairs or on their own depending on how well they have done in the previous exercises.
- Go round and check students are doing the task correctly.
- **70** When most have finished, tell them to listen to check their answers. Play the audio. Give students the opportunity to raise any queries.

> **Answers**
> **1** might   **2** can't   **3** must   **4** should   **5** might
> **6** could

7 PRONUNCIATION Weak forms: *have*

- **7a** 🔊 **71** Explain the task. Tell students to listen to sentences 1 and 2 at two speeds, to identify the pronunciation of *have* and to answer the questions. Explain that they should compare the pronunciation of *have* between the two sentences, not between the two speeds, and that the slowed down versions are just to help them hear the pronunciation clearly. Play the audio.
- Write the sentences on the board, underlining the stressed syllables. You might also write the phonemic script above each *have*.

  I *have* to *stu*dy to*night*.   He *can't* have *passed.*

> **Answers**
> In sentence 1 *have* is stressed. It is pronounced /hæf/.
> In sentence 2 *have* is not stressed. It is pronounced /əv/.

7b Put students in pairs to practise the dialogue, paying special attention to the weak forms of *have*. As they read it out, go round and listen to check that they're getting it right.

> **Teaching tip**
> **Don't stress!**
>
> One problem when teaching weak forms is that by focusing on them, you may end up stressing them. Weak forms are precisely those words that are not stressed! Instead of trying to not stress the weak forms, pay attention to those words which *are* stressed. Get the students to repeat the whole sentence or chunk, ensuring that the words around the weak forms are stressed fully. For example, don't try to get the class to repeat *have* in its weak form /əv/, but drill *You **can't** have done **bad**ly*, emphasizing *can't* and *badly*. Also let students hear and say the sentence without the words, e.g. *mmm MMM mm mm MMMmm*.

8

- Explain the task. Decide whether or not to set this as a written task or just a spoken one.
- Invite suggestions from the class. You might invite students to decide which their favourite ideas are.

Extension

Get students to act out short dialogues based on the situations, using the language they have come up with. They can add a few lines on either side, rehearse, then act them out in front of the whole class. You may need to help them add details to each situation, e.g. in situation 3, a younger brother is taunting his older sister because her teacher is downstairs talking to their parents.

> **Suggested answers**
> **2** An animal must have got into the house. I should have closed the window. / We can't have been burgled because nothing has been taken.
> **3** I must have done something wrong. I shouldn't have cheated in the exam.
> **4** Her parents might have taken her phone away as a punishment. / She should have recharged her battery.
> **5** There might be a strike today (the drivers aren't working). / There might have been an accident. / I should have given myself more time to get to where I'm going.

9 CHOOSE

The idea is for students to make their own choice of activity here. However, you might want to make the decision for the students, in which case explain why. Alternatively, you may decide to let students do more than one task.

You may be able to divide the class into groups and have each group do a different task – or you could have a vote on which task the whole class should do. For the vote:

- put students in pairs or groups to decide which they prefer.
- take a vote on each task.
- if the vote is tied, ask one student from each side to explain which is best and take the vote again. You can decide if there is still no change.
- Option 1 is a writing and speaking task. Once students have a situation, either put them in groups to read the situations out in turn and respond with spontaneous responses using today's grammatical structures, or tell students to stand up and mingle, reading their situations out to one another as they meet people.
- Option 2 is a group writing task. Let them choose their photo and brainstorm possible sentences, with one member of the group as the notetaker, the others dictating their sentences to him or her. Good photos to use for this activity include those on pages 14, 15, 20–21, 22–23, 24, 36, 46–47, 51, 58–59, 70–71, 74, 78–9, 90–91, 92–93, 94–95, 97, 104–5, 106–107, 110, 111, 126. At the end of the activity, groups read out their sentences for the rest of the class to race to find the photo in the book.
- Option 3 is a writing task. Remind students of the use of today's grammar in talking about the consequences and what they learned. Encourage them to read each other's texts by telling them to find someone with the most similar story to their own.

10D   Inside the mind of a master procrastinator

pp 124–125

- Give an example from your life of something you procrastinate about, such as starting to get fit, paying your bills or writing a novel. Explain that you know you should do it, but you haven't started yet. Invite suggestions as to why that might be, and discuss their suggestions, e.g. *Yes, that might be it* or *No, I don't think that's the reason.*

- Write on the board a definition of *procrastinate*, and tell students they are going to watch a TED Talk about procrastination.

   (verb) wait a long time to do something that you should do, often because you do not want to do it

- Read out the quote and ask students to translate it or say what they think it means in English (or both).

- ▶ **10.0** Tell them they are going to see a short text on the DVD to introduce the talk and the speaker, and play the *About the speaker* section. Then do the vocabulary exercise.

- After they finish, you might write the key words from the *About the Speaker* section of the DVD on the board and ask students to retell it aloud, or ask them to write as much of what it said as they can. Correct as necessary.

Answers to About the speaker

1 self-starter ... = b (a person who is intelligent and confident enough to do a job on their own)
2 thesis = c (a long essay that is the final part of a university degree)
3 deadline = a (a time or day you have to finish a project by)
4 rational = c (sensible and logical)
5 instant gratification = a (enjoyment from doing something fun and easy)

TED Talk About the speaker

*Tim Urban is a blogger and **self-starter** who calls himself a 'master procrastinator'. To show what he means, he talks about his time at university, when he had to write his **thesis.***

*It was supposed to take a year to write but he didn't start until three days before the deadline! He explains that part of him wants to make **rational** decisions and get the job done, but there is another part that just wants **instant gratification**.*

Tim's idea worth spreading is that procrastination can keep us from chasing our dreams, and that we're all affected by it.

AUTHENTIC LISTENING SKILLS Guessing the meaning of new words *p124*

As well as teaching aspects of phonology and listening skills, these tasks also allow:

- you to pre-teach some vocabulary.
- students to read and hear new language before they listen to the whole text.
- students to tune in to the speaker's voice and style.

- Ask for a volunteer to read the Authentic listening skills box for the whole class. Explain the task.
- **72** Play the audio.
- Invite students to share their guesses around the class. If they guess correctly, ask them whether they knew the words or were able to guess them. If they guessed them, ask them how they worked it out. For example, they may guess that a *major* is a type of student from the phrase *in college …*
- If students struggle to understand *spread out*, offer a translation in their L1 or give an example, such as a student spreading out their revision for an exam over several days or weeks.

Answers

a major is a student who studies a particular subject (American English).

papers are essays, long written assignments that you have to do at university (American English).

spread out means to divide something into smaller parts, in this case, to divide lots of work and do it over a longer period of time.

- **73** Ask students to do the same for the next section of the talk. Play the audio.
- Put students in pairs to discuss the five words and phrases. Again, if it is clear that students are not sure of the meaning, offer translations or explain in some other way.
- Elicit their guesses as to meaning. Accept any answer which is more or less correct, so if a student offers a definition which is reasonably close to the one given in the Answers, don't read out the answer here.

Answers

my normal workflow – the way you usually work: when, how much, how often

start off light – start doing only a little work

bump it up – work gradually harder and harder

kick it up into high gear – start working as hard as you can

staircase – a group of stairs in a house or other building

WATCH *p124*

Ask students to read the statements and decide how much they think they are like them. You may need to explain what *get distracted* means. This is something you can mime (by looking out of the window in the middle of your explanation, for example, or pointing to someone in the class who happens to be distracted at that moment!). Tell them about something you often get distracted by.

- Put students in pairs to share their answers from the questionnaire so that they can answer the question.
- Invite students to say who thinks they are big procrastinators, and if so, to tell the class what they procrastinate about, and why.

If you are short of time, or want a different approach to the video, you may want to watch the whole talk all the way through with only some brief checking questions. A version of this is on the DVD and is labelled as *TED Talk with activities*. At the end of each section, there is a short gist question. Pause after each question on screen so students can give their answers, then play the answer.

Answers to gist questions on DVD
Part 1

What does Tim's story about university show?

b Procrastinating is not the best way to work.

Part 2

According to Tim, what is the difference between the Instant Gratification Monkey and the Rational Decision-Maker?

c The Monkey doesn't take work seriously.

Part 3

What encouraged Tim to prepare a talk about procrastination?

b Seeing his photograph on the TED.com website.

Part 4

What did Tim learn about procrastination from the emails he received?

b The worst effects of procrastination happen when there are no deadlines.

- Explain the task. Students should complete the extract with one word. Give them a minute to read it and predict possible answers.
- ▶ **10.1** Play Part 1 straight through.
- Ask students to compare their answers in pairs. Go round and notice how well they did in order to decide how quickly to go through answers, and whether you will need to play Part 1 again.
- Check answers by asking the whole class for their ideas.

TED Talk Part 1 script ▶ 10.1

So in college, I was a government major, which means I had to write a lot of papers. Now, when a normal student writes a paper, they might spread the work out a little like this. So, you know – you get started maybe a little slowly, but you get enough done in the first week that, with some heavier days later on, everything gets done, things stay civil.

And I would want to do that like that. That would be the plan. I would have it all ready to go, but then, actually, the paper would come along, and then I would kind of do this. And that would happen every single paper.

But then came my 90-page senior thesis, a paper you're supposed to spend a year on. And I knew for a paper like that, my normal work flow was not an option. It was way too big a project. So I planned things out, and I decided I kind of had to go something like this. This is how the year would go. So I'd start off light, and I'd bump it up in the middle months, and then at the end, I would kick it up into high gear just like a little staircase. How hard could it be to walk up the stairs? No big deal, right?

But then, the funniest thing happened. Those first few months? They came and went, and I couldn't quite do stuff. So we had an awesome new revised plan. And then –

But then those middle months actually went by, and I didn't really write words, and so we were here. And then two months turned into one month, which turned into two weeks. And one day I woke up with three days until the deadline, still not having written a word, and so I did the only thing I could: I wrote 90 pages over 72 hours, pulling not one but two all-nighters – humans are not supposed to pull two all-nighters – sprinted across campus, dove in slow motion, and got it in just at the deadline.

I thought that was the end of everything. But a week later I get a call, and it's the school. And they say, 'Is this Tim Urban?' And I say, 'Yeah.' And they say, 'We need to talk about your thesis.' And I say, 'OK.' And they say, 'It's the best one we've ever seen.'

That did not happen.

It was a very, very bad thesis.

I just wanted to enjoy that one moment when all of you thought, 'This guy is amazing!'

No, no, it was very, very bad.

- Ask students to read sentences 1–6 and check they understand them.
- ▶ 10.2 Play Part 2 straight through.
- Ask students to compare their answers in pairs. Go round and notice how well they did in order to decide how quickly to go through answers, and whether you will need to play Part 2 again.

- Nominate students to answer. You may decide to let students watch the short section of part 2 where the answers can be heard again.

TED Talk Part 2 script ▶ 10.2

Anyway, today I'm a writer-blogger guy. And a couple of years ago, I decided to write about procrastination. So, here's the brain of a non-procrastinator.

Now ... here's my brain.

There is a difference. Both brains have a Rational Decision-Maker in them, but the procrastinator's brain also has an Instant Gratification Monkey. Now, what does this mean for the procrastinator? Well, it means everything's fine until this happens.

So the Rational Decision-Maker will make the rational decision to do something productive, but the Monkey doesn't like that plan, so he actually takes the wheel, and he says, 'Actually, let's read the entire Wikipedia page of the Nancy Kerrigan/Tonya Harding scandal, because I just remembered that that happened.

Then –

Then we're going to go over to the fridge, to see if there's anything new in there since ten minutes ago. After that, we're going to go on a YouTube spiral that starts with videos of Richard Feynman talking about magnets and ends much, much later with us watching interviews with Justin Bieber's mum.

All of that's going to take a while, so we're not going to really have room on the schedule for any work today. Sorry!'

- Tell students to look at the timeline before they watch Part 3. Check that students understand they must listen for when events a–c happen and in what order.
- ▶ 10.3 Play Part 3 straight through.
- Draw the timeline on the board while students are watching the talk. Ask students to compare their answers in pairs. Go round and notice how well they did in order to decide how quickly to go through answers, and whether you will need to play Part 3 again.
- Check answers by inviting students who want to write their answers on the board.

Well, turns out the procrastinator has a guardian angel, someone who's always looking down on him and watching over him in his darkest moments – someone called the Panic Monster.

Now, the Panic Monster is dormant most of the time, but he suddenly wakes up any time a deadline gets too close or there's danger of public embarrassment, a career disaster or some other scary consequence. And importantly, he's the only thing that the Monkey is terrified of. Now, he became very relevant in my life pretty recently, because the people of TED reached out to me about six months ago and invited me to do a TED Talk.

Now, of course, I said yes. It's always been a dream of mine to have done a TED Talk in the past.

But in the middle of all this excitement, the Rational Decision-Maker seemed to have something else on his mind. He was saying, 'Are we clear on what we just accepted? Do we get what's going to be now happening one day in the future? We need to sit down and work on this right now.' And the Monkey said, 'Totally agree, but let's just open Google Earth and zoom in to the bottom of India, like 200 feet above the ground, and we're going to scroll up for two and a half hours til we get to the top of the country, so we can get a better feel for India.'

So that's what we did that day.

As six months turned into four and then two and then one, the people of TED decided to release the speakers. And I opened up the website, and there was my face staring right back at me. And guess who woke up?

So the Panic Monster starts losing his mind, and a few seconds later, the whole system's in mayhem.

And the Monkey – remember, he's terrified of the Panic Monster – boom, he's up the tree! And finally, finally, the Rational Decision-Maker can take the wheel and I can start working on the talk.

8

- Tell students to read the statements before watching Part 4.
- ▶ 10.4 Play Part 4 straight through.
- Ask students to compare their answers in pairs. Go round and notice how well they did in order to decide how quickly to go through answers, and whether you will need to play Part 4 again. If they are having difficulties, stop at key points whenever the answer is given and repeat what Tim says at that point.
- Ask for a show of hands for the answer.

Answer

1 is not true. (*if you wanted a career where you're a self-starter … there's no deadlines on those things.*)

2 is true (*Now, if the procrastinator's only mechanism … is the Panic Monster, that's a problem, because in all of these non-deadline situations, the Panic Monster doesn't show up … the effects of procrastination, they're not contained; they just extend outward forever.*)

3 is true (*The frustration was not that they couldn't achieve their dreams; it's that they weren't even able to start chasing them.*)

And this entire situation, with the three characters – this is the procrastinator's system. It's not pretty, but in the end, it works. And this is what I decided to write about on the blog just a couple of years ago.

When I did, I was amazed by the response. Literally thousands of emails came in, from all different kinds of people from all over the world, doing all different kinds of things. These are people who were nurses, and bankers, and painters, and engineers and lots and lots of PhD students.

And they were all writing, saying the same thing: 'I have this problem too.' But what struck me was the contrast between the light tone of the post and the heaviness of these emails. These people were writing with intense frustration about what procrastination had done to their lives, about what this Monkey had done to them. And I thought about this, and I said, well, if the procrastinator's system works, then what's going on? Why are all of these people in such a dark place?

Well, it turns out that there's two kinds of procrastination. Everything I've talked about today, the examples I've given, they all have deadlines. But there's a second kind of procrastination that happens in situations when there is no deadline. So, if you wanted a career where you're a self-starter – something in the arts, something entrepreneurial – there's no deadlines on those things at first, because nothing's happening at first, not until you've gone out and done the hard work to get some momentum, to get things going.

Now, if the procrastinator's only mechanism of doing these hard things is the Panic Monster, that's a problem, because in all of these non-deadline situations, the Panic Monster doesn't show up. He has nothing to wake up for, so the effects of procrastination, they're not contained; they just extend outward forever. And it's this long-term kind of procrastination that's much less visible and much less talked about than the funnier, short-term deadline-based kind. It's usually suffered quietly and privately. And it can be the source of a huge amount of long-term unhappiness, and regrets. The frustration was not that they couldn't achieve their dreams; it's that they weren't even able to start chasing them.

I don't think non-procrastinators exist. That's right – I think all of you are procrastinators.

And some of you may have a healthy relationship with deadlines, but remember: the Monkey's sneakiest trick is when the deadlines aren't there.

We need to think about what we're really procrastinating on, because everyone is procrastinating on something in life. We need to stay aware of the Instant Gratification Monkey. That's a job for all of us. And it's a job that should probably start today.

Well, maybe not today, but …

You know. Sometime soon.

Thank you.

9 VOCABULARY IN CONTEXT

- **9a** ▶ 10.5 Tell students that they are going to watch some clips from the talk which contain new or interesting words or phrases. They should choose the correct meaning for each one. Play the Vocabulary in context section. Pause after each question on screen so students can choose the correct definition, then play the answer. If you like, you can ask students to call out the answers.

- Where a lot of students had given the wrong answer, explain again and give an additional example before moving on to the next extract.

> **Answers**
> 1 big deal = a (a difficult or important thing)
> 2 on his mind = c (he is worrying about)
> 3 staring = b (looking)
> 4 losing his mind = a (going crazy)
> 5 long-term = b (not temporary)
> 6 aware = c (knowing about something)

- **9b** Check students understand the words in italics and re-teach if necessary, or ask students if they can recall the example in the talk. Tell students to think of examples of the five things. Point out that they relate to some of the new words and phrases they have just learnt in Exercise 9a. Give them two minutes and make sure they note down their ideas.

- Put students in pairs to tell each other their ideas. Encourage them to find out as much as they can from their partners, e.g. if they say that they used to swim in the river, find out where, when, who with, etc. Go round and check they are doing the task correctly and notice errors, difficulties, or where they use L1. Help them by correcting or giving them the English they need. Focus especially on their use of the new words and phrases.

- At the end of the task, give some feedback about new language that came up, and errors to correct, which you may have written on the board. Nominate one or two students to tell the class the most interesting things they said or heard.

> **Suggested answers**
> - Things that people make *a big deal* about: celebrities and their private lives; sports and sports results; personal appearance; the brand or model of mobile phone, computer or trainers that people own; cars and motorbikes, etc.
> - Things you've had *on your mind* recently: examinations and assessments; school projects; a personal comment someone said online; a recent news event such as a terrorist attack or accident; money; a family relationship or friendship, etc.
> - Reasons why people sometimes *stare*: they have never seen something before or something which is unusual in a particular place; someone's new haircut or strange clothes; bad make-up or a coffee stain on a shirt; they think they recognize a person, but they are not sure; they are daydreaming, etc.

- *Long-term* goals or plans might include: career plans, life goals about relationships, success, family, money, and so on.
- Things you might not be *aware* of with headphones on: traffic, bicycles on the pavement, people shouting your name, accidents, etc.

10

- Put students in groups to discuss and answer the questions. Assign roles to ensure a productive discussion.

> **Teaching tip**
>
> **Assigning roles in discussions**
> Discussions are often easy to take part in but difficult to conclude. A good discussion must have an outcome, or result, but if no one person is responsible for the discussion, they can often lead nowhere and end up failing to meet their goals. Consider giving individual students in each group a role or responsibility and explain this to them before the discussion.
>
> **The chairperson.** Their role is to start the discussion by asking the questions, asking how the other group members want to conduct the discussion or even deciding this on their own. They should also make sure that everyone, even the quieter students, gets a chance to say what they want, by inviting them to contribute.
>
> **The secretary.** Their role is to keep a note of what was said, and to ask group members to explain things clearly so that they can write any less clear ideas down. They may also summarize what the group said for the rest of the class when asked by the teacher. It's a good idea to give this role to a strong student who can write and contribute to the discussion at the same time.
>
> **The timekeeper.** Their role is to make sure that the group achieves its goals in the time they have. This may involve asking the group to hurry up and move on to the next point if they have been talking for too long about something else.
> Students take turns at taking on these roles so that it is fair for everyone.

- Go round and listen out for a healthy exchange of ideas, offering support where needed. Encourage them to use their own experience of procrastination to inform their ideas, and prompt them for alternative solutions to the problem of distraction.
- Stop the discussions and bring the groups together. Nominate students to tell the class which of the tips were most popular in each group and why, and find out if they came up with other suggestions.

Break jobs into small steps. Advantages: big jobs don't look so big; feels motivating to tick lots of little jobs off a list. Disadvantage: may not be necessary for some jobs, so you waste time breaking them up into small steps when they are small enough already.

Download a website-blocking app. Reminds you that you shouldn't be checking social media, but they are easy to get round and unblock. Also, we all need a little distraction from time to time. No one can concentrate for hours without a break, so you might need access to fun websites.

Planning ahead helps you get organized and prioritize the jobs you have to do as long as you leave in room for flexibility in case plans have to change.

A friend can hold you accountable for your actions, i.e. you are more likely to work hard if you know you have to show someone how much you've done at the end of the week. But a friend might be very lenient, and let you do less than you said you would in order to feel free to do fun stuff themselves. Also, it may not be fair on the friendship to put such responsibility on its shoulders.

CHALLENGE

- Tell students about an unfulfilled ambition of your own, or remind them of the one you mentioned at the start of the lesson, in order to encourage them to share their unfulfilled dreams and ambitions.

- Put students in pairs to read the Challenge box and talk about something they keep meaning to do but don't seem to get round to doing. You might also tell them to try to find solutions for one another.

- After a few minutes, invite students to share with the class. Encourage them to do the things they want to.

Homework
- Set Workbook Lesson 10D exercises on page 118 for homework.

- Students either start using one of the techniques discussed in Exercise 10 to stop getting so distracted, or they take on the challenge they talked about in the final activity and plan to make it a reality in their lives. Make a note of each student's plan and follow up on it in subsequent lessons by asking them whether they have made any progress and, if so, what.

- Stronger students choose and watch another TED Talk about something related to this talk or this unit. Students browse the TED playlists until they find one. They recommend a talk that they found and explain how it relates to recent lessons.

10E Milestones pp126–127

SPEAKING p126

- Put students in pairs to talk about the questions. Check understanding of *restrictions* (rules that stop you doing something). Go round and check students are doing the task correctly and don't need help with vocabulary.

- Find out what the students know about their country's age restrictions. You might want to check online for this information if you are not sure; alternatively, ask students to look it up if they have internet access in the classroom.

- 🎧 **74** Explain the task. Play the audio.
- Let students compare answers in pairs.
- Nominate students to give their answers. Ask if any of the information is surprising to them.

> **Answers**
> vote – Turkey and Colombia: 18
> leave school – Turkey: 17 or 18; Colombia: 15
> drive – Turkey: 18; Colombia: 16

Audioscript 🎧 74

A = Alper, J = Jimena

A: *In Turkey, where I'm from, we can learn to drive when we're 18 years old.*

J: *That's very late. It's 16 in Colombia.*

A: *16?! That's crazy! If I could choose, I wouldn't let anyone drive until they're twenty at least.*

J: *Really? Why?*

A: *Do you know how many accidents are caused by teenagers? Everyone knows people tend to make dangerous decisions and take risks when they're young. That's why it's so expensive to get insurance when you're young.*

J: *Isn't one of the main reasons people learn young so that they learn well? Driving is about picking up good habits. The earlier you learn, the better you learn. At least, that's what I think.*

A: *OK, but 20 isn't too old to learn, is it? Otherwise, what's the point of going to university in your twenties?*

J: *That's different. You're not learning a skill like driving at university.*

A: *Hmm, I don't know. Anyway, what about voting? How old do you have to be to vote in elections in Colombia?*

J: *18. Is it the same in Turkey?*

A: *Yes, I think it's the same in most places. But that's too old, I think.*

J: *I agree. I don't see why we can't vote when we're 16. It's partly because of that that young people aren't interested in politics.*

A: *Absolutely! And the whole purpose of voting is to help to decide the future of the country – our futures.*

J: *Right. I mean, you can leave school at 15 – therefore, you should be able to make other big decisions then.*

A: *You can leave school at 15?!*

J: *Yes, it happens.*

A: *Wow! I think it's 17 or 18 in Turkey.*

- Explain the task. Give students a minute to read the questions. Before playing the audio again, let them try to answer from memory.
- 🎧 **74** Play the audio.
- Nominate students to share their answers. Ask if anyone can remember the exact wording but do not insist on this at this stage, since it wasn't what they were asked to do.

> **Answers**
> **1** He says teenagers have more accidents because they tend to make dangerous decisions and take risks.
> **2** She believes that the earlier you learn, the better you learn.
> **3** They think that it's partly because of the voting restrictions that young people aren't interested in politics.

- Look at the instructions. Check that students understand all the vocabulary. Do the first item with the whole class. Write on the board: *I sent him a text ____* . Elicit the correct ending and write: *I sent him a text ____ that he would understand why I'm angry.* Then ask students to find the missing word from the Useful language box (*so*).
- Let students do the rest of the activity on their own. Go round and check that students are doing the task correctly and notice errors and difficulties. Focus on these in feedback.
- When most students have finished, let them compare answers in pairs.
- Nominate students to read out the whole sentence, not just the numbers and letters.

> **Answers**
> **1** (so) f   **2** (in) e   **3** (why) h   **4** (to) d
> **5** (Consequently/Therefore) b   **6** (is) g   **7** (by) c
> **8** (of) a

Extension

Do some quick fire practice of the new structures. Write the following causes and reasons on the board, and add any others that you like. Put students in pairs to talk about them using the useful language, e.g. *The reason we have two eyes is so that we can see how far away things are more accurately.*

we have two eyes
sun cream
our eyelashes
global warming
the Egyptians wanted to bury their dead kings in style

Extension

Put students in pairs. Tell them that they are going to play a game to practise the Useful language more. Explain that you will call out the beginning of five sentences and the students should take turns to finish them with a cause or reason. They should keep going until they run out of ideas. The student who says the last reason wins a point. Read these out one at a time.
I didn't do my homework . . .
I borrowed my brother's laptop . . .
I'm not wearing any socks today . . .
I enjoyed the lesson . . .
I couldn't buy you a coffee . . .

- Decide which law is under discussion in this task. You may decide or you might have a class vote for which law it is. Alternatively, let students decide for themselves, and then put all the students who chose each law together. You may even decide whether to let them choose any other law with an age restriction.
- Explain the task. Depending on your decision about how to choose, tell students what they will talk about, or ask them what they *want* to talk about.
- Divide the class into two groups, A and B, and further divide the As and Bs into groups of four to six. The As should make a list of reasons for lowering the age limit, and the Bs reasons this might be a bad idea.
- Let the As and Bs regroup so that they are each talking to different As and Bs. This is so that they can share their arguments. Allow them time to copy each other's ideas. Ask them to think of at least three times in their argument when they might be able to use expressions from the Useful language box.

Fast finishers

Groups that finish quickly can be asked to repeat the exercise with another law.

- Put students in pairs, A and B. If there are any students without a partner because there are odd numbers, they can listen to one of the other pairs and decide whose arguments were more convincing. Explain the task.
- Go round and check students are doing the task correctly and notice errors, difficulties, or where they use L1. Make a note of any language points to go over with the class.

- Stop the task when most pairs have finished. Find out if any of the students have managed to persuade their partners that their argument is better. Find out if that's because the partners already believed their arguments.
- At the end of the task, give some feedback about new language that came up, and focus on errors to correct, which you may have written on the board. You can also share some interesting things you heard with the class.

WRITING A for and against essay *p127*

Ask students to read the essay title and find out what ages the students think they will leave home. Ask them why they think this, and also how they feel about it.

- Explain the task. If you think it may be difficult for some students to think of so many reasons, you could offer some support by writing the following prompt words on the board: *parents, money, housework, independence, emotions, travel, university.*
- Let pairs compare their lists with another pair.
- Invite volunteers to give their reasons.

- Look at the instructions. Refer students to the model essay on page 153.
- Nominate students to tell the class whether they predicted any of this writer's arguments. Ask whether anyone managed to think of different arguments to the writer's.

> **Answers**
> Overall, the writer thinks young people should move away soon after finishing school, as long as they can afford to.

10 WRITING SKILL Using discourse markers

- **10a** Direct students to the Useful language box on page 127 and explain that discourse markers make it easier for the reader to follow what the writer has written (the argument).
- Explain the task. You might get students to copy the Useful language box out in their notebooks first, leaving space under each heading for more. They can add the words and phrases that they find in the essay to these lists. You might want to put students in pairs and tell one student to have the unit page open and the other student have page 153 open to avoid a lot of flipping backwards and forwards.
- Write up the headings from the Useful language box into columns on the board. When students have finished looking, they can write what they have found in the correct columns.
- When there are no more words to put on the board, ask the class to check that they are all in the correct columns.

> **Answers**
> Sequencing: *There are a number of …, Firstly, …*
> Adding arguments: *It's also …, What's more, …, Not only that, but …*
> Introducing arguments against: *But …, However, …, Even so, …*
> Concluding: *Personally, I don't believe …*
> (Other discourse markers students may have noticed include:
> Markers introducing examples: *such as, like*
> Markers introducing results: *Consequently, …*)

- **10b** Explain the task.
- **Optional step.** You may want to give students the opportunity to try out different orders before making a final decision. To do this, put students in pairs or small groups, having photocopied the exercise enough times for each group and cut out the sentences into strips. Students can then physically move the sentences around until they have got it right. You could make this a race by handing out the strips quickly at the same time and saying 'Go!'
- When you ask students for the correct order, insist on asking them to explain their choice.

> **Answers**
> **1** f **2** c **3** a **4** b **5** d **6** g **7** e
>
> Sentence f introduces the topic. Sentences c, a and b offer reasons it might be a good idea to go straight from school to university (and the discourse markers determine the order – *Firstly, Also, Finally*). Sentences d and g offer reasons why it might not be a good idea. Again the discourse markers determine the order, *On the other hand* introducing the opposing argument and *What's more* adding a further point. The discourse marker in e clearly shows that this is a concluding statement.

Extension

Get students to change the text slightly by substituting alternative discourse markers for the existing ones. This way, you can check that they have understood the meaning and use of each one.

- Explain the task. Make sure they understand that they only need to write one essay and can choose the one they prefer. Suggest that they try to think of arguments for two or three of the essays, since they should probably choose the essay that they can think of the most arguments for and against to write.
- Tell students to refer to the model text on page 153 for help. Remind them of the structure of the model by reading out the advice at the back of the book and reminding them of

the language they have studied. You might also refer them to the Useful language for giving your opinion on page 42.

- If you are going to give students a mark, tell them it will be higher if they organize their essay in a similar way and use language they have learnt. Put students in pairs and tell them to talk about or plan their essay.
- Set the writing for homework or set a time limit of about twenty minutes to do it in class. As students are writing, go round and offer help. Play quiet instrumental music in the background if possible, provide dictionaries, and be available for students to ask questions and to check their progress. Check their work, paying special attention to their use of discourse markers. You might note some common errors to feedback on later.

Fast finishers

Students who finish quickly can think of arguments for and against for other essays in the list.

> **Suggested arguments**
>
> *A university education doesn't help prepare people for most jobs. Work experience is much more valuable.*
>
> For: a lot of what you learn at university is theoretical, not practical; the academic world teaches general concepts and knowledge, not specific skills required for each job.
>
> Against: university teaches you to think for yourself, allowing you to take the initiative in your job; you need to meet deadlines at university, often with little support.
>
> *The legal age for driving is too low and should be raised.*
>
> For: skills learnt young may be learnt faster and better; by allowing younger people to drive, parents don't have to provide as much of a taxi service for their children.
>
> Against: evidence suggests that teenage brains are more likely to take risks and not understand possible consequences of their actions; we should be discouraging people from driving in today's polluted world, not encouraging them.
>
> *Young people do better by staying in their home town rather than moving to a new city.*
>
> For: support systems, such as family, are there to help them; it means people don't have to travel as far to visit family.
>
> Against: they don't learn true independence as quickly; work and other opportunities may be limited in their home towns.
>
> *It is better to work to deadlines that other people set than to set them yourself.*
>
> For: being accountable to other people is usually more motivating to get work done; deadlines that other people set are less flexible, and therefore not so open to abuse.
>
> Against: we should learn not to be reliant on other people to make us work; many things we might want to do are personal goals, so it is hard to create the situation where other people set them for you.

When students have finished writing, put them together with other students who wrote the same essay as them to answer the question. Invite anyone with differences of opinion to explain their disagreements and find out what the rest of the class thinks.

> **Homework**
> - Set Workbook Lesson 10E and Review exercises on pages 119–121 for homework.
> - Students write another for and against essay from the choices in Exercise 11.

Communicative activities

Teacher's notes

1.1 Snatch!

Aim

To talk about the present

Language

Present simple, present continuous, present perfect

Time

30 minutes

Preparation

Two copies of worksheet for every four or five students. Cut out sentence halves (or pairs of sentences) of one of the worksheets. Separate first halves of sentences from second halves. Mix both sets up separately.

Procedure

- Write on the board:

  1 Karol lives in Posnań … a … until he moves to Brno.
  2 Karol is living in Posnań … b … , where he grew up.
  3 Karol has lived in Posnań … c … for about five years.

- In pairs, students match sentence beginnings (1–3) and endings (a–c). They explain reasons for their choices. If they are having difficulties, refer them to page 128 of the Student's Book.

- Elicit answers.

Answers

1 b – describes permanent present action;

2 a – describes temporary present situation;

3 c – describes present action that started in past.

- Demonstrate the game. Place the pack of first parts of sentences face down in a pile. Spread out sentence endings face up on the table so that all are visible.

- Four or five volunteers play a round in front of class. One player in each round is 'quizmaster' and reads out a sentence beginning from the top of the pile. They also have the other worksheet as an answer sheet. The other players are in a race to pick up the correct ending.

- The player who chooses the correct ending first wins the sentence, but must explain the reason to the quizmaster. Teacher decides if there are any differences of opinion, or if no one in the group can explain.

- Stop the demonstration. Play continues with quizmaster role moving to the player to their left, until only one

sentence ending remains. Players count sentences they have won; the player with most sentences wins.

- Divide class into groups of four or five. Hand out sentence beginnings and endings and start game. Go round and notice errors, difficulties, or where they use L1.

- When groups have finished, congratulate winners. Elicit from the class the completed sentences and explanations.

- Give feedback about errors that came up, writing them on the board. Find out what students learnt from playing.

Fast finishers

- Organize sentences into related pairs and discuss differences. Alternatively, groups divide the eighteen sentences in half (so there are nine complete sentences, shuffled, in each pile) and play 'Snap!' in pairs.

1.2 Happiness is …

Aim
To revise and extend vocabulary from the unit

Language
Adjectives describing feelings and their abstract nouns

Time
45 minutes

Preparation
One copy of the worksheet for every student

Procedure
- Give each student a worksheet. Explain that each answer is related to the word in italics. Show them the first 'across' clue. Explain that the word in italics, *delight*, is a noun, so the answer is the corresponding adjective, *delighted*. Then show the word in italics in the first 'down' clue: it is an adjective (*disappointed*), so the answer is the corresponding noun, *disappointment*. Point out that the answer to 3 across is not a derivative of *fear*. Students do the crossword in pairs.
- Go through the answers with the whole class. Write the nouns on the board (*delight, fear, friendliness, sadness, exhaustion, disappointment, loneliness, depression, embarrassment, happiness, nervousness, confusion, excitement, relaxation*).
- Explain that the crossword clues are not good definitions because they don't help you understand the meaning of the words (saying you feel *delight* when you are *delighted* doesn't clarify at all). Offer a personal definition, using the structure: *[abstract noun] is [gerund]*, e.g. *For me, delight is finding out my favourite band are coming to play a concert in my town.* Elicit more concrete examples of *delight*.
- Tell students to write personal, concrete definitions for six of the abstract nouns from the crossword.
- Go round the room and offer support and ideas, correcting errors you see (e.g. insist on the *-ing* form of the verb after *is*).
- When most students have finished, stop the activity. Nominate students to read out definitions without saying the abstract nouns; the others guess and call out the abstract noun.
- Explain that they are now going to write poems about these words using the definitions they have written.
- Divide the class into pairs. With more than 28 students, make fourteen groups. Give each pair or group responsibility for one abstract noun (decide the nouns for each group).
- Ask one student from each pair or group to go around the classroom and collect all the sentences that relate to the noun they were assigned. Once they have collected them all, tell them to decide how to order the sentences into a poem. They should write the poem and give it a title.

For example:
'Delight'
Delight is a day at the fair with my friends.
Delight is getting exactly what I wanted for my birthday.
Delight is finding out my favourite band are coming to play a concert in my town.
Delight is … (etc.)

- You could ask them to write the poems neatly in order to create a poster or a booklet of poems.
- Let students read each other's poems and choose their favourite.

Answers
Across
  1 delighted
  3 scared / afraid
 11 friendliness
 12 sadness
 13 exhausted

Down
  1 disappointment
  2 lonely
  4 depression
  5 embarrassment
  6 happiness
  7 nervousness
  8 confused
  9 excitement
 10 relaxed

Extension/Fast finishers
- Ask students to choose six other nouns they haven't chosen before and write personal definitions for them.

2.1 Talk to someone who …

Aim

To practise grammar from the unit

Language

Narrative tenses: past simple, continuous and perfect, *used to* affirmative, negative and interrogative forms

Time

40 minutes

Preparation

One copy of the worksheet for every student

Procedure

- Tell students that they are going to do a speaking activity in which they find out about each other's childhoods.
- Show the class the worksheet and say *It says 'Find someone who … was already reading when they started going to school.* Write this on the board. Ask *What question would you ask people to find out if they were reading then?* Elicit the sentence on the board: *Were you already reading when you …?*
- Elicit the other question structures they will need, e.g. *Could you … / Did you use to … / Had you already …* If students need help forming questions, tell them to write the questions before doing the speaking activity.
- Point to the second column on the worksheet. Explain that they need to ask the same question to different classmates until they find someone who says 'yes' to the question, at which point they should write that student's name. Tell them to try to get a different name for each question.
- Point to the third column. Tell them to ask for more information and make notes. Invite suggestions for questions to follow up with after finding out that their classmate could read aged three, e.g. *Who taught you so young?* or *What did you read?*
- Point out the spaces at the bottom of the worksheet. Tell them to write one or two more questions to ask.
- Ask students to stand up with the worksheet and pen. Put music on to encourage conversation. Listen to check for correct question formation and for follow-up questions. Make a note of common errors, especially concerning tenses. Correct serious errors as you hear them, such as ones concerning narrative tenses.
- When most students have completed the worksheet, ask them to return to their seats. Nominate students to share with the class the most interesting things they learnt. Correct errors on the board.

2.2 Excuse me, …?

Aim

To practise asking for, giving and understanding directions around town

Language

Expressions used for asking for and giving directions

Time

40 minutes

Preparation

One copy of the worksheet for every two students, cut in two

Procedure

- Tell students that they are going to roleplay asking for and giving directions. Elicit useful language by writing on the board the headings: *Asking for directions, Giving directions* and *Talking about landmarks.*
- Tell students to copy the headings into their notebooks and to write sentences they might say under each heading (with Student's Books closed). Elicit sentences, checking for accuracy. Drill sentences, whole class and individually, for pronunciation.
- Show the class the two maps, A and B. Explain that they are maps of the same place, but map A shows where eight places are which map B doesn't, and *vice versa.* Tell them to find out where the eight missing places are by asking their partner (and not by looking at their partner's map!).
- Point to where it says *Start here* and explain that the first time they speak they must imagine that they are in the street at this point, and that A asks B for directions to the first place on their list (i.e. the market). A must say *Excuse me* and thank B for their help, and write in the name of the place on the correct building.
- Tell them to take turns asking for directions, starting with Student A asking where the market is (then B asking for the supermarket, and so on). After each roleplay, they start from the last destination, i.e. the starting point for A's second turn is the market.
- Put students in pairs, A and B, and hand out one map each, which they must not show to each other. Set a time limit of ten minutes. Go round and make a note of errors.
- When most students have finished, let them compare their maps to check that they have marked every building correctly.
- Correct any errors you heard.

Extension

Students give directions to a mystery destination. The rest of the class call out the name of the place as soon as they think they know.

3.1 Pass the hot potato!

Aim
To practise present perfect with time expressions

Language
Present perfect simple and continuous
Time expressions: *already, yet, just, for, since, never*

Time
30 minutes

Preparation
One sheet cut up for every six students. If possible, one potato for each group

Procedure
- Divide the class into groups of four to six.
- Explain the game. In groups of six, five players take a card each, place it at their feet and stand in a circle so that others can read it. The last student sits out and is the note-taker; their job is to note all sentences and keep time. This game can also be played sitting around a table with the cards on the table in front of each player.
- The player with the potato passes it to another player by saying a correct sentence containing the word of the person they want to pass the potato to. To pass the potato to the person with the question mark, they must form a question.
- The rules are as follows.
  - Sentences must be grammatically correct. Anyone, including the note-taker, can challenge a sentence. The teacher adjudicates in any disagreements.
  - Sentences must be in the present perfect simple or continuous. To win, at least one sentence must be in the present perfect continuous.
  - Players must not repeat sentences, or say sentences which are similar, e.g. changing the subject from *we* to *he* isn't acceptable. Players cannot use sentences from a previous round.
  - Players have ten seconds to say their sentence (the hot potato will burn their hands), otherwise they pass the potato to the person to their left without making a sentence.
    For example, Paula has 'since' by her feet, Guillermo has 'already', Julio has 'just'. Julio has the potato.
    Julio: *'I haven't been to Porto since January.'* (used *since*, so passes the potato to Paula)
    Paula: *I've just had breakfast.* (back to Julio)
    Julio: *We've already been playing this game for two minutes.* (to Guillermo), etc.
  - The winner is the first person to have passed the potato to everyone in the circle with correct sentences. The winner is now the note-taker; cards are shuffled, and the next round begins.
  - Hand out a set of cards to each group. Replace the potato cards for potatoes if possible. Tell them to start.

3.2 Collocation relay

Aim
To revise and practise vocabulary from the unit

Language
Collocations and expressions related to sport, e.g. *win second prize*
Other expressions from Units 1 and 2.

Time
45 minutes

Preparation
Two copies of the worksheet for every three or four students. Cut one in half, then cut Game 1 (the completed cards) into cards and shuffle them; bring scissors and a small prize to class

Procedure
- Draw the first two domino cards on the board. Show the connection by underlining the collocation: *won … second prize*. Elicit what the first words on the third card might be: *Represent … what?* (*country, club*, etc.). Explain that sentences are unrelated to each other.
- Put students in teams of three or four. Tell them they must join all the cards in a relay line. The first and last cards are marked 'Start' and 'Finish'. The first group to finish is the winner.
- Build up tension for the start of the race. Place cards face down. Then say *Ready … steady … GO!*
- Check that teams are matching cards correctly. Help slower teams by indicating errors. Check the order of relays is correct before declaring a winner.
- Let other teams complete their relays (the winners could help). Ask the winners to read out answers before awarding the prize. Correct any errors you noticed.
- Show the class the blank cards. Explain that teams are going to prepare a similar relay for another team to order. Point out that the expressions in Game 1 came from Unit 3; they are now going to find expressions from Units 1 and 2. Elicit one or two expressions from each unit to remind them what they have learnt, e.g.
  from Unit 1: *get scared, make someone angry, take a break, directed by;*
  from Unit 2: *go for a drive, shopping centre, throw food away, go straight on.*
- Hand out the blank sheets. Explain that they should separate the collocation, e.g. *throw … | … food away,* writing the first part on one card, and the second on the next. Hand out the second unused worksheets for them to make a copy of the answers.
- Set a time limit of fifteen minutes. Check sentences are correct, and that you can match the cards.

- When groups have finished, hand out scissors for them to cut up one relay. Slower groups can shorten their relays by missing out some cards.
- When all the groups are ready, have them swap cards with another group. Don't make this a competitive race, since some relays will be easier than others.
- Go round and notice errors and difficulties.
- When most groups have finished, let them check their answers. Give feedback about errors you noticed.

4.1 Picnic planning

Aim
To practise grammar from the unit

Language
Futures, especially future arrangements

Time
40 minutes

Preparation
One copy of the worksheet for every student, cut in two

Procedure
- Show the class a copy of the diary. Tell them to imagine that it is Monday morning (if it isn't) and that they have an exciting week ahead (including English lessons!).
- Invite suggestions for an exciting week, and encourage them to include unusual or unlikely events, e.g. *attending the premiere of a new film, going parachute-jumping.*
- When students make a suggestion, say, *Fantastic! And when are you doing that?* When they tell you, pretend to write it in your diary. Tell students to spend five minutes filling in their diaries with five exciting things.
- Go around the class and check students are on task.
- When they have finished, find out from one or two students what they are most looking forward to.
- Tell the class about another exciting event to look forward to – a picnic with their classmates. Tell them that they will have to organise it beforehand, and elicit what it includes. List the following: agreeing on the day and time of the picnic (bearing in mind what they are already doing this week); deciding where they will go, what they will eat and other details (e.g. transport, shopping, cooking); and any sports or games they will play and what they will need for these.
- Demonstrate the activity with a couple of students, e.g.
  A: *Dario, let's have the picnic on Thursday afternoon.*
  B: *Thursday isn't possible for me – I'm going on X-Factor. What about Friday afternoon?*
  A: *Ah, that's when my flight to New York takes off, I'm afraid. But I'll be back by Saturday lunchtime. What about you, Suki?*
- Elicit useful future structures, i.e. present continuous for arrangements, present simple for scheduled events, *will* for predictions/spontaneous decisions, *going to* for firm intentions.
- Put students in groups of four or five. Tell them not to look at each other's diaries, but to organize a time and place for the picnic. Everyone in the group must be able to come, even if it means rearranging other events. Give them five minutes for this.
- Hand out a picnic planner to each student. Tell them to organize other details and decide who's doing what.
- After five minutes, stop the discussion and find out about each group's arrangements. Ask if you are invited!

4.2 Food sayings

Aim

To further explore the topic of the unit

Language

Food proverbs, quotes and other sayings

Time

40 minutes

Preparation

One copy of the worksheet for every student and one more for every 24 students. Cut one (two if you have more than 24 students) up and shuffle cards

Procedure

- Write on the board: *An apple a day keeps the doctor away.* Explain that this is a famous English saying. Ask monolingual classes to translate it into their L1. In multilingual classes, skip this step and ask them to explain what it means in English, i.e. If you eat apples (or fruit and vegetables) regularly, you won't get sick.

- Ask students whether they have any similar sayings in their language. Elicit suggestions.

- Hand out one card from the cut-up sheet to each student. Explain that they have half of a food-related saying and they need to find the person with the other half and sit with them. Numbered cards (1–12) are the first half and lettered cards (a–l) are the endings.

- Ask students to stand and mingle, reading out their card to everyone until they find a match.

- When everyone has a partner, elicit each full saying, checking they are all correct.

- Give pairs two minutes to discuss what their saying means. Be available to help. Nominate pairs to explain their sayings.

- Hand out one worksheet to each student. Give them a minute to match the beginnings and endings. Let them confer with other classmates to check their answers.

- Tell the class to read the sayings again and to 1) cross out any that they disagree with, 2) put a tick (✓) next to any that they strongly believe, and 3) put a question mark (?) next to any that they would like to talk about more or ask questions about.

- Go through each saying finding out the students' reaction to each and why.

- Ask the students to choose the top three sayings in terms of how relevant they are to the students' lives. When they have done that, conduct a class vote on the top three.

- Finally, have students write a food saying of their own. This can be sensible advice about healthy eating, good table manners, when, where or who to eat with, etc., or it can be silly advice or advice that reflects their personal tastes, such as *Never eat celery, unless you are a rabbit.*

- Have students write their sayings on the board, or better, on pieces of paper which they can put on the wall for other students to read.

Answers and suggested interpretations

1g Eating is too important to be forgotten when you are busy.

2j Food is necessary for making it fun when people get together.

3b Food has the power to make you see the best in people, even people that make you very angry.

4i You don't have to be rich to appreciate good food (good food doesn't have to be expensive).

5c A light-hearted way of justifying eating at any time of day.

6l The food you eat affects you in profound ways, from your health to your personality.

7e Don't eat unhealthy food, or too much food, so that you get sick and die early.

8d A funny saying (by Miss Piggy of *The Muppets*), which goes against all good advice. Eating that much is impossible!

9k Start your day with a big meal, then have smaller meals as you go through the day.

10a You decide whether your life is good or bad by what you include in it.

11f The enjoyment of food depends on how much you need it. Everything tastes good if you are very hungry.

12h Giving food only helps people temporarily; education is more useful – you don't need help.

5.1 Note to self

Aim
To practise present and past modals and modal-like structures

Language
Modals for obligation, prohibition, possibility, permission

Time
45 minutes

Preparation
One copy of the worksheet for every student. Do the activity yourself beforehand

Procedure
- Explain that the activity is a thought experiment that will help them think about the important things in life. Read out the first paragraph of the worksheet.
- Tell the class some of the things you wrote that you feel comfortable telling them. What you say will affect what they write about, so make it varied and meaningful, e.g.
  - *You love Viktoria – she's your wife. You won't have to wait long to realize why.*
  - *You haven't been able to get very fit yet. Don't ever give up. It's important and you will do it one day.*
  - *You should watch a TV series called 'The Wire'. It's quite old now, but it'll teach you a lot about the world.*
  - *You're an English teacher. It's sometimes hard teaching teenagers, but you need to keep doing it because it's such a fantastic, rewarding job.*
- Hand out the worksheets, point out the Useful language box, and set the task.
- Go round and check students are on task. Encourage them to use past and present modals, but don't force them. Make a note of errors you see, especially those concerning modal verbs.
- When they've finished, put them in small groups of three to five students to share anything that they are happy to talk about – they do not need to share *everything*. But the more personal your examples were at the start, the more likely students will be to open up.
- After five minutes, stop the discussion and say that luckily the memory loss hasn't happened yet, so they have two more minutes to add any new ideas.
- At the end, invite students to share with the class anything they would like to.
- Finally, write on the board any common or serious errors that have come up. Get students to correct them.

Extension/Homework
- Students make a selfie video for themselves. They improvise and speak continuously. They start: *Hi. I'm you. Listen, you lost your memory, so there are a few things you need to know. OK, so first thing, . . .*

5.2 What's my line?

Aim
To revise and extend vocabulary from the unit

Language
Work-related expressions and *Yes/No* questions

Time
30 minutes

Preparation
One copy of the worksheet for every five or six students, cut up

Procedure
- Shuffle a set of cards and do the first one as an example.
- Take the top card, don't show it to the class and mime a non-obvious aspect of the job: for example, for *bus driver* don't mime driving, but maybe unlocking the door and climbing in to the driver's seat, or changing a tyre.
- Tell students that they must guess your job by asking a maximum of ten *yes/no* questions, e.g. *Is your job physically demanding? Do you use a computer? Can you make a lot of money doing this job?* If they guess the job, they 'win' the card. If they don't, you keep it.
- Use this stage to correct errors in question forms and to encourage use of the vocabulary in Lesson 5A.
- The student that asked a question can guess the job if they want. If they are wrong, they are out of that round. Once a player's turn is over, other players have the opportunity to guess the job, always with the risk that if they are wrong, they are out of that round. If nobody does, the next student asks a question.
- Explain that students take turns to take a job card from the pile, that the player to their left starts with the first question and that they take turns asking questions going in a clockwise direction.
- Put students into groups of five or six and hand out one pile of jobs cards per group. Give them twenty minutes to play the game. As they play, go round and check they are playing and forming questions correctly.
- Congratulate the winners at the end of the activity. Point out any common or interesting errors.

6.1 Tricky choices

Aim
To compare what people would do in different hypothetical situations

Language
Second conditional

Time
30 minutes

Preparation
One copy of the worksheet for every six students, cut up

Procedure
- Write *Tricky choices* on the board. Ask students what *tricky* means. Show them how *tricky* and *choices* start with the same /tʃ/ sound. Ask them if they have had to make any tricky choices. You might lead by example and offer a tricky choice you've had to make in your life, such as whether to accept one job offer or another, or whether to tell someone a secret or not.
- You may decide to pre-teach the following words: *asteroid, be brought up, swap, lever, desert island, scratch, shipwreck, astronomer*. Or you can let students look them up in dictionaries or ask you when they meet the words.
- Place the cards in a pile face down on the table. Pick up a card, read it out and say what you would do in that situation; then ask others what they would do, and let the discussion continue for as long as it needs.
- Put students in groups of five or six and get them to play. Set a time limit of no more than 25 minutes.
- At the end, ask students from different groups which questions generated the most discussion, which were the silliest, most surprising, etc.

6.2 Pitch a gadget

Aim
Practise verbs describing ability

Language
allow, enable, prevent, stop you from, etc.
Vocabulary in Lesson 6B

Time
50 minutes

Preparation
One copy of the worksheet for the whole class, cut up.
If possible, enlarge the images.

Procedure
- Write *gadget* on the board. Show your mobile phone or any other gadget you have and ask students to do the same. Elicit a definition (a small piece of equipment that helps you do something, and it uses technology in some way). Write *multipurpose* on the board and show how your mobile phone is *multipurpose*. Ask students to think of other *multipurpose* gadgets, e.g. a Swiss Army penknife.
- Demonstrate the activity. Show the first image to the class or let students pass the photo around. Say that they must listen for three uses of this gadget.
- Pretend to be a sales person trying to sell the gadget. Say: *Introducing the new Handyman 3000. This clever device **allows you to** cook and use your mobile device at the same time without getting your mobile device dirty. Each of your fingers becomes a control for your mobile, tablet or PC, **enabling you to** move a mouse on the screen, turn the volume up and down on your multimedia and even write text messages without touching your device! The finger covers are cleverly designed **to prevent you from** cutting your fingers when cutting vegetables with a sharp knife. Not only that, but this section here **also lets you** grate cheese faster than a normal cheese grater. And all for the amazing price of 30 euros!*
- Put students in pairs to discuss the three uses of the *Handyman 3000*. Elicit answers from the class.

> **Answers**
> It allows you to control your mobile while you cook; it prevents you from cutting your fingers when cutting vegetables; it lets you grate cheese faster than a normal cheese grater.

- Tell students they are going to pitch their own products to potential investors. Put them into a maximum of 11 pairs or groups. Hand out one photo to each group.
- Tell them to think of as many clever uses for the gadgets as they can and prepare a presentation, which must include a name for the product, reasons you should buy it and a

price. Remind them of the verbs in Lesson 6B Vocabulary building (*enable*, *allow*, etc.).

- Go round the groups offering support.
- Tell the students that they need to 1) convince people with money to invest in their gadget, and 2) invest 10,000 euros in somebody else's gadget (not their own).
- During each presentation make a note of any common or interesting errors as they present their ideas. At the end of each presentation, invite the class to ask any questions they have about the gadget.
- When all the groups have pitched their ideas, find out which gadgets have got investment and how much. Congratulate the successful pitches.
- Conclude by correcting errors that you heard.

7.1 Biography of a brand

Aim
To revise and practise grammar of the unit

Language
Passives: present simple, past simple, past continuous, present perfect, past perfect, modal verbs

Time
30 minutes

Preparation
One copy of the worksheet for every two students, cut in two

Procedure
- Write *Vans* on the board and ask if they know anything about the company. If they don't, tell them that it makes shoes and that they are going to find out more about it.
- Show the class the two texts and point out that A has the information missing in B and *vice versa*. Write the first sentence on the board, with the missing information marked by a gap, as in text A. Elicit the question that the students need to ask to get that information: *When was the first Vans shop opened?* Remind them of the rules for making the passive in the past simple tense.
- Divide the class into two groups and hand out Text A to one group and Text B to the other.
- Give them ten minutes to write the passive questions they will need to ask to get the missing information.
- Go round the class and check. Correct errors that you see or hear. If there are some common errors being made, stop the activity and go through the rules of question formation in the passive with the class.
- When most students have finished, reorganize them in pairs of A and B. Tell them not to show their texts to each other!
- Give them ten minutes to ask and answer each other's questions, making sure that they write the answers. Go round the room checking that they are on task.
- When students have completed their text, nominate A students and B students to read out their respective gapped sentences.
- Ask them to research another fashion company for homework and write a similar text about it. They could then read these out in the following lesson, with the other students making notes.

 # 7.2 I.O.U.

Aim

To revise and extend vocabulary from the unit

Language

Money vocabulary, e.g. *owe, in debt, pay off, pay back*

Time

30 minutes

Preparation

One copy of the worksheet for every four students, top part whole and cards cut up

Procedure

- Tell students the name of the activity. Teach them that *I.O.U.* is an abbreviation for 'I owe you', so you might leave someone who has lent you £10 a note saying *I.O.U. £10*.
- Make sure students understand *flatmates* (people who share a flat) and *rent* (the money you pay for living in someone else's house or flat). Read out the first paragraph on the worksheet. Say that they will each receive some information about the flatmates, but they need to share it to answer the questions.
- Put students in groups of four. Hand out one information card to each student. If groups have three students, give one student two cards. They must not show their card.
- Give them two minutes to read the information on the card.
- Hand out one money summary to each group. Check understanding of *income, savings, payments* and *debts*. Tell the class that they must work together to answer the questions and find a solution so that they aren't thrown out of the flat. Give them ten minutes.
- Go around and check each group is on task and filling in the summary correctly. When most groups have reached a solution, stop the activity and ask spokespeople to explain their answers and suggestions to the class. Don't confirm the answer until you have heard from every group.

> **Answers**
> Flatmate 1 = Rajesh. He has £110; Flatmate 2 = Francesca. She has £130; Flatmate 3 = Josh. He has £70 if he sells his bicycle (but he's still £10 short of what he needs); Flatmate 4 = Martina. She only has £20, which is £60 short. They can pay the rent if Rajesh and Francesca lend Josh and Martina the money they need. Martina can pay them back next week, but Josh must find a job soon … he's in real financial trouble!

8.1 What she said

Aim
To report what people said accurately

Language
Reported speech and reporting verbs, e.g. *claim, admit*

Time
30 minutes

Preparation
One copy of the worksheet for every twelve students, cut into cards

Procedure
- Tell students they are going to practise reporting verbs. Elicit the reporting verbs they remember (with books closed) and write them on the board. Make sure you include all the verbs used in the activity (*remind, offer, complain, ask, recommend, suggest, promise, admit, claim*).
- Hand a student the example card and ask them to read it aloud, inserting a real name in the gap. Ask students to say back the exact words; write these on the board, then elicit the reporting verb (*agree*) and the reported speech sentence, i.e. *[Aesha] agreed to buy [Fadila's] lunch for her*.
- Put students into groups, ideally of ten.
- Give each student a card. Tell them not to show it, and to complete the sentence if there are gaps in it, and then to write the reported speech sentence on the line below. Check that their sentences are grammatically correct. Also ask them how they will say their sentence, e.g. whispering for sentence 4.
- Explain that they are now going to take turns to dictate their sentences, but that unlike a normal dictation, those who write must write what they hear using a reporting verb. They can ask each other to repeat the sentence if they need to hear it again.
- When everyone has dictated their sentences, put them in smaller groups to compare the sentences they wrote. Go round and check for accuracy. Invite students to the front to write the correct reported sentences on the board.

Answers
1 [X] reminded [Y] to do his/her homework this evening.
2 [X] offered to lend [Y] his/her calculator (today).
3 [X] complained that it was very cold in the classroom today.
4 [X] asked [Y] if he/she could copy his/her answers.
5 [X] recommended not seeing [name of film].
6 [X] suggested going for a class picnic on Saturday.
7 [X] promised the teacher that he/she wouldn't cheat in the [subject] exam.
8 [X] admitted (to) stealing [Y]'s pen.
9 [X] claimed that he/she had met [name of celebrity].
10 [X] asked [Y] if/whether he/she had watched anything good on TV last night.

8.2 Questionnaire

Aim
To explore students' communication skills

Language
Vocabulary about effective communication

Time
30 minutes

Preparation
One copy of the worksheet for every two students, cut in half

Procedure
- Tell the class that they are going to think about their communication skills. Elicit a few ideas about what these include, e.g. being a good listener, making eye contact, explaining things in ways that others can understand, not interrupting. Then dictate the following sentence stems:
  I would say that my communication skills are …
  People think that I …
  But in fact, I …
  When talking to people, I'd like to be more …
- Give students two minutes to complete the sentences so they are true for them. Then ask them to put these statements to one side until the end of the activity.
- Tell them that they are going to fill in a questionnaire on the same topic. Divide the class into two groups and give students in one group questionnaire A and the others B.
- Tell them to make questions from the statements. As an example, read out: *I find it easy to get my message across to others*. Ask what question they would ask to find this information (*Do you find it easy …*). Invite students to ask follow-up questions, such as, *Why is that, do you think?* and *Do you think it depends on who you're talking to?* Tell them to only make the questions (*not* to fill in the questionnaire). Go round and check students are doing the task correctly.
- Reorganize the class into pairs, A and B. Tell them to interview each other to complete the questionnaire with their partner's answers. Go round and check, listening for errors or difficulties with pronunciation, especially with vocabulary about communication. Make a note of occasions when students struggle.
- When the pairs have finished interviewing each other, ask them to look again at the sentences they wrote at the beginning of the activity and decide whether to keep them as they are or change any in light of what they discovered doing the questionnaire.
- Correct errors that you heard. End by asking students to share their conclusions with the class.

9.1 Thing, stuff, person

Aim

To practise the grammar of the unit

Language

Defining relative clauses

Time

40 minutes

Preparation

One copy of the worksheet for every ten students, cut up and shuffled

Procedure

- Draw on the board a frame with a question mark in it. Say *I'm thinking of something, and you get four clues to help you guess what it is, OK?* Give the following clues in this order and let them guess the object after each.

  It's a thing that eats stuff on the ground and looks like snake.

  It's a machine that some small children are scared of.

  It's something you connect to the electric system. It makes a loud noise.

  It's a machine that helps you clean your house.

- If a student shouts out the name of the object (*a vacuum cleaner*) before the end, they come to the board to draw it. Otherwise, draw it yourself.

- Explain that they are going to design and play a guessing game. Point out that you gave clues for the vacuum cleaner which got progressively easier. Their job, in groups, is to write definitions for other things and to put them in order of difficulty, from hardest to easiest. Then they are going to test another team.

- Teach them the five categories for this game: *a thing* is a countable object, e.g. a vacuum cleaner; *stuff* is uncountable material, e.g. water; *a person* is self-explanatory; *a creature* is any other living animal, and *a plant* is a fruit, vegetable, tree, etc.

- Divide the class into an even number of teams of five students or fewer. Give each team half the picture cards. Tell them not to show them to the rest of the class. Every member of the group writes a definition for every picture card on separate pieces of paper, one for each picture card. Make dictionaries available.

- When they have finished, tell them to choose the four best definitions for each object and decide the order that the definitions will be read out in a quiz for another team. Give them ten minutes for this, going round the groups, checking that the definitions make sense and the use of relative clauses is correct.

- Students now play the game. Set one team against another. One team reads out its definitions in order of difficulty. Explain the points system: they get 8 points if they guess the object after one definition, 6 after two, 4 after three and 2 after four. Then the other team reads out their definitions for their first picture card.

- Find out the winners. At the end, ask students what their favourite / most difficult / funniest definition was.

9.2 Across and down

Aim

To complete a crossword in pairs by defining words

Language

Vocabulary related to arts and entertainment

Time

30 minutes

Preparation

One copy of the worksheet for every two students, cut in half

Procedure

- Tell students that they are going to revise vocabulary about the arts, performance and entertainment from the unit in the form of a race. Explain that this is all about defining words quickly and clearly, and that in this game you can't say the word, but you can find other ways of communicating it.
- Demonstrate the game with the class. Define the following words using various techniques. Do it quickly and award a point to the first person to say the word.
  A definition: *It's a work of art that's three dimensional*; an example: *Michelangelo's David is one*. (sculpture);
  Talk about the learning moment: *It's an expression. We learnt it last week*. Do an oral gap fill: *If a piece of art affects you greatly, it [BEEP!]*. (make a big impression);
  An opposite word: *Not the actor – the part he or she plays*. (character);
  Other information about it: *It's a thing that happens in a theatre*. (a play)
- Write the techniques on the board (*definition*, etc). Put students in pairs to recall the different instances of the techniques you used to communicate. After a minute, elicit some techniques and examples. Remind them that they cannot say the word itself or use L1, or they lose a minute in the race.
- Show students the whole worksheet (making sure they cannot see the actual words) and explain that one member of each pair will have half the answers and the other will have the other half. Their job is to define the words for their partner until together they have completed the crossword.
- Divide the class in half. Hand out crossword A to one half and B to the other, telling them not to show it. Give them five minutes to check with a member of the same group that they understand all the words and can define them.
- Put students in pairs, A and B, facing each other. Say *Ready . . . steady . . . Go!* Listen out for students using L1 or cheating in any way and penalise any pairs that do so.
- Congratulate the fastest team and other teams that do it quickly. Stop the activity when enough pairs have finished.

10.1 Regrets? I've had a few

Aim

To practise the unit grammar

Language

Second and third conditionals, *If only . . .* and *I wish . . .*

Time

40 minutes

Preparation

One copy of the worksheet for every 21 students, cut up

Procedure

- To model the activity, tell the class that you are in a difficult situation and that they have to guess what it is. You will give them some clues. Read the following clues, two at a time, giving students a minute each time to discuss with a partner what the situation might be.
  If only my mobile phone was working!
  I wish I hadn't got out of the car.
  If it was warmer, I'd be able to keep walking.
  I wish I'd checked the weather forecast before coming home.
  I wouldn't have driven off the road if I'd changed the car's tyres for winter tyres.
  If I hadn't tried to get home tonight, I'd be safe and warm at Andy's house.
- To ensure that students use the grammar correctly, put the following prompts on the board: *change to winter tyres, check the weather forecast, drive off the road, get out, I wish . . ., If . . ., keep walking, mobile phone, safe and warm, try to get home, warmer*. Give students time to reconstruct the sentences before inviting volunteers to share them with the class. Compare them with the originals that you read out.
- After all six clues, tell them to decide what the full story is. Elicit their stories before revealing the original story and congratulating any pairs who guessed the full story, or close to it.

> **Answer**
> You were at your friend Andy's house and drove home in the dark. It started to snow and on the way your car came off the road. Your mobile phone wasn't working so you got out and started to walk to find help. But it was so cold that you couldn't keep walking and you have stopped. You are now somewhere in the countryside, unable to contact anyone, hoping that a car comes along.

- Put students in groups of three. Hand out one of the situations to each group. Tell students to each write two sentences prompted by the situation which use a second or third conditional sentence or start *I wish . . .* or *If only . . .*

- Go round and help students to express their ideas clearly and accurately. In their groups, have them compare sentences. Tell them that they must have six sentences which express different ideas, so if there are any repetitions, they must write new sentences.
- Put each group together with another group. They take turns to read out their sentences. Members of one group try to guess what the other group's situation is, just as you did with the class.
- When groups have finished guessing each other's situations, nominate students to share the stories, and discuss as a class which is the most difficult situation. Also, ask students what they would do in those situations.

10.2 And that's why …

Aim
To practise functional language of the unit

Language
Explaining causes and reasons, e.g. *That's why …*

Time
40 minutes

Preparation
One copy of the worksheet for every 16 students, cut up into strips

Procedure
- Put students in pairs. Ask them to tell their partner about the last time they had to make an excuse for something. After two minutes, invite students to share what their partners told them with the class.
- Tell students that they are going to practise making excuses. Point out that making excuses relates to 'Explaining causes and reasons'. Write this on the board. If it has been a few days since you did Lesson 10E, test them on their memory of the Useful language in that lesson by eliciting all the words and expressions (without them looking in their books) and writing them on the board.
- Hand out one strip of paper to each member of the class. Tell them not to show it and to think of the most complicated excuse for their problem. Explain that they will be reading out their excuse without saying the result; the listeners should be able to guess what the result is from the excuse.
- Give them five minutes, and put them in pairs to help one another. Encourage them to use the language of explaining causes and reasons. Go round and offer suggestions if necessary. Make dictionaries available.
- When they have finished, put them into groups of eight or so with people they weren't in a pair with. They must not show each other their strips of paper. Explain that they must take turns to read out their excuses, but when they get to the last sentence, they should stop and the rest of the group should call out what they think the last sentence is.
- Go round and listen for the ways they explain causes and reasons. Make a note of any errors in this area.
- When they have finished, nominate one or two students to share their favourite excuses with the class. Correct any errors that you heard.

Extension

- Take any strip and read it out. Show how you can turn it into an accusing question, e.g. *And that's why your favourite cup is broken* → *Why is my favourite cup broken?* Drill it in an accusatory tone.

- Explain that the students are going to play a game. They will stand up and go round the classroom accusing as many people as they can and eliciting excuses. Explain that if they hear an excuse that someone else has already said, they should say *Heard it!* and the person must think of a different one. If they cannot think of one, they are out of the game and must sit down. The winner is the last person still standing.

1.1 Snatch!

The water's boiling …	… Shall I make the tea?
Water boils …	… when it reaches 100 degrees.
He's always making that noise …	… It's really annoying!
He always makes that noise …	… when he's sleeping.
I'm visiting my new friend Jackie, every day …	… this week. She's in hospital.
I've visited my new friend Jackie, every day …	… since we met two weeks ago.
Anna stays in Le Havre …	… every time she comes to France. She loves it there!
Anna is staying in Le Havre …	… but she doesn't think that she'll be here much longer.
What are you cooking? …	… It smells delicious!
What do you cook? …	… It depends what ingredients I have in the kitchen.
Are you riding to school on your bike? …	… It's been perfect weather for it this week!
Do you ride to school on your bike? …	… What? Even when it rains?!
You're getting better at speaking English …	… every day! It's fantastic!
You get better at speaking English …	… if you practise!
Youssef and Brian have known each other …	… for about five years.
Youssef and Brian know each other …	… from working in the same supermarket a few years ago.
She's had headaches …	… almost every day for about a week now. She should see a doctor.
She's having headaches …	… again, like she did last year. Do you think she should see a doctor?

1.2 Happiness is …

1 Do the crossword. Each answer is a word in the same family as the word in italics.

Across

1 If you feel *delight*, you are _____.
3 The emotion is *fear*; you're feeling _____.
11 It's a *friendly* place. They like to encourage _____ there.
12 She wasn't *sad*. Those weren't tears of _____; they were tears of joy.
13 *Exhaustion* is what you experience when you are _____.

Down

1 The team was *disappointed*. The emotion is _____.
2 During a time of *loneliness*, you are _____.
4 I'm a bit sad, but I'm not *depressed*. _____ is a serious issue.
5 I don't get *embarrassed* very easily. _____ isn't something that bothers me.
6 _____ for me is about the people around me also being *happy*.
7 _____ is the state of being *nervous*.
8 You are _____ if you are in a state of *confusion*.
9 The adjective is *excited*; the noun is _____.
10 The noun is *relaxation*; the adjective is _____.

2.1 Talk to someone who …

Talk to someone who …	Name	Extra information
… has memories of being a baby.		
… could swim before they learnt to walk.		
… were speaking in sentences before they reached their second birthday.		
… was already reading when they started going to school.		
… used to walk or ride their bike to primary school on their own.		
… had already flown in an aeroplane when they learnt to walk.		
… was learning a musical instrument before they started learning English.		
… used to behave badly at school because they were bored by how easy it was.		
… had learnt how to tie their shoelaces before most of their friends could.		
… prepared their own school bag before they were ten.		
… knows how to cook, and has cooked since before they can remember.		
… has always been allowed to choose their bedtime.		
… had read a novel with no pictures before they had to do it for school.		
… has known what they want to do when they grow up for at least three years.		
… can already iron their own clothes.		
[your own idea]		
[your own idea]		

2.2 Excuse me, ...?

Student A

Take turns to ask for and give directions. Student A, ask Student B for directions to the following places:

• the market	• the stadium	• the bus station	• the town hall
• the theatre	• the library	• the museum	• *Bradaggio's restaurant*

Student B

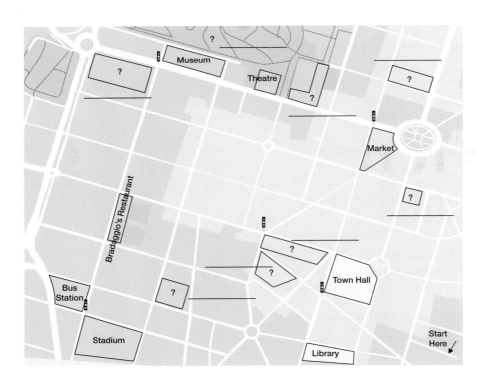

Take turns to ask for and give directions. Student B, ask Student A for directions to the following places:

• the supermarket	• Yew Tree Park	• the car park	• the art gallery
• the cinema	• the university	• the hotel	• the *Mexican Cantina*

yet	already
for	since
never	ever
not	?
been	

Game 1

START HERE	She won …	… second prize in the 50 metres freestyle.	He went on to represent …	… his country in the following year's championships.	The ball can only …
… bounce once on your side of the net.	He can run even faster in the 200-metre …	… sprint.	They beat …	… the champions two-nil.	We train in the gym and at the basketball …
… court.	They won't get gold, but they might win a …	… medal.	The stadium has a pitch and an athletics …	… track.	Motivation plays an important …
… role in success.	I think the referee made …	… a poor decision. That wasn't a goal!	I first saw her skating at a …	… rink in Norway.	He was definitely man of the match. He scored …
… two goals!	I might never achieve …	… my goal, but for me it's about trying.	Seeing my sister win that trophy made me feel …	… really proud.	They're training …
… hard, but will it be enough?	I don't know why more teenagers don't play …	… golf.	As long as you did …	… your best, that's the main thing.	The organization encourages …
… children to do more sport.	I've never done …	… yoga.	It's going to be a difficult race; I'm pushing …	… my own limits.	YOU'VE FINISHED! FINISH

Game 2

START HERE					
					YOU'VE FINISHED! FINISH

4.1 Picnic planning

Diary

	morning	afternoon	evening
Monday	*English class*		
Tuesday			
Wednesday	*English class*		
Thursday			
Friday	*English class*		
Saturday			
Sunday			

✂ -

Picnic planner

Day: _____

Time: _____

Location: _____

Number of people coming: _____

My jobs to prepare

_____

_____

_____

_____

Don't forget!

_____

_____

4.1 Food sayings

1 First we eat, …	a … you have to fill it with the best ingredients.
2 A party without cake …	b … even your own relatives.
3 After a good dinner, you can forgive anybody, …	c … why is there a light in the fridge?
4 You don't need a silver fork …	d … than you can lift.
5 If we're not meant to have midnight snacks, …	e … your own knife and fork.
6 You are …	f … to a hungry person.
7 Don't dig your grave with …	g … then we do everything else.
8 Never eat more …	h … teach a man to fish, and you have fed him for a lifetime.
9 Eat breakfast like a king, lunch like a prince, …	i … to eat good food.
10 Life is like a sandwich; …	j …. is just a meeting.
11 There is no such thing as bad food …	k … and dinner like a poor person.
12 Give a man a fish, you have fed him for today, …	l … what you eat.

5.1 Note to self

Imagine that in ten minutes you are going to lose your memory completely. Before this happens, you have just enough time to write a note to yourself to help you live your life. You don't have time to write everything, so think hard about what's really important.

They can be: practical notes, e.g. *You should remember to feed the dog in your house*; personal, e.g. *She's called Coco and she's very special to you*; necessary for survival, e.g. *You mustn't ever go in your sister's bedroom. She'll kill you!*; they may even help you live a better life: *You weren't able to swim before because you were scared of the water, but you should try it now – maybe you aren't afraid any more.*

Useful language

Don't be afraid to …   You mustn't ever …   You need to make sure that you …   You should try …
You don't need to (worry about) …   If you don't understand … you can talk to …
You had to … when you were younger. This means that now you can't / have to / …
You've never been able / allowed to … but you might be able to now.

Note to self

_____

_____

_____

_____

_____

_____

_____

_____

_____

_____

_____

_____

_____

_____

_____

_____

_____

_____

_____

_____

_____

_____

5.2 What's my line?

accountant	explorer	politician
flight attendant	factory worker	postman / postwoman
architect	farmer	president
athlete	hairdresser	prison guard
babysitter	hotel receptionist	reporter
bank manager	housewife / househusband	sailor
butcher	journalist	scientist
cameraman / camerawoman	judge	secretary
chef	lawyer	security guard
cleaner	librarian	shop assistant
dancer	mechanic	soldier
dentist	musician	swimming instructor
designer	painter	taxi driver
detective	photographer	tour guide
driver	piano teacher	unemployed
engineer	poet	waiter / waitress

A billionaire is planning the first manned mission to Mars. You are the perfect candidate to be an astronaut. It's a great opportunity, but it's quite possible you won't return to Earth.	A genetics test shows that you were swapped at birth by accident and have been brought up in a family that is not your biological family.
Your best friend, sitting next to you in your university entrance exam, asks you for the answer to a question. The teacher isn't looking. There is a one percent chance that they will see you cheating.	A train is going to crash, probably killing ten passengers. You control a lever which changes the track, saving the passengers but killing three people standing on the second track.
There is a fire in your house and you can only save one thing (all the people are safe).	There's only one fruit left to eat for the rest of your life.
The group is having a party. You can invite anyone, including famous people.	You get the chance to live a day you've already had over again.
You are told you can either lose your mobile phone forever or lose the little finger of one hand.	A medical situation means you have to choose – your sense of smell or your sense of taste?
For one month you are only allowed to shower or brush your teeth, not both.	You can speak another language fluently (that isn't English).
You get one superpower.	You can go anywhere in the world right now!
You get to be invisible for a day.	You can meet one person from history.
You are going to change into a different species of animal for the rest of your life. You can keep your human intelligence and identity. What animal would you be?	You alone survive a shipwreck on a desert island. All the food and water you need is there. You save one luxury from the ship (it's nothing that you can use to call for help).
You win a prize to go on a date with any celebrity.	You are given the chance to go back to any time in history.
You've just passed your driving test. You bump into a parked car in a quiet street and scratch their car, but nobody sees you. You could just drive away.	You're offered a well-paid job in another country, but it would mean not seeing your friends or family for long periods of time.
You are an astronomer. You've discovered an asteroid is flying towards Earth. Only you know that everyone on the planet is going to die, and there are only four days left.	You can have twenty years of incredible happiness, but only if you accept that you will die at the end of the period.

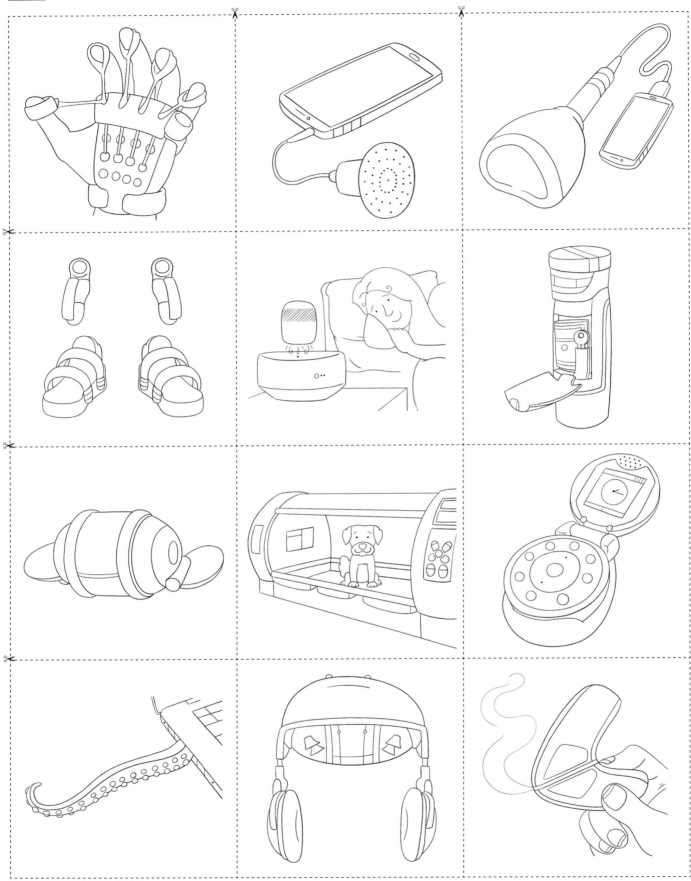

7.1 Biography of a brand

Student A

Vans shoes have been worn by young people since (1) _____ (*When / open?*), when the first Vans shop was opened by two brothers, Paul and James Van Doren and two friends. It was named *The Van Doren Rubber Company*. That day, only (2) _____ (*How many / buy?*) pairs of shoes were bought, but the customers couldn't have their shoes immediately. An important idea in Vans clothing is customization, which means the fabric and colour can be chosen by the customer, so Paul and James had to go to (3) _____ (*Where / make?*), where the shoes were made, and bring them back to the shop that afternoon. At the beginning, the company only had three styles, all of which were priced at under $5.00.

Vans is associated with (4) _____ (*What / associate with?*). The brand logo has been used on their shoes for more than 40 years but in fact the original version had been designed by (5) _____ (*Who / design?*), who loved skateboarding, when he was just 13. Originally, the design was painted on his skateboards. But his dad liked it, so soon it was used by the company as (6) _____ (*How / use?*).

By the 1970s, over 70 shops had been opened, and nowadays Vans are an established global brand. As well as shoes, clothes and equipment are sold for other sports, such as surfing and snowboarding.

Vans have worked hard to maintain their links with young people. In 1995 the (7) _____ (*What / sponsor?*) was sponsored by them for the first time, and this yearly tradition is still going strong. Their skating roots have never been forgotten, either, and (8) _____ (*What / build?*) have been built by them. The first one was opened in 1998 in Los Angeles. More have since been created (9) _____ (*Where / create?*).

- -

Student B

Vans shoes have been worn by young people since March 16, 1966, when the first Vans shop was opened by two brothers, Paul and James Van Doren and two friends. It was named (1) _____ (*What / name?*). That day, only twelve pairs of shoes were bought, but the customers couldn't have their shoes immediately. An important idea in Vans clothing is customization, which means (2) _____ (*What / choose?*) can be chosen by the customer, so Paul and James had to go to a nearby factory, where the shoes were made, and bring them back to the shop that afternoon. At the beginning, the company only had three styles, all of which were priced (3) _____ (*How much / price at?*).

Vans is associated with skateboarding. The brand logo has been used on their shoes for (4) _____ (*How long / use?*) but in fact the original version had been designed by James' son Mark, who loved skateboarding, when he was just 13. Originally, the design was painted (5) _____ (*Where / paint?*). But his dad liked it, so soon it was used by the company as its logo.

By the 1970s, (6) _____ (*How many / open?*) shops had been opened, and nowadays, Vans are an established global brand. As well as shoes, clothes and equipment are sold for other sports, such as (7) _____ (*What other sports / sell for?*).

Vans have worked hard to maintain their links with young people. In 1995 the rock festival Warped Tour was sponsored by them for the first time, and this yearly tradition is still going strong. Their skating roots have never been forgotten, either, and several skate parks have been built by them. The first one was opened (8) _____ (*When / open?*) in Los Angeles. More have since been created in America and London.

It's the end of the month and there isn't much money left. Four flatmates need to work out how much each of them has in total because the rent needs to be paid today.

Who are the four flatmates?

Who can help out?

Which of them can't afford to pay their part of the rent today?

Who is in most financial trouble? Why?

Money summaries

Flatmate 1 Name: _____

Income: £ _____

Savings: £ **0**

Payments: £ _____

Debts: £ _____

Debts owed to him: £ _____

Total: £ _____

Flatmate 2 Name: _____

Income: £ _____

Savings: £ **120**

Payments: £ _____

Debts: £ _____

Debts owed to her: £ _____

Total: £ _____

Flatmate 3 Name: _____

Income: £ _____

Savings: £ ____

Payments: £ _____

Debts: £ _____

Debts owed to him: £ **0**

Total: £ _____

Flatmate 4 Name: _____

Income: £ _____

Savings: £ ____

Payments: £ _____

Debts: £ _____

Debts owed to her: £ _____

Total: £ _____

Information cards

1. Rajesh had totally run out of money but he got paid £200 today from work.
2. Martina has found a job. She gets paid £300, but not until next week, so her female flatmate has lent her £50 for a pair of shoes for work.
3. One male flatmate has to sell his bicycle if he has any chance of paying the rent. He can get £120 for it second-hand even though it's worth more.

1. Martina's mum and dad lent her £50 for food (they never ask her to pay them back).
2. Josh did a job for a weekend at a restaurant. He made £150 but he's spent two-thirds of it.
3. Rajesh is going to his brother's wedding next weekend. The suit he wants costs £170.

1. Francesca has £120 in her bank account for emergencies.
2. The male flatmate who hasn't lent money to anyone donated £10 pounds to a children's charity.
3. Last week, Rajesh lent the other male flatmate £20.

1. Rajesh did the food shopping for everyone in the flat, which cost £120 pounds. The others owe him their share.
2. Josh must pay back the flatmate who lent him £40 pounds because she can't pay the rent without it.
3. Each flatmate pays £80 rent per week.

8.1 What she said

Example: '[Name of student], do you want me to buy your lunch for you? OK, I will.' (AGREE)

_____

1 'Hey, [name of student], don't forget to do your homework this evening.' (REMIND)

_____

2 '[Name of student], you can borrow my calculator today, if you like.' (OFFER)

_____

3 'Brrr! It's very cold in the classroom today.' (COMPLAIN)

_____

4 '[Name of student], please can I copy your answers?' (ASK)

_____

5 'I don't think you should see [name of film]. It's terrible!' (RECOMMEND)

_____

6 'Hey everyone! Why don't we go for a class picnic on Saturday?' (SUGGEST)

_____

7 '[Name of teacher], I promise I won't cheat in the [subject] exam.' (PROMISE)

_____

8 'OK, [name of student], it was me who stole your pen. I'm sorry." (ADMIT)

_____

9 'Actually, I've met [name of celebrity]. It's true!' (CLAIM)

_____

10 '[Name of student], did you watch anything good on TV last night?' (ASK)

_____

8.2 Questionnaire

Student A

1 Ask your partner to say how true these statements are for them, from 'I strongly agree' to 'Never or hardly ever'. Ask follow-up questions to find out more.

	I strongly agree	Sometimes	Not very often	Never or hardly ever
1 I find it easy to get my message across to others.				
2 I use a lot of complicated words to show how intelligent I am.				
3 I like to offer advice about people's problems.				
4 I am generally nervous about speaking to other people.				
5 My friends and family tell me I talk too much.				
6 It is difficult for me to express my thoughts in words.				
7 I often do most of the talking in conversations.				
8 In class, I prefer to sit at the back of the room.				
9 I make connections easily and usually get on well with people I have just met.				

2 **Now answer your partner's questions.**

✂- -

Student B

1 **Answer your partner's questions.**
2 **Now ask your partner to say how true these statements are for them, from 'I strongly agree' to 'Never or hardly ever'. Ask follow-up questions to find out more.**

	I strongly agree	Sometimes	Not very often	Never or hardly ever
1 I get distracted during conversations – most people have nothing to say.				
2 I look at people's eyes when I'm listening.				
3 I like to be the last person to speak on a subject.				
4 I only listen to other people in order to know when it's my turn to speak.				
5 I interrupt people a lot.				
6 I show that I am listening by responding with questions, noises and facial expressions.				
7 I pay attention to other people's body language, gestures and facial expressions.				
8 I finish people's sentences for them when I know what they are going to say.				
9 I feel comfortable and confident in group situations.				

a butterfly	a cactus	a desktop fan ('a fan')	a drawing pin
a horse	a little brother	a millionaire	a pair of scissors
a skateboard	a trumpet	an alien	an onion
electricity	flour	grass	a video game
oxygen	sand	a painting	toothpaste

9.2 Across and down

Student A

Student B

10.1 Regrets? I've had a few!

You are going to an interview for a place at university. It rained on the way to the train station and you are wet. You didn't buy a ticket online, the ticket office is closed and the ticket machine isn't working. You get on the train and get fined £50 for travelling without a ticket. You have to get off at the next station. If you arrive late, you won't get a place at university.

- -

You decided to drive to your friend's house for a party he was having. The car got a puncture (a hole in the tyre), but you didn't have a spare tyre because you didn't replace it the last time this happened. It's getting dark and you are miles from anywhere.

- -

It was a sunny morning so you went to the beach. After a swim, you lay down on your inflatable mattress. You fell asleep. When you wake up, you are burnt from the sun from head to toe. You also realize that you are now about 500 metres from land.

- -

It was hot in the night so you decided to sleep in the garden. You wake up covered in mosquito bites, then realize you can't get into the house because you forgot to bring the key.

- -

You have technical skills at web design. A friend of yours asked you to help him start an internet business. You happily gave him your help, but, now that the website is online, you see that it is a dishonest website that tries to get people to give it money for nothing.

- -

You saw your best friend cheating in an exam. You and she have talked about cheating in the past and she's always been against it. It's not like her to do this. What's more, this exam is really important for you, and it won't be fair if she does better than you.

- -

You found £1,000 in a bag in the park some time ago. There was no one there to claim it, so you took it and have since spent it all. You've just heard from a friend whose mother works at a local children's charity that they lost £1,000 in the park, so the money you spent was probably theirs.

… your favourite cup is broken.

… there's water all over the bathroom floor.

… I haven't done your homework.

… there's a strange smell in here.

… there's tomato ketchup on the wall.

… Dad's iPhone is in the washing machine.

… your bicycle is not outside where you left it.

… I'm wet.

… there's an angry dog in the garden.

… I'm giving you your birthday present two weeks late.

… I can't give you your MP3 player back.

… there's a scratch on the car.

… the TV isn't working.

… I didn't get home until four in the morning.

… I only got 2 out of 10 in the Maths exam.

Workbook answer key

1 In touch with your feelings

1A

Vocabulary Describing emotions

1
1 afraid   2 unhappy   3 angry   4 upset   5 bored   6 worried
7 pleased   8 excited

2
1 upset   2 afraid   3 worried   4 unhappy   5 pleased
6 excited   7 angry   8 bored

3
1 angry   2 pleased   3 bored   4 excited   5 worried
6 unhappy

4
1 b   2 a   3 h   4 g   5 d   6 e   7 f   8 c

5
1 d   2 e   3 a   4 b   5 c

6
1 about   2 by   3 about   4 with   5 about   6 of
7 of   8 by

7
1 My job makes me feel stressed.
2 Are you very scared of heights?
3 Living on your own can be lonely.
4 She was delighted with her exam results.
5 I'm confused about the meaning of this word.
6 We're very pleased that you came.
7 They have nothing to be ashamed of.
8 I'm worried about moving to a new city.

8
1 nervous, relaxed   2 excited, delighted   3 annoyed, upset
4 lonely, pleased   5 embarrassed, confused   6 stressed, nervous

9
Students' own answers.

10
1 jealous   2 impatient   3 grateful   4 disappointed
5 proud   6 selfish

11
1 cheerful   2 selfish   3 lonely   4 upset   5 embarrassed
6 proud

12

positive	negative
cheerful	angry
delighted	ashamed
excited	bored
grateful	confused
pleased	impatient
relaxed	lonely
	scared
	selfish
	upset
	worried

Pronunciation -ed adjectives

13
1 /d/   2 /t/   3 /t/   4 /ɪd/   5 /d/   6 /ɪd/   7 /d/

14
1 a   2 a   3 c   4 b   5 a

Listening

15
Students' own answers.

16
1 b   2 a   3 b   4 c   5 c   6 a

17
1 scared   2 delighted   3 nervous   4 relaxed
5 annoyed, stressed   6 confused   7 grateful, embarrassed

18
1 Ralph Powell   2 Gerri Pennington   3 Bruce Collins
4 Jamie Cawley

Grammar subject / object questions

19
1 d   2 c   3 e   4 a   5 b   6 f

20
1 What TV programmes ~~do~~ make you angry?
2 Who **do** you talk to when you are confused?
3 Who ~~does~~ laugh**s** most in your family?
4 Why **do** they feel excited?
5 How many people ~~do~~ think this is wrong?
6 Whose cake ~~does~~ taste**s** the best?

21
1 Why does Jo look so angry?
2 How much food did they eat?
3 Whose bike has a puncture?
4 What did Pepe say to them?
5 How often do you go swimming?
6 How many people came to the party?

22
1 did they collect   2 gave you the flowers   3 does she cry
4 makes you feel stressed   5 do you listen to music
6 people did he invite

23
Students' own answers.

1B

Vocabulary building Suffixes

1

+ment	+ness	+ion
disappointed	friendly	confused
embarrassed	happy	depressed
excited	lonely	exhausted
	nervous	
	sad	
	selfish	

2
2 disappointment   3 confusion   4 excitement   5 sadness
6 depression   7 embarrassment

Reading

3

b

4

1 consistently **2** imaginary **3** benchmark **4** life expectancy
5 stark **6** rank **7** corruption **8** evaluation

5

1 F **2** T **3** F **4** NG **5** T **6** F **7** T **8** NG

6

1 Switzerland **2** United States **3** Iceland **4** Madagascar
5 Denmark **6** Australia **7** Togo **8** United Kingdom

1C

Grammar Talking about the present

1

1 g **2** c **3** f **4** e **5** b **6** d **7** a

2

1 Water ~~is freezing~~ **freezes** at 0 degrees Celsius.
2 The phone ~~rings~~ **is ringing.** Can you answer it?
4 I'm bored. I ~~am wanting~~ **want** to watch TV.
5 **A** It's 6 o'clock already, we need to go. **B** Sorry, Freya, ~~I've come~~ **I'm coming.**
8 I ~~feed~~ **'m feeding** the cat while John and Angie are on holiday this month.

3

1 reads **2** enjoy **3** We've shopped **4** She's always shouting
5 doesn't set **6** think **7** never go **8** I'm laughing

4

1 Anna bakes bread every day.
2 How long have you know the truth?
3 Jack is always asking me to help him.
4 How are you feeling right now?
5 The internet is changing the way we communicate.
6 The moon rotates at ten miles per hour.
7 Life has become very difficult recently. / Recently, life has become very difficult.
8 I usually watch TV to relax.

5

1 It's always breaking down **2** 's always going to bed late
3 They're always interfering **4** She's always asking
5 You're always forgetting **6** You're always working
7 He's always feeling **8** You're always complaining

6

1 have shared **2** enjoys **3** runs **4** 's always asking
5 don't like **6** swim **7** watch **8** reads **9** does
10 's also learning **11** 's cooking **12** (is) listening
13 finds **14** cleans **15** 've always been

7

1 b **2** b **3** a **4** b **5** a **6** a **7** a **8** a

1D

Authentic listening skills Content words

1

'At <u>Cambridge</u>, <u>thousands</u> of <u>miles</u> away from <u>home</u>, I <u>realized</u> I was <u>spending</u> more <u>hours</u> with my <u>laptop</u> than I did with any other <u>human</u>.'

2

homesick, lonely, crying, emotions

Watch

3

4

1 c **2** b **3** a **4** b **5** c **6** b

5

1 want to share **2** especially close to my heart **3** visually impaired
4 tracked your mood **5** down the line **6** fighting a losing battle
7 golden opportunity

Vocabulary in context

6

1 characteristics **2** joy **3** homesick **4** wrinkles **5** curiosity
6 gender

1E

Speaking

1

1 What sort **2** When did it **3** Who's **4** What else has
5 what's it about **6** Where is it **7** would you recommend

2

1 <u>What</u> sort of film is it? **2** <u>When</u> did come out? **3** <u>Who's</u> in it?
4 What <u>else</u> has she been in? **5** So <u>what's</u> it about?
6 <u>Where</u> is it set? **7** Oh, OK. So would you <u>recommend</u> it?

3

1 When did it come out? g **2** Who directed it? f **3** So what's it about? d **4** What's the acting like? c **5** Would you recommend it? e
6 Where's it set? b **7** What sort of film is it? a

4

Students' own answers.

5

Students' own answers.

Writing A review

6

3 *The Pursuit of Happyness* is a moving film, …
6 This is not a feel-good movie, …
1 *The Pursuit of Happyness*
5 However, though the story is …
4 In my opinion, …
2 2006, Drama / Biography, …

7

yes

8

1 *The Pursuit of Happyness* - title
2 2006, Drama / Biography, … - basic information
3 *The Pursuit of Happyness* is a moving film, … - a description of the plot
4 In my opinion, … - what the writer liked
5 However, though the story is … - what the writer didn't like
6 This is not a feel-good movie, … - a recommendation

9

1 tearjerker **2** feel-good **3** biography **4** thought-provoking
5 action-packed **6** moving

10

Students' own answers

11

1 I really loved was the ending.
2 I found a bit disappointing were the special effects.
3 I didn't like was the soundtrack.
4 the portrayal of the prison that wasn't very realistic.
5 I enjoyed the most were the song and dance scenes.

Review

1

1 confused **2** scared **3** relaxed **4** lonely **5** annoyed
6 stressed **7** embarrassed **8** delighted

2

1 do you eat   **2** go   **3** 've tried   **4** doesn't taste   **5** prefer
6 has   **7** sells   **8** 've started   **9** 'm saving   **10** 've decided

3

1 What did they decide to do?   **2** How often did you go to the gym?
3 Whose daughter played the piano?   **4** How many friends did she
invite?   **5** What did he ask Jenna?   **6** What made you feel
embarrassed?   **7** How many students passed the exam?

4

1 delighted   **2** bored   **3** lonely   **4** nervous   **5** worried
6 relaxed   **7** interested   **8** confused   **9** embarrassed
10 excited

5

1 a   **2** a   **3** a   **4** b

6

1 He won't be a minute – he ~~just puts~~ **'s just putting** his coat on.
2 The kettle ~~boils~~ **is boiling**. I'll turn it off.
3 Karl and Penny ~~live~~ **have lived** in York since 2001.
4 I~~'ve~~ usually run in the park on Sundays.
5 If water ~~is freezing~~ **freezes**, it ~~is turning~~ **turns** to ice.
6 We~~'re knowing~~ **'ve known** Kevin for about two years.

2 Enjoy the ride

2A

Vocabular Travel

1

1 airport   **2** visiting   **3** tourists   **4** bus   **5** hotels   **6** drives
7 traveller   **8** holiday

2

1 train   **2** airport   **3** tourist   **4** station   **5** hotel   **6** drive
7 ticket   **8** taxi

3

1 train   **2** visitors   **3** travelling to   **4** fly   **5** hotel   **6** bus

4

1 commute   **2** route   **3** voyage   **4** cruise   **5** expedition
6 ride   **7** backpacking   **8** flight

5

1 voyage   **2** ride   **3** backpacking   **4** flight   **5** route
6 cruise   **7** commutes   **8** expedition

6

1 e   **2** d   **3** a   **4** c   **5** b

7

1 got off   **2** getting to know   **3** get to   **4** got to   **5** getting
6 Get off   **7** got to know / gets to know   **8** get

8

1 cruise   **2** excursion   **3** flight   **4** ride   **5** destination
6 expedition

9

1 d   **2** a   **3** b   **4** f   **5** e   **6** c

10

1 depart, way   **2** leave, sightseeing   **3** board   **4** know
5 stay   **6** land

Listening

11

1 c   **2** g   **3** e   **4** h   **5** b   **6** a   **7** f   **8** d

12

1 b   **2** c   **3** b   **4** a   **5** b   **6** c   **7** b   **8** a

13

b

14

1 c   **2** a   **3** b   **4** a   **5** c   **6** b   **7** c   **8** a

Grammar Adjectives ending in *-ed* and *-ing*

15

1 interesting   **2** bored   **3** embarrassed   **4** surprising
5 confusing   **6** annoyed   **7** depressing

16

1 amazing, disappointed   **2** surprising   **3** confused   **4** terrifying
5 excited   **6** relaxing

17

1 depressing   **2** exhausted   **3** boring   **4** confused
5 frightening   **6** annoyed   **7** amazing   **8** disappointed

18

1 bored   **2** unexcited   **3** boring   **4** confused   **5** surprised
6 amazed   **7** amazing   **8** unexpected

19

1 terrifying/frightening   **2** relaxed   **3** frightened   **4** confusing
5 embarrassing   **6** insulting   **7** worried/frightened

2B

Vocabulary building Compound nouns

1

1 back   **2** public   **3** sky   **4** tour   **5** horse   **6** sight   **7** view
8 line

Reading

2

a 5   **b** 1   **c** 2   **d** 3   **e** 4

3

1 b   **2** a   **3** d   **4** b   **5** c

4

1 F   **2** F   **3** F   **4** T   **5** T   **6** F

2C

Grammar Narrative forms

1

1 used to have, every Friday   **2** didn't use to work   **3** were walking,
when they heard   **4** called, when, arrived   **5** didn't use to be
6 missed, we'd woken up   **7** While I was checking, texted

2

Infinitive	Past Simple	Past Continuous	Past Perfect
go	went	was/were going	had gone
run	ran	was/were running	had run
talk	talked	was/were talking	had talked
sit	sat	was/were sitting	had sat
take	took	was/were taking	had taken
fly	flew	was/were flying	had flown
catch	caught	was/were catching	had caught

3

One day last week I <u>was reading</u> a book and <u>listening</u> to the radio. I
<u>was enjoying</u> some great classical music when suddenly I heard an
announcement. There was a huge thunderstorm coming our way!
I hurried to close the windows, and called my sister Tami, who <u>was
riding</u> her bike to volleyball practice. I told her about the storm, and she
asked if our dad <u>was driving</u> home from work and could pick her up. So
I quickly called him to see if he could find Tami before the storm came.
He'd left work already and was on his way home, so he said he'd pick
her up in about five minutes. Once Tami was in the car with her bike
in the back and they <u>were driving</u> home together, the storm hit. There
was an incredible amount of rain, thunder, and lightning – I was so
glad they were safely on their way home.

4

When Omar was in the sixth form, he studied maths and all three sciences – physics, chemistry and biology. In his last year, he got an opportunity to do a course at a local university. He was studying all the time, taking exams at school and university! Omar <u>had always enjoyed</u> biology and chemistry in school and wanted to learn more about biochemistry. He<u>'d talked</u> to some of his friends who <u>had done</u> courses at the university while they were still at school, and they all said that they<u>'d learnt</u> a lot and <u>had enjoyed</u> it. Omar <u>had been</u> a bit worried that his schedule might be too full, but he didn't really mind because he loved the university classes – they were so interesting and the professors were amazing. Omar especially loved being able to use the university library, and did all his homework there. He<u>'d told</u> so many of his friends about his great experience that they all wanted to take classes at the university, too.

5

1 read **2** was walking **3** had **4** use, saw **5** used to have, sold
6 Had you tried, hadn't tried **7** take, took **8** used to walk

6

1 we didn't eat breakfast at the hotel
2 weren't taking the exam
3 She didn't make a lot of new friends
4 I wasn't looking for a book
5 I hadn't eaten my lunch
6 They weren't working in the garden
7 I didn't use to work at a bank.
8 Renting an apartment in the city didn't use to be so expensive.

7

1 a **2** a **3** b **4** b **5** b **6** a **7** b

8

1 a **2** a **3** b **4** a **5** a **6** b **7** b

Pronunciation Weak forms: *used to*

9

1 /juːzt/ **2** /juːzt/ **3** /juːzd/ **4** /juːzt/ **5** /juːzt/ **6** /juːzd/

2D

Authentic listening skills Understanding accents

1

1 cars **2** destination **3** don't only find **4** pairs of urban scenes
5 user votes **6** recalled **7** More generally **8** people you love

Watch

2

1 b **2** a **3** c **4** a **5** c **6** c

3

a 1 **b** 7 **c** 6 **d** 5 **e** 2 **f** 3 **g** 4 **h** 8

Vocabulary in context

4

1 team up with **2** shy **3** a handful of **4** surrounded by
5 shame **6** Don't get me wrong

2E

Speaking

1

1 Do you know the way to Buckingham Palace?
2 Go all the way until you get to the crossroads.
3 At the traffic lights, go straight on.
4 After 200 metres, cross the roundabout.
5 Go past a bookshop on your right.
6 The train station is on your left.
7 It's not very far from here.
8 It's no more than a kilometre away.

2

1 Do you <u>know</u> the way to <u>Buckingham Palace</u>?
2 Go <u>all</u> the way until you get to the <u>crossroads</u>.

3 At the <u>traffic</u> lights, go <u>straight</u> on.
4 After <u>200</u> metres, <u>cross</u> the roundabout.
5 Go <u>past</u> a bookshop on your <u>right</u>.
6 The <u>train</u> station is on your <u>left</u>.
7 It's <u>not</u> very far from <u>here</u>.
8 It's <u>no</u> more than a <u>kilometre</u> away.

3

1 c **2** h **3** d **4** i **5** a **6** g **7** b **8** e **9** f

4

Students' own answers.

5

Students' own answers.

Writing A story

6

1 b **2** a **3** a **4** b **5** a

7

1 c **2** e **3** d **4** a **5** b

8

a 3 **b** 4 **c** 2 **d** 1

9

1 alone **2** a week **3** bad weather **4** lost **5** found
6 concludes **7** adventure **8** sunshine

10

Students' own answers.

Review

1

1 e **2** d **3** a **4** b **5** c **6** f

2

1 F A destination is the place where you ~~begin~~ **end** / **finish** your journey.
2 F An expedition is usually a ~~short~~ **long** trip.
3 T
4 T
5 T
6 F A cruise is a journey on a ~~train~~ **ship**.

3

1 interesting **2** annoying **3** terrifying **4** confusing **5** worried
6 surprising

4

1 fell / was falling, boring **2** exhausted **3** Had you ever been / Have you ever been, exciting **4** came **5** were shocked
6 told, disappointing **7** told, amazing

5

1 a **2** c **3** d **4** b **5** b **6** a **7** d

3 Active lives

3A

Vocabulary Sports

1

1 baseball **2** swimming **3** skiing **4** running **5** football
6 yoga

2

Team Sports	Individual Sports
basketball	badminton
cricket	boxing
ice hockey	ice skating
rugby	surfing
volleyball	tennis

3

1 Baseball is my least favourite sport. / My least favourite sport is baseball.
2 Boxing can be a very dangerous sport.
3 Football is played in more than 200 countries.
4 Running is good for your heart.
5 Swimming is a popular sport in Australia.
6 Doing yoga makes you feel calm.

4

1 f   2 a   3 d   4 b   5 c   6 e

5

1 rink   2 court   3 pitch   4 track   5 mountain   6 pool

6

1 b   2 b   3 c   4 c   5 a   6 a   7 b

7

1 diving   2 Gymnastics   3 karate   4 Sailing   5 climbing
6 basketball

8

1 achieve   2 beat   3 win   4 encourage   5 train   6 scored
7 represent

9

1 playing   2 doing   3 go   4 go   5 play   6 does   7 goes

10

1 riding   2 ice skating   3 played   4 snowboarding   5 polo
6 table-tennis   7 windsurfing

Listening

11

1 a   2 b   3 c   4 b   5 c   6 a   7 c   8 b

12

d

13

1 b   2 c   3 b   4 a

14

1 b   2 c   3 a   4 c

Grammar Past simple and present perfect

15

Past simple	Present perfect simple
2, 6, 7, 8	1, 3, 4, 5

16

1 enjoyed, found   2 did, rode, wanted   3 built   4 designed, made
5 didn't understand, preferred   6 entered, won

17

1 have been
2 have lived/'ve lived
3 has not known/hasn't known, has known/'s known
4 has always wanted
5 has not practiced/'s not practised, has not improved/'s not improved
6 has decided / 's decided
7 has not yet thought/hasn't yet thought
8 have told

18

1 have decided   2 joined   3 has never skipped
4 has now recovered   5 began   6 has only eaten

19

1 have participated   2 ran   3 have called   4 jumped
5 travelled   6 completed   7 have always wanted   8 was

3B

Vocabulary building Phrasal verbs

1

1 warm up   2 keep up   3 work out   4 give up   5 take on
6 join in   7 knocked out   8 taking up

Reading

2

1 c   2 b   3 a   4 a   5 a

3

b, d

4

a, d

5

1 b   2 a   3 e   4 d   5 c

3C

Grammar Present perfect simple and continuous

1 has she been playing   2 haven't called   3 I've already tried, still
4 She's been talking, for   5 have you been   6 It's been snowing
7 hasn't taken, yet

2

infinitive	present perfect simple	present perfect continuous
take	have/has taken	have/has been taking
choose	have/has chosen	have/has been choosing
represent	have/has represented	have/has been representing
try	have/has tried	have/has been trying
encourage	have/has encouraged	have/has been encouraging
win	have/has won	have/has been winning
feel	have/has felt	have/has been feeling

3

1 a   2 b   3 b   4 d   5 a   6 c   7 b   8 c

4

1 b   2 d   3 c   4 a   5 f   6 e

5

1 No, I still haven't changed it. / No, I still haven't changed the light bulb. / No, I still have not changed it. / No, I still have not changed the light bulb.
2 No, I haven't washed it yet. / No, I haven't washed the frying pan yet. / No, I have not washed it yet. / No, I have not washed the frying pan yet.
3 Yes, I've already turned it on. / Yes, I've already turned the oven on. / Yes, I've already turned on the oven. / Yes, I have already turned it on. / Yes, I have already turned the oven on. / Yes, I have already turned on the oven.
4 Yes, I have just locked it. / Yes, I have just locked the door.
5 No, I still haven't put them in the washing machine. / No, I still haven't put the towels in the washing machine. / No, I still have not put them in the washing machine. / No, I still have not put the towels in the washing machine.
6 Yes, I've already put it in the freezer. / Yes, I've already put the ice cream in the freezer. / Yes, I have already put it in the freezer. / Yes, I have already put the ice cream in the freezer.

6

1 a   2 a   3 a   4 b   5 a   6 a

7

2 Have you ever seen such beautiful scenery?
3 How long have you been working on that maths question?
4 Has he eaten dinner yet? / Has he eaten dinner?
5 How many times have you taken the train to school this week? / How often have you taken the train to school this week?
6 Have you ever taken the bus to the airport?
7 How long has she been reading that novel?

8

1 has been   2 brought   3 disliked   4 yet   5 has gone   6 just
7 deserved   8 never

Pronunciation Weak forms: *for*

9

1 /fɔː(r)/   2 /fə(r)/   3 /fə(r)/   4 /fə(r)/   5 /fɔː(r)/   6 /fə(r)/

3D

Authentic listening skills Signposts

1 And then, after a year of training,
2 And on day four,
3 And I thought,
4 And he came up to me and he said,

Watch

2
1 7 years | Seven years   **2** the first   **3** 23 | twenty-three
4 2 days | Two days   **5** 5 | five   **6** 4 months | Four months

3
1 c   **2** a   **3** b   **4** a   **5** c   **6** a   **7** b

Vocabulary in context

4
1 barely   **2** swollen   **3** fresh water   **4** costume
5 'I believe in you, Sis.'   **6** ensure

3E

Writing An opinion essay

1

Expressing an opinion	Making a general statement
1, 3, 6, 7	2, 4, 5, 8

2
1 b   **2** d   **3** a   **4** c

3
1 e   **2** d   **3** b   **4** f   **5** a   **6** c

4
1 third sentence   **2** benefits   **3** team sports   **4** good
5 working   **6** good   **7** an opinion

5
Students' own answers.

Speaking

6
1 see, D   **2** got, A   **3** understand, D   **4** not, A   **5** Yes, D   **6** not, D
7 right, A   **8** true, A   **9** good, A   **10** totally, A   **11** but, D
12 agree, D

7
1
↘   **2** ↗   **3** ↘   **4** ↗   **5** ↗   **6** ↘   **7** ↗   **8** ↗   **9** ↗   **10** ↗
11 ↘   **12** ↘

8
1 e ii   **2** d iv   **3** a iii   **4** c i   **5** b vi   **6** f v

9
Students' own answers

10
Students' own answers

Review

1
1 a limit   **2** your best   **3** exercise   **4** your opponent
5 your goal   **6** a win

2
1 She only goes running to keep fit.
2 I try to push my own limits.
3 They trained hard before the race.
4 Who is going to represent our school?
5 How many gold medals has he won for gymnastics?
6 Our coach encouraged us to work as a team.

3
1 has held, has not cut/hasn't cut   **2** made, weighed   **3** has belonged, consisted   **4** has been   **5** has held   **6** won, shook

4
1 took   **2** They've been making   **3** had been looking
4 had been laughing   **5** hadn't repaired   **6** confirmed

5
1 I've been ill since last Saturday.
2 Alex has been trying on shoes for an hour.
3 She has never wanted to live in Australia.
4 I've known David for three years.
5 They haven't met their new teacher yet.
6 Lenny has been studying all day.
7 Pete and Sarah have already moved to Bristol.

4 Food

4A

Vocabulary Describing food

1
1 chicken   **2** pasta   **3** prawns   **4** coffee   **5** apple
6 lemon / melon   **7** curry   **8** tomato

2

Sweet	Spicy	Salty
cake	chilli powder	crisps
chocolate	curry	French fries
ice cream		
strawberry		

3
1 e   **2** a   **3** b   **4** f   **5** c   **6** d

4
1 fresh   **2** wheat   **3** delicious   **4** Raw   **5** suitable   **6** junk

5
1 cooked   **2** fresh   **3** boiled   **4** fried   **5** tasty   **6** steamed
7 natural

6
1 Cooked   **2** Natural   **3** boiled   **4** fresh   **5** Fried   **6** tasty
7 Steamed

7
1 unhealthy   **2** junk   **3** raw   **4** fresh   **5** healthier   **6** taste / are

8
1 c   **2** a   **3** g   **4** b   **5** d   **6** e   **7** f

9
2 A starter is the ~~last~~ **first** thing you eat when you ~~are~~ **have** dinner.
3 A main course is usually a ~~small~~ **large** / **big** dish.
4 Vegetarians eat mainly ~~meat~~ **vegetables**.
5 Steaming fish is ~~less~~ **more** healthy / **healthier** than frying it.
6 A cake is a type of ~~starter~~ **dessert**.

10

Starter	Main Course	Dessert
bread and olives	mashed potato	apple pie
salad	pasta	chocolate cake
soup	roast chicken	ice cream
	steak	

Listening

11
1 oven-baked   **2** gingerbread   **3** celebrating   **4** wicked
5 century   **6** sugar   **7** sweet-tasting   **8** edible   **9** bakers

12
a 4   **b** 2   **c** 7   **d** 1   **e** 3   **f** 6   **g** 8   **h** 5

13

c

14

1 c 2 a 3 b 4 c 5 a 6 a 7 b

Grammar Future plans, intentions and arrangements

15

1 'll probably 2 'm bringing, opens 3 may decide 4 're going to check 5 'll find 6 're going to make 7 'll email, 're meeting 8 will be 9 may possibly invite

16

1 aren't going to find 2 won't grow 3 may not be 4 probably won't have to 5 aren't bringing 6 won't grow 7 isn't going to work 8 don't discover, won't go

17

1 c 2 b 3 b 4 b 5 c 6 a 7 a 8 a

18

1 is going to work 2 see 3 plans 4 is going to make 5 'm going to steam / am going to steam 6 are going to bake 7 opens 8 is going to come up with

19

2 Everyone **is** preparing a dish that is popular in their own country.
3 Chen is going **to** bring his favourite Chinese dish.
4 Marisol will cook̶i̶n̶g̶ a Mexican dish that's very spicy.
6 Kasia may t̶o̶ make a special dessert – if she can remember where the recipe is.
7 If he can find the right ingredients, Milan will t̶o̶ make fish stew.
8 When we w̶i̶l̶l̶ have everything in the cafeteria, it will smell so good.

4B

Vocabulary building Compound adjectives

1

1 a deep-fried b oven-baked c home-made d sweet-tasting e sun-dried

2

a well-known b old-fashioned c good-looking d over-cooked e half-finished

Reading

2

a 4 b 4 c 3 d 1 e 2 f 5

3

1 T 2 T 3 F 4 NG 5 T 6 F

4

1 c 2 b 3 a 4 b 5 c 6 b 7 c

4C

Grammar Making predictions

1

Christine grew up in a small town. Her family had lived there for many years. She loved walking to school with her sisters and cousins, and stopping by her grandparents' house on the way home. When she was in secondary school, her aunt asked Christine what she wanted to do in the future. Christine said, 'I'm going to go to university. I'll probably study biology. I might have to do more training, but then I'm going to be a doctor.' Her aunt replied, 'That sounds great, Christine! I expect you'll have to work very hard if that's your ambition. I wanted to be a doctor when I was younger, but I didn't have enough money for university. I had to work after school. I'm sure you will do well at school if you study a lot and ask for help when you need it.'

2

1 will meet, finishes 2 'll 3 gets, will be 4 won't 5 may, are 6 ask, I'll 7 be taking, won't 8 going to, have spoken

3

1 does 2 'll 3 won't 4 is 5 might 6 will 7 going to 8 she'll

4

1 b 2 a 3 a 4 b 5 b 6 b 7 b

5

1 My uncle will plant more flowers this spring.
2 Melanie is going to buy balloons for Josh's birthday.
3 I'm going to listen to the programme. / I am going to listen to the programme.
4 We'll have learnt about Ancient Rome by the end of term. / We will have learnt about Ancient Rome by the end of term.
5 We'll be eating dinner when you arrive. / We will be eating dinner when you arrive.
6 My parents will buy me a new car after graduation.

6

1 If the play is bad, the audience won't clap.
2 They'll be flying to Tanzania in January. / In January they'll be flying to Tanzania.
3 I'm not going to study in the US next year. / Next year I'm not going to study in the US.
4 When will you have worked here for a year?
6 Ms Shultz won't be collecting the assignments in class.
7 She'll have downloaded the songs by the time we get to the party.

7

1 e 2 d 3 g 4 f 5 a 6 c 7 b

8

1 b 2 b 3 b 4 a 5 b 6 a 7 a 8 a

Pronunciation Sentence stress in future

9

1 Anna won't be eating seafood.
2 The chef will be preparing something special.
3 They won't have arrived in Shanghai yet.
4 He'll have left by the time you get there.
5 What will you be doing tomorrow?
6 She won't have completed her work.

4D

Authentic listening skills Pausing

1

1 end of a sentence 2 adverbial time phrase 3 between a long subject and verb 4 commas 5 before an important phrase

Watch

2

a, c, d, f, h

3

1 a 2 b 3 c 4 a

Vocabulary in context

4

1 b 2 c 3 b 4 a 5 b 6 c

4E

Speaking

1

1 b 2 d 3 h 4 g 5 a 6 f 7 c 8 e

2

1 I think I might 2 I expect I'll 3 I'm thinking of 4 I'm hoping to 5 I'm aiming to 6 I'm looking forward to 7 I'd really like to 8 I'm interested in

3

Students' own answers.

4

Students' own answers.

Writing **A social media update**

5

Tip	Example
Leave out the subject in sentences.	Having a wonderful time.
Use exclamations.	It's amazing here!
Use descriptive vocabulary.	We enjoyed a fabulous feast.
Use emotionally powerful words.	*We were furious because the bus left early.*
Talk about recent events	This morning, I had the best melon I've ever tasted.
Talk about future plans and hopes.	In the next few days, we're hoping to do more sightseeing.

6

1 e **2** c **3** f **4** a **5** d **6** b

7

1 on the way here **2** magnificent **3** terrified **4** camping **5** traditional **6** meat dishes **7** delicious **8** planning

8

1, 3, 5, 6, 8, 10, 12

9

Students' own answers.

Review

1

1 b **2** c **3** d **4** a **5** f **6** e

2

1 since I've eaten **2** junk **3** it is easy / it's easy **4** boil it **5** healthy enough **6** meat-eater

3

1 Will the food arrive in time for us to eat?
2 The chef is making risotto next week. / Next week the chef is making risotto.
3 How will the customers find out about the daily specials?
4 Tomorrow might be the best time for everyone to get together.
5 I will measure the ingredients very carefully.
6 The inspectors are going to ask for more information.
7 My cousin might help his parents at their café tomorrow. / Tomorrow my cousin might help his parents at their café.
8 The soup is going to get cold if we don't eat soon.

4

1 is **2** going to **3** going to **4** won't / will not **5** will / 'll / 's going to **6** starts / begins

5

2 going to be **3** may / might **4** staying / going to stay / going to be staying **5** graduate **7** don't think I'll / don't think I will / do not think I'll / do not think I will

5 Work

5A

Vocabulary Describing work

1

Emergency Services	Desk jobs	Retail
firefighter	accountant	salesperson
paramedic	chief executive	shop manager
police officer	lawyer	

2

1 nurse **2** teacher **3** lawyer **4** chef **5** accountant **6** architect

3

1 e **2** a **3** b **4** f **5** d **6** c

4

1 c **2** a **3** b **4** f **5** e **6** d

5

1 career prospects **2** demanding **3** flexible **4** working on **5** industry **6** stressful **7** creative

6

1 f **2** c **3** a **4** d **5** b **6** e

7

1 for **2** on **3** on **4** in **5** for **6** on **7** in

8

1 I like being in charge of a large team.
2 He has been out of work for three months.
3 Working on big projects is stressful for me.
4 Being a writer is such a creative job.
5 I am looking for a job with career prospects.
6 She hopes to work in the entertainment industry.
7 There aren't many jobs, so it's very competitive.

9

1 find **2** quit **3** found **4** needs **5** need **6** quit

10

1 T
2 F – A vacancy is a job that is available for someone to do.
3 F – A challenging job is a job that needs a lot of effort.
4 T
5 T
6 F – A person who is retired is at the end of their career.
7 T

Listening

11

1 should **2** must **3** was able to **4** are allowed to **5** can't **6** didn't need to

12

1 T **2** F **3** T **4** F **5** F **6** T **7** F **8** T

13

1 b **2** b **3** c **4** a **5** c **6** b **7** c

14

1 c **2** b **3** a **4** c **5** b **6** a **7** b

Grammar Verb patterns: verb + *-ing* or infinitive with *to*

15

Verb + *-ing*	Infinitive with *to*
He's the kind of person who doesn't like disappointing people.	I think the owner is planning to hire more people.
She'll go on searching for a job until she finds something.	I've promised to talk to the bank about a business loan.
We only hire people who don't mind accepting challenges.	Remember to check your spelling before you submit the application form.
Why don't you try looking on the company website?	We agreed to continue the discussion tomorrow.

16

1 to look **2** working **3** applying, asking **4** to get **5** to find **6** to travel, to go **7** to fly **8** looking

17

1 spending **2** sitting, sending, talking **3** to go **4** to spend **5** working **6** to find **7** being

18

1 giving **2** to miss **3** to be **4** telling **5** working **6** to solve
7 talking

19

1 Our hard-working and creative employees have learnt ~~producing~~ **to produce** smartphone apps more efficiently.
2 Neither of my parents likes to ~~working~~ long hours. / Neither of my parents likes ~~to~~ working long hours.
3 I don't want **to** be in charge of people who don't do their jobs well.
4 Most university graduates expect ~~finding~~ **to find** well-paid jobs.
5 I agreed ~~attending~~ **to attend** the training course because we want the company **to** remain competitive.
6 Have you considered ~~to~~ research**ing** jobs in the tech industries?
7 Customers often go on ~~to~~ complaining even when you've told them there's nothing you can do. / Customers often go on to ~~complaining~~ **complain** even when you've told them there's nothing you can do.

5B

Vocabulary building Ways of seeing

1

1 recognized **2** observed **3** glanced **4** identified
5 spotted **6** noticed

Reading

2

1 b **2** c **3** a **4** b **5** d

3

1 F **2** T **3** F **4** NG **5** NG **6** T

4

1 c **2** c **3** c **4** b **5** a

5C

Grammar Present and past modal verbs

1

1 have to make **2** mustn't text **3** needs to win **4** have to get
5 can ask **6** need to take **7** should take

2

ability or possibility	advice	prohibition
Can you send an application after the closing date? Do you think she'll be able to help with the project? I could pay for lunch if you like.	I think you ought to ask him for help with your CV. Should I ask her for an interview? You should come to the office party.	Ron couldn't take a day off because he didn't have enough holiday. She isn't allowed to use the phone at work. You mustn't eat lunch at your desk.

3

1 P **2** NA/P **3** D/S **4** NA/P **5** D/S **6** NA/P
7 D/S **8** P **9** P

4

1 You should read the lesson before class. / Before class, you should read the lesson.
2 You aren't allowed to eat in class.
3 You should talk in class when the teacher asks questions.
4 You need to ask the teacher for help if you don't understand something. / You don't need to ask the teacher for help if you understand something. / If you don't understand something, you need to ask the teacher for help. / If you understand something, you don't need to ask the teacher for help.
5 You may want to study with your classmates.
6 You can't miss more than three lessons in a term.

7 You mustn't chat with your friends in class. / In class, you mustn't chat with your friends.
8 You can take three books from library each week. / Each week, you can take three books from the library.

5

2 We can't miss more than three lessons during the term.
3 He doesn't have to tell his teacher if he isn't going to be in class.
4 They can talk to their friends after the lesson.
5 I need to borrow the car to drive to work.
6 Tomas has to finish the report before 5pm.
7 I can't go to Nairobi with Jemma.
8 She has to work, so she isn't able to go to the museum with us.

6

1 need to **2** shouldn't **3** can **4** might **5** isn't allowed to
6 ought to **7** mustn't

7

1 to catch **2** take **3** to skip **4** hand in **5** win **6** study
7 throw **8** to help

8

1 h **2** c **3** b **4** d **5** g **6** e **7** a **8** f

5D

Authentic listening skills Understanding contrasts

1

1 repeating structures **2** replacing with opposites
3 contrasting words **4** contrasting words **5** repeating structures

Watch

2

1 a **2** b **3** a **4** c **5** a **6** a **7** c

3

1 a **2** d **3** b **4** c

Vocabulary in context

4

1 tough **2** assignment **3** turn out **4** count on **5** term
6 a piece of cake

5E

Speaking

1

1 I'd say I was quite a creative person.
2 I'm willing to work long hours.
3 I'm quite good at talking to people.
4 I've had lots of restaurant experience.
5 I'm working on my English.
6 I've always wanted to work outdoors.
7 I think this job would give me new skills.
8 What does the job involve?
9 I was just wondering if I would have to wear a uniform.
10 Are we allowed to wear jewellery?

2

1 I've always wanted to
2 I think this job would give me
3 I'm quite good at
4 I'd say I was quite an
5 I'm willing to
6 I've had lots of experience
7 I'm working on
8 I was just wondering if I would have to
9 are we allowed to

3

Student's own answers.

4

Student's own answers.

Pronunciation quite

5

1 NS   2 S   3 NS   4 S   5 S   6 NS   7 NS   8 S

Writing A formal letter of application

6

1 b   2 a   3 c   4 c   5 b

7

1 full postal address   2 today's date   3 formal greeting
4 reason for writing   5 relevant experience   6 personal qualities
7 asking about the job   8 information about availability
9 requesting a reply   10 polite ending

8

1 F   2 T   3 F   4 T   5 T   6 F   7 F   8 T

9

June 2018: no specific date
Hi: informal language
I'm: contraction
It's obvious that I am the perfect … : sounds arrogant
Drop me a line … : informal language
Thanks: informal language

10

Students' own answers.

Review

1

1 d   2 f   3 b   4 a   5 c   6 e

2

1 demanding   2 well-paid   3 creative   4 competitive
5 well-paid   6 stressful

3

1 quitting   2 working   3 to give   4 locking   5 to help
6 to take   7 counting

4

1 can't forget ~~taking~~ **to take**
3 might to remember ~~calling~~ **to call**
4 ~~go~~ mustn't **go** on taking / mustn't take
5 wasn't allowed **to** stop ~~to~~ having wasn't allowed to have

5

1 a   2 c   3 a   4 b   5 d   6 b   7 d   8 a

6 Superhuman

6A

Vocabulary The human body

1

1 elbow   2 throat   3 knee   4 nose   5 finger   6 stomach
7 chest   8 hand

2

1 head   2 neck   3 shoulder   4 chest   5 stomach   6 knee
7 foot

3

1 seasick   2 virus   3 temperature   4 broken   5 pain   6 patient

4

1 b   2 a   3 c   4 f   5 d   6 e

5

1 food   2 bacteria   3 nutrients   4 absorb   5 digestion   6 tongue

6

1 absorbed   2 tongue   3 Digestion   4 food   5 nutrients
6 bacteria

7

1 digestive system   2 foods   3 nutrients   4 muscles
5 bacteria   6 digestion

8

1 cells   2 oxygen   3 taste   4 break   5 skeleton   6 Muscles
7 breathe

9

Internal	External
intestines	eyebrow
liver	fingernail skin
ribs	wrist
spine	
vein	

10

1 vein   2 tendon   3 ribs   4 blood   5 bacteria

Listening

11

1 b   2 d   3 c   4 a   5 b   6 d

12

1 c   2 a   3 b   4 a   5 b   6 c   7 a

13

b

14

1 c   2 a   3 b   4 b   5 c   6 b

Grammar Zero and first conditional

15

Zero conditional	First conditional
Call your doctor if the pain is really bad.	Drinking tea with honey may help if you have a sore throat.
If you have a high temperature, you shouldn't go to school.	I can make you a sandwich if you're hungry when you arrive.
If your clothes no longer fit, it's time to go on a diet!	If you see Helen, tell her I'm not very well.
	Your bones will become weak if you don't drink enough milk.

16

1 wash, reduce   2 should treat, recognize   3 receive, recover
4 Go, feel   5 isn't, don't apply   6 goes, take   7 should see, is

17

1 will catch   2 will feel / 'll feel   3 touch   4 will introduce / 'll
introduce   5 will improve   6 won't be / will not be   7 relax

18

1 treats   2 will destroy   3 'll injure   4 give   5 won't catch
6 breathe   7 Wear   8 continue

19

1 increase, will begin / 'll begin   2 won't get, warm up   3 end up, will take
4 will contact, observes   5 won't / will not get, remember   6 won't /
will not improve, follow

6B

Reading

1

a 2   b 1   c 4   d 5   e -   f 3

2

1 b   2 a   3 e   4 d   5 c

3

1 skin   2 brain   3 bone   4 sophisticated   5 skeleton
6 muscle   7 headset   8 functional

Vocabulary building Verbs describing ability

4
1 save **2** allows **3** stop **4** prevent **5** lets **6** help **7** enable

6C

Grammar Second conditional

1
1 I would be really disappointed **if** I didn't pass.
2 **If** we won the match**,** we would be the champions.
3 **If** I improved my English**,** I could get a job in London.
4 I could answer questions in the lesson **if** I did the homework.
5 I'd know what to do **if** I listened to his advice.
6 They would fly to Tamil Nadu **if** they had enough money.
7 **If** Marcy took a holiday**,** she might feel more relaxed.

2
1 No, aren't (able to talk) / can't (talk)
2 doesn't/does not like bright colours
3 No, doesn't (like fish)
4 Alani doesn't/does not like learning languages
5 No, isn't/is not (able to climb Mount Everest) / can't/cannot (climb Mount Everest)
6 Yes, does (have to work), No, can't/cannot (go to the theatre) / isn't/is not able to (go to the theatre)
7 No, doesn't/does not (like baseball)
8 Yes, does (have a cold), No, isn't/is not (going to play tennis)

3
1 I'd **2** had, would **3** had **4** were, I'd **5** would be, made
6 could **7** would, had **8** were, would

4
1 'm/am not able, have a lesson **2** don't drive, longer / more than
3 don't/do not have/haven't got **4** isn't/is not, don't/do not live
5 not going **6** doesn't /does not have, doesn't /does not write

5
1 ~~would ran~~ **ran** **2** ~~had~~ **have** **4** ~~call~~ would/could call
5 I could write **7** I'd / I would

6
1 I would be slim if I ate less chocolate.
2 If only I could talk to you right now.
3 If the pharmacy were open, Akira would collect her medicine.
4 I wish I lived in Oslo.
5 They'd be worried if she didn't call every day.
6 If I had a toothbrush, I'd brush my teeth.
7 I wish I didn't have to go to bed!

7
1 a **2** b **3** b **4** a **5** a **6** b **7** a

Pronunciation *I wish* and *If only*

8
1 I <u>wish</u> I <u>didn't</u> have a <u>headache</u>.
2 If <u>only</u> I <u>knew</u> what to <u>say</u>.
3 I <u>wish</u> I could <u>dance</u>.
4 If <u>only</u> I <u>hadn't</u> broken my <u>leg</u>.
5 I <u>wish</u> I <u>did</u> more <u>exercise</u>.
6 If <u>only</u> I could <u>find</u> better <u>food</u>.
7 I <u>wish</u> I <u>had</u> more <u>time</u>.
8 If <u>only</u> I <u>hadn't</u> lost my <u>phone</u>.

6D

Authentic listening skills Following the argument

1
It is the most amazing experience, beyond most other things I've experienced in life. I literally have the freedom to move in 360 degrees of space and an ecstatic experience of joy and freedom. <u>And the incredibly unexpected thing is that</u> other people seem to see and feel that too. Their eyes literally light up, and they say things like, 'I want one of those', or, 'If you can do that, I can do anything'. <u>And I'm thinking</u>, it's because in that moment of them seeing an object they have no frame of reference for, or so transcends the frames of reference they have with the wheelchair, they have to think in a completely new way. <u>And I think</u> that moment of completely new thought perhaps creates a freedom that spreads to the rest of other people's lives. <u>For me, this means</u> that they're seeing the value of difference, the joy it brings when instead of focusing on loss or limitation, we see and discover the power and joy of seeing the world from exciting new perspectives.

Watch

2

Limitations	Freedoms
fear	doing something unexpected
pity	feeling joy
preconceptions	having a new toy
restrictions	taking a journey

3
1 freedom **2** illness **3** new toy **4** on the street **5** reaction
6 see **7** changed **8** identity

4
1 f **2** e **3** a **4** b **5** d **6** c

Vocabulary in context

5
1 b **2** c **3** a **4** b **5** b **6** a

6E

Speaking

1
1 i **2** e **3** h **4** a **5** c **6** d **7** j **8** b **9** g **10** f

2
1 photo **2** obviously **3** sort **4** children **5** looks **6** must
7 behind **8** looks **9** background **10** table

3
Students' own answers.

4
Students' own answers.

Writing An informal email describing people

5

Ways of starting an informal email	Ways of ending an informal email
How are things?	Give my love to your family.
It was great to get your news!	Please write soon.
Sorry I haven't written for a while.	Say 'hi' to everyone for me.
Thanks so much for your email.	Speak to you soon!

6
1 at the mo **2** ages **3** loads **4** my place **5** in a rush
6 thrilled **7** BTW **8** say 'hi' to **9** my stuff

7
1 g **2** f **3** c **4** e **5** h **6** b **7** d **8** a

8
1 Khalid **2** Takumi **3** Takumi **4** Khalid **5** Khalid **6** Takumi
7 Khalid **8** Takumi **9** Khalid **10** Takumi

9
Students' own answers.

Review

1
1 Oxygen is needed by all the major organs.
2 The brain is like a computer that controls the body.
3 Skin protects the body from dangerous bacteria.

4 The heart moves blood through the body.
5 Blood vessels carry oxygen to the brain.
6 The skeleton is made of a set of bones.
7 Each cell has a different job.
8 Muscles are used to move parts of the body.

2
1 b **2** c **3** e **4** a **5** f **6** d

3
1 have **2** don't work **3** don't drink **4** put **5** don't trust
6 'll start / will start **7** exercise **8** See

4
1 If you eat more protein, it ~~help~~ **will help** / **helps** your muscles grow.
2 If you ~~will~~ exercise a lot, you need to eat more so your body has the energy it needs.
3 If you ~~will~~ want your muscles to grow, drink a protein drink before you work out.
4 If you ~~will be~~ **are** serious about building muscle, you should lift weights every other day.
5 If you eat a small meal every three hours, your body ~~build~~ **will build** / **builds** muscle throughout the day.
6 Your body will build muscles as you sleep if you ~~will~~ eat certain foods before bed.

5
1 would/'d be, forgot **2** could skip **3** would/'d be, did
4 studied, would/'d know **5** wouldn't be, had **6** was/were, could go
7 listened, would/'d know **8** felt, would/'d breathe

7 Shopping around

7A

Vocabulary Money and shopping

1

Beginning	End
advertise	recycle
create	throw away
design	
grow	
manufacture	

2
1 material **2** options **3** advertise **4** manufacture **5** pick
6 Recycling **7** growing

3
1 a **2** b **3** a **4** c **5** d **6** a **7** b **8** b

4
1 around **2** special **3** away **4** debt **5** donate **6** back
7 refund **8** spend

5
1 for **2** back **3** more **4** for **5** more **6** off **7** for **8** back

6
1 browsing **2** refund **3** borrow **4** quality **5** brand **6** on
7 earns **8** logo

7
1 d **2** a **3** b **4** c **5** f **6** e

8
1 pay off **2** bargain **3** browse **4** lend **5** brand **6** sold out
7 shop around

9
1 return **2** loan **3** interest **4** owes / owed **5** consumers **6** seller

10
1 online **2** buyer **3** lend **4** return **5** owe **6** seller
7 stock **8** purchase

Listening

11
1 a **2** c **3** c

12
c

13
1 b **2** a **3** c **4** a **5** b **6** c

14
1 a **2** c **3** a **4** b **5** c **6** b **7** a

Grammar The passive

15
1 P **2** A **3** P **4** P **5** A **6** P **7** A **8** A

16
1 has been changed **2** don't recommend **3** is donated, is played
4 spent **5** sells **6** was returned, has been given

17
1 Sometimes, great deals can be found on the Internet.
2 Who had been identified as the previous owner?
3 Gift cards are usually given to new customers.
4 What has been donated to the auction?
5 These suits are only sold in our Edinburgh store.
6 Last year's prices have been increased by 10%.

18
1 were sold / have been sold **2** can be repaired
3 had been damaged **4** has already been returned **5** is worn
6 has been sent / was sent **7** can be bought

19
2 are damaged **3** had been sold **4** were taken
5 Have, been delivered **6** is manufactured **7** has been made
8 had been thrown away

7B

Reading

1
1 b **2** a **3** d **4** b **5** c

2
1 T **2** F **3** NG **4** T **5** T **6** F

3
1 b **2** c **3** c **4** b **5** d

Vocabulary building Adverbs

4
1 perfectly **2** temporarily **3** occasionally **4** fast **5** carefully
6 professionally **7** carefully **8** well

7C

Grammar *have / get something done*

1
1 have the pool cleaned **2** got the parcel delivered **3** have my laptop repaired **4** get your fence painted **5** has her dog walked
6 got the brakes tested **7** have it sent

2
1 have / had my hair cut **2** has / had a family portrait taken
3 got a new sound system installed **4** got coffee and biscuits brought
5 had my eyes checked **6** has / had the piano tuned
7 had pizza delivered **8** get your car washed

3
1 our teacher **2** don't know **3** don't know **4** don't know
5 the students **6** Marissa **7** don't know **8** don't know

4

1 We had breakfast ~~delivering~~ **delivered** to our room while we were on holiday.

2 We ~~have our tickets checked~~ **had our tickets checked** as we went into the concert.

4 He has the weekly report ~~got copy~~ **copied** before he sends it to Joe.

5 She had the invitations **be sent** a week before the party.

7 The librarian had the books **put** ~~has got~~ back on the shelves.

5

2 She / Nadia got the lights fixed. / She / Nadia had the lights fixed.

3 She / Nadia didn't get her phone fixed. / She / Nadia didn't have her phone fixed.

4 She / Nadia got the windows cleaned. / She / Nadia had the windows cleaned.

5 She / Nadia got her hair cut. / She / Nadia had her hair cut.

6 She / Nadia didn't get her teeth cleaned. / She / Nadia didn't have her teeth cleaned.

6

2 had / got his glasses fixed   3 had / got a sign made
4 had / got his calls forwarded   5 had / got the bill sent
6 had / got breakfast brought   7 had / got the kitchen tap repaired

7

1 a   2 b   3 a   4 a   5 b   6 a   7 b

Pronunciation Sentence stress

8

1 Have you <u>ever</u> had anything <u>stolen</u>?
2 I've <u>never</u> had my <u>room</u> <u>painted</u>.
3 Have you <u>ever</u> had something <u>made</u>?
4 Has she <u>ever</u> had her <u>eyes</u> <u>tested</u>?
5 Have they <u>ever</u> had their <u>groceries</u> <u>delivered</u>?
6 We've <u>never</u> had the <u>television</u> <u>repaired</u>.

7D

Authentic listening skills Reformulating

1

1 c   2 b   3 b   4 a   5 c

Watch

2

a 1   **e** 2   **b** 3   **d** 4   **g** 5   **h** 6   **f** 7   **c** 8

3

1 efficient   2 made   3 it's good for the environment
4 be an addition to   5 they might be used in another area

Vocabulary in context

4

1 b   2 c   3 a   4 b   5 b   6 a   7 c

7E

Speaking

1

1 It's OK, I'm just browsing.   2 have you got these in a larger size?
3 I need a size 'L'.   4 I'm after something smarter.   5 We've only got red ones   6 where are the changing rooms?   7 Is it the right size?
8 It looks really good on you.   9 I'll buy it.

2

1 jus<u>t</u> browsing   2 go<u>t</u> these   3 somethin<u>g</u> smarter   4 go<u>t</u> red
5 changin<u>g</u> rooms   6 righ<u>t</u> size   7 loo<u>ks</u> really

3

1 c   2 f   3 e   4 g   5 d   6 b   7 a

4

Students' own answers.

5

Students' own answers.

Writing An announcement

6

2, 6, 8, 10

7

1 a   2 b   3 b   4 a   5 b

8

1 d   2 b   3 e   4 c   5 a

9

1 Selling price   2 Central Madrid   3 for general travel
4 Lots of smaller   5 Suitable for   6 students   7 Brand new
8 quality   9 selling because   10 bargain price   11 Cash payment

10

Students' own answers.

Review

1

1 company   2 bargain   3 donate   4 logo   5 lend   6 browse
7 borrow

2

1 debt   2 I'd donate / I would donate   3 shop around
4 get a refund   5 take it   6 loan

3

1 present simple   2 present perfect   3 present simple
4 past simple   5 past perfect   6 present perfect   7 present simple
8 past perfect

4

1 are often bought online   2 salesperson has reduced the item
3 loan had been paid back   4 The designer removed the logo
5 bank sent the payment

5

1 c   2 a   3 b   4 d   5 a

6

1 Our teacher got new computers installed.
2 I have a cake made every year for my father's birthday. / Every year(,) I have a cake made for my father's birthday.
3 They get the grass cut on Thursdays. / On Thursdays(,) they get the grass cut.
4 We had that photo taken five years ago. / Five years ago(,) we had that photo taken.
5 Chao got his laptop repaired before he went to university. / Before he went to university, Chao got his laptop repaired.
6 The school is having a new website made.

8 Effective communication

8A

Vocabulary Effective communication

1

1 b   2 a   3 f   4 d   5 c   6 e

2

1 I don't understand what you are saying.
2 Send me a text if you need me.
3 How well can you communicate in English?
4 I spoke to the teacher about the test.
5 Is anyone listening to me?
6 I understand your point of view.
7 I got an important message from my boss.

3

1 N   2 N   3 N   4 N   5 V   6 N   7 V   8 V

4

1 pay attention   2 get my message out   3 get distracted
4 interpersonal skills   5 post on social media   6 respond to texts
7 share photos   8 make connections

5

1 get 2 respond 3 pay 4 send 5 share 6 make

6

1 a text 2 connection 3 messages 4 to a phone 5 chat
6 on an email

7

1 a conversation 2 an argument 3 a discussion 4 a chat
5 a debate

8

1 I need to get my message out.
2 Jack's teacher has terrible interpersonal skills.
3 She is trying to connect with old friends.
4 Be careful what you post on social media.
5 Don't get distracted by your friends.
6 He likes to share photos on his website.
7 Pay attention when someone is talking.

9

1 debating 2 discuss 3 argue 4 questioning 5 phone
6 chatting

10

1 gossip 2 quarrel 3 agreement 4 reminder 5 criticism
6 speech

Listening

11

1 b 2 d 3 c 4 b 5 a 6 c

12

c

13

1 T 2 F 3 F 4 T 5 T 6 T 7 F 8 F

Grammar Reported speech (1)

14

1 D 2 R 3 R 4 R 5 D 6 R 7 R

15

1 a 2 b 3 b 4 a 5 a 6 b

16

1 told, had 2 had, was 3 cooked, cooked 4 was learning
5 had got 6 was

17

1 She complained that she had
2 He replied that he had enjoyed working
3 She suggested that she could show
4 He admitted that he wasn't
5 She claimed that she had worked
6 He replied that he needed to find

18

1 were going to study 2 knew 3 was, had not seen/hadn't seen
4 could help 5 had written 6 waited 7 had already passed
8 would know

8B

Reading

1

1 T 2 F 3 NG 4 T 5 T 6 F

2

a 4 b 3 c 5 d 1 e 2 f 2 g 4

3

1 d 2 e 3 b 4 c 5 a

Vocabulary building Negative prefixes

4

1 unbelievable 2 unable 3 irrelevant 4 impossible
5 unusual 6 informal

8C

Grammar Reported speech (2)

1

1 said he'd enjoyed 2 complained that she hadn't had
3 replied that he liked 4 agreed to meet 5 reminded Claire
6 asked me to come

2

1 b 2 a 3 b 4 b 5 a 6 b 7 a 8 b

3

direct speech	example	reported speech	example
present simple	'I speak French.'	past simple	She said that she spoke French.
present continuous	'I am speaking French.'	past continuous	She said that she was speaking French.
past simple	'I spoke French.'	past perfect	She said that she had spoken French.
present perfect	'I have spoken French.'	past perfect	She said that she had spoken French.
will/won't	'I'll speak French.'	would/wouldn't	She said that she would speak French.
can/can't	'I can't speak French.'	could/couldn't	She said that she couldn't speak French.

4

1 tomorrow 2 our 3 yesterday 4 then 5 they 6 that day
7 that 8 there

5

1 meet the president. 2 the day before 4 admitted he lost /
admitted that he lost 5 Brigit asked 6 told Sara 7 reminded me
that he couldn't come

6

1 she 2 moving, replied that 3 agreed to help 4 the next day
5 me to join 6 promised to 7 that she'd played 8 hadn't replied

7

1 said that she was going to jump / said she was going to jump
2 asked my brother if he'd fed the dog yet. / asked my brother if he had
  fed the dog yet. / asked him if he'd fed the dog yet. / asked him if he had
  fed the dog yet. / asked my brother whether he'd fed the dog yet. /
  asked my brother whether he had fed the dog yet. / asked him whether
  he'd fed the dog yet. / asked him whether he had fed the dog yet.
3 asked Tori if she went to the cinema / asked Tori whether she went to
  the cinema / asked her if she went to the cinema / asked her
  whether she went to the cinema
4 promised he would text Jen to ask her if she had left / promised he
  would text her to ask her if she'd left
5 explained that he had / explained he had tickets to the match on
  (the) Saturday, so he couldn't go to the play with me
6 asked my brother if he had any homework to do / asked my brother
  whether he had any homework to do / asked him if he had any
  homework to do / asked him whether he had any homework to do
7 offered to take my sister to the shops after her / offered to take her to
  the shops after her
8 invited me to go sailing

8

1 Paul argued that we all connect on social media <u>before</u> we meet in
  person.
2 <u>Paul</u> argued that we all connect on social media before we meet in
  person.
3 Paul argued that we all connect on <u>social media</u> before we meet in person.
4 Can you believe Sarah shared <u>those photos</u> of me on her blog?

5 Can you believe <u>Sarah</u> shared those photos of me on her blog?

6 Can you believe Sarah shared those photos of me on her <u>blog</u>?

9

1 b **2** c **3** c **4** c **5** a **6** b

8D

Authentic listening skills Understanding fast speech

1

1 a **2** b **3** b **4** a **5** c **6** b **7** c

Watch

2

1 conversations **2** a disagreement **3** online, but not face to face **4** a professional interviewer **5** disagrees with **6** the skills she uses in her profession as an interviewer

3

1 d **2** a **3** c **4** e **5** f **6** b

Vocabulary in context

4

1 b **2** c **3** a **4** b **5** b **6** a

8E

Speaking

1

1 see **2** afraid **3** say **4** What **5** Unfortunately **6** frustrating **7** hear **8** hear **9** just **10** such **11** thing **12** but

2

1 I'm sorry to <u>hear</u> that. **2** That is frus<u>tr</u>ating. **3** That's such a shame. **4** <u>What</u> a pity. **5** I <u>see</u>. **6** I <u>hear</u> what you're saying, <u>but</u> … **7** I <u>understand, but</u> … **8** You see, the <u>thing</u> is … **9** It's <u>just</u> that … **10** Un<u>fort</u>unately, … **11** I'm a<u>fraid</u> that … **12** I'm sorry to <u>say</u> …

3

Suggested answers:

1 Oh, I'm sorry to hear that **2** Oh, no **3** Oh, dear, bad luck. That's such a pity. **4** What a shame **5** That's frustrating **6** Oh, I see

4

Students' own answers.

Writing An email of complaint

5

1 A **2** R **3** A **4** C **5** C **6** R **7** C **8** A

6

1 formal greeting **2** reason for writing **3** background to the problem **4** details of the problem **5** how she feels **6** what she wants them to do **7** items attached **8** request for a reply **9** formal ending

7

Students' own answers.

Review

1

1 d **2** a **3** f **4** e **5** b **6** c

2

1 a **2** b **3** a **4** d **5** a **6** c **7** b

3

2 'The project is taking longer than I expected.'

3 'You need to finish your projects by Thursday.'

4 'No one has followed the directions.' / 'No one followed the directions.'

5 'The test will make up 30% of your final marks.'

6 'We always enjoy English lessons.'

7 'I can lend you a dictionary.'

4

1 paid, talked **2** interrupted **3** forgot, could check **4** hadn't spoken, had visited **5** was, spoke

5

1 admitted **2** invited **3** was making, could **4** told **5** the next day **6** he'd do **7** there, that

9 Unexpected entertainment

9A

Vocabulary Creative arts

1

1 f **2** a **3** d **4** b **5** c **6** e

2

1 a **2** b **3** b **4** b **5** d **6** a **7** d

3

People	Venues
audience	gallery
listeners	stadium
viewers	studio
visitors	theatre

4

1 f **2** c **3** b **4** d **5** e **6** a

5

1 b **2** b **3** c **4** c **5** a **6** b

6

1 tune **2** stadium **3** verse **4** listeners **5** broadcast **6** characters **7** form of entertainment

7

1 gallery **2** performance **3** drawing **4** plays **5** portrait **6** mural **7** lyrics

8

Positive	Negative
appealing	awful
creative	boring
imaginative	slow
inspirational	tedious
moving	

9

1 a **2** c **3** d **4** b **5** a **6** d

10

1 lifelike **2** abstract **3** modern **4** imaginative **5** award-winning **6** controversial

Listening

11

1 b **2** a **3** c **4** a **5** b **6** c **7** a **8** b

12

c

13

1 g **2** i **3** d **4** j **5** e **6** b **7** a **8** h **9** c **10** f

14

1 c **2** a **3** b **4** a **5** a **6** c **7** b **8** c

Grammar

15

1 that **2** that **3** - **4** who **5** which **6** that **7** that **8** who

16

1 N **2** U **3** N **4** N **5** U **6** U **7** N **8** N

17

1 which has many famous paintings by Latin American artists / which has famous paintings by many Latin American artists

2 is a museum which focuses on Polish modern artists

3 which includes painters from many different European and South American countries

4 who paint colourful murals all over the world
5 who was known for his paintings of famous and important people
6 that sometimes hosts exhibitions of up-and-coming artists

18
1 S   **2** O   **3** O   **4** S   **5** O   **6** S   **7** S   **8** O

19
2 The painter bought new paintbrushes that/which were made in Italy.
3 The ancient Romans decorated their homes with paintings that/which were later discovered by archaeologists.
4 M.C. Escher was a famous graphic artist who/that was from the Netherlands.
5 Tango is a well-known dance that/which is from Argentina and Uruguay.
6 Graphic novels are a new kind of literature that/which are enjoyed by kids around the world.

9B

Vocabulary building Expressions with *make*

1
1 make a living   **2** make friends   **3** make the most   **4** make a decision   **5** make sense   **6** make time   **7** make a difference

Reading

2
1 b   **2** a   **3** b   **4** a   **5** b   **6** b
3
1 play   **2** performance   **3** concert   **4** audiences   **5** exhibitions
4
1 b   **2** c   **3** a   **4** c   **5** d   **6** d

9C

Grammar Defining and non-defining relative clauses

1

defining relative clause	non-defining relative clause	no relative clause
4, 5	3, 6	1, 2

2
1 b   **2** c   **3** a   **4** a   **5** c   **6** b   **7** c   **8** b
3
1 which   **2** that / which   **3** that / who   **4** which   **5** which   **6** who
4
1 My friend <u>who</u> lives in Oregon invited us to go walking along the Pacific Trail.
2 Yesterday's concert, which was the last one this year, had the biggest audience ever.
3 The man <u>who</u> was sitting opposite me was very quiet.
4 The seafood <u>which</u> we had at that restaurant near the beach was delicious.
5 My mum, who has always been interested in art, went to Florence last month.
6 Our friends <u>who</u> moved to Singapore email us every week.
7 He gave all the money to Angela, who decided to spend it on a car.
5
1 that   **2** article, which   **3** article that   **4** who   **5** that's
6 dictionary that   **7** who   **8** that
6
1 a   **2** b   **3** b   **4** b   **5** a   **6** b
7
1 She's the teacher who won the big award.
2 Her hair, which is very short, is dark brown.
3 My friend who moved to La Paz texts me every now and then.
4 Many people loved his third song, which he wrote in 2015.
5 Thad is my friend who starred in the school play.
6 The song that she wrote was not good enough to put on the album.
7 Tracy told us a story, which wasn't true, about her time in Helsinki.

8
1 instrument that / instrument which / instrument
2 postcard, which
4 menu which / menu that / menu
5 photographer who took / photographer that took
6 neighbour, who loves
7 man that / man who / man
8 ruler which / ruler that / ruler

Pronunciation Relative clauses
9
1 N   **2** D   **3** N   **4** N   **5** D   **6** D

9D

Authentic listening skills Collaborative listening
1
1 b   **2** c   **3** a   **4** d

Watch

2
1 is never very exciting.
2 NRK came up with a new kind of TV programme that, surprisingly, people liked.
3 watching the cruise ship journey on TV even though the fog means it's hard to see the coastline.
4 Even though knitting is boring, Norwegians find this form of TV fascinating.
5 jokes that viewers won't see anything exciting in the following report.

3
1 3,000   **2** 100 years   **3** 87 days   **4** 14 hours   **5** 7 hours and 4 minutes   **6** 8,040   **7** 148   **8** 1.2 million   **9** 23

Vocabulary in context
4
1 b   **2** c   **3** a   **4** b   **5** b   **6** a

9E

Speaking
1
1 The museum is a **must**-see.
2 It was alright, I **suppose**.
3 The new Bond film is **well** worth seeing.
4 What **did** you think about it?
5 I highly **recommend** it.
6 You might like it if you've got **nothing** else to do.
7 Is it **worth** visiting?
8 I didn't **think** it was great.
9 I don't **normally** like musicals, but this has a good story too.
10 You won't want to **miss** this.
11 Is **it** any good?
12 You **must go**!
13 It'll **appeal** to anyone who enjoys thrillers.
14 It's worth **watching**.

2
1 G   **2** S   **3** G   **4** A   **5** G   **6** S   **7** A   **8** S   **9** S   **10** G
11 A   **12** G   **13** S   **14** G

3
1 what did you think about   **2** must-see   **3** I don't normally like
4 it worth   **5** highly recommends it   **6** send you   **7** recommend it
8 want to miss this   **9** it any good   **10** think it was great
11 alright, I suppose   **12** well worth   **13** you might like it
14 You must go   **15** don't normally like

4
Students' own answers.

5
Students' own answers.

Writing An email describing a place and its culture

6

1 that   2 which   3 that   4 where   5 who   6 where

7

a 5   **b** 3   **c** 1   **d** 4   **e** 2   **f** 6

8

1 e   2 c   3 f   4 a   5 h   6 g

9

Students' own answers.

Review

1

1 musical, theatre   2 play, characters   3 gallery, drawings
4 listeners, programme   5 Live, form   6 concert, lyrics

2

1 She's taking an art class which ~~it~~ meets on Saturdays at the college.
2 The gallery ~~who~~ **that/which** is owned by my artist friend is open at the weekend.
3 Our teacher showed us photos of objects which she had seen ~~them~~ in the museum.
4 Performance art is not something ~~who~~ **that/which** I usually understand. / Performance art is not something ~~who~~ I usually understand.
5 The paintings **that/which** are most valuable are in the gallery downstairs.
6 Not all the countries that competes in the Eurovision Song Contest are European.
7 Jazz is a kind of music which not everyone can appreciate ~~that~~.

3

2 I met a director who has won many awards for her films about nature.
3 The actors who were chosen for the film are travelling to the set by helicopter.
4 The artist's inspiration for the drawing was a windmill that/which he had seen in the Netherlands. / The artist's inspiration for the drawing was a windmill he had seen in the Netherlands.
5 The poet writes about subjects which/that come from his personal life.
6 The painter started with a red square which/that represented loneliness for her.

4

1 This is the picture <u>that</u> my cousin Lydia painted.
4 Charles is the friend <u>who</u> I was telling you about.
6 The birthday card <u>that</u> I sent my brother was hilarious.
8 The flight <u>that</u> I took to Kuala Lumpur was late.

5

1 c   2 a   3 d   4 b   5 d   6 **b**

10 Time

10A

Vocabulary Phrasal verbs about time

1

1 during   2 before   3 before   4 after   5 wait   6 early   7 once

2

1 Don't be late for the football match.
2 The people kept talking during the film.
3 Don't exercise until your doctor says it's OK.
4 Try to arrive at the theatre early.
5 Both teams should research their arguments before a debate.
6 I can't lend you any more money until next month.
7 She liked steak before she became a vegetarian.

3

1 c   2 f   3 a   4 b   5 d   6 e

4

1 catch up   2 wait around for   3 looking forward to
4 fall behind   5 hanging out   6 put off

5

1 F – If you never get round to exercising, you ~~exercise a lot~~ **never exercise**.
2 T
3 T
4 F – If you run out of time, you have ~~a large amount of~~ **no time left**.
5 T
6 T
7 F – When you hang out, you are usually **not** busy.

6

1 get round to   2 wait around for   3 take time off   4 fall behind
5 bring, forward   6 hold on

7

1 fall behind   2 catch up   3 put off   4 fit, in   5 bring, forward
6 run out of time

8

1 past   2 future   3 place   4 soon   5 last   6 late   7 time

9

1 in the first place   2 as soon as   3 at last   4 in the past
5 on time   6 In the future   7 run late

10

1 currently   2 finally   3 currently   4 meanwhile   5 meanwhile
6 finally

Listening

11

b

12

1 d   2 c   3 b   4 c   5 a   6 c

13

b

14

1 c   2 a   3 a   4 b   5 c   6 b   7 a

Grammar Third conditional

15

Zero / first conditional	Second conditional	Third conditional
2, 4, 6, 11	3, 5, 10	1, 7, 8, 9

16

1 b   2 a   3 c   4 a   5 c

17

1 had brought   2 wouldn't have ruined   3 would have been
4 hadn't been   5 had rained   6 would have arrived
7 hadn't been broken   8 hadn't forgotten

18

1 c   2 a   3 c   4 c   5 b   6 a   7 c

19

1 knew, would have arrested
2 wouldn't have caused, had been paying
3 hadn't been singing, would have paid
4 hadn't rained, wouldn't have been
5 wouldn't have skidded, hadn't been
6 had indicated, would have known
7 wouldn't have hit, hadn't stepped

20

1 If you ~~would study~~ **had studied** harder, you would have received better marks.
2 If he ~~would have took~~ **had taken** better notes, he could have studied more easily.
3 They would have got better marks if they ~~would have~~ **had** remembered to hand in their homework.
4 If we ~~wouldn't skip~~ **hadn't skipped** our lessons, the test would have been much easier.
5 We would have created a study group if we ~~would know~~ **had known** each other's phone numbers.
6 If she ~~would~~ **had** done the assignments on time, she wouldn't have fallen behind.
7 If only we ~~would have~~ **had** taken better notes when we read the articles.
8 I wish that we ~~would do~~ **had done** some practice tests to help us study. We would have got better results.

10B

Vocabulary building Expressions with *time*

1
1 c **2** c **3** d **4** b **5** b

Reading
2
a 4 **b** 3 **c** 1 **d** 3 **e** 5 **f** 4
3
1 F **2** T **3** NG **4** T **5** T **6** F
4
1 b **2** a **3** e **4** c **5** d

10C

1

In 1526, explorer Hernán Cortés recorded tales of fabulously rich towns hidden in the Honduran interior. He must have heard similar stories from a variety of people. If early explorers hadn't heard stories of a ruined city rising above the jungle, archaeologist Chris Fisher might not have flown to the mountains of La Mosquitia in early 2015 to look for the ruins of a lost city. Fisher did not believe in the legends of 'Ciudad Blanca' – a mythical city built of white stone. He thought it can't have existed.

Though the Mosquitia are among the most mysterious of ancient cultures in the Americas, Fisher *did* believe the mountains of La Mosquitia must contain the ruins of a real lost city, which had been abandoned for at least 500 years.

When archaeologists first began to explore Mosquitia in the 1930s, they uncovered some settlements. They thought the area may once have been occupied by a widespread, sophisticated culture. Some archaeologists have proposed that a group of Maya warriors may have taken control of Mosquitia. Others think that the local culture could have simply embraced the characteristics of the Maya.

There is no evidence yet that the Mosquitia built with stone. When their buildings were decorated and painted, they may have been as remarkable as some of the great temples of the Maya. But once abandoned, they dissolved in the rain and rotted away. If the Mosquitia had built their buildings of stone, we might know more about them.

2
1 a **2** b **3** b **4** b **5** a **6** a **7** a **8** a
3
1 yes **2** yes **3** no **4** yes **5** no **6** yes **7** no
4
1 hadn't moved **2** would have gone **4** might have won
6 would have gone
5
1 a **2** a **3** b **4** a **5** a

6
1 shouldn't **2** might not **3** can't **4** should **5** might not
6 may not
7
1 b **2** a **3** b **4** b **5** a **6** a **7** a

Pronunciation Weak forms: *have*

8
1 He could have done better if he had studied.
2 <u>Have</u> you had any luck finding a job?
3 They can't come because they <u>have</u> to study tonight.
4 I should have started earlier. Now it's too late.
5 We might have missed the plane if we hadn't taken a taxi.
6 Would you really <u>have</u> helped me if I'd asked you?
7 The test must have been very difficult.
8 <u>Have</u> the exam results been posted yet?

10D

Authentic listening skills Guessing the meaning of new words

1
1 a **2** b **3** b **4** c

Watch
2
a 4 **b** 6 **c** 2 **d** 5 **e** 1 **f** 3
3
1 saving him or her from a potentially bad outcome
2 procrastinated for the first five months before planning it
3 people from many different backgrounds emailed him
4 more than one kind
5 they may never achieve their goals

Vocabulary in context
4
1 b **2** c **3** c **4** b **5** b **6** a

10E

Speaking
1
1 The purpose of studying is to develop your abilities.
2 Boredom at school is caused by studying things that don't interest you.
3 That's why I like learning practical subjects.
4 The point of learning something is to enjoy your life more.
5 I like cooking because of its very practical nature.
6 We have to eat in order to live.
7 Consequently, cooking is the most practical skill.
8 Therefore, eating and cooking should be enjoyable.
9 I learnt to cook so that I could enjoy food more.
10 One of the main reasons is that I like the creativity of cooking.
11 That's the reason I want to be a chef.

2
1 h **2** g **3** j **4** i **5** f **6** a **7** k **8** c **9** e **10** b **11** d
3
1 The purpose of **2** One of the main reasons is that **3** That's the reason **4** in order to **5** That's why **6** because of **7** is caused by
8 Therefore **9** so that **10** Consequently **11** the point of
4
Students' own answers.

Writing A for and against essay

5
1 b **2** a **3** b **4** c

6

1 structure **2** the topic **3** relevant **4** in favour of **5** reasons
6 linking words **7** First of all **8** third paragraph **9** discourse marker
10 own opinion

7

1 f **2** d **3** b **4** a **5** c **6** e

8

Students' own answers.

Review

1

1 I won't wait around for you much longer.
2 I'm so busy that I'm falling behind at work.
3 It took so long to catch up.
4 Can you take time off this year?
5 I never get round to calling her.
6 I put off studying and failed my test.

2

1 a **2** d **3** b **4** b **5** c **6** a **7** d

3

1 b **2** a **3** d **4** a **5** c **6** b **7** d **8** d

4

1 I might not have met my best friend if we had gone to different schools.
2 If I hadn't found my passport, I wouldn't have been able to fly home last week.
3 Shana must have eaten all the sweets.
4 You shouldn't have streamed all that music.
5 He must have done well in his exam.
6 I shouldn't have cut my hair.
7 The river would be lower if it hadn't rained so much last week.

Grammar practice answer key

1 In touch with your feelings

1

1 correct **2** What does Ingrid do? **3** Which bus goes …
4 correct **5** What were you doing … **6** Who did Lina love …

2

2 a Who enjoys their maths classes?
b Which classes do the children enjoy?
3 a What did Evgeny do yesterday?
b How many movies did Evgeny watch yesterday?
4 a Who likes the new teacher?
b Who* do most of the class like?
5 a What has Karina lost?
b Who has lost her bag?
6 a What did Kei tell Naomi?
b Who did Kei tell the secret to?
* In object questions, 'who' can be replaced with 'whom'. However, 'whom' is very formal and very few people use it any more, except in a few very formal expressions, such as in a letter addressed to no one specific person: 'To whom it may concern …'

3

1 do you go, is planning **2** Are you coming, I need **3** normally take, aren't working, I'm cycling, always takes **4** have you had, I'm borrowing **5** You're always playing, I'm finishing **6** I'm looking, haven't seen, I don't know, I'm doing

4

1 are getting, are eating / eat **2** is going up **3** are using / use **4** is becoming

5

1 How long have you known your best friend?
2 How long is your journey to school?
3 How long have you been at this school?
4 How long does this lesson last?
5 How long have you been able to swim?
6 How long have you known how to speak English?

6

1 b **2** c **3** g **4** a **5** f **6** e **7** d

7

A: What jobs do your parents do?
B: Well, my mum is a doctor but my dad isn't working / doesn't work at the moment. He is studying to be a computer programmer.
A: Oh really? Why's that?
B: He has been a restaurant manager for most of his life, but he wants to do something different.
A: And he likes / does he like computers?
B: Oh, yes, he is always playing / always plays with computers at home. My computer is never working / never works because my dad thinks he can 'improve' it!
A: Oh no! Well, I hope he learns how to fix your computer on this course!

2 Enjoy the ride

1

1 bored **2** surprising **3** worried **4** frightening, relaxed
5 interesting, tired **6** confused **7** terrifying **8** exhausting

2

1 ~~embarrassed~~ embarrassing **2** ~~frightening~~ frightened **3** correct
4 ~~boring~~ bored **5** relaxed ~~relaxing~~ **6** correct
7 ~~depressed~~ depressing **8** correct

3

1 c **2** b **3** a **4** e **5** d **6** f

4

1 use to go (not possible) **2** both correct **3** both correct
4 use to move (not possible) **5** both correct **6** both correct

5

1 Who taught you **2** he was travelling **3** Did you see
4 had already started **5** Did you use to* **6** I lost

* did you used to / didn't used to is becoming widely accepted in written English these days, according to written corpus data. However, it is generally regarded as an error by examinations organizations, so students would be advised to follow tradition and write did you use to.

6

1 until he had checked **2** used to spend **3** was (still) eating
4 had already met **5** were arguing **6** hadn't brought

3 Active lives

1

1 have always loved **2** invited **3** have been **4** was
5 turned over **6** didn't give up **7** have spent **8** have just bought
9 haven't taken **10** took **11** haven't seen **12** has gone

2

1 We ~~have~~ played three matches yesterday.
2 She hasn't tried ~~yet rollerblading~~ rollerblading yet, but I'm sure she will.
3 The team ~~competed~~ have / has competed / been competing in the tournament for more than 30 years.
4 Oh no! You ~~hurt~~ have hurt your arm. It looks really sore.
5 A: Where's Tariq?
B: He's ~~been~~ gone to the changing rooms to get ready.
6 José and I have played together ~~since~~ for three years.
7 They ~~hasn't~~ haven't won many matches so far this year.
8 I've ~~met~~ been meeting him since 2014.

3

1 taken, been raining **2** I've injured, haven't wanted **3** has known, started **4** swum, I've been swimming **5** hasn't chosen, I've been training **6** won, been playing **7** been reading, finished

4

1 A: How long have you been playing hockey?
B: Six years. In that time, I've played for three different teams.
A: And have your teams won any tournaments?
B: We haven't won any big trophies, but we won the local tournament last month.
A: Congratulations!
2 A: Where have you been?
B: I've been working out at the gym.
A: You haven't had a shower yet, that's for sure! You smell terrible!
B: Give me a chance! I've just got home!
3 A: Who's that player with the ball? He's been playing well so far.
B: That's Gareth Bale. You must have heard of him! He's been playing for Madrid all season.
A: Of course I've heard of him! But I didn't know what he looked like.

5

1 How many Grand Slams has she won?
2 How much have they spent so far?
3 How long has she been a member?
4 How long have you known each other?
5 How long have you been cycling?
6 How much did it cost?

6

1 Have you ever run a marathon?
2 He's just bought some new trainers.
3 They've never won before.
4 Has she played for the team yet?
5 We've never met a famous person.
6 I haven't had time to wash my football boots yet. They're very dirty!
7 I've already done some exercise today. / I've done some exercise already today. / I've done some exercise today already.
8 Have you just arrived? Get your swimming costume on!

4 Food

1

1 going to work   2 does the plane   3 I'll   4 I'm going to
5 are you going to   6 are you going to   7 I'm spending, visit
8 might

2

1 will get, arrives   2 gets, won't be   3 'll / will understand, talk
4 find out, will (you) text   5 'll / will call, give

3

1 'll carry   2 'm helping / going to help   3 won't be   4 'll call
5 'm cooking / going to cook   6 'll make

4

1 What are you doing / going to do this weekend?
2 I'll text you after I speak to her.
3 Are you seeing anyone this evening?
4 I won't make a noise.
5 Do you think you'll go back to that restaurant?
6 I'm not going to see / not seeing her

5

1 'll / will be eating   2 'll / will have passed   3 won't be staying
4 'll / will have gone   5 won't have crossed / won't be crossing*
6 Will you be joining

* The action of crossing the line (or not) can be seen as happening at the same time as it is getting dark (continuous), or before it gets dark (perfect).

6

1 'll / will want   2 'll definitely come   3 Are you / will you be leaving
4 'll / will be   5 won't be   6 'll see   7 'll be wearing

5 Work

1

1 tried talking   2 tried to open   3 remember putting
4 remember to set   5 went on to win   6 went on chatting
7 stop doing   8 stopped to look   9 regret to inform
10 regret doing   11 forgot to pay   12 forget arriving
13 mean missing   14 mean to hurt

2

1 have to (not *must* in questions)   2 are allowed to (permission)   3 managed to (not *could* with specific possibility)   4 couldn't (past lack of ability)   5 should (*ought* followed by *to*)   6 don't often have to (no obligation)   7 didn't need to (not *needn't* in past)   8 aren't allowed (*can't* is not followed by *to*)

3

1 must   2 can't   3 must   4 can't

4

1 had to wear a suit   2 must eat   3 couldn't take breaks
4 Do you have to wear a helmet   5 can't use the printer   6 didn't have to buy a new phone   7 could smoke   8 have to / must arrive
9 mustn't / can't drink coffee or tea

5

1 d̶i̶d̶n̶'t̶ ̶h̶a̶v̶e̶ wasn't allowed   2 m̶u̶s̶t̶ have to   3 m̶u̶s̶t̶n̶'t̶ don't have to / don't need to / needn't   4 needn't t̶o̶ do   5 m̶u̶s̶t̶n̶'t̶ can't

6 Superhuman

1

1 wake up   2 shouldn't drink   3 continues   4 can / may pass
5 should cover   6 may / can pass   7 have   8 can / may go
9 gets   10 don't look after

2

1 h̶e̶'l̶l̶ ̶f̶e̶e̶l̶ he feels   2 i̶f̶ unless / w̶o̶n̶'t̶ will   3 s̶h̶o̶u̶l̶d̶ will / may / can
4 U̶n̶l̶e̶s̶s̶ If / h̶a̶p̶p̶y̶ not happy / c̶a̶n̶ can't   5 I̶ ̶p̶h̶o̶n̶e̶ I'll phone
6 w̶i̶l̶l̶ ̶r̶a̶i̶n̶ rains   7 s̶h̶o̶u̶l̶d̶ will / might / may / can
8 w̶i̶l̶l̶ should / y̶o̶u̶ ̶w̶i̶l̶l̶ see

3

1 would choose   2 paid   3 was or were (both possible)
4 couldn't   5 weren't   6 had   7 didn't   8 might

4

1 helped his classmates, wouldn't be angry with him   2 could come out / would be able to come out, didn't have   3 wouldn't have to look after, their parents didn't both work   4 wasn't broken, could print
5 wish they could   6 wasn't closed, wouldn't have to study at home
7 be able to drive to work, a car wasn't parked   8 Patricio still lived here / Patricio lived here still

5

1 real future possibility – see, I'll   2 an unlikely future situation – would, won   3 an imagined present situation – had, we'd
4 real future possibility – will, pass   5 an imagined present situation – wasn't, I'd   6 an imagined present situation – would, weren't
7 an imagined present situation – would, could   8 real future possibility – I'll, is

7 Shopping around

1

1 a (agent is obvious)   2 a (agent is people in general)
3 a (agent is repeated)

2

1 is affected   2 were   3 are   4 may have been   5 made
6 is   7 has been   8 isn't

3

1 has been designed   2 have been put   3 We were encouraged
4 are kept   5 had been encouraged   6 was designed
7 were also placed   8 is played

4

1 We had the house cleaned by a cleaning company after the party. / After the party, we had the house cleaned by a cleaning company.
2 Please get the fire alarm fixed before something terrible happens.
3 He received so many unwanted calls from companies that he had his phone number changed.
4 I had / I'm having / I'm going to have my old trainers repaired instead of buying a new pair.
5 Where can I get this suit cleaned?
6 Before they moved in, they had all the walls painted. / They had all the walls painted before they moved in.

7 You should have your car tested every year.
8 Get your university application checked for errors before you send it.

5
1 to get / have the oil changed **2** to get / have it cleaned
3 got / had some flowers sent **4** gets / has his hair cut
5 get / have a/my photo taken **6** got / had some (Chinese) food delivered

8 Effective communication

1
1 say **2** told **3** said **4** asked **5** ask **6** tell

2
1 went **2** hadn't enjoyed **3** were starting **4** would find out
5 couldn't see **6** had visited, had studied **7** had found
8 were, had to visit

3
1 She told the reporter that she'd been in Antarctica with her team for six months. **2** She explained that she was studying small fish that live(d) there. **3** She said she had arrived last November (the previous November), at the beginning of summer.* **4** She told him that the temperature was -25° that day. **5** She said that she didn't want to leave that magical place. **6** But she explained that she couldn't stay. She had to catch the plane to New Zealand the next/following day.*

* To replace tomorrow, next week and so on when the time referenced is no longer tomorrow or next week, etc. we can use the next day/week, etc. or more formally the following day/week, etc. To replace yesterday, last week, etc. we can use the day/week before or the previous day/week, etc.

4
1 He asked her what kind of camera she used for her videos.
2 He asked her how many videos she had posted on YouTube.
3 He asked her if she was happy with the number of people who watch(ed) her videos. **4** He asked her if she posted videos every day.
5 He asked her if she had ever made a video that people didn't like/ hadn't liked. **6** He asked her if she would ever stop posting on YouTube.

5
1 complained that they had **2** asked Paulo if/whether he
3 replied that it hadn't **4** added that he wasn't **5** explained that he was **6** claimed that he had **7** admitted that he had
8 told him/Paulo to buy

6
1 e **2** d **3** c **4** h **5** g **6** f **7** a **8** b

9 Unexpected entertainment

1
1 who **2** – (no relative pronoun necessary) **3** which **4** – **5** –
6 which **7** –

2
1 My sister is the one who told me about the exhibition.
2 This is the book (which/that) I read when I was on holiday.
3 This is the song which/that won the award for best R&B track.
4 That's the architect who went on to design the new library.
5 She's the dancer (who/that) I spoke to after the performance.

3
1 All the galleries that/which are taking part in this year's art festival can be found on the website. **2** Every picture is made of old glass (which/that) the artists found in rubbish bins and recycling centres.
3 Older programmes which/that were made before 2005 won't be available online until 2019. **4** Please show tickets which/that were bought online at the main theatre box office. **5** Viewers who/that want to vote for the best singer need to call this number.

4
1 I was born in 2001, which was the year the animated movie *Shrek* came out. **2** My favourite author is Marguerite Abouet, who wrote the AYA graphic novels. **3** The only musical I've ever seen is Les Misírables, which has been playing in the capital for years.
4 *She's Just A Shadow* stars Tao Okamoto, who is one of several new successful Japanese actors. **5** Have a look at his Facebook page, which has a photo of his new baby nephew.

5
1 Commas not necessary – defining relative clause. **2** Commas not necessary – defining relative clause. **3** The music, which is played by a DJ, is broadcast by radio to the dancers' headphones. **4** Often two or three DJs work at the same time, which means that dancers can choose the type of music they want to dance to. **5** Commas not necessary – defining relative clause. (Many nightclub owners are allowed to play loud music late at night, so it is not adding information about all nightclub owners.)

10 Time

1
1 I'd gone **2** have learnt **3** had taken **4** If only
5 wouldn't, hadn't worked **6** had eaten **7** I'd spent
8 I'd, wouldn't

2
Sentences 3, 4, 7 and 8 express regret.

3
1 had been able, would have kept **2** would have been, had travelled
3 had been, wouldn't have got **4** would have solved, had followed
5 had been **6** hadn't passed, would have continued

4
1 you ever wish you had gone **2** only I hadn't eaten that burger
3 I hadn't bought an expensive jacket, I would have had enough money
4 wouldn't have needed to go back to the shop if he had remembered
5 would have been (much) quicker if I had taken

5
1 might **2** might **3** must **4** can't **5** should
6 might / should **7** can't **8** shouldn't

6
1 No, that ~~mustn't~~ can't be him. **2** I could ~~had~~ have done …
3 I ~~must~~ should/could have gone yesterday … **4** You ~~can~~ could have told me … **5** you **might must** have done something …